Artificial Intelligence in Highway Safety

Subasish Das
Texas A&M Transportation Institute
Texas A&M University, USA

CRC Press is an imprint of the
Taylor & Francis Group, an **informa** business
A SCIENCE PUBLISHERS BOOK

Cover credits: Debangana Banerjee

First edition published 2023
by CRC Press
6000 Broken Sound Parkway NW, Suite 300, Boca Raton, FL 33487-2742

and by CRC Press
4 Park Square, Milton Park, Abingdon, Oxon, OX14 4RN

CRC Press is an imprint of Taylor & Francis Group, LLC

Library of Congress Cataloging-in-Publication Data (applied for)

ISBN: 978-0-367-43670-4 (hbk)
ISBN: 978-1-032-20473-4 (pbk)
ISBN: 978-1-003-00559-9 (ebk)

DOI: 10.1201/9781003005599

Typeset in Palatino Roman
by Innovative Processors

Dedicated to

Anandi and Suha

Preface

In recent years, artificial intelligence (AI) has become a driving force in many research areas. Both AI and highway safety have gained much attention individually. The recent increase of AI applications (in various sectors of transportation engineering) has become a new trend in solving complex engineering problems due to their advantages of precision and performance efficiency. For this reason, the application of AI in highway safety has recently garnered the interest of many researchers. This book is a result of my efforts to provide information on the latest applications of AI in highway safety-related issues. This book not only draws on my own previous and ongoing works on AI in highway safety, but also reflects the emerging knowledge and experience in this disruptive field. This book is intended as a reference for undergraduate and graduate students in transportation engineering and will also be useful for those interested in research.

This book is not intended to be a comprehensive reference for AI algorithms. Only highway safety research-related AI basics are provided in this book. For more in-depth knowledge of the algorithms, readers can consult an abundance of AI books. This book's purpose is to provide transportation engineering students with a basic knowledge of AI concepts and their applications in highway safety problems. I hope to get the readers interested in finding state-of-the-art AI solutions for solving highway safety engineering problems. This book includes basic conceptual information about popular algorithms with the inclusion of case studies and example problems with codes. For the convenience of the readers, all relevant data and codes are made public by open-sourcing codes and data in GitHub (https://github.com/subasish/AI_in_HighwaySafety). The majority of the codes used in this book were developed using R (https://www.r-project.org/). I published most codes of this book in RPubs (https://rpubs.com/subasish). Additional example problems and relevant codes are also included in the GitHub repo and RPubs which are not included in the current version of the book.

I want to thank my wife Anandi and my daughter Suha for their enormous support. Without their support, this book would never have been completed. Valerie and Magdalena helped me enormously in editing this book. I am indebted to them. I would like to thank Debangana Banerjee for developing an excellent book cover for this book. I have delayed the submission deadlines several times. I would like to thank my publisher Vijay Primlani for his patience.

This is my first book. I know that there are many shortcomings in it. I will keep improving this book in the upcoming editions. You are most welcome to send your comments and feedback to me at subasishsn@gmail.com.

Subasish Das, Ph.D.

February 12, 2022

Contents

List of Abbreviations

AAM	Advanced Air Mobility
AADT	Annual Average Daily Traffic
AASHTO	Association of American State Highway Transportation Officials
AV	Automated/Autonomous vehicles
AI	Artificial Intelligence
AIC	Akaike Information Criterion
ALE	Accumulated Local Effects
BIC	Bayes' Information Criterion
BRNN	Bidirectional Recurrent Neural Networks
CA	Correspondence Analysis
CART	Classification and Regression Tree
CAV	Connected and autonomous/automated vehicles
CMF	Crash Modification Factor
CNN	Convolutional Neural Network
CVSP	Commercial Vehicles Safety Plan
DAA	Data Archiving Application
DBN	Deep Belief Network
DDSA	Data Driven Safety Analysis
DLR	Diagnostic Likelihood Ratio
DMS	Dynamic Message Sign
DOT	Department of Transportation
DSA	Differential Search Algorithm
DUI	Driving Under the Influence
EB	Empirical Bayes
EDRNN	Encoder-Decoder Recurrent Neural Networks
EV	Electric Vehicle
FARS	Fatality Analysis Reporting System
FHWA	Federal Highway Administration
FB	Full Bayesian
GAN	Generative Adversarial Networks
GBM	Gradient Boosting Machine

GIS	Geographic Information Systems
GLM	Generalized Linear Model
HISP	Highway Safety Improvement Program
HSM	Highway Safety Manual
ICA	Independent Component Analysis
ICE	Individual Conditional Expectation
ICT	Information and Communications Technology
IDF	Inverse Document Frequency
KDT	Knowledge Discovery in Text
KNN	K Nearest Neighbor
LADOTD	Louisiana Department of Transportation and Development
LAPGAN	Laplacian Generative Adversarial Network
LEHD	Longitudinal Employer-Household Dynamics
LIME	Local Interpretable Model-Agnostic Explanations
LSTM	Long Short-Term Memory
LDA	Latent Dirichlet Allocation
MaaS	Mobility as a Service
ML	Machine Learning
MLP	Multilayer Perceptron
MOD	Mobility on Demand
MPO	Metropolitan Planning Organization
MUTCD	Manual on Uniform Traffic Control Devices
NB	Negative Binomial
NCHRP	National Cooperative Highway Research Program
NEISS	National Electronic Injury Surveillance System
NHTSA	National Highway Traffic Safety Administration
NIPALS	Nonlinear Iterative Partial Least Squares
NLU	Natural Language Understanding
NLP	Natural Language Processing
NOAA	National Oceanic and Atmospheric Administration
NPV	Negative Predictive Value
NPMRDS	National Performance Management Research Data Set
PBCAT	Pedestrian and Bicycle Crash Analysis Tool
PCA	Principal Component Analysis
PDP	Partial Dependence Plot
PPV	Positive Predictive Value
PTASP	Public Transportation Agency Safety Plan
PUN	Pretrained Unsupervised Network
RBM	Restricted Boltzmann Machine
ReLU	Rectified Linear Unit
RF	Random Forests
RNN	Recurrent Neural Network
RTM	Regression to the Mean
SD	Stanford Dependencies
SHAP	SHapley Additive exPlanations

SHSP	Strategic Highway Safety Plan
SPF	Safety Performance Function
STM	Structural Topic Model
SVD	Singular Value Decomposition
SVM	Support Vector Machine
SVR	Support Vector Regression
TBPTT	Truncated Backpropagation Through Time `
TCA	Taxicab Correspondence Analysis
TIGER	Topologically Integrated Geographic Encoding and Referencing
TPR	True Positive Rate
TSP	Highway Safety Planning
USDOT	United States Department of Transportation
VID	Video Identification Number

CHAPTER

1

Introduction

1.1. Highway Safety

Highway safety has become an emerging research area due to the rise in disruptive technologies such as connected and automated vehicles (CAV). One critical marketing aspect of autonomous vehicles (AV) is their capability to remove the human error component from the driving paradigm. It is generally said that over 90% of traffic crashes are due to human errors.

Highway safety is mainly associated with the reduction of either traffic crashes or the severity of crashes. Crash data analysis methodologies have a history of over a hundred years (see Figure 1). These methodologies mainly aim to improve highway safety by reducing crashes or crash-related injuries. Although many highway safety researchers alternatively use the term 'accident,' the usage of the term 'crash' is preferable as crash solely indicates 'road traffic crashes.' The term 'accident' can alternatively indicate any kind of accident, such as an industrial accident. From 1910, the term 'crash' was first introduced as an alternative to 'collision.' The first accident theory evolved during the early 20th century. Five major theories have evolved over the years: crashes as random events, crash proneness theory, causal crash theory, systems theory, and behavioral theory (Elvik et al., 2009).

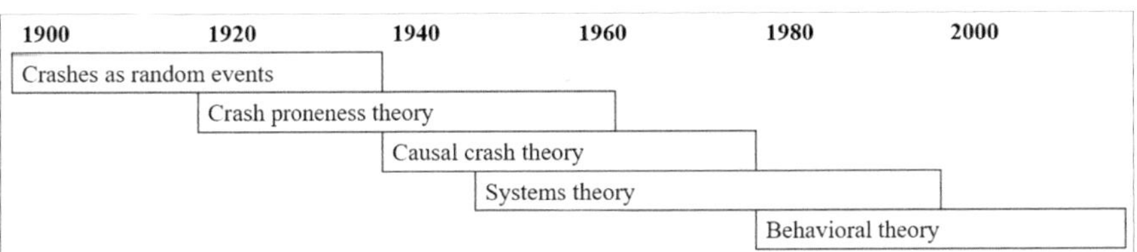

Figure 1. Theories on highway safety research.
Adapted from: Elvik et al., 2009

Analytical tools and methods for measuring the prospective impacts of crashes as a result of decisions made in design, planning, operations, and maintenance are provided in the first edition of the Highway Safety Manual (HSM). Agencies are aided by the information within the HSM in their attempts to include safety in decision-making procedures. The HSM is specifically written for practitioners at the local, metropolitan planning organization (MPO), county, or state level. The HSM is not proposed to be nor establishes legal guidelines for professionals or users about the information contained within it. The use or nonuse of the HSM cannot create or impose any standard of conduct or any duty toward any person or the public. Publications such as the Association of American State Highway Transportation Officials (AASHTO)'s "Green Book," entitled 'A Policy on Geometric Design of Highways and Streets,' other AASHTO and agency manuals, or guidelines, and policies, or the Federal Highway Administration's (FHWA) Manual on Uniform Traffic Control Devices (MUTCD), are not superseded by the HSM. Additionally, the first edition of the HSM is limited to roadway geometry and a few operational characteristics such as aggregate level traffic volume. Many significant operating measures, such as operating speed, have not been considered in the HSM models. Countries such as Sweden, Australia, and New Zealand adopted safe system approaches (focusing on four pillars: safe roads, safe road users, safe speeds, and safe vehicles) decades ago. Adopting safe system approaches showed significant safety improvement. In 2022, the United States Department of Transportation (USDOT) adopted safe system (by adding a new pillar known as 'post-crash care') as the key safety strategy.

There is a need for new methodologies that can provide better safety improvements. The current book can be considered as a starting point in exploring different AI techniques and how to apply them in highway safety improvements. A brief overview of highway safety and its major components is provided in Chapter 2.

1.2. Artificial Intelligence

1.2.1. Idea of Artificial Intelligence

As a result of their intelligence, humans are known as *Homo sapiens* (man the wise). Humans have attempted for thousands of years to better their welfare by learning how to think such that they can understand, predict, and influence the world. Human-level intelligence is created within the field of artificial intelligence (AI), and it can be used in solving many difficult and unsolved problems.

AI recently became a field of science and engineering (see Figure 2 to understand the sub-domains of AI). Soon after World War II, work in this area started in earnest, and the name was coined in 1956. There are a large variety of subfields contained in AI, including general topics, such as perception and learning, and more specific topics, such as proving mathematical theorems, playing Go, driving an AV, writing poetry, and diagnosing diseases. AI is truly a universal field and is relevant to intellectual tasks. Some major fields of AI include:

- **Machine learning:** Detecting and extrapolating patterns, and adapting to new circumstances.
- **Natural language processing:** Enabling automated knowledge extracted from unstructured data.

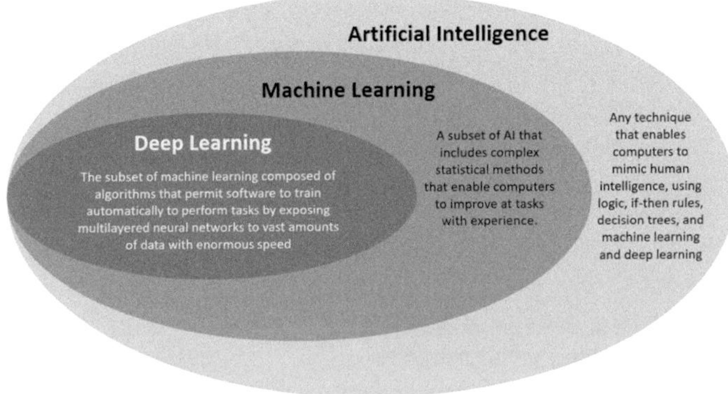

Figure 2. AI, machine learning, and deep learning.

- **Knowledge representation:** Showing what is heard or known.
- **Automated reasoning:** Answering questions to multi-faceted environments.

1.2.2. History of AI

The concept of "the mind" is not very old. It arose during the seventeenth century, along with modern science and modern mathematics. These historical roots of AI would require a separate book by itself. Many AI books provide different perspectives on its history. Some of the key milestones are listed in Table 1, but this table is not comprehensive. Readers need to consult other relevant books to know all roots associated with the history of AI. Figure 3 illustrates the timeline of the major AI algorithms over the years.

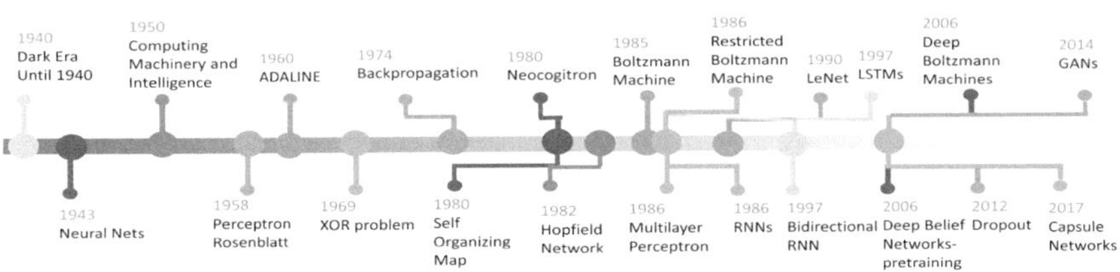

Figure 3. History of key AI algorithms.

1.2.3. Statistical Model vs. AI Algorithm: Two Cultures

One can think of data as being presented by a vector of input variables x (explanatory variables) entering on one side and the target variables y exiting on the other (see Figure 4). Essentially, a response variable is a function of

Table 1. Some of the key milestones of AI

Year	Milestones
1931	Kurt Gödel's first-order predicate logic.
1937	The limits of intelligent machines with the halting problem were identified.
1943	Neural networks were modeled and the connection to propositional logic was made by McCulloch and Pits.
1950	Machine intelligence was defined with the Turing test
1951	Marvin Minksy's neural network machine was developed.
1955	Arthur Samuel's learning checkers program, which plays better than its developer, was developed.
1956	First Artificial Intelligence conference, was organized by McCarthy in Dartmouth College.
1958	McCarthy's invention of high-level language LISP.
1959	The Geometry Theorem Prover was built by Gelernter (IBM).
1961	Human thought was imitated by the General Problem Solver (GPS) by Newell and Simon.
1965	The resolution calculus for predicate logic was invented by Robinson.
1966	Eliza carried out dialog with people in a natural language.
1969	The perceptron, a very simple neural network, can only represent linear functions, was shown in the book Perceptrons by Minsky and Papert.
1972	The logic programming language PROLOG was invented by Alain Colmerauer.
1976	MYCIN, an expert system for the diagnosis of infectious diseases, capable of dealing with uncertainty, was developed by Shortliffe and Buchanan.
1981	The *Fifth Generation Project* was begun by Japan with the goal of building a powerful PROLOG machine.
1986	Renaissance of neural networks by Hinton, Rumelhart, and Sejnowski, among others.
1990	Probability theory was brought into AI with Bayesian networks by Pearl, Cheeseman, Whittaker, Spiegalhalter.
1992	The power of reinforcement learning was shown by the Tesauros TD-gammon program.
1993	Proposal made by Worldwide RoboCup to build soccer playing autonomous robots.
1995	Vapnik developed support vector machines from statistical learning theory, which are very important today.
1997	Gary Kasparov was defeated by IBM's chess computer Deep Blue.
2009	The first Google self-driving car was driven on the California freeway.
2011	Two human champions were beaten by IBM's "Watson" .
2014	Generative adversarial network was introduced by Ian Goodfellow
2015	Deep learning enabled quality image classification. Google self-driving cars were driven over one million miles and operated within cities.
2016	The Go program AlphaGo by Google DeepMind beat one of the world's best Go players, Korean Lee Sedol

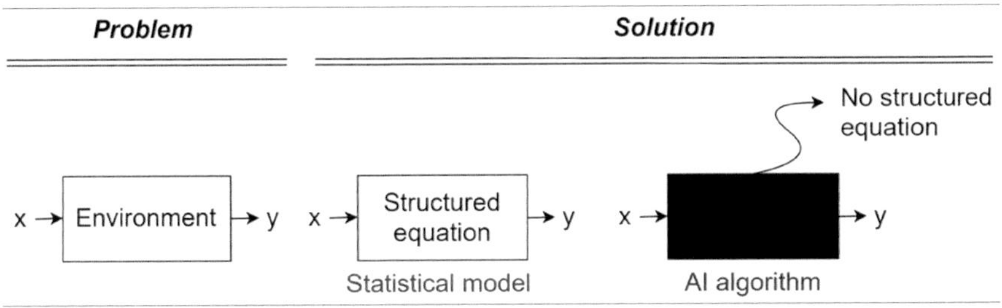

Figure 4. Statistical model vs. AI algorithm.

parameters, independent variables, and random noise. The parameter values can be estimated from the data and then a model with a structured equation can be used for prediction. So, the real word problem of the unknown environment can be depicted by the structural form of a statistical model. On the other hand, AI employs a different method to find the solution. It aims to find a function in the form of an algorithm that operates on x to predict the response y. These algorithms do not produce a structured equation, but rather they provide emphasis. Thus, AI models are sometimes known as 'black box' models.

The most common method for performing highway safety research is historical crash data analytics or predictive analysis. Historical traffic crash data, along with related contributing factors like roadways, traffic, and surrounding variables, are employed to develop crash prediction models. A basic interpretation of complicated crash data is provided by the crash prediction model. Two basic categories are the basis of the overall crash data analysis: classification analysis (crash injury types) and frequency analysis (crash counts). A visual of the trade-offs associated with these methods (the traditional statistical model in black triangles, triangles 1, 2 and 3, the data-driven or machine learning or AI model in the purple triangle $\Delta m1m2m3$, the endogeneity/heterogeneity model in the dotted red triangle $\Delta e1e2e3$, the causal inference model in the green triangle $\Delta c1c2c3$, and the explainable AI model in the deep blue dotted triangle $\Delta x1x2x3$) regarding three performance measures (causal inference capability, predictive accuracy, and big data applicability), shown at each node of the largest grey triangle, ΔABC, is shown in Figure 5. If the node of any methodology-based triangle is close to any of the performance measure nodes (e.g., A, B, or C), it indicates that the methodology is good at that specific performance measure. For example, a data-driven or machine learning model in the purple triangle $\Delta d1d2d3$ has two nodes $d1$ and $d2$ which are closer to predictive capability (node A) and big data suitability (node B), respectively. However, the third node $m3$ is far away from causality/inference capability (node C). The explainable AI model's inference capability is higher than that of other AI models (see the location of $x3$) shown in the figure. The overall interpretation is that data-driven methods (AI and explainable AI) are good at prediction and big data analysis; however, this method falls short in interpretation (Mannering et al., 2020). With the rise of interpretable or explainable AI, data-driven methods can also mitigate the gap in inference capability (see $\Delta x1x2x3$).

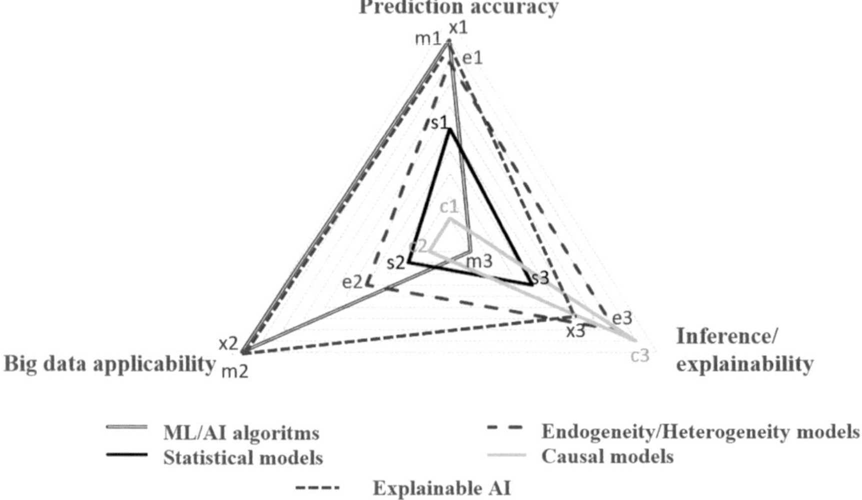

Figure 5. Tradeoffs between key modeling techniques.

1.3. Application of Artificial Intelligence in Highway Safety

With the massive amount of highway safety-related data, easily accessible computational power, and numerous AI algorithms, highway safety research has evolved from traditional statistical analysis to combine the power of AI and statistical learning. More and more data-driven studies on highway safety topics have been published recently. Many insights and patterns have been revealed that were not found with traditional data collection techniques, such as surveys and conventional statistical analysis methods. However, with a plethora of literature available now on the topic, there is a need for conducting a thorough literature review on AI applications in the highway safety field. Readers can consult a study (Das et al., 2020), which provides a comprehensive review on applications of AI algorithms in highway safety.

1.4. Book Organization

This book is organized into eleven chapters, each covering aspects of artificial intelligence in highway safety. Each chapter contains relevant case studies, example problems, or both. It is followed by appendices that further offer explanations over topics and practice over areas such as identifying datasets, performing data fusion, developing interactive maps, and applying different AI techniques.

Chapter Conclusion

This chapter offers a brief introduction to highway safety and AI, including AI history, algorithms, and applications within highway safety. The enormous growth of AI applicability in highway safety indicates that many current research problems associated with highway safety can be resolved by AI in the future.

References

Das, S., Wei, Z., Agarwal, V. and Kong, X., 2020. Artificial Intelligence in Transportation Safety: A Systematic Literature Analysis. Preprint.

Elvik, R., Vaa, T., Hoye, A. and Sorensen, M., 2009. The Handbook of Road Safety Measures, Second Edition. Emerald Group Publishing.

Mannering, F., Bhat, C., Shankar, V. and Abdel-Aty, M., 2020. Big data, traditional data and the tradeoffs between prediction and causality in highway-safety analysis. Analytic Methods of Accident Research, 25.

CHAPTER

2

Highway Safety Basics

2.1. Introduction

Highway safety research encompasses the study of traffic crashes and their effects on transportation systems. The emphasis is mostly on crash outcomes (i.e., fatalities and serious injuries) rather than citation data and driver's safety understanding.

The term "accident" indicates that the outcome is unexpected or unintended. Motor vehicle accidents are also called "crashes," which indicates that they can be avoided. Regardless of which term is used, "crash" and "accident" both refer to collisions involving motor vehicles, drivers and passengers, motorcyclists, bicyclists, pedestrians, and other roadway users. Safety experts conduct research on these crashes to learn about effective prevention measures.

Science-oriented road safety is the empirical study of roadway crashes or accidents. Highway safety includes the number of crashes or crash effects, by type and injury pattern, that are expected to take place on the entity during a specific period.

As one can see in this definition, the focus is placed on event outcomes, such as injuries and property damage. If possible, these metrics should be used to measure safety. Other measures, such as violations, incidents, or near misses, may indicate safety problems, but they are categorized as measures to characterize the outcome of an event. An entity can refer to highway facilities such as an interstate on-ramp, a signalized intersection, or a rural highway segment; it can also refer to driver or vehicle groups. The observed safety may not be consistent with the expected safety at a certain entity. The expected safety typically represents the true safety level of an entity, while the observed safety is subject to spontaneous variations in crashes. In the U.S. in 2019, 36,560 people died in roadway crashes. The projected number of roadway fatalities was 36,120 for 2020. Figure 6 shows the fatal crash frequencies by key facility types (rural vs. urban).

Understanding both substantive and nominal safety is necessary for the context of design decision-making and design exceptions (see Figure 7). Nominal safety refers to the importance of a roadway design element or alternative meeting the minimum design criteria. A highway or proposed design has nominal safety if the minimum ranges or values are attained by its design features (like shoulder

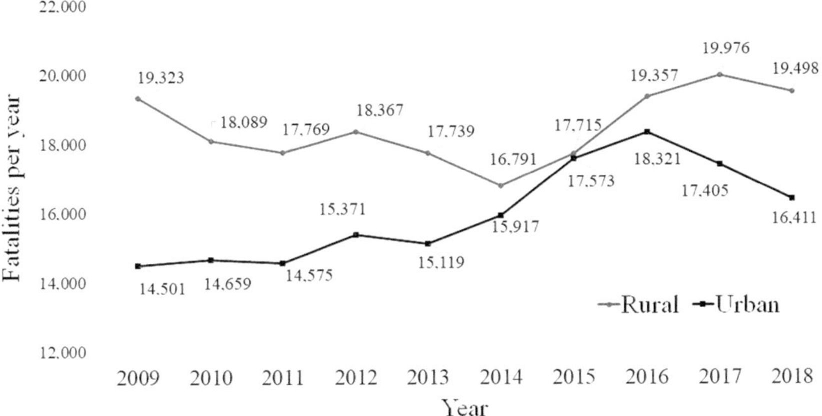

Figure 6. Traffic crashes by rural and urban facilities (2009-2018).

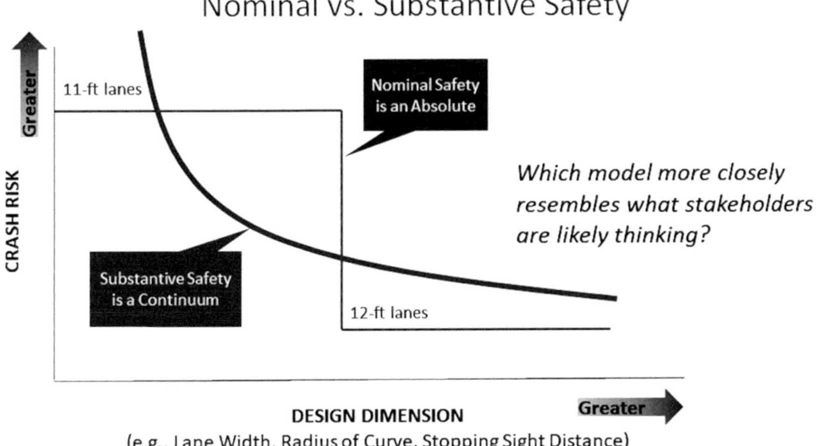

Figure 7. Nominal safety vs. substantive safety.

width, lane width, sight distance, and alignment). The nominal safety measurement is just a comparison of the criteria of design element dimensions to the adopted design. For example, the criterion for Interstate lane width is 12 feet; 12-feet lane widths proposed by a design alternative is considered a nominally safe design, while 11-feet lane widths are not considered nominally safe.

The level of nominal safety does not always directly correspond to a roadway's long-term or substantive safety performance, due to the fact that a roadway can be nominally safe (i.e., the design criteria is met by all design elements) yet also be substantively unsafe (i.e., relative to expectations, it reflects or demonstrates a high crash issue). In the same way, a roadway can be nominally unsafe (the design criteria are not met by one or more design elements) but still have high substantive safety. Many explanations account for this, but the main reason is that many factors are the basis for the criteria (only one being safety) and are obtained from streamlining models and assumptions that are broadly applied.

2.2. Influential Factors in Highway Safety

Safety is often defined as a function of significant variables such as environment, roadway, and driver factors (see Figure 8). The modules within the Highway Safety Manual (HSM) are focused on the type of facility where the crashes occur; it is expected that crash occurrence will vary based on road type.

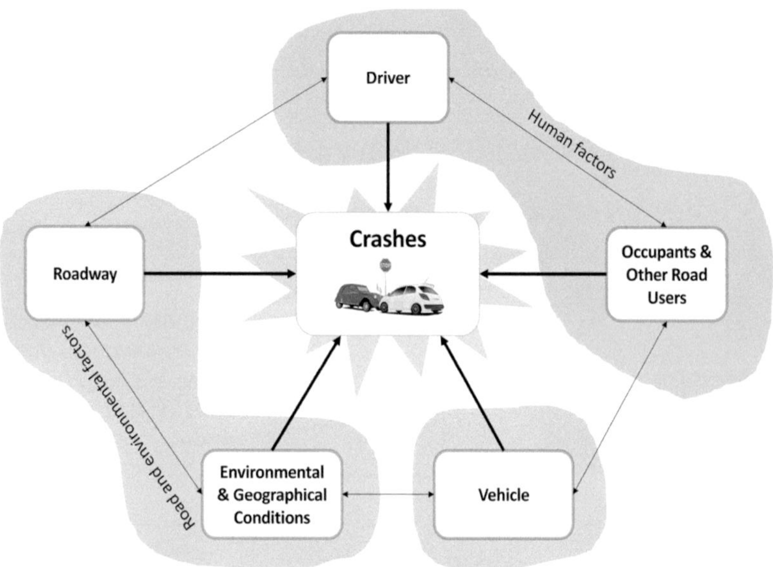

Figure 8. Key factors associated with traffic crash occurrences.

Highway safety can also be viewed from the perspective of a driver. Unlike road safety models that analyze safety based on the transportation network, other models analyze safety from the perspective of the road user; these models consider driver actions and the environment. The relationships between drivers and factors that affect their safety are also explored with statistical models. Although conventional safety analysis considers human error as the key factor, approaches such as safe system consider error to be associated with system's failure (see Figure 9). Certain classes of road users are subject to substantial research as they need special attention; these include:

- Young and inexperienced drivers.
- Older drivers.

- Heavy vehicle operators.
- Rural vs. urban drivers.
- Aggressive drivers and speeders.
- Motorcyclists.
- Pedestrians.
- Bicyclists.

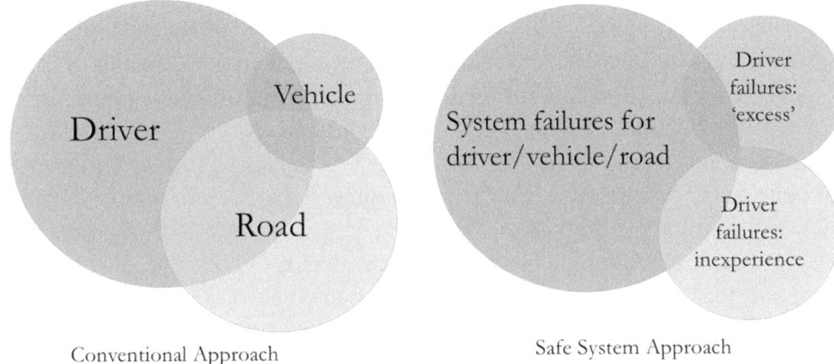

Figure 9. Crash contributing factors.

2.3. 4E Approach

There are many different approaches to address roadway safety; however, no single method can solve all issues within roadway safety entirely. There are four key areas for addressing road safety acknowledged by road safety professionals: engineering, education, enforcement, and emergency responses. These can also be called the 4 Es of road safety. The 4 Es are typically used to measure and correct existing road safety issues or to create crash prevention strategies.

2.3.1. Engineering

Engineers investigate road safety issues that are connected to the roadway, roadside, and vehicle. The engineer's role is to guarantee that all transportation systems and modes are built to cover the needs and mitigation of transportation user limitations.

2.3.2. Education

The purpose of highway safety education is to alter the actions of road users (i.e., limit unsafe behaviors and promote safe behaviors). Education is a critical tool for improving road safety. In more than 60 percent of crashes, the human element is cited as the main cause, and in more than 90 percent of crashes, it is identified as a contributing factor. Educational campaigns can be used either as a singular countermeasure or in conjunction with engineering and enforcement measures.

Education can be used as a single measure to enhance road rules knowledge and driving skills, and to raise road safety awareness in general.

2.3.3. Enforcement

Unfortunately, education and engineering cannot solve road safety issues completely. For instance, an educational campaign can explain the dangers of excessive speed, and an engineer can design a roadway with a specific speed limit, but some drivers may still choose to exceed the posted speed limit, despite engineering and education efforts. Therefore, enforcement is necessary to change road user behaviors. A relatively large proportion of crash-related injuries and deaths are associated with speeding, driving under the influence (DUI), and incorrect seat belt use. In other countries, such as Australia, the enforcement of driver behaviors has achieved a high rate of success in minimizing crash-related injuries and fatalities. Safety belt use in the U.S. has been steadily improving because of enforcement and educational campaigns. The use of automated enforcement techniques (e.g., red light running and speed detection cameras) in the U.S. has been met with resistance. Furthermore, the strength of DUI campaigns in the U.S. does not meet the standards set by other developed countries.

2.3.4. Emergency

After a crash occurs, it is the responsibility of emergency responders to rescue victims from the crash, provide medical care, and protect other road users from harm. Emergency responders usually handle post-crash problems, but it is important for these workers to possess a well-conceived crisis-response plan before the crash occurs as well. Emergency responders include traffic engineers, emergency medical services, law enforcement, and fire and rescue services, each with a specific purpose. Law enforcement officers, along with traffic engineers, are generally responsible for investigating crashes and controlling traffic. Fire and rescue workers remove crash victims from their vehicles, if necessary, and often provide medical care. Depending on the jurisdiction, emergency medical services may act under a separate public agency or a privately contracted company. Emergency responders also rely on support from others, such as towing and recovery services, transportation agencies, traffic reporting media, and hazardous materials contractors. Emergency responders can all work in collaboration through effective incident management to minimize the consequences of crashes.

Need to know

The 4E approach is comparable with the safe system approach which can provide a meaningful improvement in highway safety in the U.S. The safe system approach focuses on five key objectives: safer people (education), safer roads (engineering), safer vehicles (engineering), safer speeds (enforcement), and post-crash care (emergency). To learn more about the safe system approach, interested readers can consult the Safe System GitHub page developed by the author (https://github.com/subasish/safesystems).

2.4. Intervention Tools

Intervention methods include statistical models that can identify "sites with promise," or sites where safety performance needs improvement, and tools that can be used to identify effective countermeasures and interventions, such as the Haddon Matrix and road safety audits. The Haddon Matrix is a method used to mitigate sites with many safety problems, while a road safety audit is a more proactive method intended to recognize and address safety issues before problems occur at a site (see Table 2). Five major intervention tools are:

- Statistical models
- The Haddon Matrix
- Road safety audits
- Countermeasure effectiveness
- Multidisciplinary case studies

Table 2. Haddon matrix for an urban area (HSIP Manual)

Period	Human	Vehicle/ Equipment	Physical Environment	Socio Economic
Pre-Crash	Speed, impairment, improper passing, distraction.	Brake failure, issues with headlight, tyre problems.	Insufficient traffic control devices, absence of shoulder.	Cultural norms in preventing speeding and drunk driving.
Crash	No seabelt.	Malfunctioning safety belts, poorly engineered airbags.	Low design standards of safety countermeasures.	Low vehicle inspection standards.
Post-Crash	High susceptibility, alcohol.	Poorly designed fuel tanks.	Poor emergency communication systems.	Insufficient trauma support systems.

The first nine cells of the Haddon Matrix display the time phases of a crash in correlation to human, vehicle, and physical environment factors. It is common to add a fourth column of factors that can include socio-economic factors, environmental conditions (e.g., weather), or other categories. The Haddon Matrix is filled out by evaluating the details associated with the crash site. When the matrix is completed, it offers insight into potential safety issues and concerns as well as potential countermeasures.

2.5. Data Sources

Transportation and safety practitioners and decision-makers use state and local road safety data that include information on:

- Crashes.
- Injury surveillance and EMS information.
- Roadway information.
- Driver characteristics.
- Vehicle-related information.
- Enforcement-related information such as prior convictions and citations.
- Other types of data which will be described in this module.

2.6. Crash Frequency Models

Crash frequency analysis is one of the most common safety analysis procedures. The problem can be considered as a discrete count data (regression) problem. Conventionally, Poisson and negative binomial (NB) models are the most common models for performing count data models. Many variants of Poisson and NB models have been introduced by researchers.

2.7. Crash Severity Models

Crash severity analysis can be considered to be a classification problem analysis. The severity of crashes is generally divided into four main groups: fatal (K), incapacitating injury (A), non-incapacitating injury (B), minor injury (C), and no injury or property damage only or PDO (O). These five severity types are considered as KABCO scales. Many advanced statistical and AI models have been applied in crash severity analysis by researchers.

Lord and Mannering (2010) created a comprehensive review of crash count data analysis methods in their study. For a comprehensive review of crash severity modeling, readers can consult Savolainen et al. (2011). Mannering and Bhat (2014) provided an update to the Lord and Mannering (2010) and Savolainen et al. (2011) studies by exploring crash severity models and count data models. Das (2016) developed a hyperlinked web page for a one-stop place for further information, listing 592 papers.

2.8. Effectiveness of Countermeasures

The safety effectiveness evaluation can be divided into three different groups:

- Observational B/A studies.
- Observational cross-sectional studies.
- Experimental B/A studies.

2.8.1. Observational B/A Studies

The most commonly utilized method in highway safety analysis out of these three are observational B/A studies. In this method, data is collected and evaluated for the before and after periods of a project operation. There are numerous methods in B/A studies for evaluating individual countermeasures and projects, which are presented in the remaining subsections.

Naïve B/A Studies

In the simple or naïve B/A studies, the before period crash frequency is compared to the after-period crash frequency. These methods don't need a tremendous amount of data and are easy to conduct and easily interpretable. However, these methods don't consider traffic volumes, regression to the mean (RTM) bias, or temporal effects, or trends like other local factors, crash reporting, and alterations in driver behavior. These methods aren't suggested when utilized in countermeasure evaluations for developing quality CMFs due to these shortcomings.

Naïve B/A Studies with Linear Traffic Volume Correction

A B/A study that has a linear traffic volume correction and that accounts for temporal changes in traffic volumes is a naïve B/A study deviation in which the crash rates (rather than crash counts) for the periods before and after a treatment are executed and compared. This makes it more of a reliable method than naïve B/A studies. The following is used to calculate crash rates:

$$Crash\ Rate_i = \frac{C_{Observed,\ i}}{AADT_i} \tag{1}$$

Where:
The crash rate at site i in a defined time (an example being three to five years) is $Crash\ Rate_i$.
The average crash count at site i in a defined time is $C_{Observed,i}$.
The annual average daily traffic at site i in a defined time is $AADT_i$.

Both project and countermeasure evaluations can be conducted with this method, but the effects of RTM and variations in other factors over time are not considered. If RTM has no or limited potential and there aren't any changes during the before and after periods in crash reporting or driver behavior, this method could be appropriate for CMF development.

EB Method

The anticipated crash frequency with no treatment is estimated and compared to the actual number of crashes during the after period in the Empirical Bayes (EB) method. It is an incredibly reliable method for CMF development because alterations in traffic volumes, RTM bias, and temporal effects are accounted for. A weighted average principle is the basis of the EB method; a weight factor, w, is utilized to calculate the *expected crash frequency*, $C_{Expected}$, by adding observed ($C_{Observed}$) and predicted ($C_{Predicted}$) crash frequencies:

$$C_{Expected} = w \cdot C_{Predicted} + (1 - w) \cdot C_{Observed} \tag{2}$$

Where,
w represents a weight factor. It differs based on the overdispersion parameter that is acquired from the SPF.
$C_{Expected}$ stands for the expected crash count.
$C_{Predicted}$ stands for the predicted crash count, typically computed by utilizing the CMFs and SPF.
$C_{Observed}$ stands for the observed crash count.

Both predicted and observed crash frequencies are accounted for in the EB method to overcome potential bias due to RTM, but it is possible that if a high overdispersion parameter is gathered from the SPF, there will be high uncertainty in the number of predicted crashes. To mitigate this issue, a weight factor is applied. The measure of the weighted adjustment factor decreases as the overdispersion parameter increases, so the observed is given greater emphasis in comparison to the predicted crash frequency. Typically, if the information utilized to form a model is significantly dispersed, the dependability is lower than the resulting predicted crash frequency. It is reasonable in this instance to put a greater amount of weight on the observed crash frequency and less on the predicted. However, if the information utilized to form a model has low overdispersion, the consistency of the resultant SPF is typically higher. It is reasonable in this instance to put less weight on the observed crash frequency and more on the predicted (Tsapakis et al., 2019).

Full Bayesian

Full Bayesian (FB) is an important method that any study design is able to use, including cross-sectional study designs and observational B/A, and it is appropriate for countermeasure evaluations. Full Bayesian can be used for smaller data samples (unlike the EB method), making it more suitable in situations where the amount of after-period data is small. The differences between EB and FB approaches have been examined in many research studies, which have found that the FB method is able to perform as well as the EB method, even with large sample sizes.

A previous distribution of the FB model and data is used to simulate the posterior distribution of expected/predicted crashes. Through the posterior distribution of the predicted crashes for the control and treatment groups in the after and before periods, the CMFs can be estimated in order to assess the efficacy of the safety treatment. The FB approach estimates the anticipated crash counts for the after and before periods to compensate for the RTM effects, without direct use in the comparison of the observed crash frequency (Tsapakis et al., 2019).

Difference in Differences

Evaluating the differences in a treatment's effect on a group of sites which were the treated versus the untreated sites in a control group through the use of observational data is mirrored in the difference in differences (DID) method, which a variety of fields have used. Conventional B/A observational studies examine the same locations in the before and after periods to figure out the impact on the safety of a treatment, but, during that time frame, other variables may change if the impact of a countermeasure takes a considerable amount of time to be noticeable. Therefore, it is possible that the treatment is not the only effect on the change in the crash count.

The performance measures are compared in the treatment group before and after execution in other B/A evaluation methods, but the DID is founded on the discrepancy across the treatment and control groups of the two B/A differences. Potential biases within the treatment group that might be due to external factors that are unrelated to the treatment and within the after-period between the control and treatment groups that might be a result of permanent differences between the groups are removed by this double differencing (Tsapakis et al., 2019).

2.9. Benefit Cost Analysis

In B/C analysis, the monetary value of the anticipated crash count difference is calculated, added, and then compared to the cost of the countermeasure. In B/C analysis, crash frequency is not simply evaluated in terms of monetary cost, but instead is compared to the total construction cost (i.e., cost-effectiveness is given as the annual cost per crash reduced).

Societal comprehensive crash costs are used to convert the predicted reduction in crash severity and frequency into monetary values. Table 3 presents the national comprehensive crash unit costs used in Texas as part of the 2018 HSIP and those published by FHWA; all crash injury severity levels are coupled with a certain amount of dollars.

Table 3. National comprehensive crash unit costs and TxDOT's HSIP crash costs

Crash Severity	FHWA Comprehensive Crash Unit Cost	TxDOT's Crash Cost (2018 HSIP)
Fatal (K)	$11,295,400	$3,500,000
Incapacitating Injury (A)	$655,000	$3,500,000
Non-incapacitating Injury (B)	$198,500	$500,000
Possible Injury (C)	$125,600	Not Applicable in HSIP
Property Damage Only (O)	$11,900	Not Applicable in HSIP

The project costs include right-of-way procurement, construction, operation, and maintenance. The cost-effectiveness assessment includes determining the ratio of the total cost of the project to the difference before and after execution in the crash count.

2.10. Transportation Safety Planning

A comprehensive, multimodal, systemwide, proactive process that combines safety into effective transportation decision-making is offered in Transportation Safety Planning (TSP). Ensuring that safety is integrated into surface transportation planning and decision-making relies on the work of transportation planners. Transportation planners can, with their safety specialist partners, support the mission of TSP and enhance communication, collaboration, and synchronization for the reduction of serious severity outcomes and fatalities. This can be done through their understanding and knowledge of safety and safety planning. Below is a brief description of the key elements of TSP:

FAST Act Implementation Highlights

PM and HSIP Rule – FHWA issued two final rules related to safety–they first updated the rule for the Highway Safety Improvement Program (HSIP) and then established the Performance Measures (PM) for the program. Both rulemakings were initiated to implement MAP-21 requirements, but requirements from FAST were incorporated to expedite implementation. The new performance measures in this rule will help State DOTs and metropolitan planning organizations make investment decisions that will result in the greatest possible reduction in fatalities and serious injuries.

- **Highway Safety Improvement Program (HSIP):** HSIP is a Federal-aid program that reduces injuries and the number of crashes for highway safety improvement projects. It must depict the headway in executing highway safety improvement projects, assess their usefulness, and depict the degree to which they have aided in the reduction of serious injuries and fatalities on public roads.
- **Strategic Highway Safety Plan (SHSP):** An SHSP is a data-driven, statewide safety plan that is a major component of the HSIP and is typically considered as the "umbrella" safety plan for all state plans at the local, regional, and state levels. It gives a comprehensive framework for the reduction of serious injuries and fatalities on all public roads and highways and directs investment decisions towards countermeasures and strategies that have the most potential for preventing them. Federal law requires state and metropolitan transportation planning to have a Highway Safety Plan (HSP): A HSP is administered by the National Highway Traffic Safety Administration (NHTSA) and is an annual work program that outlines programs and projects that primarily address behavioral safety issues, like impaired and distracted driving, speeding, motorcyclist safety, pedestrian and bicycle safety, and failure to use required safety equipment.

- **Commercial Vehicles Safety Plan (CVSP):** The Federal Motor Carrier Safety Administration (FMCSA) requires states to create a CVSP as an annual work program. The performance-based CVSP identifies a State's commercial motor vehicle safety objectives, activities, strategies, and performance measures.
- **Public Transportation Agency Safety Plan (PTASP):** The Federal Transit Administration (FTA) necessitates public transportation system operators to implement a PTASP founded on the safety management system approach.
- **Regional and Local Safety Plans:** The SHSP is thought of as the main safety plan for any state, but Metropolitan Planning Organizations (MPOs), Tribes, and local jurisdictions are allowed specific planning areas to make a decision to develop their own safety document to prioritize safety needs, projects, and programs. These plans ought to be consistent with the State SHSP's goals and objectives; for example, the outcomes of the plans' crash analyses can be utilized to prioritize and inform the highway safety projects.

2.11. Workforce Development and Core Competencies

Roadway safety is a major focus of the FHWA's Fixing America's Surface Transportation Act (FAST Act). Highway safety professionals must have 'critical knowledge in the form of core competencies' to perform their work efficiently. The current workforce faces two critical issues: 1) the rise of emerging technologies requires new skill sets and knowledge, and 2) the loss of a workforce with a wealth of knowledge and experience.

This section contains a brief summary of the occupational descriptors of transportation-related jobs. It also includes the prototype framework and a tool to help highway agencies identify effective and efficient training and educational opportunities.

2.11.1. Occupational Descriptors

To understand the transportation engineering-related job descriptions, this study examined job specifications and job postings within the transportation workforce at various levels through a well-validated dictionary of occupational descriptors (see Table 4). After an extensive search of transportation engineering jobs, four relevant titles and associated job descriptions were found. Table 4 lists these titles and their associated tasks. The task indicators explain the common job duties at various levels, and safety engineering is one of the critical components of these tasks.

Table 4. Transportation engineering job descriptions

Traffic Technicians
• Communicate with the public to respond to complaints or requests, answer questions about traffic, and discuss traffic control plans, policies, ordinances, and procedures. • Create charts, graphs, diagrams, and other visual aids to show conclusions and observations. • Assess data related to crash rates, traffic flow, or potential developments to find the best methods for expediting traffic flow. • Create work orders for necessary repairs, maintenance, or traffic system changes. • Organize, design, and upgrade traffic control systems to adjust to current or future traffic and promote usability and efficiency. • Explore factors impacting traffic conditions, such as lighting conditions and visibility, and to examine their effectiveness. • Collect, organize and code data from machine count tapes, hand count sheets, and radar speed checks for computer input. • Measure and document traffic speed with electrical timing devices or radar equipment. • Place the pavement markings for striping crews to follow. • Conduct technical supervision of traffic technicians or laborers for traffic control devices. • Use counters and document data to analyze the vehicle type, traffic volume, and movement of vehicular or pedestrian traffic at particular times. • Install automatic counters securely using power tools and collect them at the end of the counting periods. • Keep up with and make minor field repairs or adjustments to survey equipment, including replacing parts of traffic data gathering devices. • Go to development or work sites to determine the impact of the projects on traffic, assess the adequacy of traffic control and safety plans, and recommend traffic control measures if necessary. • Create street closure procedures for construction projects. • Communicate traffic information to the public (e.g., road conditions). • Observe street or utility projects to ensure compliance with traffic control permit conditions. • Design plans or long-term strategies for creating adequate parking space. • Survey motorists about particular intersections or highways to collect road-condition information.
Transportation Engineers
• Examine construction plans, design calculations, and cost estimations to guarantee accuracy, completeness, and alignment with engineering standards or practices. • Create or design plans for new transportation systems, such as commuter trains, airports, drainage structures, streets, highways, bridges, and roadway lighting. • Collaborate with utility companies, contractors, and government agencies about plans, details, and work schedules. • Plan or engineer erosion, drainage, or sedimentation control systems for transportation projects.

- Create budgets, schedules, and detailed plans for project labor and materials.
- Design changes for existing transportation structures to promote safety or functioning.
- Study traffic problems and implement changes to improve traffic flow or safety.
- Create a budget for transportation projects.
- Provide statistics, maps, or other information at public hearings and meetings related to construction.
- Conduct technical, administrative, or statistical reports on traffic-operation issues, including safety measures, traffic crashes, and pedestrian volume and behaviors.
- Assess transportation systems, traffic control devices, and lighting systems to evaluate the need for changes or expansion.
- Inspect development plans to estimate potential traffic implications.
- Examine finished transportation projects to evaluate safety or adherence to applicable standards or regulations.
- Supervise the surveying, staking, and layout of construction projects.
- Assist with contract bidding, negotiation, and administration.
- Create transportation scenarios to assess the effects of various activities, like new constructions, or to determine potential transportation solutions.
- Research and test certain building materials to ensure that they meet requirements and standards.
- Oversee the upkeep or repairs of transportation systems and their components.
- Examine finished construction projects for adherence to environmental guidelines.
- Examine building materials with respect to environmental standards.
- Create plans to destroy damaged or unused roadways or other transportation structures in an environmentally sound manner and prepare the land for sustainable development.
- Examine the environmental impact of transportation projects.
- Create sustainable transportation systems or structures, by employing proper materials or products.
- Help in the development of computer software and processes for transportation.

Transportation Managers

- Organize and supervise subordinate staff to guarantee that their work is conducted in accordance with organizational requirements.
- Oversee activities such as routing, dispatching, and tracking transportation vehicles.
- Direct operations so that workers follow administrative policies and procedures, environmental policies, union contracts, government regulations, and safety rules.
- Act as the point of contact for all employees within assigned territories.
- Execute schedule or policy changes for transportation services.
- Track spending to keep expenses consistent with authorized budgets.
- Conduct safety audits, hold company safety meetings, and meet with individual employees to promote safe work practices.
- Make recommendations to management, such as scheduling changes or increasing fees and tariffs.
- Conduct investigations to verify and address customer or shipper concerns.

(*Contd.*)

- Lead operations to acquire equipment, facilities, and human resources.
- Examine spending and other financial data to create strategies, policies, or budgets to boost profits and improve services.
- Work with other managers or employees to develop and execute policies, processes, and goals.
- Plan or execute changes to save energy, such as shortening routes, optimizing capacity, using alternative modes of transportation, or eliminating idling.
- Oversee repairing personnel and maintaining vehicles, equipment, or facilities.
- Hold employee orientations and training sessions about subjects such as handling hazardous materials, quality improvement, and computer usage.
- Recommend or approve capital spending to acquire new equipment or property to improve the efficiency and services of operations.
- Collaborate with government agencies to investigate the causes of transportation crashes, coordinate cleanup efforts, and enhance safety practices.
- Establish operation standards and policies, including safety procedures for handling hazardous materials.
- Create criteria, procedural manuals, application instructions, and contracts for federal or state public transportation programs.
- Create or execute plans to increase the control of transportation services from the regional to the national or global level.
- Oversee central load control centers to improve transportation efficiency and effectiveness.
- Manage clerks that classify tariffs and prepare billing.
- Work with equipment and material suppliers to negotiate, authorize, and oversee the fulfillment of their contracts.
- Assess transportation vehicles and auxiliary equipment to be purchased with respect to factors such as fuel economy and aerodynamics.
- Choose technologies for transportation and communications systems to minimize the costs and environmental impact.
- Assist those receiving transportation grants with administrative or technical issues.
- Lead procurement procedures such as vendor contracts, equipment research and testing, or approval of requisitions.
- Take part in contract negotiations or grievance settlements with unions.

Transportation Planners

- Recommend upgrades of projects for transportation systems based on population, economic factors, land-use, and traffic projections.
- Identify issues and priorities for regional or local transportation planning.
- Attend public meetings or hearings to explain construction proposals, receive feedback from stakeholders, and reach agreements on project designs.
- Conduct transportation surveys to determine public concerns.
- Analyze and interpret data from traffic modeling software, GIS systems, and related databases.
- Prepare transportation planning reports and provide suggestions.

- Create new or upgraded transportation infrastructure, like renovated roads, pedestrian projects, bus stops, or parking lots.
- Examine transportation information, such as land use policies, the environmental impacts of construction, and long-term planning requirements.
- Work with engineers to investigate, evaluate, and resolve complicated transportation design challenges.
- Assess the needs and costs of transportation projects.
- Work with other professionals to create long-term transportation strategies for local, regional, and national levels.
- Gather the necessary documentation to secure project approvals and permits.
- Create computer models to help with transportation planning.
- Create or test new methods and models for transportation analysis.
- Conduct or review engineering studies and specifications.
- Examine development plans and assess their impact on transportation systems, infrastructure requirements, and adherence to applicable transportation requirements.
- Assess the impact of federal or state legislative proposals on transportation.
- Create environmental documents, including environmental assessments or impact statements.
- Represent jurisdictions in the approval of land development projects at the administrative or legislative level.
- Publish and update data such as urban borders or roadway classification.

Source: Occupational Information Network (https://www.onetonline.org/).

2.11.2. Core Competencies

The term "core competencies" refers to 'critical capabilities or resources' needed for success in a particular area. As applied to highway safety, "core competencies" include a knowledge base, a basic skill set, and an analytical capability to make key highway safety decisions. This study focused on safety-related content in the civil engineering departments' transportation courses and public health programs' injury prevention courses. The findings of this study showed an evolving need for core competencies to be addressed in highway safety courses that are offered in the U.S. (Dixon et al., 2021).

The core competencies do not represent all the knowledge and skills necessary for a safety professional to be successful. Instead, they represent the core components that one must know in the overall field of highway safety. Other relevant knowledge and skills needed include an understanding of statistics and evaluation processes, public affairs, engineering judgments, effective communications, and social marketing. Upon examination of a typical course syllabus, core competencies are similar to the identified key learning modules as presented by other disciplines in similar fields. Different sectors of highway safety such as engineering, public policy, road user behavior, and injury prevention require a core understanding of key knowledge and skill sets. The top core competencies are:

- Multidisciplinary nature of road safety.
- Agency-related setups for safety management.
- Crash data sources, characteristics, and usage.
- Key contributing factors, safety countermeasures, and evaluation.
- Have a highway safety management program developed, implemented, and administered.

Table 5 shows an outline of key topics in a conventional highway safety course.

Table 5. Outline of key topics

Topic	Objectives	Content
Introduction to Road Safety		
Traffic Crash—a global underemphasized problem.	Be familiar with the gravity of the problem.	1. Crash statistics (global, U.S. and state). 2. Comparing traffic crashes with other types of fatalities.
Impact of crashes on a society.	Recognize the multidimensional aspects of safety..	1. Public health problem. 2. Economic problem. 3. Liability problem/Social problem.
Dissecting a crash.	Identify influential and contributing factors to a crash and its severity.	1. Basic crash mechanism. 2. Haddon matrix. 3. How roadway, vehicle, and environmental conditions contribute to a crash occurrence and its severity.
Introduction to the 4E approach.	Understand the significance of the 4E approach.	1. Roadway users' characteristics. 2. Vehicle characteristics. 3. Roadway characteristics. 4. Environment. 5. Emergency service.
Basic Safety Concepts		
Defining Safety.	Understand the scientific definition of safety.	1. How do customers define safety. 2. Objective and subjective safety. 3. Safety definition.
Safety Data		
Safety Related Data.	Understand how the crash data can be used to measure safety and the issues related to crash counts.	1. Regression to the mean. 2. Issues with the data quality. 3. Direct measurement. 4. Surrogate measurement.

Fundamental Statistics		
Fundamental Statistics.	Refresh fundamental statistics related to safety analysis.	1. Mean and variance estimation. 2. Accuracy and standard error. 3. Related probability distribution faction. 4. Introduction to the Empirical Bayes method.
Development of Safety Models		
Introduction	Understand the purpose, development history and issues in safety models.	1. The need for safety predictive models in the project decision making process. 2. Introduction to parametric and non-parametric modeling techniques. 3. Conceptual safety predictive model.
Development of Safety Models.	Understanding the basic steps in the safety modeling process and having the ability to develop models with local crash data.	1. Data cleaning process. 2. Exploratory data analysis. 3. Formulating model structure. 4. Parameter estimation. 5. Model fitness evaluation.
Safety Predictive Models from HSM		
Safety Predictive Models from HSM.	Be familiar with the safety models for three types of highways for potential safety management applications.	
Safety Evaluations		
Introduction to safety evaluation.	Understand the purpose and requirements for safety evaluation.	Safety evaluation objectives and definitions.
Methodology	Understand the correct way to evaluate safety and apply the fundamental concept to roadway safety to estimate project safety or crash countermeasures.	1. The logical basis for safety evaluation. 2. General evaluation types. 3. Observational nature of roadway safety evaluation. 4. Before-and-after study. 5. Cross-sectional study.
Case studies	Be able to perform safety evaluation analysis.	1. Atchafalaya I-10 Speed study. 2. Lane conversion (4U to 5T) study.

Source: Sun, X., 2015. Development of a Highway Safety Fundamental Course. Report No. FHWA/LA.14/524

Resources

The author of this book is the co-principal investigator of NCHRP 20(07)-384 Core Competency (CC). Please see the link below for more comprehensive information on university courses on highway safety:

https://github.com/subasish/NCHRP-20-07-384-CC-Courses

Example Problem 1

Do bicycle-related injuries vary by gender and age? Answer the research question by using a nationally representative data source.

Solution: To answer this question, a dataset from the National Electronic Injury Surveillance System (NEISS) has been used. The following code chunks show the coding to answer the question. The code results are not shown (few major plots are shown to explain the results).

Example Problem 1 (Code Chunk 1)

```
## Please check my RPUBS for additional codes: https://rpubs.com/subasish
## Codes are also published here:  https://rpubs.com/subasish/331572

## import libraries
library(neiss)
data(injuries)
data(products)

## import supporting libraries
library(ggplot2)
library(dplyr)
library(reshape2)

## identify bicycle injuries
prod_bike <- subset(products, code==5040|code==5033|code==1202)
prod_bike

injuries_bike <- subset(injuries, prod1==1202| prod1==5040| prod1==5033)
dim(injuries_bike)

library(ggplot2)
injuries_bike$location <- as.factor(injuries_bike$location)
whereinjury <- injuries_bike %>% group_by(location) %>% summarise(total = sum(weight))
ggplot(data = whereinjury,
     aes(x = location, y = total)) +
      geom_bar(stat = „identity“, fill = „red“, alpha = 0.8)+theme_bw()+
      theme(legend.position=“none“, axis.title.x = element_blank(),
           axis.text.x= element_text(angle=45, hjust = 1)) +
      ylab("Estimated number of Bicycle injuries") +
      ggtitle("Location of Bicycle Injuries")
```

Figure 10 shows the locations of bicycle-related injuries. The most common location is the street or highways, and the least common location is a farm or industrial place.

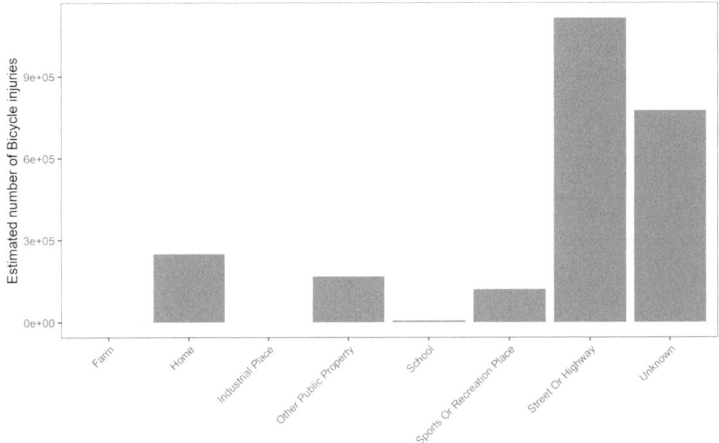

Figure 10. Location of bicycle injuries.

Example Problem 1 (Code Chunk 2)

```
injuries_bike$sex <- as.factor(injuries_bike$sex)
whereinjury <- injuries_bike %>% group_by(location, sex) %>% summarise (total =
sum(weight)) %>%
      arrange(desc(total))
ggplot(data = whereinjury[whereinjury$sex != "None listed",],
     aes(x = location, y = total, fill = sex)) +
      geom_bar(alpha = 0.8, stat = "identity", position = "dodge") + theme_bw()+
      scale_fill_manual(values = c("blue", "red")) +
      theme(axis.title.x = element_blank(), legend.title=element_blank(),
          axis.text.x= element_text(angle = 45, hjust = 1)) +
      ylab("Estimated number of injuries") +
      ggtitle("Location of Injuries")
injuries_bike <- subset(injuries, prod1==1202| prod1==5040| prod1==5033)
dim(injuries_bike)

library(ggplot2)
injuries_bike$location <- as.factor(injuries_bike$location)
whereinjury <- injuries_bike %>% group_by(location) %>% summarise(total =
sum(weight))
ggplot(data = whereinjury,
     aes(x = location, y = total)) +
      geom_bar(stat = "identity", fill = "red", alpha = 0.8) + theme_bw() +
      theme(legend.position = "none", axis.title.x = element_blank(),
          axis.text.x = element_text(angle = 45, hjust = 1)) +
      ylab("Estimated number of Bicycle injuries") +
      ggtitle("Location of Bicycle Injuries")
```

Figure 11 shows the location of injuries by gender. The most common location for both a male or a female to be injured is a street or highway. The general findings show that males are more commonly injured than females.

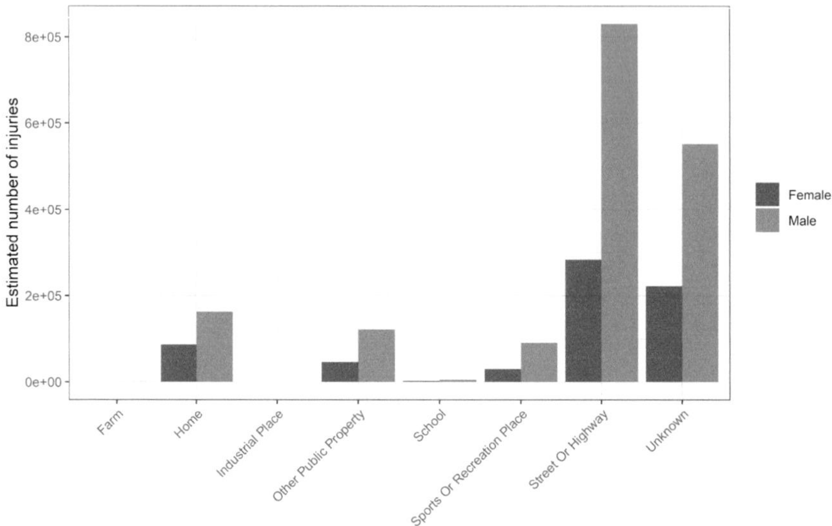

Figure 11. Location of injuries by gender.

Example Problem 1 (Code Chunk 3)

```
sexageinjury <- injuries_bike %>%
  group_by(sex, age = as.numeric(cut(age, breaks = (seq(0,100, by = 1))))-1) %>%
  summarise(total = sum(weight))
sexageinjury
medianpop <- population %>% filter(year >= 2009) %>% group_by(age, sex) %>%
  summarise(n = median(n))
totalinjuries <- left_join(medianpop, sexageinjury, by = c("age" = "age"))
totalinjuries <- totalinjuries %>% filter(sex.x == tolower(sex.y)) %>%
  select(age, sex = sex.x, population = n, injuries = total)
totalinjuries
toiletinjury <- injuries_bike %>%
      group_by(sex, age = as.numeric(cut(age, breaks = (seq(0,100, by = 1))))-1) %>%
      summarise(total = sum(weight))
totalinjuries <- left_join(medianpop, toiletinjury, by = c("age" = "age"))
totalinjuries <- totalinjuries %>% filter(sex.x == tolower(sex.y)) %>%
      select(age, sex = sex.x, population = n, injuries = total) %>%
      mutate(rate = injuries/population*1e5) %>%
     melt(id = c("age", "sex"), measure = c("injuries", "rate"))
```

```
levels(totalinjuries$variable) <- c("Estimated Number of Injuries", "Injury Rate per
100,000 Population")
ggplot(data = totalinjuries,
      aes(x = age, y = value, color = sex)) +
       facet_wrap(~variable, ncol = 1, scales = "free_y") +
       geom_line(size = 1.2, alpha = 0.9) + theme_bw() +
       scale_color_manual(values = c("blue", "red")) +
       theme(legend.title=element_blank(), legend.justification=c(0,0.38),
            legend.position=c(0,0.38)) +
       ylab("Number") + xlab("Age") +
       ggtitle("Bicycle Related Injuries by Age and Sex")
```

Figure 12 shows the estimated number of bicycle-related injuries by age and gender. Males face a higher estimated number of injuries than females. Injuries are most common for both sexes in the age group of 10-15 years.

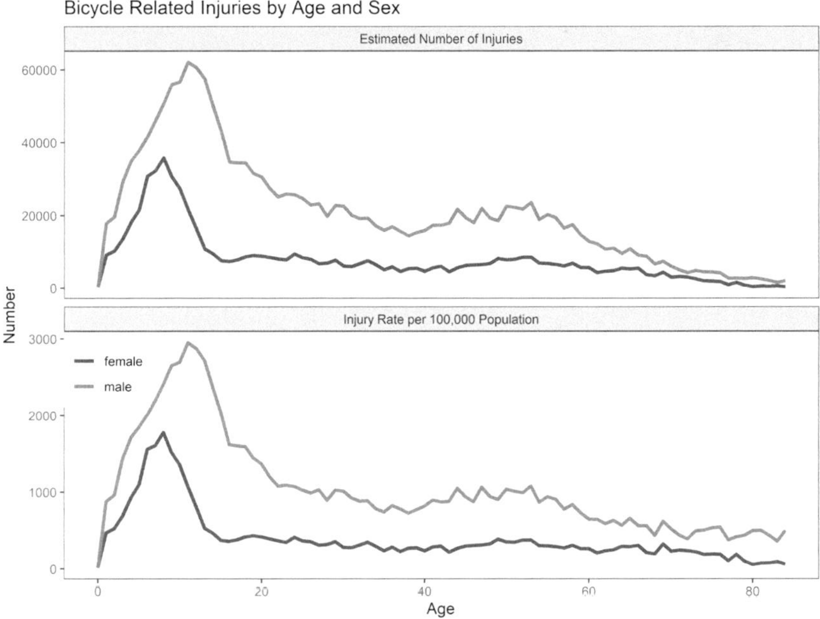

Figure 12. Number of injuries and injury rates by gender.

Example Problem 2

How does the traffic fatality rate change over the years? Show the results graphically.

Solution: To answer this question, Fatality Analysis Reporting System (FARS) data has been used. The following code chunks show the coding to answer the question. The code results are not shown (few major plots are shown to explain the results).

Example Problem 2 (Code Chunk 1)

```
## Collect traffic fatality rate data from FARS
## For this example, FARS data is collected from 1994 to 2013.

## Please check my RPUBS for additional codes: https://rpubs.com/subasish
## Codes are also published here:  https://rpubs.com/subasish/156137

library(dplyr)
library(tidyr)
library(grid)
library(scales)
library(ggplot2)
us <- data %>%
  filter(State == "USA") %>%
  gather(Year, Fatality, X1994:X2013) %>%
  separate(Year, c("left","Year"), sep="X") %>%
  select(-left)%>%
  arrange(Year)
head(us)

us_base <- us[us$Year==1994,3]
us$us_baseline <- us_base

us <- us %>% mutate(us_change = (Fatality-us_baseline)/us_baseline)
head(us)

states <- data %>%
  filter(State != "USA") %>%
  gather(Year, Fatality, X1994:X2013) %>%
  separate(Year, c("left","Year"), sep="X") %>%
  select(-left) %>%
  arrange(Year) %>%
  filter(Fatality != "NA")

state_base <- states %>%
  filter(Year == 1994) %>%
  select(State, State_Baseline = Fatality)

states <- states %>%
  left_join(state_base) %>%
  arrange(State) %>%
  mutate(state_change = (Fatality-State_Baseline)/State_Baseline)

states$Year <- as.numeric(states$Year)
us$Year <- as.numeric(us$Year)
```

```
rank <- states %>%
  filter(Year == 2013) %>%
  arrange(desc(state_change)) %>%
  mutate(rank = seq(1,length(State), by=1)) %>%
  filter(rank < 6 | rank > 46 )

p <- ggplot(states, aes(Year, state_change, group=State)) +
  theme_bw() +
  theme(plot.background = element_blank(),
      panel.grid.minor = element_blank(),
      panel.grid.major.x = element_blank(),
      panel.grid.major.y = element_line(linetype = 3, color = "grey50"),
      panel.border = element_blank(),
      panel.background = element_blank(),
      text=element_text(size=20),
      axis.ticks = element_blank(),
      axis.title = element_blank()) +
  geom_line(color="grey90", alpha=.9)+
  labs(title="Changes in Traffic Fatality Rates [1994-2013]")+
  scale_x_continuous(breaks = c(1995, 2000, 2005, 2010))

p <- p +
  geom_line(data=us, aes(Year, us_change, group=1), linetype=5, size = 1.2)

p <- p +
  geom_line(data=filter(states, State==44),
        aes(Year, state_change, group=State), color="#D8B70A", size = 1.5)
p <- p +
  geom_line(data=filter(states, State==9),
        aes(Year, state_change, group=State), color="#046C9A", size=1.2) +
  geom_line(data=filter(states, State==35),
        aes(Year, state_change, group=State), color="#C27D38", size=1.2)

p1 <- p + annotate("text", x = 2014.2, y = 0.07, label = "N. Dakota (5%)",
color="#C27D38", size=5)
p2 <- p1 + annotate("text", x = 2014, y = -0.21, label = "Texas (-22%)", color="#D8B70A",
size=5)
p3 <- p2 + annotate("text", x = 2014, y = -0.37, label = "USA (-37%)", color="black",
size=5)
p4 <- p3 + annotate("text", x = 2014, y = -0.71, label = "D.C. (-72%)", color="#046C9A",
size=5)
p4
```

Figure 13 shows the traffic fatality changes over the years from 1994 to 2013. Texas, the USA, and D.C. all have downward trends, whereas North Dakota is increasing slightly. North Dakota had the highest positive change in fatality rate in 2013, whereas D.C. had the lowest.

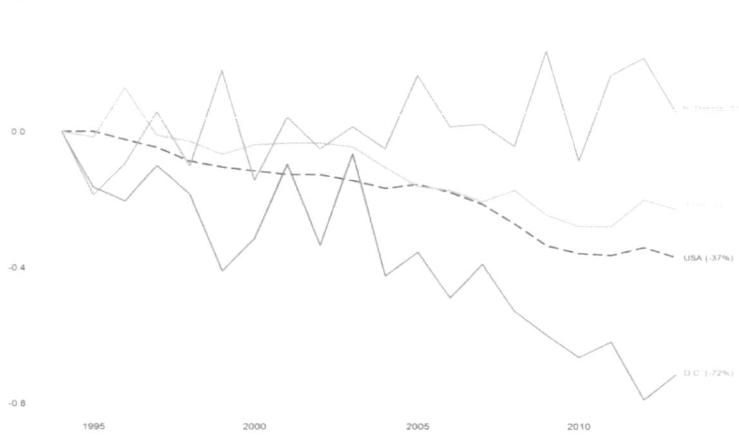

Figure 13. Comparison of traffic fatality rates.

Coding help 1

Develop a searchable 'CMF Clearinghouse' webtool.

Solution: CMF Clearinghouse is an excellent tool for identifying suitable countermeasures. However, the website is not flexible and easily searchable. DataTables (https://datatables.net/) is an excellent tool to use to resolve this problem. The following code can help in generating a searchable CMF clearinghouse (see Table 6).

Coding Help 1 (Code Chunk 1)

```
### Data Source: http://www.cmfclearinghouse.org/

## Please check my RPUBS for additional codes: https://rpubs.com/subasish
## Codes are also published here:  https://rpubs.com/subasish/506776

library(DT)
library(readxl)
setwd("~folder location")
cmf <- read_excel("CMFClearinghouse.xlsx", sheet="V0")
cmf$CMF <- as.numeric(cmf$CMF)
cmf$CMF <- round(cmf$CMF, 3)
datatable(cmf, extensions = 'Responsive', options(digits = 3))
```

Coding help 2

Draw speed crash schematics using R.

Solution: Data for this reproducible example (see Figure 14 for the output) was collected from the National Performance Management Research Data Set (NPMRDS).

Table 6. Partial display of the searchable CMF clearinghouse

Show 10 entries Search:

	CMF ID	Countermeasure	Subcategory	Category	CMF	CRF	Crash Type
1	1	Decrease lane width from 11 feet to 9 feet	Lane width	Roadway	1.21	-21	All
2	2	Decrease lane width from 11 feet to 10 feet	Lane width	Roadway	1.09	-9	All
3	3	Increase lane width from 11 feet to 12 feet	Lane width	Roadway	0.95	5	All
4	4	Four to five lane conversion	Number of lanes	Roadway	1.11	-11	All
5	5	Four to five lane conversion	Number of lanes	Roadway	1.1	-10	All
6	6	Four to five lane conversion	Number of lanes	Roadway	1.11	-11	All
7	7	Five to six lane conversion	Number of lanes	Roadway	1.03	-3	All

Coding Help 2 (Code Chunk 1)

```
etwd("~Folder Name")
tmc <- read.csv("TMC2.csv") # check https://github.com/subasish/AI_in_HighwaySafety for data

## Please check my RPUBS for additional codes: https://rpubs.com/subasish
## Codes are also published here: https://rpubs.com/subasish/190283

library(ggplot2)
library(ggrepel)
## Warning: package 'ggrepel' was built under R version 3.2.5
cbPalette <- c("#046C9A", "#46ACC8", "#E1AF00", "#DC863B")
ggplot(tmc) + geom_segment(aes(color=Direction, x=miles,
xend=miles1, y=Direction, yend=Direction), size=1.5,
arrow=arrow(length=unit(0.4,"cm"))) +theme_bw()+
  geom_point(aes(x=miles1,y=Direction, color=Direction), size=2)+
  geom_point(aes(x=2,y=1),size=7, color="green")+
  geom_point(aes(x=2,y=3),size=7, color="grey")+
  geom_label_repel(aes(x=miles1,y= Direction, label=speed1, color = Direction),
                fontface = 'bold', force=60,
                box.padding = unit(0.25, "lines"),
                point.padding = unit(0.5, "lines"))+
  scale_color_manual(values=cbPalette)+
  geom_vline(xintercept = 2, color="red", linetype = "longdash", size=1.5)+
 annotate("text", label = "Crash time: 08:11:45 AM", x = 2.05, y=3.1, size = 5, color =
"red", angle=90)+
```

(Contd.)

```
geom_segment(aes(x=1.6,y= 0.8, xend = 2, yend = 1),
        color='red', size=0.5, arrow = arrow(length = unit(0.5, "cm")))+
annotate("text", x=1.5,y= 0.75, label = "Crash on Northbound",
      size=4, color='red') +
 geom_segment(aes(x=1.6,y=   2.8, xend = 2, yend = 3),
         color='red', size=0.5,arrow = arrow(length = unit(0.5, "cm")))+
 annotate("text", x=1.5,y=   2.75, label = "Crash on Opposite Bound",
      size=4, color='red') +labs(x="Distance (in miles)")
```

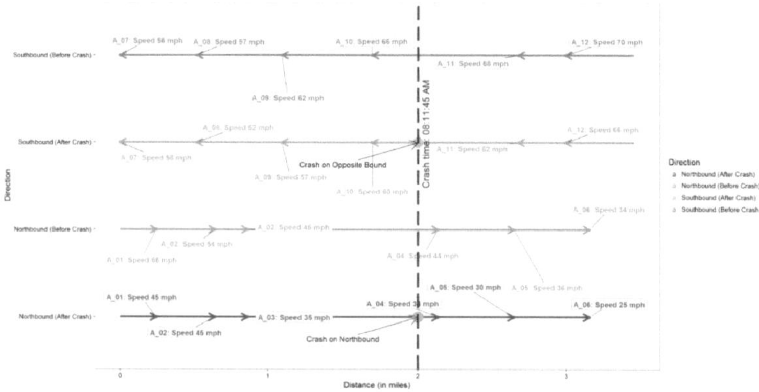

Figure 14. Speed crash schematics.

Coding help 3

Show an example of manipulation of Tables and Maps interactively.

Solution:

It is very interesting to make a table and map talk to each other. The following scripts can make this task easy. The end result can be seen in Figure 15. The web version is here: https://rpubs.com/subasish/519027.

Coding Help 3 (Code Chunk 1)

```
SharedData1 <- read.csv("file:///~folder_location/FARS_2014_2016_PBType_withPersonVehicleAccident.csv") # check ### https://github.com/subasish/AI_in_HighwaySafety for data

## Please check my RPUBS for additional codes: https://rpubs.com/subasish
## Codes are also published here:  https://rpubs.com/subasish/519027

sd1 <- SharedData1[,c(1, 218, 219, 34, 8, 9)]
colnames(sd1)[2] <- "lat"
colnames(sd1)[3] <- "long"

library(crosstalk)
library(leaflet)
library(DT)
```

```
sd <- SharedData$new(sd1[sample(nrow(sd1), 150),])

# Create a filter input
##filter_slider("HOUR", "Hour", sd, column=~HOUR, step=0.1, width=250)

# Use SharedData like a dataframe with Crosstalk-enabled widgets
bscols(
  leaflet(sd) %>% addTiles() %>% addCircleMarkers(),
        datatable(sd,    extensions="Scroller",    style="bootstrap",    class="compact",
width="100%",
          options=list(deferRender=TRUE, scrollY=300, scroller=TRUE)))
```

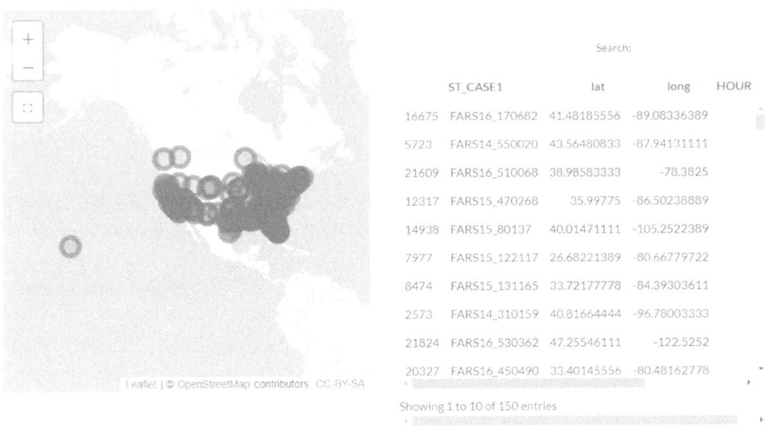

	ST_CASE1	lat	long	HOUR
16675	FARS16_170682	41.48185556	-89.08336389	
5723	FARS14_550020	43.56480833	-87.94131111	
21609	FARS16_510068	38.98583333	-78.3825	
12317	FARS15_470268	35.99775	-86.50238889	
14938	FARS15_80137	40.01471111	-105.2522389	
7977	FARS15_122117	26.68221389	-80.66779722	
8474	FARS15_131165	33.72177778	-84.39303611	
2573	FARS14_310159	40.81664444	-96.78003333	
21824	FARS16_530362	47.25546111	-122.5252	
20327	FARS16_450490	33.40145556	-80.48162778	

Figure 15. Speed crash schematics.

Chapter Conclusion

This chapter provides a brief introduction of highway safety concepts. It starts with some key core concepts of highway safety education. It also provides an overview of the 4E approach, along with different intervention tools, data sources, and models within highway safety. Observational B/A studies are also looked at. This chapter concludes with information on core competencies and resources of highway safety courses offered by different universities. In the end, a couple of example problems are provided, and some coding help is offered.

Further Reading

AASHTO, 2010. Highway Safety Manual, 2010. AASHTO, Washington DC.

Das, S., 2021. Data Dive into Transportation Research Record Articles: Authors, Coauthorships, and Research Trends. TR News, pp. 25-31.

Das, S., 2021. Traffic volume prediction on low-volume roadways: A Cubist approach. Transportation Planning and Technology 44, pp. 93-110.

Dixon, K., Das, S. and Potts, I., 2021. NCHRP 20-07 (384) Report: Core Competencies for Key Safety Analysis. National Academies.

Elvik, R., Vaa, T., Hoye, A. and Sorensen, M., 2009. The Handbook of Road Safety Measures: Second Edition. Emerald Group Publishing.

Fitzpatrick, K., McCourt, R. and Das, S., 2019. Current Attitudes among Transportation Professionals with Respect to the Setting of Posted Speed Limits. Transportation Research Record. Journal of the Transportation Research Board 2673, pp. 778-788.

Hauer, E., 1997. Observational Before-after Studies in Road Safety: Estimating the Effect of Highway and Traffic Engineering Measures on Road Safety. Elsevier Science Incorporated, Tarrytown, N.Y.

Hauer, E., 2014. The Art of Regression Modeling in Road Safety. Springer.

Kong, X., Das, S., Zhou, H. and Zhang, Y., 2021. Characterizing phone usage while driving: Safety impact from road and operational perspectives using factor analysis. Accident Analysis & Prevention 152.

Lord, D., Qin, X. and Geedipally, S.R., 2021. Highway Safety Analytics and Modeling. Elsevier.

Mannering, F. and Bhat, C., 2014. Analytic methods in accident research: Methodological frontier and future directions. Analytic Methods in Accident Research, Vol. 1, pp. 1-22.

McCourt, R., Fitzpatrick, K., Koonce, P. and Das, S., 2019. Speed limits: Leading to change. ITE Journal 89, pp. 38-43.

Park, E.S., Fitzpatrick, K., Das, S. and Avelar, R., 2021. Exploration of the relationship among roadway characteristics, operating speed, and crashes for city streets using path analysis. Accident Analysis & Prevention 150.

Sun, X. and Das, S., 2014. A Comprehensive Study on Pavement Edge Line Implementation. LTRC Project.

Sun, X. and Das, S., 2015. Developing a Method for Estimating AADT on all Louisiana Roads. LTRC Project.

Tarko, A., 2019. Measuring Road Safety with Surrogate Events. Elsevier.

Washington, S., Karlaftis, M.G., Mannering, F. and Anastasopoulos, P., 2020. Statistical and Econometric Methods for Transportation Data Analysis. CRC Press.

Zubaidi, H.A., Obaid, I.A., Alnedawi, A. and Das, S., 2021. Motor vehicle driver injury severity analysis utilizing a random parameter binary probit model considering different types of driving licenses in 4-legs roundabouts in South Australia. Safety Science 134.

References

Das, S., 2016. Statistical and Algorithmic Models on Crash Analysis: Research Papers and Abstracts. Accessed May 2021. http://subasish.github.io/pages/TRB2016/crash.html

Lord, D., and Mannering, F., 2010. The statistical analysis of crash-frequency data: A review and assessment of methodological alternatives. Transportation Research Part A: Policy and Practice, 44, (5), pp. 291-305.

Tsapakis, I., S. Sharma, B. Dadashova, S. Geedipally, A. Sanchez et al., 2019. Evaluation of Highway Safety Improvement Projects and Countermeasures. TxDOT Report.

Savolainen, P., Mannering, F., Lord, D., and Quddus, M., 2011. The statistical analysis of highway crash-injury severities: A review and assessment of methodological alternatives. Accident Analysis & Prevention, 43, (5), pp. 1666-1676.

CHAPTER
3

Artificial Intelligence Basics

3.1. Introduction

With the massive amount of highway safety-related data, easily accessible computational power, and numerous machine learning algorithms, highway safety research has evolved from traditional statistical analysis to combining the power of machine learning into statistical learning. More and more data-driven studies on highway safety topics have been published recently. Many insights and patterns have been revealed that were not found with traditional data collection techniques, such as surveys and conventional analysis methods. However, with a plethora of literature available now on the topic, there is a need for conducting a comprehensive literature review on AI applications within the highway safety field.

This chapter offers a brief summary of the basics of AI concepts. Figure 16 shows the main branches of AI.

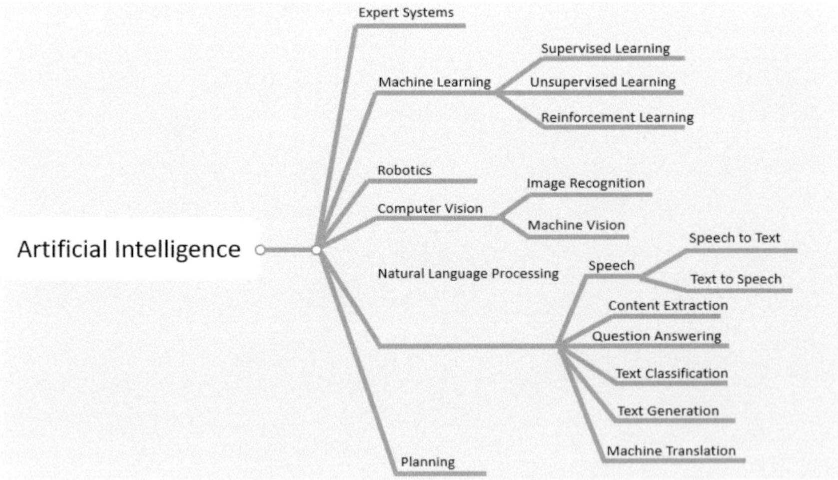

Figure 16. Main branches of AI.

3.2. Machine Learning

A major branch of the AI domain is machine learning, which is able to be divided into five major sub-domains: supervised learning, unsupervised learning, semi-supervised learning, reinforcement learning, and deep learning. Some major applied domains of machine learning are natural language processing (NLP), robotics, computer vision, expert systems, and planning.

3.2.1. Supervised Learning

The response variable is defined in supervised learning (SL), and the learning algorithm uses a large dataset along with the corresponding response variable and dependent variables. The algorithm is then taught the key characteristics of each data point to determine the response. The mechanism is inclined to estimate the outcome or correct answer for any given data point based on key features.

For example, a list of 20,000 freeway roadway segments is considered for analysis. The researcher started to collect as many geometric variables as possible. By exploring the historical crash counts, the individual impact of each variable is compared with the number of crashes. If the data has been trained based on different features and the associated number of crashes over time, the algorithm is able to correctly estimate the number of crashes. Here is another example of computer vision. Thousands of bridge condition pictures are given to a program, and the computer vision algorithm is given the correct label of the bridge condition. From this, the algorithm is able to learn the characteristics within the images that distinguish the conditions of different bridges.

In another example of SL, a machine is given a dataset relating to the stock market, and it is given a corresponding label for each data point that tells it about the stock's activity on a certain day. The machine is able to learn the final index or stock price for each data point. Now, the machine can identify the stock investment choice of a new data point, based on the previous data it was given.

3.2.2. Unsupervised Learning

No response variable is provided in unsupervised learning. The algorithm in unsupervised learning is designed to identify trends in a large amount of data to find similarities. It is then able to produce an algorithm that can identify clusters of similar data points and categorizes a new item within an existing cluster.

Here is an unsupervised learning example. A crash dataset of alcohol-impaired driving is provided. The dataset has different variables at the driver level such as driver age, driver gender, driver license type, driver condition, driver severity type, and first harmful event. Without defining a response variable, the dataset has been used to identify clusters or groups of different variable attributes. Different clusters can provide information about different scenarios. Agencies can consider these findings while developing policies and guidelines.

3.2.3. Semi-supervised Learning

Semi-supervised learning is a blend of unsupervised and supervised learning. In semi-supervised learning, a machine uses a large dataset, and only some of the data points are labeled. The machine uses clustering methods, like in unsupervised learning, to create groups based on the data, and it uses the labels it was given to assign labels to the rest of the data.

Semi-supervised learning can be beneficial in saving a lot of time and effort. For example, a list of 10,000 crash narrative reports is taken to identify marijuana-impaired crashes. For supervised learning, the crash reports need to be tagged as marijuana-impaired and non-marijuana-impaired crashes, which is a significant effort. For semi-supervised learning, there is a need for a subset of crash narrative reports to be tagged properly. Among the reports, the algorithm will find similarities with the narrative reports and assign labels to the groups of similar crash reports based on the few defined crash narratives. Therefore, each crash narrative will be given a label that can be used to help the algorithm continue learning. Semi-supervised learning is clearly very effective in handling a large number of unlabeled data points.

3.2.4. Reinforcement Learning

In recent years, the most promising field of machine learning has been reinforcement learning. This method can be useful in continuously changing situations, such as real-life traffic conditions. In this situation, the machine must adjust its response to a continuously changing external situation. Reinforced learning enables the machine to sense the external environment as well as its own state to choose an action that will optimize a certain predefined goal.

3.2.5. Deep Learning

A very promising field of machine learning is deep learning. Chapter 7 provides more information on deep learning.

3.3. Regression and Classification

3.3.1. Regression

No model can be expected to make perfect predictions in the real world. Furthermore, as the same value of the explanatory x can lead to different target y's, y may not be a complete function of x. This could occur when there is some randomness in y.

Assuming that calculating a linear function of the independent variables (in example x) is how to obtain the dependent variable (i.e., y), followed by the addition of a zero-mean normal random variable, results in a simple model which in written form is,

$$y = xT\beta + \xi, \tag{1}$$

where random effects are modeled by ξ. ξ is always assumed to contain a zero mean. β is a vector of weights, which would be predicted or estimated. When for a certain set of independent variables x^* a value of y is predicted with this model, then the value that takes ξ cannot be predicted. The mean value (zero) is the best prediction. The model predicts $y = 0$ if $x = 0$.

Definition: Linear Regression

A linear regression model contains the exploratory vector x and predicts $xT\beta$ for some vector of coefficients β. Using the data, the coefficients are determined to develop the best predictions.

Choosing β: β can be determined by two methods- a probabilistic way and a non-probabilistic way. Although these two methods differ in core principles, many researchers consider them as interchangeable.

Probabilistic Approach: By assuming that ξ is a zero-mean normal random variable that has an unknown variance, one can consider $P(y|x, \beta)$ as normal with a mean measure of $x^T\beta$ with some likelihood functions. Here, σ^2 is the variance of ξ. The likelihood function is:

$$\begin{aligned} \log\log L(\beta) &= \sum_i \log\log P(x_i, \beta) \\ &= -\frac{1}{2\sigma^2}\sum\nolimits_i (y_1 - x_i^T\beta)^2 + term\ \beta. \end{aligned} \tag{2}$$

Maximization of the log-likelihood is parallel to the minimization of the negative log-likelihood. Also, the location of the minimum is not changed by the term $\frac{1}{2\sigma^2}$, so β is associated with the minimization of $\Sigma_i(y_i - x_i^T\beta)^2$. The minimization can be expressed as:

$$\left(\frac{1}{N}\right)\left(\Sigma_i(y_i - x_i^T\beta)^2\right) \tag{3}$$

Non-probabilistic Approach: For the estimated values of β, there remains an estimation of the values of the unmodelled effects ξ_i, by assuming $\xi_i = y_i - x_i^T\beta$. It is evident that the unmodeled effects should be minimized. The mean of the squared values is a good measure of size, which can be minimized as:

$$\left(\frac{1}{N}\right)\left(\Sigma_i\,(y_i - x_i^T\beta)^2\right) \tag{4}$$

Using the expressions of vectors and matrices, it can be described as:

$$\left(\frac{1}{N}\right)(y - \chi\beta)^T(y - \chi\beta) \tag{5}$$

which indicates:

$$\chi^T\chi\beta - \chi^T y = 0 \tag{6}$$

Residuals and R-squared

For a reasonable feature choice, it is expected that $\chi^T\chi$ the vector, residual, can be written as:

$$e = y - \chi\widehat{\beta} \tag{7}$$

This shows the discrepancy between the true value at each point and the model's predicted value. Due to the fact that the mean-squared error value relies on the measurement units of the dependent variable, it is not a suitable measure of the goodness of the regression. The **mean-squared error** can be expressed as:

$$m = \frac{e^T e}{N} \tag{8}$$

There is a significant quantitative measure that doesn't depend on the units of how accurate a regression is. If the dependent variable is not a constant, it has some variance. This model ought to describe some characteristics of the dependent variable's value, meaning the dependent variable's variance ought to be larger than the residual variance. If perfect predictions were made by the model then the residual variance should be zero.

Regression Basics

Consider $y = \chi\widehat{\beta} + e$, where e is the residual. Consider χ has a column of ones, and β is considered to minimize e^Te. The properties are:

1. $e^T\chi = 0$, i.e., e is orthogonal to any column of χ.
2. $e^T1 = 0$.
3. $1^T(y - \chi\widehat{\beta}) = 0$.
4. $e^T\chi\widehat{\beta} = 0$.

One can calculate $mean(\{y\})$ and $var[y]$ now that y is a one-dimensional dataset assembled into a vector. Similarly, the implication of mean and variance for $\chi\widehat{\beta}$ and e is known as they are one-dimensional datasets arranged into a vector. This gives an important result:

$$var[y] = var\left[\chi\widehat{\beta}\right] + var[e] \tag{9}$$

This allows for considering a regression describing the variance in y; when the ability to explain y gets better, $var\ [e]$ goes down. On the contrary, a normal measure of a regression's goodness is the percentage of the variance of y it can explain, which is also called R^2 or the R-squared value. It can be written as:

$$R^2 = \frac{var\left[\chi\widehat{\beta}\right]}{var[y]} \tag{10}$$

which shows how effectively the regression explains the training data. A perfect model will have $R^2 = 1$ (which is rare), and good predictions give high values of R^2. Two estimates for the value of R^2 are acquired in ways that attempt to consider the quantity of data and the number of variables within the regression that can be determined from looking at the summary given for linear regression by *R*. The disparities aren't significant between these numbers and R^2.

Bias and Variance

It is a good approach to look at an abstract way in the process of finding a model. Doing so shows three distinctive effects that trigger erroneous predictions from models. One of these is an **irreducible error**. Even a perfect model choice is able to have misconstrued predictions due to the fact that more than one prediction could be correct for the same data. This could also be thought of as the possibility for multiple future data points to all have the same x but a different y. In this case, making wrong predictions is unavoidable. **Bias** is the second effect; some collections of models must be utilized by users, however, the collection's best model may be unable to predict the data effects. Errors due to the inability of the best model to accurately predict data are attributed to bias.

Variance is considered as the third effect; the user has to choose a model from the collection, and it is not likely to be the best model in many cases. The reason is that the estimates of the parameters are not exact due to a limited amount of data. Errors due to a chosen model that isn't the family's best are attributed to variance. Figure 17 shows a diagram of model complexity, demonstrating the relationship of error and model complexity with total error, variance, and bias (Washington et al., 2020).

Need to know

The trade-off between bias and variance is important. In general, one expects that the best model in the family can provide a precise estimation with a low variance. However, when a model is small or simple it may face difficulty reproducing the data (by generating a large bias). Likewise, a large or complex model typically has high variance, but low bias. All modeling requires handling this trade-off between variance and bias, so it is difficult to be precise about a model's complexity. One reasonable proxy is the number of parameters needed to be estimated to determine the model.

The influential error source is biased when low degree monomials are used, and when high degree monomials are used it causes variance. Feeling that the primary difficulty is bias is a common mistake, and, subsequently, people tend to use incredibly complex models. This typically results in huge errors in variance due to poor estimates of model parameters. People with modeling experience fear variance over bias.

This discussion of variance and bias suggests that simply using all the explanatory variables that can be thought of or obtained is not a good idea, as it could result in a model with more variance issues. Rather, a model which utilizes a big enough subset of the explanatory variables such that the bias is not a problem and small enough to control the variance must be chosen. Choosing explanatory

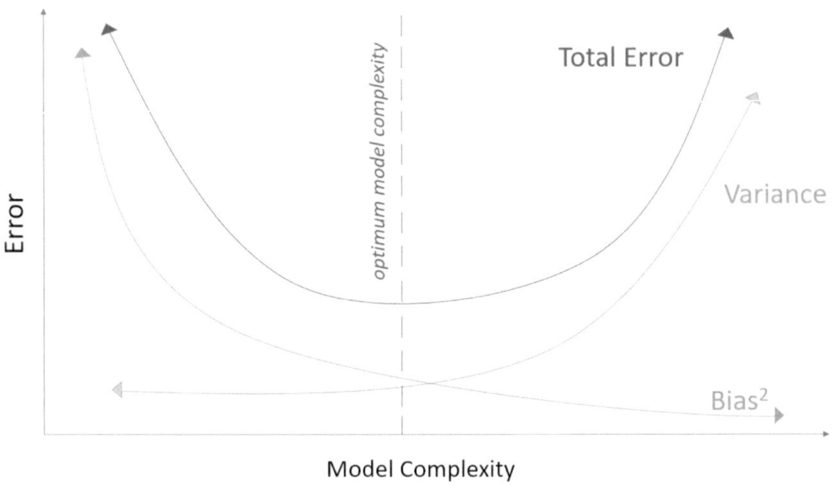

Figure 17. Model complexity.

variables requires some strategy; the simplest (but not best) approach is searching for a good set among sets of explanatory variables. However, it can be difficult to know when one has been found (Washington et al., 2020).

Model Selection based on AIC and BIC

In a regression analysis, it is common to have multiple explanatory variables. An assortment of non-linear functions could be computed with only one measurement. The fitting cost will be reduced by inserting variables into a model, but that does not mean that there will be better predictions. Which explanatory variables will be used needs to be chosen. Poor predictions might be made by a linear model that has fewer explanatory variables due to the fact that it is incompetent at precisely representing the independent variable, and poor predictions also might be made by one that has more explanatory variables due to the fact that the coefficients cannot be estimated as well. These effects need to be balanced to choose the explanatory variables that will be used (and thus the model that will be used).

As more complex models are associated with lower training errors, the most complex model is typically the model that has the lowest training error. Training error is not the best method for error testing due to the fact that lower bias on the model's part is indicated by lower training error; greater variance, however, is expected with lower bias, which the training error does not consider. Penalizing the model for its complex nature is one strategy, wherein some penalty that reflects the model's complexity is added to the training error, so as the model becomes more complex, the training error goes down and the penalty increases. Subsequently, it is expected to observe a point wherein the sum is at a minimum.

Constructing penalties has many methods, such as Akaike Information Criterion (AIC), which is a method originally due to *H* that, instead of utilizing the training error, utilizes the log-likelihood of the model's maximum value. For this value *L* is used, and *k* is used for the number of parameters that are predicted to fit the model. Thus, the AIC can be written as:

$$2k - 2l \tag{11}$$

Note that a better model is linked to a larger log-likelihood. Subsequently, a lower AIC value is typically associated with a better model. If one assumes the noise to be a zero-mean normal random variable, then for regression models estimating the AIC is direct. The noise variance, and thus the model's log-likelihood, is given by estimation of the mean-squared error. Two points are important to watch; first, *k*, the total number of parameters that are predicted to fit the model (e.g., in a linear regression model, wherein one models *y* as $x^T \beta + \xi$ to estimate $\widehat{\beta}$ and the variance of ξ (in order to get the log-likelihood), *d* parameters need to be estimated; $k = d + 1$ in this situation). Second, typically log-likelihood is known only up to a constant, thus, various constants are frequently used by different software, which can be tremendously confusing. Bayes' information criterion (BIC) is an alternate measure, which can be written as:

$$2klogN - 2L \tag{12}$$

where *N* is the size of the training dataset. This is frequently narrated as $2L - 2klogN$, but the form above was given so one desires the smaller value each time, like with AIC. A lot of literature compares BIC and AIC. AIC is typically considered to have firmer theoretical foundations, but is somewhat known for overestimating the required number of parameters (Washington et al., 2020).

3.3.2. Classification

During hard classification, the probabilities are either converted using thresholds or returned by the algorithm, and, for each observation, there are four potential cases (see Table 7):

- True Negative (*TN*): the algorithm predicts it to be negative, and the response is truly negative.
- False Positive (*FP*): the algorithm predicts it to be positive, but the response is truly negative.
- True Positive (*TP*): the algorithm predicts it to be positive, and the response is truly positive.
- False Negative (*FN*): the algorithm predicts it to be negative, but the response is truly positive.

Every observation can be categorized into one of these four cases. The possibilities form a confusion matrix, as shown below in Table 7.

Table 7. Four Potential Cases

Actual/Predicted	Predicted Negative (0)	Predicted Positive (1)
Actual Negative (0)	True Negative (*TN*)	False Positive (*FP*)
Actual Positive (1)	False Negative (*FN*)	True Positive (*TP*)

Below are several common performance metrics, in which cases are hard classified:

- **Misclassification:** To calculate a binary classifier, the misclassification rate, also called the error rate, is the most often used metric. This rate represents the probability of an incorrect classification prediction. It can be expressed as:

$$Misclassification\ rate = Pr(\widehat{Y} \neq Y) = \frac{FN + FP}{TN + FN + TP + FP} \tag{13}$$

- **Accuracy:** The accuracy calculates the rate of correct classifications.

$$Accuracy = Pr(\widehat{Y} \neq Y) = 1 - Misclassification\ rate \tag{14}$$

- **Sensitivity:** The sensitivity (which can be defined as the true positive rate) measures the percentage of positive responses correctly classified and can be determined from the confusion matrix.

$$Senstivity = Pr(\widehat{Y} = 1 \mid Y = 1) = \frac{TP}{TP + FN} \tag{15}$$

True positive rate (*TPR*) and recall are other terms that represent sensitivity. The measure of sensitivity is popular in medical tests. For machine learning and natural language processing, the term recall is often used.

- **Specificity:** The specificity (also referred to as the true negative rate or *TNR*) measures the percentage of the negative responses accurately classified and can be determined from the entries of the confusion matrix.

$$Specificity = Pr(\hat{Y} = 0 \mid Y = 0) = \frac{TN}{TN + FP} \tag{16}$$

- **Positive predictive value (*PPV*):** The PPV is the likelihood of the correct classification of a positively classified observation. It can be determined from the entries of the confusion matrix:

$$PPV = Pr(\widehat{Y} = 1 \mid Y = 1) = \frac{TP}{TP + FP} \tag{17}$$

- **Negative predictive value (*NPV*):** The *NPV* is the likelihood of the correct classification of a negatively classified observation. It can be determined from the entries of the confusion matrix.

$$NPV = Pr(\widehat{Y} = 0 \mid Y = 0) = \frac{TN}{TN + FN} \tag{18}$$

- **Diagnostic likelihood ratio (*DLR*):** The *DLR* is a measure of accuracy for a binary classifier. In the context of statistics, this ratio is simply a likelihood ratio, but as an accuracy measure, it is known as a diagnostic likelihood ratio (*DLR*). Both positive and negative *DLR* metrics are defined:

$$Positive\ DLR = \frac{TPR}{FPR} \tag{19}$$

$$Negative\ DLR = \frac{TNR}{FNR} \tag{20}$$

- **F-Score:** The F-Score (also referred to as the F1-Score or F-measure) can be defined as the harmonic mean of precision (PPV) and recall (TPR), and is a tool utilized to evaluate the performance of the binary classifier. It is commonly utilized in information theory to assess the performance of the search, document classification, and query classification functions.

$$F-Score = \frac{2}{\frac{1}{PPV}+\frac{1}{TPR}} = 2 \times \frac{PPV \times TPR}{PPV + TPR} \tag{21}$$

3.4. Sampling

All components in any field of analysis consist of a 'population.' Sampling includes selecting some part of a population that can provide a representative estimate of something about the whole population. A sample requires being representative of the population to obtain statistical reliability. Sampling design has two broad categories: probability sampling and non-probability sampling. In scientific research, probability sampling is mostly used. Unrestricted sampling infers sampling methods that consider taking a random sample at large from a population. The other sampling methods consider some local or global restrictions to make sampling more robust. These methods are known as restricted sampling. Figure 18 shows different kinds of sampling methods, including probability and non-probability sampling.

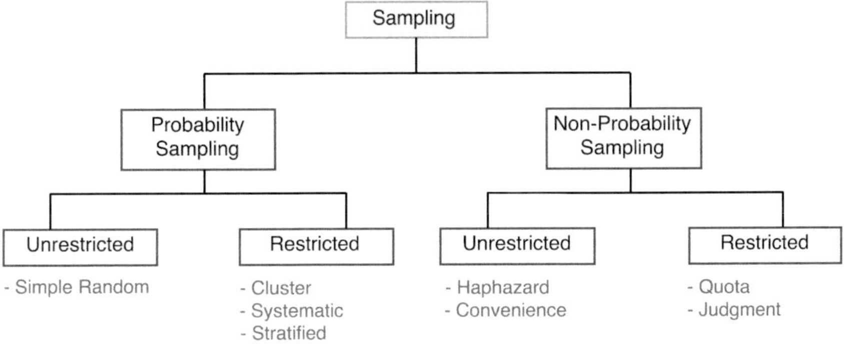

Figure 18. Types of sampling design.

3.4.1. Probability Sampling

Probability sampling indicates a sampling design wherein each unit of the population has an equal likelihood of being drawn in a sample. This method is delimited by statistical regularity (a sample would represent the main traits of the population).

Simple Random Sampling: Simple random sampling ensures a sampling technique wherein each unit of the population has an equal likelihood of being picked. This method has two categories: with and without replacement. Simple random sampling with substitution allows the return of the element drawn from the population before the next draw. Repeat selection is not allowed by the technique without replacement. Unbiased estimates of the population mean with an unbiased estimate of variability, used to evaluate the result's reliability, are offered by simple random sampling. n distinct units are chosen from the N units in the population so that each possible arrangement of n units is equally likely to be the sample chosen in simple random sampling without replacement. Figure 19 illustrates a sampling technique used in simple random sampling. It shows that from a population of 25 units, 8 random units are picked.

It is common to use the selection of a spatially random sample by dividing the local roads into particular length segments, but local road geographic information systems (GIS) databases are less developed in comparison to those for more major roadways. This makes the application of simple random sampling difficult.

Cluster Sampling: In this sampling, a central unit consists of a cluster of secondary units, typically in close vicinity of each other. Clustered primary units contain spatial arrangements, i.e., square or long collections of adjacent plots in spatial settings. All secondary units of the primary unit would be considered in the sample if cluster sampling considers any secondary unit of a primary sample. Obtaining estimators of low variance is the principle of clustering; the population should be divided into clusters so that one cluster is similar to another in this

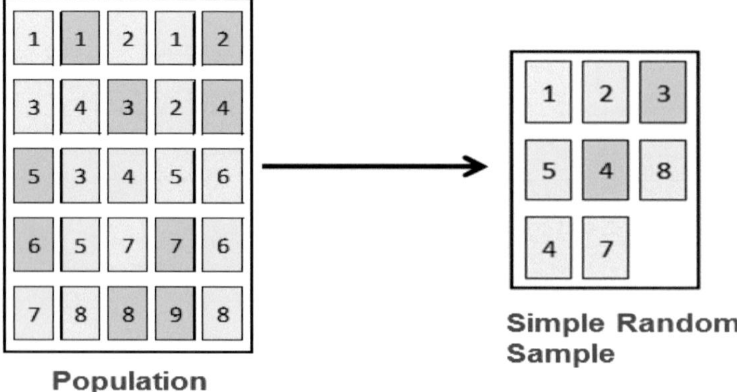

Figure 19. Simple random sampling.

method. The concepts of cluster sampling are illustrated by an example in Figure 20. The population has 25 units and comprises five clusters, and the target is to select a sample of 10 units. Two clusters (in this case, cluster 2 and cluster 5) are randomly selected.

Systematic Sampling: A systematic sampling design selects a single starting unit at random and determines a fixed interval for all other units in the population. This method is also called quasi-random sampling, as random sampling is usually conducted as the first choice. For example, if a population has $N = 2{,}000$ units and n is taken as 200 units, then the sampling fraction would be 10. A random sample would be selected between 1 and 10, and it would be systemically continued 200 times. Figure 21 illustrates systematic sampling by proving an example. The population has 25 units. To get a sample of eight units, the first unit is randomly selected between 1 and 3. This is systematically continued eight times to complete the sample.

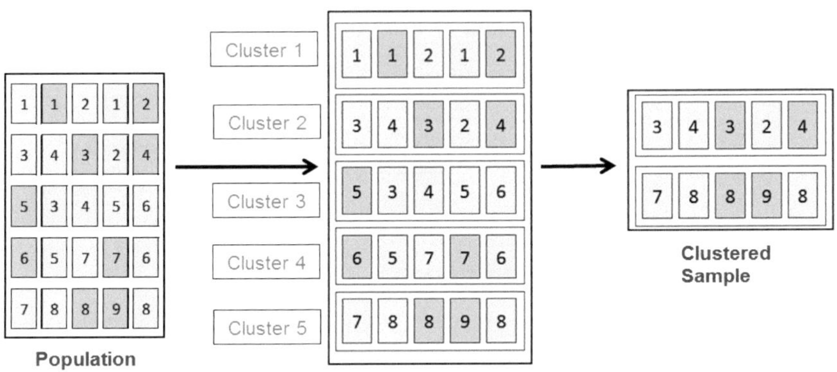

Figure 20. Cluster sampling.

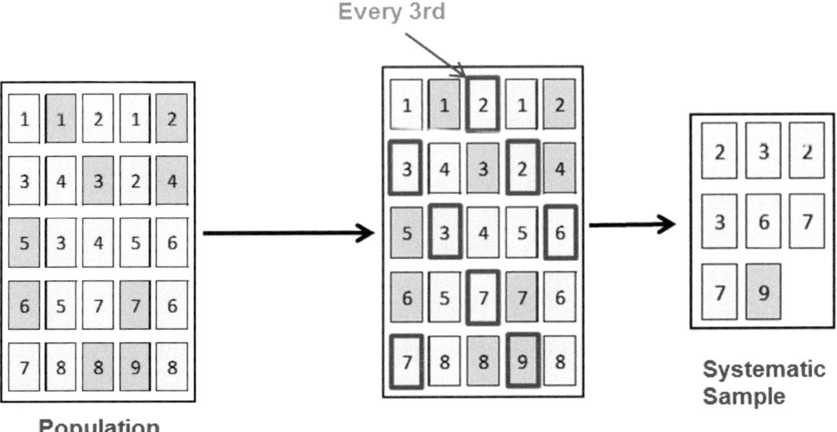

Figure 21. Systematic sampling.

Stratified Sampling: In this sampling method, the population is divided into regions or various strata, and units are selected from each stratum. The assumption of stratification is to divide the population so that the units within a stratum are as similar to each other as possible since this method contemplates within-stratum variances of estimators for the entire population. The sampling design in each stratum being simple random sampling is ensured by stratified random sampling. The concept of stratified sampling is illustrated by providing an example in Figure 22. From a population with 25 units and 3 strata, a sample of 10 units is selected.

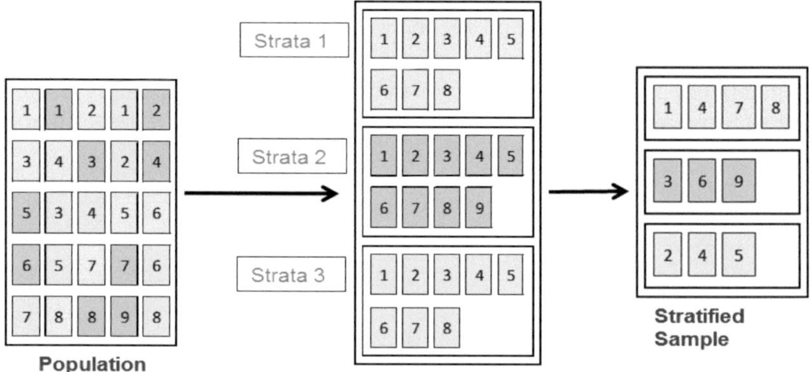

Figure 22. Stratified sampling.

3.4.2. Non-probability Sampling

Non-probability sampling is not popular for scientific research. This method does not consider any basis of probability and statistical regularity.

3.4.3. Population Parameters and Sampling Statistics

Assume that a population has N units and a simple random sample of n units is taken from it. A measurement that describes the entire population is known as a population parameter. Population mean and population variance are two common population parameters. The y-values' average in the entire population is the population mean μ:

$$\mu = \frac{1}{N}(y_1 + y_2 + ... + y_N) = \frac{1}{N}\Sigma_{i=1}^{N} y_i \tag{22}$$

The population variance is defined as

$$\sigma^2 = \frac{1}{N-1}\Sigma_{i=1}^{N} (y_i - \mu)^2 \tag{23}$$

A measurement that describes the sample is called a sample statistic. Two common sample statistics are sample mean and sample variance. The sample mean y is the mean of the y-values in the entire sample:

$$\underline{y} = \frac{1}{n}(y_1 + y_2 + ... + y_n) = \frac{1}{n}\Sigma_{i=1}^{n} y_i \tag{24}$$

The sample variance is

$$s^2 = \frac{1}{n-1} \Sigma_{i=1}^{n} (y_i - \underline{y})^2 \tag{25}$$

The interval is known as a 100 (1 – α)% confidence interval, and the quantity (1 – α) can be described as the confidence coefficient. The general selections for the value of α are 0.01, 0.05, and 0.1. With $\alpha = 0.01$, for example, the confidence coefficient is 0.99. In simple random sampling, a 99% confidence interval procedure means there is a 99% likelihood of the interval including the true value of the population mean μ. For the population mean μ, an approximate 100 (1 – α)% confidence interval is

$$\underline{y} + t\sqrt{\left(\frac{N-n}{N}\right)\frac{s^2}{n}} \tag{26}$$

3.4.4. Sample Size

The sample mean $\underline{y}$ is an unbiased estimator of the population mean μ with sample variance $var\ (\underline{y}) = \frac{(N-n)\sigma^2}{Nn}$ in simple random sampling. Sample size can be estimated as:

$$z\sqrt{\frac{(N-n)}{N}\frac{\sigma^2}{n}} = d \tag{27}$$

Solving for n results in the necessary sample size for the population mean:

$$n = \frac{1}{\frac{d^2}{z^2\alpha^2} + \frac{1}{N}} = \frac{1}{\frac{1}{n_0} + \frac{1}{N}} \tag{28}$$

Where:
n = Sample size
Z = Value of the standard normal statistic for an alpha confidence level (two sided)
α = Allowable probability of error
d = Maximum allowable difference between the estimate and the true value
N = Population size

$$n_0 = \frac{z^2\alpha^2}{d^2} \tag{29}$$

Resources

Readers can consult the following link for a curated list of AI concepts, tools, and algorithms:
https://github.com/owainlewis/awesome-artificial-intelligence
The following link shows the applicability of different ML algorithms:
https://rpubs.com/subasish/170751

Example Problem 1

Show a reproducible example of crash count data modeling.

Solution

To solve this problem, crash data from Louisiana has been used. The following code chunks show the coding to answer the question. The code results are not shown (few major plots are shown to explain the results).

Example Problem 1 (Code Chunk 1)

```
## Please check my RPUBS for additional codes: https://rpubs.com/subasish

setwd("~folder location")
dat= read.csv("TAHIR_rwd1.csv")
table(dat$HwyClass)
head(dat)

dat1= subset(dat, HwyClass=="Rural Two-Lane")
dim(dat1)
dat1= dat1[, c(4, 5, 7:11)]

# Set the graphical design
ggplot2::theme_set(ggplot2::theme_light())

# Set global knitr chunk options
knitr::opts_chunk$set(
 fig.align = "center",
 fig.height = 3.5
)

# Required packages
library(dplyr)
library(ggplot2)
library(caret)
library(vip)
library(rsample)

# stratified sampling with the rsample package
split <- initial_split(dat1, prop = 0.7, strata = "Total_Crash")
ames_train <- training(split)
ames_test <- testing(split)

model1 <- lm(Total_Crash ~ AADT, data = ames_train)


# Fitted regression line (full training data)
p1 <- model1 %>%
 broom::augment() %>%
 ggplot(aes(Total_Crash, AADT)) +
 geom_point(size = 1, alpha = 0.3) +
 geom_smooth(se = FALSE, method = "lm") +
 ggtitle("Fitted regression line")
```

```
# Fitted regression line (restricted range)
p2 <- model1 %>%
 broom::augment() %>%
 ggplot(aes(Total_Crash, AADT)) +
 geom_segment(aes(x = AADT, y =Total_Crash,
 xend = AADT, yend = .fitted),
 alpha = 0.3) +
 geom_point(size = 1, alpha = 0.3) +
 geom_smooth(se = FALSE, method = "lm") +
 ggtitle("Fitted regression line (with residuals)")

# Side-by-side plots
grid.arrange(p1, p2, nrow = 1)
summary(model1)
(model2 <- lm(Total_Crash ~ Length+ AADT+LaneWidth+ShWidth+Curve+MinPSL,
 data = ames_train))

# Fitted models
fit1 <- lm(Total_Crash ~ Length+ AADT,
 data = ames_train)
fit2 <- lm(Total_Crash ~ Length*AADT, data = ames_train)

# Regression plane data
plot_grid <- expand.grid(
 Length = seq(from = min(ames_train$Length),
 to = max(ames_train$Length),
 length = 100),
 AADT = seq(from = min(ames_train$AADT),
 to = max(ames_train$AADT),
 length = 100)
)
plot_grid$y1 <- predict(fit1, newdata = plot_grid)
plot_grid$y2 <- predict(fit2, newdata = plot_grid)

# Level plots
p1 <- ggplot(plot_grid, aes(x = Length, y =AADT,
 z = y1, fill = y1)) +
 geom_tile() +
 geom_contour(color = „white“) +
 viridis::scale_fill_viridis(name = "Predicted\nvalue", option = "inferno") +
 theme_bw() +
 ggtitle("Main effects only")
p2 <- ggplot(plot_grid, aes(x = Length, y = AADT,
 z = y2, fill = y1)) +
 geom_tile() +
 geom_contour(color = "white") +
```

(*Contd.*)

```
 viridis::scale_fill_viridis(name = "Predicted\nvalue", option = "inferno") +
 theme_bw() +
 ggtitle("Main effects with two-way interaction")

gridExtra::grid.arrange(p1, p2, nrow = 1)

model3 <- lm(Total_Crash ~ ., data = ames_train)

# print estimated coefficients in a tidy data frame
broom::tidy(model3)

set.seed(123) # for reproducibility
(cv_model1 <- train(
 form = Total_Crash ~ AADT,
 data = ames_train,
 method = "lm",
 trControl = trainControl(method = "cv", number = 10)
))

# model 2 CV
set.seed(123)
cv_model2 <- train(
 Total_Crash ~ AADT+ Length,
 data = ames_train,
 method = "lm",
 trControl = trainControl(method = "cv", number = 10)
)

# model 3 CV
set.seed(123)
cv_model3 <- train(
 Total_Crash ~ .,
 data = ames_train,
 method = "lm",
 trControl = trainControl(method = "cv", number = 10)
)

# Extract out of sample performance measures
summary(resamples(list(
 model1 = cv_model1,
 model2 = cv_model2,
 model3 = cv_model3
)))
```

Figure 23 shows the comparison between main effects and main effects with interaction. The trends show that interaction makes association non-linear.

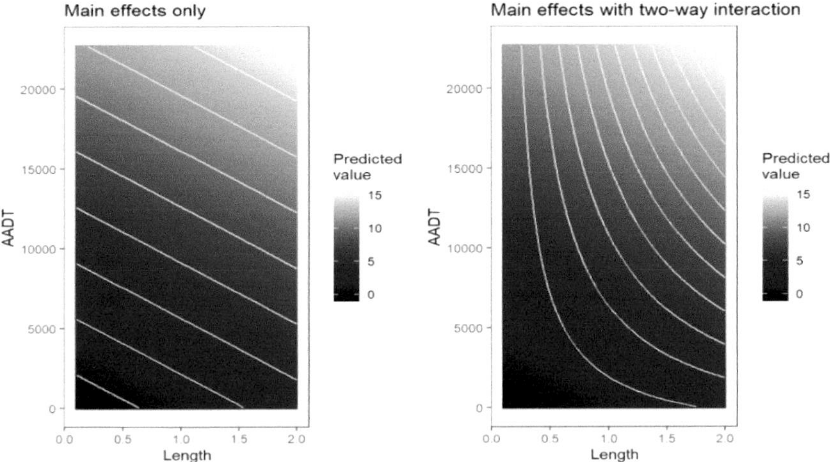

Figure 23. Comparison between main effects and main effects with interaction.

Example Problem 2
Develop an AI model based on Chicago Crash data

Solution

For this example, data was collected from Chicago. The following code chunks show the coding to answer the question. The code results are not shown (few major plots are shown to explain the results below).

Example Problem 2 (Code Chunk 1)

```
### Made some changes in variable selection. Otherwise, complete replicate of
### https://juliasilge.com/blog/chicago-traffic-model/

## Please check my RPUBS for additional codes: https://rpubs.com/subasish
## Code is uploaded here: https://rpubs.com/subasish/770232

library(tidyverse)
library(lubridate)
library(RSocrata)
library(data.table)
library(themis)
library(baguette)
### install.packages(„baguette")
library(lubridate)
library(ggplot2)
theme_set(theme_bw(base_size = 16))
```

(Contd.)

```
### the following codes are from Julia Silge's blog. However, variable selection and
some steps are ### different.
years_ago <- today() - years(4)
crash_url <- glue::glue("https://data.cityofchicago.org/Transportation/Traffic-Crashes-
Crashes/85ca-t3if?$where=CRASH_DATE > '{years_ago}'")
crash_raw <- as_tibble(read.socrata(crash_url))
names(crash_raw)

crash <- crash_raw %>%
 arrange(desc(crash_date)) %>%
 transmute(
 injuries = if_else(injuries_total > 0, "injuries", "none"),
 crash_date,
 crash_hour,
 report_type = if_else(report_type == "", "UNKNOWN", report_type),
 num_units,
 posted_speed_limit,
 weather_condition,
 lighting_condition,
 roadway_surface_cond,
 lighting_condition,
 alignment,
 crash_type,
 first_crash_type,
 trafficway_type,
 prim_contributory_cause,
 latitude, longitude
 ) %>%
 na.omit()

dim(crash)
head(crash)

crash$year= year(crash$crash_date)
table(crash$year)

crash= subset(crash, year==2018| year==2019| year==2020)
dim(crash)

theme_set(theme_bw(base_size = 18))
crash %>%
 mutate(crash_date = floor_date(crash_date, unit = "week")) %>%
 count(crash_date, injuries) %>%
 filter(
 crash_date != last(crash_date),
 crash_date != first(crash_date)
 ) %>%
```

```
ggplot(aes(crash_date, n, color = injuries)) +
geom_line(size = 1.5, alpha = 0.7) +
scale_y_continuous(limits = (c(0, NA))) +
labs(
x = NULL, y = "Number of traffic crashes per week",
color = "Injuries?"
)
```

Figure 24 shows the amount of traffic crashes from 2018-2021. The top line represents crashes with injuries, and the bottom line represents crashes without injuries.

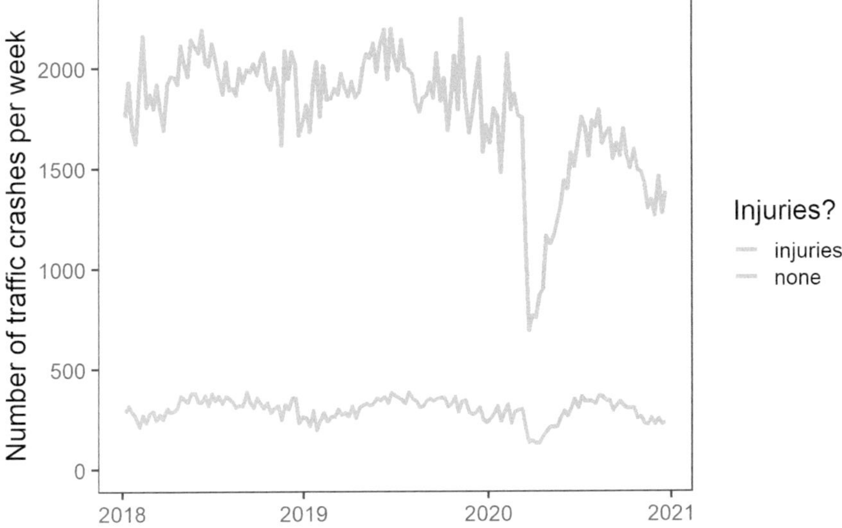

Figure 24. Injury and no injury crashes during 2018-2021.

Example Problem 2 (Code Chunk 2)

```
crash %>%
filter(latitude > 0) %>%
ggplot(aes(longitude, latitude, color = injuries)) +
geom_point(size = 0.5, alpha = 0.4) +
labs(color = NULL) +
scale_color_manual(values = c("deeppink4", "gray80")) +
coord_fixed()
```

Figure 25 shows a map of Chicago traffic crashes, including injury and non-injury crashes.

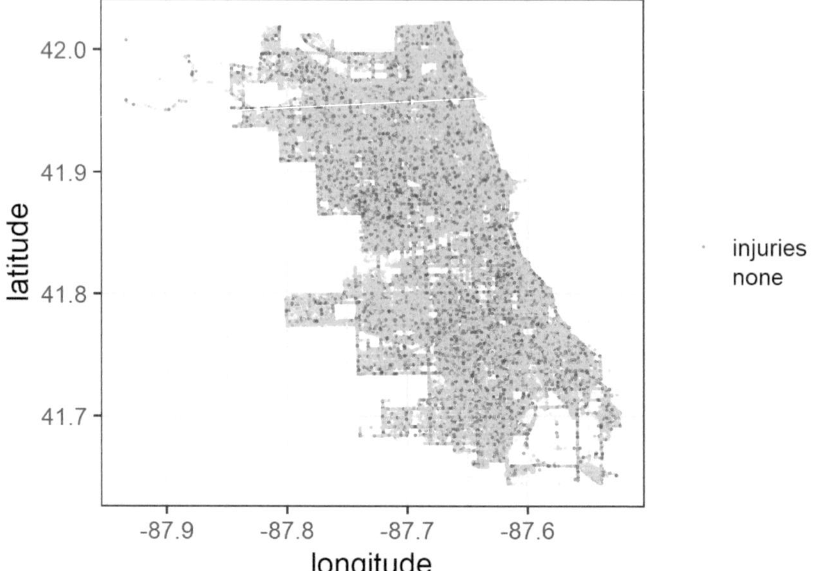

Figure 25. Map showing injury and no injury crashes.

Example Problem 2 (Code Chunk 3)

```
names(crash)

crash= crash[, -c(2, 3, 4, 15:17)]
names(crash)
library(tidymodels)

set.seed(2021)
crash_split <- initial_split(crash, strata = injuries)
crash_train <- training(crash_split)
crash_test <- testing(crash_split)

set.seed(2020)
crash_folds <- vfold_cv(crash_train, strata = injuries)
crash_folds



crash_rec <- recipe(injuries ~ ., data = crash_train) %>%
 step_other(weather_condition, first_crash_type,
 trafficway_type, prim_contributory_cause,
 other = "OTHER"
 ) %>%

step_downsample(injuries)
```

```
bag_spec <- bag_tree(min_n = 10) %>%
 set_engine("rpart", times = 25) %>%
 set_mode("classification")

crash_wf <- workflow() %>%
 add_recipe(crash_rec) %>%
 add_model(bag_spec)


#doParallel::registerDoParallel()
#crash_res <- fit_resamples(
 #crash_wf,
 #crash_folds,
 # control = control_resamples(save_pred = TRUE)
#)


crash_fit <- last_fit(crash_wf, crash_split)
collect_metrics(crash_fit)
crash_imp <- crash_fit$.workflow[[1]] %>%
 pull_workflow_fit()

crash_imp$fit$imp %>%
 slice_max(value, n = 10) %>%
 ggplot(aes(value, fct_reorder(term, value))) +
 geom_col(alpha = 0.8, fill = "midnightblue") +
 labs(x = "Variable importance score", y = NULL)
```

Figure 26 shows a variable importance plot. The crash type has the highest variable importance, and alignment has the lowest variable importance.

Example Problem 2 (Code Chunk 4)

```
collect_predictions(crash_fit) %>%
 roc_curve(injuries, .pred_injuries) %>%
 ggplot(aes(x = 1 - specificity, y = sensitivity)) +
 geom_line(size = 1.5, color = „midnightblue“) +
 geom_abline(
 lty = 2, alpha = 0.5,
 color = "gray50",
 size = 1.2
 ) +
 coord_equal()
```

Figure 27 shows an ROC curve over a graph of 1-specificity vs. sensitivity. It peaks and flattens out around a sensitivity of 1.00.

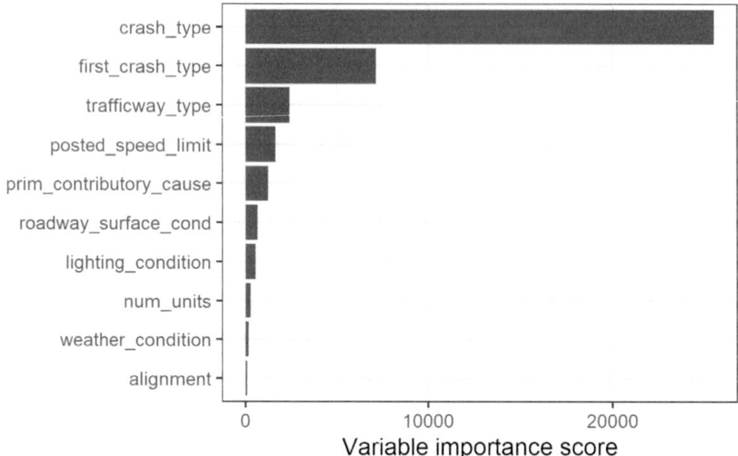

Figure 26. Variable importance plot.

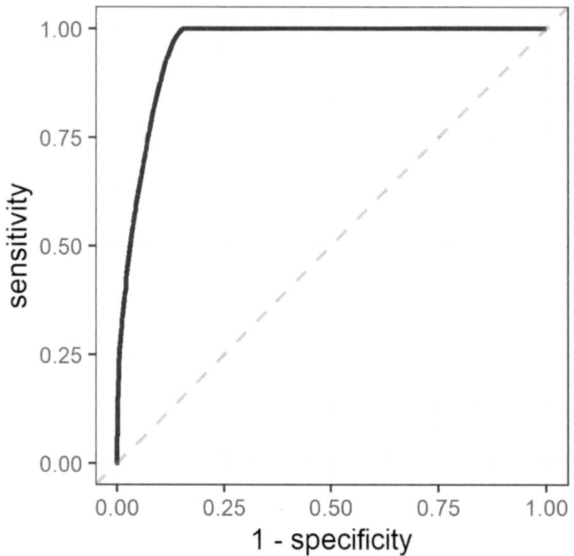

Figure 27. ROC curve.

Chapter Conclusion

This chapter introduces the key branches of AI, including sections on machine learning (covering supervised learning, unsupervised learning, semi-supervised learning, reinforcement learning, and deep learning), regression and classification, and sampling (covering probability sampling, non-probability sampling, population parameters, sampling statistics, and sample size). Concepts of regression and classification are introduced with the inclusion of the concept of sampling. More details on the relevant algorithms are described in the following chapters. Some example problems are included to aid in understanding the AI tools in highway safety engineering.

Further Reading

Andriole, S.J., 1985. Applications in Artificial Intelligence. Petrocelli Books, Inc., USA.
Bartoletti, I., Leslie, A. and Millie, S.M., 2020. The AI Book: The Artificial Intelligence Handbook for Investors, Entrepreneurs and FinTech Visionaries. John Wiley & Sons.
Burkov, A., 2019. The Hundred-Page Machine Learning Book. Andriy Burkov.
Gawda, A.E., Kacprzyk, J., Rutkowski, L. and Yen, G.G., 2017. Advances in Data Analysis with Computational Intelligence Methods. Dedicated to Professor Jacekurada, 1st ed. Springer Publishing Company, Incorporated.
Claster, W.B., 2020. Mathematics and Programming for Machine Learning with R: From the Ground Up. CRC Press.
Cormen, T.H., Cormen, T.H., Leiserson, C.E., Rivest, R.L. and Stein, C., 2001. Introduction to Algorithms. MIT Press.
Forsyth, D., 2018. Probability and Statistics for Computer Science. Springer, USA.
Haugeland, J., 1989. Artificial Intelligence: The Very Idea. MIT Press, Boston, USA.
Knox, J., Wang, Y. and Gallagher, M., 2019. Artificial Intelligence and Inclusive Education: Speculative Futures and Emerging Practices. Springer.
Mitchell, M., 2019. Artificial Intelligence: A Guide for Thinking Humans. Farrar, Straus and Giroux.
Monarch, R. (Munro), 2021. Human-in-the-Loop Machine Learning: Active Learning and Annotation for Human-centered AI. Manning Publications.
Neapolitan, R.E. and Jiang, X., 2018. Artificial Intelligence: With an Introduction to Machine Learning, Second Edition. CRC Press.
Russell, S. and Norvig, P., 2009. Artificial Intelligence: A Modern Approach, 3rd ed. Prentice Hall Press, USA.
Skiena, S.S., 2009. The Algorithm Design Manual. Springer Science & Business Media.
Smith, B.C., 2019. The Promise of Artificial Intelligence: Reckoning and Judgment. MIT Press.
Theodoridis, S., 2020. Machine Learning: A Bayesian and Optimization Perspective. Academic Press.
Zerilli, J., Danaher, J., Maclaurin, J. and Gavaghan, C., 2021. A Citizen's Guide to Artificial Intelligence. MIT Press.

Reference

Washington, S., Karlaftis, M.G., Mannering, F. and Anastasopoulos, P., 2020. Statistical and Econometric Methods for Transportation Data Analysis. CRC Press.

CHAPTER

4

Matrix Algebra and Probability

4.1. Introduction

To understand AI algorithms, it is important to have adequate knowledge of matrix algebra and probability. Undergraduate or graduate level coursework on matrix algebra and probability can be beneficial for the readers to understand the critical concepts.

As in multivariate statistical methods, matrix algebra is a very important tool. This section covers a review of matrix algebra. Additionally, key statistical concepts are also briefly described in this chapter. It is easier to do computations with matrix algebra than it is with simple algebra. Summation operators are offered before the introduction of standard matrix notation. Some common summation operators are

$$\sum_{i=1}^{N} X_i = X_1 + X_2 + \ldots + X_N$$

$$\sum_{i=1}^{N} C = NC$$

$$\sum_{i=1}^{N} (X_i + Y_i) = \sum_{i=1}^{n} X_i + \sum_{i=1}^{n} Y_i$$

$$\sum_{i=1}^{N} (X_i C + K) = C \sum_{i=1}^{n} X_i + NK$$

An $n \times p$ matrix is be written as

$$\left[x_{11} \cdots x_{1p} \vdots \ddots \vdots x_{n1} \cdots x_{np}\right] \quad (1)$$

in which j = the column index and i = the row index of matrix X. Matrix X's columns relate to independent variables that are taken from each observation and matrix X's rows correspond to observations in the data set in multiple statistical modeling applications. Thus, a matrix $X_{n \times p}$ has observations on n individuals, with each having p observed or measured attributes.

A matrix with the same count of rows and columns, or when $n = p$, is known as a square matrix. A column vector (or simply a vector) is a matrix containing only one column, and a matrix with only one row is a row vector. If two matrices have equal dimensions, and all of the corresponding elements are equal in the matrices, then the matrices are equal.

Transposing the rows and columns in matrix A gives the transpose, represented as A' or A^T, such that

$$A^T = [a_{11}\ a_{12}\ a_{13}\ a_{21}\ a_{22}\ a_{23}\ a_{31}\ a_{32}\ a_{33}]^T$$
$$= [a_{11}\ a_{21}\ a_{31}\ a_{12}\ a_{22}\ a_{32}\ a_{13}\ a_{23}\ a_{33}] \quad (2)$$

Matrices must have the same dimension if they are being subtracted or added. The corresponding difference or sum of the two matrices' individual components gives the difference or sum of the two matrices, such that

$$A + B = \left[a_{11} \cdots a_{1p} \vdots \ddots \vdots a_{n1} \cdots a_{np} \right] + \left[b_{11} \cdots b_{1p} \vdots \ddots \vdots b_{n1} \cdots b_{np} \right]$$
$$= \left[a_{11} + b_{11} \cdots a_{1p} + b_{1p} \vdots \ddots \vdots a_{n1} + b_{n1} \cdots a_{np} + b_{np} \right] \quad (3)$$

4.2. Matrix Algebra

4.2.1. Matrix Multiplication

There are two ways to perform matrix multiplication: a matrix can be multiplied with another matrix or a scalar. The scalar–matrix product is produced by multiplying each element in the matrix by the scalar. One can find the product of two matrices by calculating and then adding across the cross-products of the rows of matrix A with the columns of matrix B. In the multiplication of matrices, the order matters; subsequently, a matrix is pre- or post- multiplied by another matrix. Matrix dimensions are critical in computing products of matrices. To produce the product AB, the number of columns of matrix A must be equal to the number of rows of matrix B. When matrix A is post multiplied by B, it will result in matrix C, the size of which will have columns equal to the number of columns in matrix B and rows equal to the number of rows in matrix A.

4.2.2. Linear Dependence and Rank of a Matrix

If one vector can be expressed as a linear combination of the other, then the column vectors are linearly dependent. Otherwise, the vectors are linearly independent.

Scalar multiples of the columns of matrix $A_{n \times m}$ can be looked at as the sum of the linear combination of column and scalar vectors $\lambda_1 C_1 + \lambda_2 C_2 + ... + \lambda_m C_m = 0$. A minimum of two rows are linearly dependent if a scalar combination $\lambda_1, \lambda_2, \ldots, \lambda_m$ is located so that the sum of the linear combination equals zero. The matrix is considered linearly independent if the set of all 0 is the only set of scalars that this holds. Data analysis difficulties can result from the linear or near-linear dependencies showing up in statistical modeling. Two columns containing equal information, that differ by a constant only, is suggested by two columns having a linear dependency.

Need to know

The matrix's rank is described by the maximum number of linearly independent columns that are in the matrix (the matrix's rank is 3 in the last example), and if there are no column vectors that are linearly dependent then a matrix is considered to be full rank. A full rank matrix of independent variables implies that a different dimension in the data or different information in statistical modeling applications is measured by each variable.

4.2.3. Matrix Inversion (Division)

Division in algebra is parallel to matrix inversion. A number that is multiplied by its reciprocal or inverse always results in 1 in non-matrix algebra, such that (10)*(1/10) = 1. A matrix denoted by A^{-1} is the inverse of a matrix A in matrix algebra. Due to the inverse property, $A^{-1}\,A = AA^{-1} = I$, in which I is the identity matrix (a diagonal matrix with components along the main diagonal and zeros making up all other components):

$$[1 \cdots 0 \vdots \ddots \vdots 0 \cdots 1] \tag{4}$$

Matrix inverses are defined only for square matrices. If a matrix has an inverse (not all do), the inverse is unique. For a square $r \times r$ matrix, the inverse only exists if the matrix has a full rank (which is considered to be nonsingular). A $r \times r$ matrix with a rank that is less than r does not have an inverse and is said to be singular.

The matrix operations below are then performed to compute the unknown quantities in vector B

$$AB = C$$

$$A^{-1}\,AB = A^{-1}C \text{ (premultiply both sides by } A^{-1}\text{).}$$
$$IB = A^{-1}\,C \text{ (a matrix multiplied by its inverse is } I\text{).}$$
$$B = A^{-1}\,C \text{ (a matrix multiplied by } I \text{ is itself).} \tag{5}$$

For the solutions of the unknown in matrix B, one only needs to find the inverse of matrix A.

It is a formidable computation to compute matrix inversions for matrices bigger than 3 × 3, and these problems subsequently justify using computers extensively. For these operations, statistical analysis software is utilized in statistical modeling applications. For calculating the individual ij^{th} elements of the inverse of matrix A (matrix A^{-1}), the general formula is

$$a^{ij} = \frac{C_{ij}}{|A|} \tag{6}$$

where $|A|$ is the determinant of A and C_{ij} is the ji^{th} cofactor of A. Cofactors, determinants, and matrix inversion computations can be compared with greater detail by reviewing references on matrix algebra.

4.2.4. Eigenvalues and Eigenvectors

Eigenvectors are the characteristic vectors whereas eigenvalues are the matrix's characteristic roots. There are many applications of eigenvalues of a matrix. The solutions to the sets of equations below give results that are helpful for evaluating a square matrix A:

$$AE = \lambda E \tag{7}$$

where λ is a vector of eigenvalues, A is a square matrix, and E contains the matrix eigenvectors. Matrix manipulations can be used to obtain the eigenvalues that solve Equation 7, restricting the solutions so that $E^T E = 1$ (to get rid of the indeterminacy), and then solving

$$|A - \lambda I| = 0 \tag{8}$$

The solutions of these equations are nonzero only if the matrix $|A - \lambda I|$ contains a zero determinant or is singular. The symmetric matrix's eigenvalues will always be real, and luckily the majority of matrices solved for eigenvectors and eigenvalues in statistical modeling endeavors are symmetric.

The original formulation that is shown in Equation 8 can be utilized to locate eigenvectors now that the eigenvalues vector has been determined. Equation 8 can be altered to get

$$(A - \lambda I)\, E = 0 \tag{9}$$

The eigenvectors of matrix A can be found using Equation 9. Remember that the constraint $E^T E = 1$ has to be imposed to get a unique solution.

4.2.5. Useful Matrices and Properties of Matrices

Statistical modeling has many important matrices. A matrix is symmetrical if $A = A^T$; subsequently, a symmetrical matrix has to be square. A square matrix with off-diagonal elements that are all zeros is a diagonal matrix, of which there are two kinds: the scalar matrix and the identity matrix. The identity matrix is a diagonal matrix with elements on the main diagonal that are all ones, as shown denoted by I in Equation 9. Pre- or post-multiplying any $r \times r$ matrix A by an $r \times r$ identity matrix I gives A, so that $AI = IA = A$. The scalar matrix, a diagonal matrix, can be represented as an $r \times r$ matrix A by the $r \times r$ scalar matrix λI which is parallel to multiplying A by the scalar λ. I denotes a column vector with all components equal to 1, and J denotes a square matrix with all components equal to 1.

4.2.6. Matrix Algebra and Random Variables

Matrix algebra is very effective for working with random vectors, variables, and matrices, and it is very helpful for manipulating matrices that are utilized for developing statistical methods and models. Some simple matrices utilized in the statistical modeling of random phenomena, along with other matrices as necessary, are introduced in the section below. A matrix of random variables of size $n \times p$ is a typical starting point in many statistical modeling applications

$$X_{n\times p} = \left[x_{11} \cdots x_{1p} \vdots \ddots \vdots x_{n1} \cdots x_{np} \right] \tag{10}$$

in which the p columns in matrix X signify variables (e.g. segment width, presence of intersection, driver age.), and the n rows in matrix X embody observations throughout sampling units (e.g. autos, road sections, individuals.). A mean matrix $\underline{X}$ (representing the averages across individuals) can be shown as:

$$E[X] = \underline{X} = \left[E[X_{11}] \cdots E\left[x_{1p}\right] \vdots \ddots \vdots E[x_{n1}] \cdots E\left[x_{np}\right] \right] \tag{11}$$

in which the averages of the components from the mean matrix $\underline{X}$ are computed as follows,

$$E\left[x_{ij}\right] = \frac{\sum_{i=1}^{n} x_{ij}}{n}; \; j = 1, 2, ..., p. \tag{12}$$

Subtracting matrix $E[X]$ from X gives a deviations matrix. Building on the fact that $VAR[X_i] = E[X_i - E[X_i]]$, in matrix form (with the sizes of the matrices displayed) the variance–covariance matrix of matrix X is gathered as follows,

$$VAR[X]_{p\times p} = E\left\{ \left[X_{n\times p} - E[X]_{n\times p} \right]^T_{p\times n} \left[X_{n\times p} - E[X]_{n\times p} \right]_{p\times n} \right\} \tag{13}$$

Calculating the variance-covariance matrix using standardized variables gives a correlation matrix, where,

$$z_{ij} = \frac{x_{ij} - x_j}{\sigma_j}; \quad i = 1, 2, ..., p.$$

replaces the original x_{ij} terms.

4.3. Probability

4.3.1. Probability, Conditional Probability, and Statistical Independence

The probability of the occurrence of an event (for example, a crash or near-crash event) is the ratio of times that it occurs in a long-run sequence to the total number of examinations. Probability is denoted in notation as

$$P(A) = \frac{count\ (A)}{trials};\ trials \to \infty \tag{14}$$

where *count* (*A*) is the number of times that the incident *A* occurs, and trials (*n*) is the number of experiment repetitions or the number of recorded observations where event *A* could have occurred. As the number of trials tends to infinity, *P*(*A*) converges in probability, so one views back the idea that before getting a reliable estimate of probability, multiple trials are needed to be observed. A Bayesian statistician, however, is able to use subjective information to produce estimates of probability.

Conditional probability can be defined as the probability of an event, such as event *A*, if event *B* has occurred already, and it is given in notation as

$$P(B) = \frac{P(AB)}{P(B)} \tag{15}$$

where the joint probability of events *A* and *B* happening together is *P*(*AB*). Statistical modeling relies on conditional probability, as many statistical models predict or explain, given the independent variables *X*, the probability of an outcome, *Y*, such that the model provides $P(Y|X)$.

Conditional probabilities make up statistical hypothesis tests. The general form of a classical or frequentist statistical hypothesis test is given as

$$P(true\ null\ hypotheis) = \frac{P(data)\ p(true\ null\ hypothesis)}{P(true\ null\ hypothesis)} \tag{16}$$

It is common that on the right side of Equation 16, the denominator is the unknown and desired value. Subsequently, the classical hypothesis test doesn't offer the null hypothesis' probability of being true, but rather the data's conditional probability (given a true null hypothesis) of being observed. However, objective evidence is given by the conditional probability regarding the plausibility of the null hypothesis.

Conditional probability is also based on Bayes' theorem (utilized to bypass the classical hypothesis test results philosophical and practical problems), which is derived as follows:

$$P(B) = \frac{P(AB)}{P(B)}$$

$$P(A) = \frac{P(AB)}{P(A)}$$

$$P(B) = \frac{P(A)\ P(A)}{P(B)}\ (Bayes'\ Thoerem) \tag{17}$$

The development of some statistical methods has been helped by the use of statistical independence (the condition in which the probability of the occurrence of another event B does not affect the probability of the occurrence of event A). If events A and B are independent

$$P(AB) = P(A)P(B) \tag{18}$$

The conditional probability formula in Equation 18 can be used to show that for statistically independent events,

$$P(B) = \frac{P(AB)}{P(B)} = \frac{P(A)\,P(B)}{P(B)} = P(A) \tag{19}$$

The above equation shows that the probability that event A occurs if event B has already occurred is the probability of event A occurring if events A and B are statistically independent; this makes sense because event A is not impacted by event B.

4.3.2. Estimating Parameters in Statistical Models

Parameters are necessary and important parts of statistical models. A model often begins with a theory that is known to generate data, suggesting that it could require any number of variables and could take the general form,

$$Y = f(\theta; X) + \varepsilon \tag{20}$$

where θ is a vector of estimated model parameters, X is a matrix of variables across n observations to effect Y, ε is a vector of disturbances, and Y is a vector of outcomes. There are different techniques for coordinating functions f that relate θ and the matrix X to the outcome vector Y, i.e., the ordinary least squares regression model links the X terms to Y through the expression $Y = \beta X + \varepsilon$ where θ is the vector of estimated parameters or the β. Observational data is generally used in this approach to estimate the parameters.

There are many different methods for estimating parameters in statistical models, such as maximum likelihood, weighted least squares, ordinary or unweighted least squares, and method of moments. Maximum likelihood and ordinary least squares (two parameter estimation methods that are often used) are briefly presented to give the reader a basic understanding of these concepts.

Minimizing the squared differences between predicted and observed observations makes up the concept of ordinary least squares estimation, such that

$$Q = MIN(Y_i - \widehat{Y}_i)^2 \tag{21}$$

wherein $\widehat{Y}_i$ is the value of Y that the statistical model predicts for the ith trial or observation. A function of the X terms and the collection of estimated parameters θ is the predicted value of Y. In least squares estimation, solving Equation 21 gives the parameter estimates. To use least squares estimation to get parameter estimates requires no assumptions about statistical distributions.

Maximum likelihood methods are fundamentally different but still provide estimates of parameters in statistical models. Maximum likelihood depends on the idea that different samples are created by different populations, and so some populations compared to others are more likely to give a particular sample; e.g., if a random sample of $y_1, y_2, \ldots, y_n$ was drawn then some parameter θ (which functions as the sample mean) is the most likely to create that sample. Figure 28 shows two distinctive statistical distributions A and B, which denote two distinctive assumed sample means. In the figure, the sample mean θ_B for distribution B is less likely to create the sample of y than the sample mean θ_A, which distribution A is associated with. The parameters most probable to have created the observed data (y) among all possible θ is sought by maximum likelihood estimation.

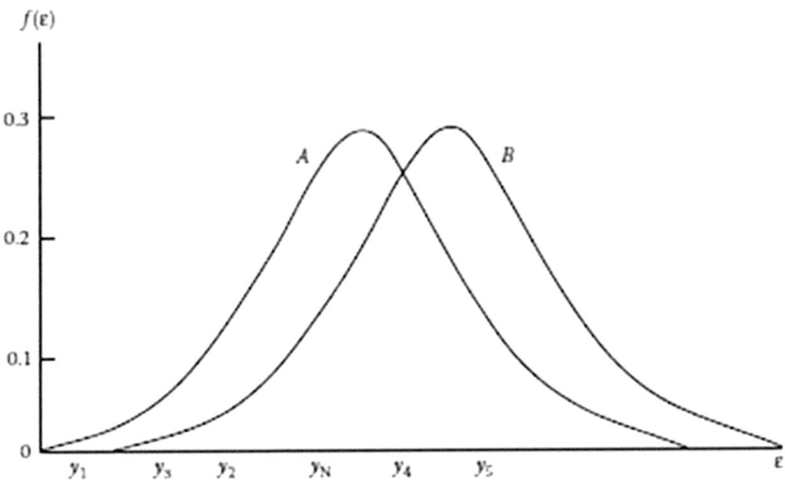

Figure 28. Illustration of maximum likelihood estimation.

4.3.3. Useful Probability Distributions

Econometric and statistical analysis relies on probability distributions. A simplistic way of answering probability-related questions (like an event's occurrence probability) is to identify the characteristics behind underlying data-generating processes. A large number of commonly studied phenomena are approximated by well-understood probability distributions. Normal distributions approximate many samples, like vehicle speeds on a segment of a freeway, quite well.

Considered here are four common statistical distributions: the standard normal Z distribution, the t distribution, the χ^2 distribution, and the F distribution.

Need to know

The two primary types of probability distributions are discrete and continuous. Discrete distributions come from ordinal data or count data (strictly continuous data that can only take on integer values). Variables that are able to, within a range of values, take any value that is measured on the interval or ratio scale are capable of generating continuous distributions. Two properties related to probability distributions are that the sum of all probabilities over all possible outcomes is 1 and that the probability of any outcome lies between 0 and 1.

The Z Distribution: The central limit theorem is where the derivation of the Z distribution comes from. If the average X is computed on a sample of n observations gathered from a distribution with a known finite variance σ^2 and mean μ, then, irrespective of the characteristics of the population distribution, the sampling distribution is approximately standard normally distributed for the test statistic Z^*. As an example, the population can be normal, binomial, Poisson, or beta distributed. A bell-shaped curve, with a mean equal to zero and a variance equal to one, brands the standard normal distribution. A random variable Z^* is calculated as follows:

$$Z^* = \frac{X \quad \mu}{\frac{\sigma}{\sqrt{n}}} = Z_a \tag{22}$$

In which α represents a confidence level, and Z^* is a random variable whose distribution, as n tends to infinity, approaches a standard normal distribution. This result is very useful, as it says that a test statistic calculated using Equation 22 will, as the sample grows larger, near the standard normal distribution no matter what the population distribution that the samples are drawn from is. Subsequently, in practice, an effectively normally distributed sampling distribution of the mean results from sample sizes of 20 or more.

Studying normal distributions with any variance and mean is aided by the Z distribution. By employing the standard normal transformation,

$$Z_i = \frac{X_i - \mu}{\sigma} \tag{23}$$

original variables that are gathered from any normal distribution X_i can be standardized to new variables Z_i which are standard normally distributed.

The *t* Distribution: Many statistical tests discussed here use the t distribution. The basis for hypothesis testing and confidence interval estimation when σ^2 is known is formed using the Z^* statistic, but it is normal to exchange it with its unbiased estimator s^2 when σ^2 is not known, resulting in a test statistic t^*

$$t^* = \frac{X - \mu}{\frac{s}{\sqrt{n}}} = t_a(v = n - 1) \tag{24}$$

wherein t^* is approximately t distributed with $n - 1$ degrees of freedom.

The standard normal and t distributions are similar. The degree to which the t distribution is more spread out than the normal distribution is determined by the distribution's degrees of freedom. As the sample size grows, the t distribution nears the standard normal Z distribution. The population the samples are drawn from must be normal for the t distribution.

The χ^2 Distribution: Since it arises in numerous situations, the χ^2 distribution is extremely useful. According to statistical theory, the standard normal variable Z squared is χ^2 distributed with 1 degree of freedom. Let $Z_1, Z_2, \ldots, Z_n$ be k independent standard normal random variables. If each random variable is squared, then a χ^2 distribution with k degrees of freedom will be followed by their sum, such that

$$X^2 = \sum_{i=1}^{n} {}^{2}_{i} = X^2_{(k)} \tag{25}$$

This χ^2 statistic reveals that the addition of independent squared normal random variables is where the χ^2 distribution comes from. The χ^2 random variable cannot be negative as a sum of squares, so the χ^2 distribution is slanted to the right and the χ^2 random variable is bounded by zero on the lower end. The χ^2 distribution approaches the normal distribution as degrees of freedom increase. In fact, the χ^2 distribution nears a normal distribution with a variance equal to two times the degrees of freedom, and the mean is equal to the degrees of freedom as they increase.

The χ^2 distribution with $v = n - 1$ degrees of freedom is roughly the predicted variance of a random sample of size n taken from a normal population with variance σ^2. The sampling distribution of the test statistic χ^2 is such that

$$X^2 = \frac{(n-1)s^2}{\sigma^2} = \frac{\sum_{i=1}^{n} (X_i - \underline{X})^2}{\sigma^2} \approx \chi^2_a = (v = n - 1) \tag{26}$$

Two distributions can be compared using the χ^2 distribution. The χ^2 distribution can be employed to test whether the actual frequencies parallel the predicted frequencies if the frequencies of events are witnessed in some frequency bins or categories under both the expected and the observed distributions. The way that the test statistic is written is as:

$$X^2 = \sum_{i=1}^{I} \sum_{j=1}^{J} \frac{(O_i - E_i)^2}{E_i} \approx \chi^2_a(I - 1, J - 1), \tag{27}$$

where the number of columns and rows in a two-way contingency table are J and I. Multiway tables, where, for example, there could be I rows, J columns, and K elements associated with each $i\,j^{th}$ bin, can be accommodated by the test statistic. The degrees of freedom become $(I-1)(J-1)(K-1)$. The expected frequency could result from a model of statistical independence (a frequency distribution founded on a presumed statistical distribution such as the normal distribution) or an empirical distribution (wherein two empirical distributions are compared). The reliability of the test statistic can be compromised by small and expected frequencies when using the test statistic (Washington et al., 2020).

The *F* Distribution: The F distribution, which was discovered in 1924 by Sir Ronald A. Fisher (an English statistician whom it is now named after), is another extremely useful statistical distribution. The ratio of two independent χ^2 random variables, both divided by their own degrees of freedom, is used to approximate this distribution. As an example, let χ_1^2 be an χ^2 random variable that has 1 degree of freedom, and χ_2^2 be an χ^2 random variable that has 2 degrees of freedom.

If there are two variables F distributed with $\chi_1 = 1$ and $\chi_2 = 2$ degrees of freedom, respectively,

$$F^* = \frac{\frac{\chi_1^2}{v_1}}{\frac{\chi_2^2}{v_2}} \approx F_\alpha(v_1, v_2) \tag{28}$$

Testing if two samples come from a single population with variance σ^2 or testing the variance ratio of two samples taken from a population that is normal is a useful application of the F distribution. The test statistic F^*'s sampling distribution is about F distributed with v_1 (numerator) and v_2 (denominator) degrees of freedom if we have independent random samples of sizes n_1 and n_2 with estimated variances s_1^2 and s_2^2, respectively, such that

$$F^* = \frac{s_1^2}{s_2^2} = F_\alpha(v_1 = n_1 - 1, v_2 = n_2 - 1) \tag{29}$$

The F distributions are asymmetric, which is a quality that is "inherited" from the χ^2 distributions; their shape also looks like that of the χ^2 distributions. Note that $F_{(2,10)} \neq F_{(10,2)}$

4.3.4. Mean, Variance and Covariance

The Mean: For one-dimensional data, it can be written as:

$$mean(\{x\}) = \frac{\sum_i x_i}{N} \tag{30}$$

The mean of each data point is each component of the mean $(\{x\})$, but there isn't a simple analogue of the median (so one could ask how does one order high dimensional data?).

Notice that one has

$$mean(\{x - mean(\{x\})\}) = 0 \tag{31}$$

(i.e., the dataset resulting from subtracting from a dataset has a zero mean).

Covariance: Standard deviation, variance, and correlation can be observed as an example of a more general data operation- obtaining two factors from all the vectors in a dataset of vectors, giving two 1D datasets of N items, and using $\{x\}$ for one and $\{y\}$ for the other. The ith element of $\{x\}$ corresponds to the ith element of $\{y\}$ (the i'th element of $\{x\}$ is one part of some larger vector x_i and the i'th element of $\{y\}$ is another component of this vector). The covariance of $\{x\}$ and $\{y\}$ can be defined.

Covariance

Assuming two sets of N data items, $\{x\}$ and $\{y\}$, the covariance can be calculated by

$$cov(\{x\},\{y\}) = \frac{\Sigma_i \left(x_i - mean(\{x\})\right)\left(\left(y_i - mean(\{y\})\right)\right.}{N}$$

The inclination of corresponding elements (defined by t elements ordered in the dataset, so x_1 corresponds to y_1, x_2 corresponds to y_2) of $\{x\}$ and $\{y\}$ to be bigger than (resp. smaller than) the mean is measured by the covariance. The covariance should be positive if $\{x\}$ is typically bigger (resp. smaller) than its mean for data points where $\{y\}$ is also bigger (resp. smaller) than its mean. The covariance should be negative if $\{x\}$ is typically bigger (resp. smaller) than its mean for data points where $\{y\}$ is smaller (resp. bigger) than its mean. Notice that

$$std(x)^2 = var(\{x\}) = cov(\{x\}, \{x\}) \tag{32}$$

Substituting the expressions can prove this. The covariance of a dataset measures its inclination to not be constant due to the fact that variance is a measure of the inclination of a dataset to differ from the mean. The relationship between correlation and covariance is even more important and is shown in the box below.

Important Equation

$$cov(\{(xy)\}) = \frac{cov(\{x\},\{y\})}{\sqrt{cov(\{x\},\{x\})}\sqrt{cov(\{y\},\{y\})}}$$

Sometimes this is a beneficial way to consider correlation; it says that the inclination of $\{x\}$ and $\{y\}$ to be bigger (resp. smaller) than their averages for the same data points, *in comparison* to the amount that they change on their own, is measured by the correlation.

The Covariance Matrix: Using covariance instead of correlation permits the unification of some ideas. Particularly, it is simple for data items that are

d-dimensional vectors to calculate one matrix that contains all covariances between all the pairs of components (referred to as a covariance matrix).

Covariance Matrix

The covariance matrix is:

$$Covmat(\{x\}) = \frac{\sum_i (x_i - mean(\{x\}))(x_i - mean(\{x\}))^T}{N}$$

It is quite usual to write a covariance matrix as Σ, and this convention will be followed here.

Σ is often used to represent covariance matrices, regardless of what dataset it is (context is used to determine exactly which dataset is intended). In general, when referring to the j, k^{th} entry of a matrix A, $A_{j\,k}$ is written, so the covariance is $\Sigma_{j\,k}$ between the jth and k'^{th} data components (Washington et al., 2020).

Properties of the Covariance Matrix

- The j, k'th entry of the covariance matrix is the covariance of the jth and the k'th components of x, which is written
- The j, jth entry of the covariance matrix is the variance of the jth component of x.
- The covariance matrix is symmetric.
- The covariance matrix is always positive semidefinite; it is positive definite, *unless* there is some vector **a** such that $a^T(x_i - \text{mean}(\{x_i\}) = 0$ for all i.

Mean and Covariance Under Affine Transformations

Assume a d-dimensional dataset $\{x\}$. Choosing a matrix A and vector b, and creating a new dataset $\{m\}$, wherein $m_i = Ax_i + b$, provides an affine transformation for this data. Here A just has to have a second dimension d.

Computing the covariance and mean of $\{\boldsymbol{m}\}$ is easy. One has

$$mean(\{\boldsymbol{m}\}) = mean(\{Ax + \boldsymbol{b}\}) = Amean(\{x\}) + \boldsymbol{b} \tag{33}$$

Multiplying the original mean by A and adding $\boldsymbol{b}$ gives the new mean; equivalently, by transforming in the same way the points were transformed the old mean.

It is also simple to compute the new covariance matrix. One has

$$Covmat(\{\boldsymbol{m}\}) = Covmat(\{Ax + \boldsymbol{b}\})$$

$$= \frac{\sum_i \left(\boldsymbol{m}_i - mean(\{\boldsymbol{m}\})\right)\left(\boldsymbol{m}_i - mean(\{\boldsymbol{m}\})\right)^T}{N}$$

$$= \frac{\sum_i \left(Ax_i + \boldsymbol{b} - Amean(\{x\}) - \boldsymbol{b}\right)\left(Ax_i + \boldsymbol{b} - Amean(\{x\}) - \boldsymbol{b}\right)^T}{N}$$

$$\frac{A\left[\sum_i \left(x_i - mean(\{x\})\right)\left(x_i - mean(\{x\})\right)^T\right]A^T}{N} = ACovmat(\{x\})A^T \quad (34)$$

One can attempt to pick affine transformations that result in "good" covariance matrices and means. Choosing $\boldsymbol{b}$ is common so that the new dataset's mean is zero, but a large amount of information about it can be revealed through an appropriate choice of A.

Need to know

Transform a dataset $\{x\}$ into a new dataset $\{\boldsymbol{m}\}$, where $\boldsymbol{m}_i = Ax_i + \boldsymbol{b}$. Then mean($\{\boldsymbol{m}\}$) = $Amean(\{x\}) + \boldsymbol{b}$ $Covmat(\{\boldsymbol{m}\}) = ACovmat(\{x\})\,A^T$

Eigenvectors and Diagonalization

If $M = M^T$, then a matrix M is **symmetric**, and it must be square. Assume that $\boldsymbol{u}$ is a $d \times 1$ vector, S is a $d \times d$ symmetric matrix, and λ is a scalar. If one has

$$S\boldsymbol{u} = \lambda \boldsymbol{u}, \quad (35)$$

$\boldsymbol{u}$ is considered an **eigenvector** of S and the matching **eigenvalue** is λ. To have eigenvectors and eigenvalues, matrices do not need to be symmetric, but the ones that are symmetric are the ones of interest.

The eigenvalues are real numbers in the case of a symmetric matrix, and there are d distinct eigenvectors that are normal to each other and can be scaled to have unit length; they can be stacked into an orthonormal matrix $U = [\boldsymbol{u}_1, ..., \boldsymbol{u}_d]$ (orthonormal meaning that $U^T U = I$).

This means there is an orthonormal matrix U and a diagonal matrix Λ so that

$$SU = U\Lambda \quad (36)$$

There is a g number of such matrices because the equation continues to work with a new Λ, which is obtained through reordering the original Λ's diagonal elements, and it is possible to reorder the matrix U's eigenvectors. Tracking this complexity doesn't have a reason, but instead, the convention is adopted that the components of U are arranged so that the components of Λ are arranged with the greatest value first along the diagonal, giving a very specific procedure.

Diagonaizing a Symmetric Matrix

Any symmetric matrix S can be converted to a diagonal form by computing

$$U^T SU = \Lambda$$

There are procedures through numerical and statistical programming environments to compute U and Λ. It is assumed that the elements of U are ordered so that the elements of Λ are sorted along the diagonal, with the largest value coming first.

Orthonormal Matrices Are Rotations

Orthonormal matrices should be thought of as rotations as they do not change lengths or angles. For x a vector, and R an orthonormal matrix, $\boldsymbol{m} = Rx$

$$\text{such that, } \boldsymbol{u}\ T\boldsymbol{u} = x^T R^T Rx = x^T Ix = x^T x,$$

which means that R doesn't change lengths. For y, z, both unit vectors, the cosine of the angle between them is

$$y^T x.$$

Due to the argument above, the inner product of Ry and Rx is the same as $y^T x$; this means that R doesn't change angles, either.

The Multivariate Normal Distribution

It is suggested that it is necessary to use simpler probability models by the high dimensional data facts shown above. The **multivariate normal distribution**, also called the **Gaussian distribution**, is the most important model. This model has two sets of parameters, the covariance Σ and the mean μ. The covariance is a $d \times d$-dimensional matrix (a symmetric matrix) for a d-dimensional model and a d-dimensional column vector is the mean. For the definitions to have meaning, the covariance matrix must be positive definite. The distribution $p(\mu, \Sigma)$ form is

$$p(\mu, \Sigma) = \frac{1}{\sqrt{(2\pi)^d \det(\Sigma)}} \exp\left(-\frac{1}{2}(x-\mu)^T \Sigma^{-1} (x-\mu)\right) \tag{37}$$

The names of the parameters are explained by the following facts:

Parameters of Multivariate Normal Distribution

Assuming a multivariate normal distribution,

- $E[x] = \mu$, which means that the mean of the distribution is μ.
- $E[(x-\mu)(x-\mu)^T] = \Sigma$, which means that the entries in Σ represent covariances.

Assume now a dataset of items x_i, wherein i goes from 1 to N, and that one wishes to use a multivariate normal distribution to model this data. $\hat{\mu}$, the mean's maximum likelihood estimate, is,

$$\hat{\mu} = \frac{\Sigma_i x_i}{N} \tag{38}$$

(Σ), the covariance's maximum likelihood estimate, is,

$$\hat{\Sigma} = \frac{\Sigma_i (x_i - \hat{\mu}) \Sigma_i (x_i - \hat{\mu})^T}{N} \tag{39}$$

These facts mean that the majority of what is intriguing about Gaussians (or multivariate normal distributions) is already known (Washington et al., 2020).

Chapter Conclusion

This chapter provides a brief introduction of matrix algebra and some basic concepts of probability. Some of the key topics discussed in this chapter are matrix multiplication, matrix division, the rank of a matrix, eigenvalues, eigenvectors, and properties of matrices. This chapter also narrates on conditional probability, statistical independence, least squares, maximum likelihood, mean, variance, and covariance. As highway safety analysis requires advanced statistical knowledge, there is a need for a clear understanding of matrix algebra and probability theory.

Further Reading

Gentle, J., 2007. Matrix Algebra: Theory, Computations, and Applications in Statistics (Springer Texts in Statistics), Springer.

Reference

Washington, S., Karlaftis, M.G., Mannering, F. and Anastasopoulos, P., 2020. Statistical and Econometric Methods for Transportation Data Analysis. CRC Press.

CHAPTER

5

Supervised Learning

5.1. Introduction

Supervised learning is one of the popular machine learning algorithms in highway safety studies. Many studies used different supervised learning algorithms to solve highway safety-related regression and classification problems. The current chapter is mostly focused on classification or regression problems. It should be noted that this chapter does not provide discussions on all applied supervised AI algorithms in highway safety issues.

5.2. Popular Models and Algorithms

5.2.1. Logistic Regression

Logistic regression is a classification learning algorithm, not actually a regression. The name arises from statistics because the mathematical formulation of linear regression has similarities to logistic regression. To explain logistic regression, the binary classification case is used, and it can be naturally extended to include multiclass classification.

The aim is still to model y_i as a linear x_i equation in logistic regression, but, with a binary y_i, it is not straightforward. A function that ranges from minus infinity to plus infinity is a linear combination of features such as $wx_i + b$; in contrast, there are only two possible values of y_i. Before the existence of computers, when scientists were required to perform manual calculations, they were eager to discover a linear classification model. They discovered they would only have to discover a simple continuous function whose codomain is (0, 1) if negative labels are defined as 0 and positive labels as 1. In this case, x will be assigned a negative label if the value returned by the model for input x is closer to 0. The example will receive a positive label in any other case. A function that has this trait is the **sigmoid function** or the **standard logistic function**:

$$f(x) = \frac{1}{1 + e^{-x}} \tag{1}$$

where e is the base of the natural logarithm (also called *Euler's number*; e^x is also called the *exp*(x) function in Excel and in multiple programming languages). If the values of x and b are optimized appropriately, the output of $f(x)$ can be understood as the probability of y_i being positive. As an example, if it's higher than or equal to the threshold 0.5, it is said that the class of x is positive; if not, it's negative.

In practice, the threshold choice could differ depending on the problem. We return to this in Chapter 5 where model performance assessment is discussed.

So, the logistic regression model looks like this:

$$f_{w,b}(x) \stackrel{def}{=} \frac{1}{1 + e^{-(wx+b)}} \tag{2}$$

One is able to see the term $wx + b$ from linear regression, but how does one now find the best values w * and b * for the model? In linear regression, the empirical risk (defined as the average squared error loss, also called the **mean squared error** or MSE) is minimized.

5.2.2. Decision Tree

An acyclic table, which can be used to make choices, is called a decision tree. A particular function j of the feature vector is investigated in all branching nodes of the graph. The left branch is followed if the value of the function is beneath the given threshold; otherwise, the right branch is followed. The judgment on the class to which the example belongs is taken when the leaf node is reached.

There are different formulations of the decision tree learning algorithm. In this book only one (called **ID3**) is considered. The optimization criterion here is the average log-likelihood:

$$\frac{1}{N}\sum_{i=1}^{N} y_i \ln f_{ID3}(x_i) + (1 - y_i) \ln \left(1 - f_{ID3}(x_i)\right) \tag{3}$$

where f_{ID3} is a decision tree.

It seems similar to logistic regression by now. However, it is different from the logistic regression learning algorithm which, by finding an optimal solution, generates a **parametric model** $f_{w^*,\, b^*}$.

The ID3 algorithm optimizes it roughly to the optimization criteria by building a **non-parametric model**.

$$f_{ID3}(x) \stackrel{def}{=} Pr(y = 1 \mid x) \tag{4}$$

The algorithm for learning ID3 operates as follows. Let a set of named examples be denoted by S. At the outset, there is only a start node in the decision tree that includes all examples:

$S \stackrel{def}{=} \{(x_i, \gamma_i)\}_{i=1}^{N}$. A constant f_{ID3}^{S} model is used in the beginning:

$$f_{ID3}^{S} = \frac{1}{|S|}\sum_{(x,\, y) \in S} y. \tag{5}$$

For any input x, the prediction provided by the above model, $f_{ID}^{S}(x)$, will be the same.

Then one searches through all features j = 1, ... D and all thresholds t and splits the set S into two subsets:

$$S_{-=}^{def} \{(x, y) | (x, y) \in S, x^{(j)} < t\} \text{ and } S_{+=}^{def} \{(x, y) | (x, y) \in S, x^{(j)} \geq t\} \quad (6)$$

The two new subsets would go to two new leaf nodes, and one evaluates, for all potential pairs (j, t), how good the split is with pieces S_- and S_+. Last, one picks the best of such values (j, t), splits S into S_+ and S_-, forms two new leaf nodes, and continues recursively on S_+ and S_- (or quits if no split results in a model that is sufficiently better than the previous one).

Now, one should ask what is implied by the words "evaluate how good the division is." By using the criterion called *entropy*, the goodness of a split is calculated in ID3. A calculation of uncertainty about a random variable is entropy. When all the values of the random variables are similarly likely, it achieves its limit. When the random variable may have only one value, entropy approaches its lowest. The entropy of a series of examples S is given by the following:

$$H(S) = -f_{ID3}^{S} \ln f_{ID3}^{S} - (1 - f_{ID3}^{S}) \ln (1 - f_{ID3}^{S}) \quad (7)$$

The entropy of a split of a set of examples by a certain feature j and a threshold t, $H(S_-, S_+)$, is just a weighted sum of two entropies:

$$H(S_-, S_+) = \frac{|S_-|}{|S|} H(S_-) + \frac{|S_+|}{|S|} H(S_+) \quad (8)$$

So, in ID3, one finds a split at each step, at each leaf node, that minimizes the entropy or one stops at this node of the leaf.

In any of the below situations, the algorithm stops at a leaf node:

- All examples in the leaf node are classified correctly by the one-piece model.
- One cannot find an attribute to split upon.
- The split reduces the entropy less than some $\in$ (the value for which has to be found experimentally).
- The tree reaches some maximum depth d (also has to be found experimentally).

Need to know

Since the decision to break the dataset on each iteration in ID3 is local (does not depend on potential splits), an optimal solution is not guaranteed by the algorithm. By using methods such as backtracking during the search for the ideal decision tree, the model can be strengthened at the expense of potentially taking longer to create a model.

5.2.3. Support Vector Machine

Presume a labeled dataset made up of N pairs (x_i, y_i), with x_i as the ith feature vector, and y_i as the ith class label (see Figure 29). Presume two different classes, and that y_i is −1 or 1. One wishes to predict the sign of y or at any point x. A linear classifier is used, so one will predict for a new data item x

$$sign(\boldsymbol{a}^T x + b) \tag{9}$$

and the specific classifier that is used comes from one's choice of $\boldsymbol{a}$ and b.

Suppose there is a named dataset of N pairs (x_i, y_i). Here, x_i is the vector of the ith function, and y_i is the mark of the ith class. Say that there are two groups, and that either 1 or −1 is y_i. For some point x, one wishes to predict the sign of y. A linear classifier is used, so that one will predict sign $(\boldsymbol{a}^T x + b)$ for a new data item x, and the option of $\boldsymbol{a}$ and b is given to the unique classifier one uses.

$\boldsymbol{a}$ and b can be thought of as standing for a hyperplane, provided by the points wherein $\boldsymbol{a}^T x + b = 0$ is given. Note that the amplitude of $\boldsymbol{a}^T x + b$ increases when point x travels farther away from the hyperplane. An instance of a **decision boundary** is when the positive data is isolated from the negative data by this hyperplane. As a point crosses the judgment boundary, the mark expected for that point adjusts. There are limits for choices with both classifiers. A beneficial approach for constructing classifiers is looking for the judgment boundary that gives the best actions.

A Linear Model with a Single Feature

Assume the use of a linear model with one feature. For an example with feature value x, this predicts sign $(ax + b)$. Equivalently, the model tests x against the threshold $-\dfrac{b}{a}$.

By selecting values that minimize a price function, one will select $\boldsymbol{a}$ and b. Two priorities must be achieved by the cost function. First, a term that guarantees that each example of training is on the correct side of the judgment boundary (or, at least, not too much on the wrong side) is necessary. The second priority is that the cost function requires a word that can punish errors on query examples. The form of the suitable cost function is:

$$\textit{Training error cost} + \lambda \textit{ penalty term} \tag{10}$$

in which λ represents an unknown weight that achieves the two objectives. The value of λ will eventually be set by a search process.

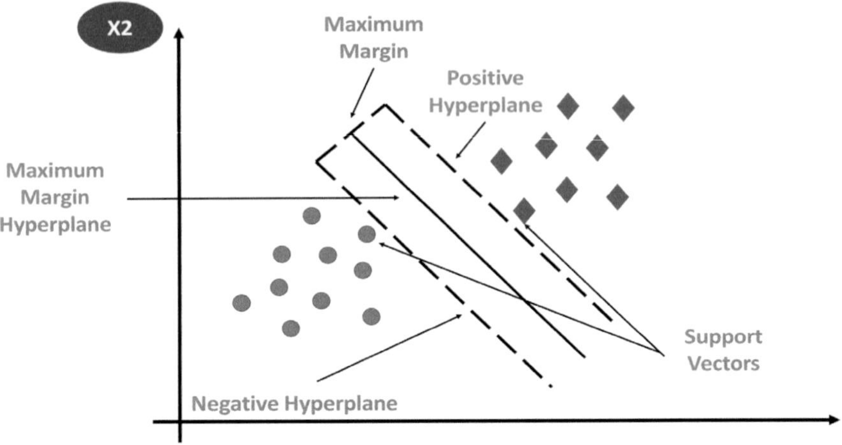

Figure 29. Concept of SVM.

The Hinge Loss

The equation

$$\gamma_i = a^T x_i + b \tag{11}$$

represents the value used for example *i* by the linear function. The function $C(\gamma_i, y_i)$ compares γ_i with y_i. The following represents the training error cost:

$$(1/N)\sum_{i=1}^{N} C(\gamma_i, y_i) \tag{12}$$

The hinge loss can be shown by

$$C(\gamma_i, y_i) = max(0, 1 - y_i\gamma_i) \tag{13}$$

and it has the properties mentioned below:

- If the signs for γ_i and y_i are different, then C should be large. Additionally, as x_i moves on the wrong side away from the boundary, the cost increases linearly.
- If the signs for γ_i and y_i are the same, but $y_i \gamma_i < 1$, then x_i is located near the decision boundary, meaning there is a cost, which increases as x_i nears the boundary.
- If $y_i \gamma_i > 1$, then the sign is correctly predicted by the classifier and there are no costs as x_i is far from the boundary.

To mitigate this loss, a classifier is trained by making strong negative or positive predictions for each example, and for ones that it is incorrect about, making predictions with a minimal magnitude possible. A **support vector machine** or **SVM** is a linear classifier taught with hinge loss.

Regularization

Since there is one odd property of the hinge loss, the penalty term is required. Assume that all training instances are appropriately identified by the pair $\boldsymbol{a}$, b, such that $y_i(\boldsymbol{a}^T x_i + b) > 0$. Then, by scaling $\boldsymbol{a}$ and b, one can still guarantee that the hinge loss is zero for the dataset, so one can pick a scale such that $y_j(\boldsymbol{a}^T x_j + b) > 1$ for each example index j. This scale has not been altered by the outcome of the classification rule on training data. If $\boldsymbol{a}$ and b give zero hinge failure, then $2\boldsymbol{a}$ and $2b$ do so as well. This ought to be bothersome, for it means one cannot uniquely select the parameters of the classifier.

One can do so by applying a penalty term to favor solutions in which $\|\boldsymbol{a}\|$ is small for the hinge loss. It is sufficient to ensure that $(1/2)\boldsymbol{a}^T\boldsymbol{a}$ is small (the 1/2 element makes the gradient cleaner) to get an $\boldsymbol{a}$ of small length. This penalty word would guarantee that there's a particular selection of classifier parameters when the hinge loss is zero. It is often referred to as **regularization** to incorporate a punishment word to facilitate the solution to a learning question. The penalty term is frequently called a **regularizer** because it appears to deter broad (and therefore have a high potential failure on future test results) solutions but is not clearly backed by training data. The parameter λ is also called the **regularization parameter**.

Utilizing the hinge loss to establish the training cost and regularizing the penalty term $(1/2)\boldsymbol{a}^T \boldsymbol{a}$ indicates that the cost function is

$$S(\boldsymbol{a}, b; \lambda) = \left[(1/N)\sum_{i=1}^{N} \quad max\,(0, 1 - y_i(\boldsymbol{a}^T x_i + b))\right] + \lambda\left(\frac{a^T a}{2}\right) \quad (14)$$

There are now two challenges to overcome. First, suppose λ is known; one then needs to find values for $\boldsymbol{a}$ and b that minimize $S(\boldsymbol{a}, b; \lambda)$. Second, there currently isn't a method for choosing λ, so an appropriate value will have to be searched for.

Finding a Classifier with Stochastic Gradient Descent

For the price feature, the standard methods for seeking a minimum are unsuccessful. Next, $\boldsymbol{u} = [\boldsymbol{a}, b]$ should be written for the vector gained by stacking the vector $\boldsymbol{a}$ along with b. One has a *function*, $g(\boldsymbol{u})$, and one wants to get a $\boldsymbol{u}$ value that minimizes it. Often, a problem like this can be solved by creating the gradient and discovering a value of $\boldsymbol{u}$ that changes the gradient to zero, but this doesn't work here (because problems are created by the max). One needs to use a numerical approach.

The point $\boldsymbol{u}^{(n)}$ is taken and updated to $\boldsymbol{u}^{(n+1)}$, and then searched to see whether a minimum is the product in typical numerical methods. This approach begins from a starting point. For general problems, the starting point chosen may or may not be important, but for the dilemma a random starting point is good. Typically, the update is gained through calculating the path $\boldsymbol{p}^{(n)}$ such that η, $g(\boldsymbol{u}^{(n)} + \eta\, \boldsymbol{p}^{(n)})$ is smaller than $g(\boldsymbol{u}^{(n)})$. Such a trajectory is accepted as a **descent direction**, and one needs to evaluate how far to go in the direction of descent, a method called **line search**.

Choosing a Step Length: It takes some work to pick a step length η. Since one doesn't want to test the function g, one cannot check for the move that gives the user the best g value (doing so requires looking at each of the g_i terms). Instead, the methodology can investigate large shifts in the values of the classifier's parameters initially, and smaller ones later slowing it down; hence, one employs a huge step length η at the outset. It is also called a **steplong schedule** or **learning schedule** to pick how η gets smaller.

Searching for λ

A good meaning for λ is not known to us. By selecting a set of different values, using each value to fit an SVM and using λ that results in the best output is the prime objective. Experience has demonstrated that a method's output is not deeply susceptible to the λ value, so one is able to look at values that are spaced very far apart. Taking a small number (e.g., $1e-4$), and multiplying it by powers of 10 (or 3 if one has a fast computer and is fussy) is normal. So, one could look at $\lambda \in \{1e-4, 1e-3, 1e-2, 1e-1\}$, for instance. One understands how to match a given value of λ to a SVM. Choosing the value that results in the best SVM and using that to get the best classifier is the challenge (Lantz, 2013).

5.2.4. Random Forests (RF)

Random Forests (RF) have many decision tree classifiers and combine multiple decision trees into a single, efficient model through the "bagging" concept of Breiman. It utilizes the self-help approach (i.e., the bootstrap resampling technology) by recurrently choosing random k ($k < N$) sample sets to create novel training sample sets from the initial training samples of N. Some samples may be gathered more than once during the overall collection process. In each of the random bagging sampling rounds, around 36.8 percent of the training data won't be sampled, relating to out-of-bag (OOB) data; this uncollected data doesn't engage in model fitting during testing but may be utilized for detection of model generalization capabilities. For the creation of random forests, the training sample is utilized to produce k buffeting decision or regression trees (CART) and then to assign the test sample return values by average use or a majority vote decision. Strong generalization capacity and low variance tolerance with no additional pruning can in general be accomplished by random forests due to the fact that randomness can easily minimize model variance. Of course, during preparation, the fitting model degree can worsen, which leads to higher bias, but it's just relative. The CART algorithm is a binary tree, however, meaning that only two branches will lead to each non-leaf node. The vector is likely to be used several times if a non-leaf node is a multi-level (over two) discrete variable, and simultaneously, if a non-leaf node is a continuous variable, it is viewed as a discrete variable by the decision tree (Huang, 2019).

The CART used in RF is based on the Gini coefficient's set of functions. The Gini coefficient is chosen according to the requirement that the maximum purity of each child node is achieved, with all observations belonging to the same classification on that child node. In that case, with the lowest volatility but maximum purity, the Gini coefficient meets its minimum value. CART's Gini coefficient can be expressed as follows:

$$Gini(p) = 2p(1 - p) \tag{15}$$

If while traversing each segmentation point of each feature $A = a$ is used, then D is split into two sections, respectively D_1 (the sample set that meets $A = a$) and D_2 (the sample set that meets $A\ a$). The Gini coefficient of D, under the condition of function $A = a$, is:

$$Gini(D, A) = \frac{D_1}{D} Gini(D_1) + \frac{D_2}{D} Gini(D_2) \tag{16}$$

where $Gini(D, A)$ is the uncertainty of D.

Each CART in RF finds the segmentation point that has the lowest feature Gini coefficients till the stop condition is met, breaking the data set into two subsets and constantly crossing all potential segmentation points of the feature within the tree a. Figure 30 shows a diagram of a Random Forest over a dataset X.

Need to know

Compared to other traditional algorithms, the CART algorithm in RF differs. Every selected feature in an RF tree is generated randomly from all m features, which has lowered the tendency of overfitting. Specific eigenvalues or feature combinations aren't used to determine the model, and control of the model's fitting ability indefinitely is not improved by the increase of randomness. An RF, unlike ordinary decision trees, also improves the establishment of decision trees. Ordinary decision trees require picking an optimal feature among all m sample features on the node to do the left and right subtree division of the decision tree, but each tree of the RF is a part of selected features, and in order to divide the left and right subtrees of the decision tree an optimal feature is selected among these few features, enhancing the generalization ability of the model and increasing the effect of randomness. Assuming that for each tree m sub-features are chosen, then the smaller the m sub is, the worse is the fitting degree of the model to the training set, and there will be an increase in the generalization ability, an increase in bias, and a decrease in the variance of the model. The opposite effects will occur with a larger m sub. The value of the m sub is typically thought to be a parameter, and in order to get an appropriate value through tuning it will be constantly adjusted.

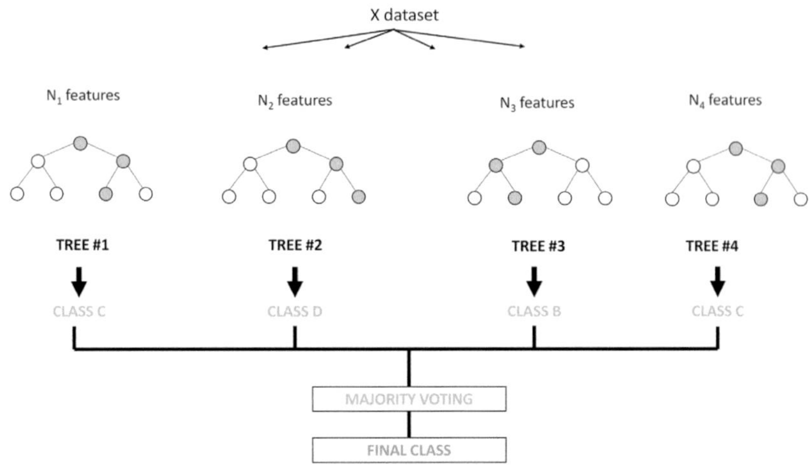

Figure 30. Random forest.

5.2.5. Naïve Bayes Classifier

According to theory, based on the given data and assumptions, the optimal Bayes classifier gives the best possible classification outcomes.

In text mining, this is extremely valid (but not only) since the designation of a right class-label c_j depends on the number of attributes in social-media contributions or text documents. Their repertoire can be very broad after accumulating many training samples (which is nice from the chance computing point of view), thousands or tens of thousands of specific terms (or general terms).

Each word has its probability in every class and there are very many possible attribute combinations, even if the data is reduced by, for example, eliminating insignificant terms. Let a_1, a_2, ..., a_N be the given attributes (vocabulary words). In any class, each word has its likelihood and there are many potential variations of attributes, even though the data is diminished by, for instance, removing irrelevant words.

Let the given attributes be a_1, a_2, ..., a_N (vocabulary words). The best description, c_{MAP}, can be written as:

$$c_{MAP} = c_j \in Cargmaxp(a_1, a_2, ..., a_N | c_j)\, p(c_j) \tag{17}$$

For large values of N, the computational complexity is given by the item $p(a_1, a_2, ..., a_N)$ in Eq. 21. Because of the possible mutual conditional dependence of attributes, it is necessary to compute probabilities of all their possible combinations for a given c_j. The computational complexity is provided by the item $p(a_1, a_2, ..., a_N)$ for large values of N. Because of the possible reciprocal conditional dependence of attributes, it is important for a given c_j to compute the probabilities of all their possible combinations (Lantz, 2013).

The definition of the so-called naïve Bayes classifier, which is based on a presumption (theoretically not very accurate) that there is no interdependence between the attributes (which is 'naïvity'), resulted in a way to make the calculation simpler and technically applicable. This suggests that it is possible to use a simplified equation for the classification to evaluate c_{MAP}, which can be called c_{NB} (for NB like Naïve Bayes):

$$c_{MAP} = c_j \in C argmax p(c_j) \prod_i p\left((a_i \mid c_j)\right) \tag{18}$$

In other words, only the a posteriori probabilities of observable attributes times the a priori likelihood of a class event per classified textual object must be determined using the probabilities of attributes in the training results. The classification result could be more often inaccurate because of the theoretical incorrectness, based on how much the principle of freedom is broken.

The naïve Bayes classifier is quite common despite this incorrectness since its findings are very appropriate in thousands of current applications. However, when reading the classification outcomes, one should be vigilant - this inaccuracy could be one of the explanations for the rare incorrect classification that e-mail users recognize well: non-spam classified as spam and vice versa.

5.2.6. Artificial Neural Networks

An artificial neuron can be interpreted as a function of transfer $\varphi(.)$ with $n + 1$ inputs x_i weighted by w_i, where $x_i \in R$, $-\infty < w_i < +\infty$:

$$\hat{y} = \varphi(w \cdot x) = \varphi\left(\sum_{i=0}^{n} w_i x_i\right) = \varphi\left(\theta + \sum_{i=0}^{n} w_i x_i\right) \tag{19}$$

where for the dot product of the vectors $w \cdot x$ with the constant value of $x_0 = 1.0$ there is a bias (threshold) $\theta = w_0\, x_0 = w_0 \cdot 1.0$ that determines the value of the transfer function $\varphi(.)$ from which the neuron is activated and provides its output $\neq$ 0.0. Hence, the neuron generally makes the transformation $R'' \rightarrow R$.

Determining the specific φ function depends on the type of application and known or anticipated properties of the approximated unknown function $\hat{y} = \hat{f}(x)$. A commonly used nonlinear transfer function φ is *sigmoid* (known also as *logistic*), $S(x)$, where the dot product of the $w \cdot x$ vectors with the constant value of $x_0 = 1.0$ there is the bias (threshold) $\theta = w_0 x_0 = w_0 \cdot 1.0$, which specifies the value of the $\varphi(.)$ transition function from which the neuron is activated and giving its output $\neq 0.0$. Therefore, the neuron usually generates the $R'' \rightarrow R$ transition (Lantz, 2013).

The determination of the basic φ function is based on the type of operation and the proven or expected features of the approximate unknown function $\hat{y} = \hat{f}(x)$. *Sigmoid* (also called *logistic*) $S(x)$ is a widely used nonlinear transfer function φ, where,

$$S(x) = (1 + e^{-1}), S(x) = 0, \lim_{x \to +\infty} S(x) = 1 \tag{20}$$

and where, as the neuron returns 1 for classification, the normal threshold is for $S(x) \geq 0.5$, otherwise 0. However, for some purposes, there are also a variety of alternatives normally needed by particular applications; information can be found in the literature.

Neurons can be mixed to estimate uncertain complex nonlinear (including discontinuous or non-differentiable) functions in layers in a network and can also be used for classification or regression advantageously. The error function E (or classification in this case) of the approximation is commonly defined as follows:

$$E = \frac{1}{2}(y - \hat{y})^2 \tag{21}$$

where y is a known correct value and $\hat{y}$ is a value returned for the given training data sample by the trained network. The square of the difference $y - \hat{y}$ eliminates negative error values and highlights larger errors whose removal takes precedence over smaller errors (multiplication by 1/2 is just for formal reasons, so that the number 2 in the exponent may not be considered in the derivative when looking for the steepest descent of the error). To correct the output of $\varphi(w \cdot x)$ for the input sample x, only the weight vector w can be modified because the values of x are given. This modification affects the significance of the n weighted individual components (attributes x_i) of the input vector $x = (x_1, x_2, \ldots, x_n)$, whose combination determines the required output value of the approximated function $\widehat{f}(\boldsymbol{x})$ in which y is a proven right value and $\hat{y}$ is a value returned by the qualified network for the given training data set. The $y - \hat{y}$ discrepancy square reduces negative error values and illustrates larger errors whose elimination takes precedence over smaller errors (multiplication by 1/2 is for formal purposes only, so that when checking for the steepest descent of the error the number 2 in the exponent will not be considered in the derivative). Only the weight vector w can be changed to correct the output of $\varphi(w \cdot x)$ for the input sample x since the values of x are given. The importance of the n weighted individual components (x_i attributes) of the input vector $x = (x_1, x_2, \ldots, x_n)$ is influenced by this change, whose combination specifies the necessary output value of the approximate function $f(\boldsymbol{x})$. There are, of course, no w_i weights known before beginning the training phase.

The instantaneous location of a point describing a certain iterative solution within an n–dimensional space is often determined by these weights. The target is preferably the optimum solution, the highest classification accuracy (alternatively the lowest classification error) in our case, which is the global maximum of the desired function $f(\boldsymbol{x}) \approx f(\boldsymbol{x})$.

The initial values of w_i determine the starting point and, since it is generally not known where to start from, these coordinate values can only be generated randomly. It will be possible to evaluate the starting subspace (or point) more precisely in a case where some original, if restricted, information is available. Because of a potential error in the performance of the qualified network, it is important to change the attribute weights accordingly. It is generally achieved progressively in each iteration stage with the individual layers in the direction from the output to the input layer, so the term 'backup error propagation' is also used. Further information can be found in the various existing literatures (Lantz, 2013).

Advantages and disadvantages of the key algorithms		
Algorithms	**Advantages**	**Disadvantages**
Support vector machine (SVM)	• Can utilize predictive power of linear input combinations. • Higher prediction accuracy. • Minimized generalization error. • Easy to explain or interpret.	• Not powerful in handling computational scalability and mixed data types. • Sensitive to kernel choice and tuning parameters. • Slow for big data training.
Decision Trees	• Some tolerance to correlated inputs. • Handle missing values. • Suitable for both numerical and categorical data. • Work well with big data.	• Cannot work on (linear) combinations of features. • Relatively less predictive in many situations. • Practical decision-tree learning algorithms cannot guarantee to return the globally optimal decision tree. • Overfitting issue.
Logistic regression	• Easy to interpret. • Provides confidence intervals • Quickly update the classification model to incorporate new data.	• Cannot handle the missing values of continuous variables. • Multicollinearity problem. • Sensitive to extreme values of continuous variables.
Neural networks	• Precise prediction accuracy. • Some tolerance to correlated inputs.	• Not robust to outliers. • Susceptible to irrelevant features. • Not suitable for big data.

5.2.7. Cubist

Cubist is a type of rule-based ensemble regression model. In Cubist, a simple model tree is generated with a separate linear regression model for each terminal node. The paths along the model tree are compressed into rules, and these rules are streamlined and trimmed. The min_n parameter is the primary method of limiting the tree sizes, while max_rules limits the number of rules.

Cubist ensembles are produced using *committees*, which are related to boosting. Once the first model within the committee is generated, the second model adjusts the outcome data based on whether the first model under- or over-predicted the outcome. The new outcome y^* is computed for iteration m using

$$y^*_{(m)} = y - (\hat{y}_{(m-1)} - y) \quad (22)$$

If the previous iteration of a sample is over-predicted, the outcome for the next iteration will be adjusted so that it is more likely to be under-predicted to compensate. This modification process will continue for each ensemble variation.

There is also an opportunity for a post-hoc adjustment after the model is created using the training set. When the model predicts a new sample, it can be adjusted by its closest neighbors from the original training set. For K neighbors, the model-based predicted value is adjusted by the neighbor using:

$$\frac{1}{K}\sum_{l=1}^{K} w_l\left[t_1 + (\hat{y} - \hat{t}_l)\right] \quad (23)$$

in which t represents the training set prediction and w represents an inverse weight to the distance to its neighbor.

5.2.8. Extreme Gradient Boosting (XGBoost)

Boosting meta-algorithms typically employ a similar algorithm, called a weak learner, in their ensemble. In the weak learner algorithm, a classification error of less than 50% is adequate assuming there are two classes; however, a more accurate rate is desired.

Additional classifiers with similar properties are added slowly to upgrade the overall outcome and improve the results of classification. Each additional classifier may be successfully used separately if it is randomly selected during the training phase, while other samples are left to colleagues. Thus, the classification ability of the ensemble will be enhanced. The initial criterion is the determination of the number of weak learners, n_{wl}. This variable is related to the random separation of the training set into the correct number of training subsets, n_{wl}, one subset per learner.

There is no clear algorithm for the n_{wl} value to be calculated in advance. The basic requirement is that any sample from the training set D is included in the training phase. Additionally, the number of training samples per weak learner must remain approximately the same, provided that each learner has an equal vote in the final process. The classifications for an unlabeled item are given by each trained learner, and the result is determined by the majority.

The theory is quite basic, but, unfortunately, it is more difficult in practice. Typically, simpler classification tasks are distinguished by the fact that the initial trained classifier operates correctly on most of samples m_1, where $m_1 \gg m_i$, $i = 2 \ldots, n_{wl}$. In the absence of training samples, the presumption that only a small number of samples still need to be addressed by the appropriate classifiers leads to insufficient training. As a result, some training samples available in D remain unused and it produces non-optimal results, given the circumstances.

Usually, the solution is applied to replicate the entire boosting process multiple times to ensure the optimum value for m1, which is roughly equal to the distribution of samples in training subsets, and utilize all training samples, if possible. To do this, multiple heuristics are used to attempt the fulfillment of requirements.

Let $x_i = \{x_{i1}, x_{i2}, \ldots, x_{ij}\}$ define a vector of observed values on the ith observation for j features, wherein $i \in \{1, 2, 3, \ldots, I\}$ and $j \in \{1, 2, 3, \ldots, J\}$. The target outcome for the ith observation is the value of y_i. To forecast the result using additive functions, a tree ensemble model is produced as

$$\hat{y}_1 = \Phi(x_i) = \sum_{t=1}^{T} f_t(x_i), \tag{24}$$

in which f_t represents the correlating tree structure and T represents the number of trees. Each tree is described by a function q that connects an observation to the lth leaf, wherein $1 \in \{1, 2, 3, \ldots, L\}$, and a weight ($w$) on each leaf, is defined as

$$f(x) = w_{q(x)}, \;\; w \in R^L, \;\; q: R^J \rightarrow L. \tag{25}$$

Once the weights are determined and the tree structure is generated, by first assigning a leaf on each tree to be observed based on the traits of the feature set, and then calculating the weights on the corresponding leaves, a predicted outcome is achieved.

The algorithm develops trees by optimizing the following objective function:

$$L(\Phi) = \sum_{i} l(y_i, \hat{y}_i) + \sum_{t} \Omega(f_t) \tag{26}$$

in which l is a differentiable loss function that quantifies the difference between the predicted and observed outcomes. In this equation, the complexity of the model is limited by Ω, which is defined as a regularization term to prevent overfitting. In this study, in the context of a classification problem that has two outcomes, l is defined as a logistic loss function:

$$l(y_i, \hat{y}_i) = y_i \; ln \, ln \, (1 + e^{-\hat{y}_i}) + (1 - y_i) \; ln \, ln(1 + e^{-\hat{y}_i}) \tag{27}$$

The term regularization can be defined as,

$$\Omega(f_t) = \gamma L + \frac{1}{2}\lambda \,||\, w \,||^2, \tag{28}$$

where the number of leaves in the tree structure is represented by L, and γ and λ represent the penalties of the tree's complexities. A type of L2 regularization is represented by the term $\lambda||w||^2$ on the weights of the leaves.

The objective function is optimized additively; this process begins with a constant prediction, and then, to minimize the loss function, one searches for a new tree, and it is added at each iteration as shown here:

$$\hat{y}_i^{(0)} = 0$$
$$\hat{y}_i^{(1)} = \hat{y}_i^{(0)} + f_1(x_i)$$
$$\hat{y}_i^{(2)} = \hat{y}_i^{(1)} + f_2(x_i)$$
$$\hat{y}_i^{(t)} = \hat{y}_i^{(t-1)} + f_t(x_i) \tag{29}$$

Thus, at the iteration t, the objective function is written as

$$L^{(t)} = \sum_i l(y_i, \hat{y}_i^{(t-1)} + f_t(x_i)) + \Omega(f_t) \tag{30}$$

A second-order Taylor approximation was employed by Chen and Guestrin (2016) to refine this objective function rapidly, and the $L^{(t)}$ second-order Taylor approximation is

$$L^{(t)} \simeq \sum_i \left[l(y_i, \hat{y}_i^{(t-1)}) + g_i f_t(x_i) + \frac{1}{2} h_i f_t^2(x_i) \right] + \Omega(f_t), \tag{31}$$

in which for the loss function, g_i and h_i respectively are the first- and second-order gradient statistics, considering the predicted value from the preceding step, $\hat{y}_i^{(t-1)}$. These variables can be calculated as

$$g_i^{(t)} = \frac{\partial l(y_i, \hat{y}_i^{(t-1)})}{\partial \hat{y}_i^{(t-1)}} = -\frac{(y_i - 1)e^{\hat{y}_i^{(t-1)}} + y_i}{e^{\hat{y}_i^{(t-1)}} + 1} \tag{32}$$

$$h_i^{(t)} = \frac{\partial^2 l(y_i, \hat{y}_i^{(t-1)})}{\partial (\hat{y}_i^{(t-1)})^2} = \frac{e^{\hat{y}_i^{(t-1)}}}{\left(e^{\hat{y}_i^{(t-1)}} + 1\right)^2} \tag{33}$$

It can be demonstrated that the lth leaf's optimal weight could be determined for a fixed tree structure at iteration t by,

$$w_l = -\frac{\sum_{i \in S_l} g_i}{\sum_{i \in S_l} h_i + \lambda'} \tag{34}$$

It is possible to determine if the prediction is improved by a particular tree structure by calculating the gain score with the equation,

$$Gain = \left[\sum_{l=1}^{L} \frac{(\sum_{i \in S_l} g_i)^2}{\sum_{i \in S_l} h_i + \lambda} - \frac{(\sum_i g_i)^2}{\sum_i h_i + \lambda} \right] - \gamma, \tag{35}$$

where S_l is a collection of observations assigned to the lth leaf.

During the development of trees and the addition of new branches, Equation 35 is used to evaluate each possible split. For each structure, the XGBoost algorithm begins from a single leaf structure and, so long as there is a split with a positive gain, the addition of branches continues.

5.2.9. Categorical Boosting (CatBoost)

CatBoost is one of the most recent algorithms for a gradient boosting decision tree (GBDT) which is able to handle categorical functions (Huang, 2019). The unique qualities of this approach are described below:

- It can handle categorical attributes during training. During training, the CatBoost algorithm uses the complete dataset. The target statistics (TS) method handles categorical features efficiently with minimal information loss. A random permutation is performed by the CatBoost to calculate an average label value for each of the dataset's examples. In the permutation, the examples with the equivalent category value are placed ahead of the previous ones. If a permutation is $\Theta = [\sigma_1, \ldots, \sigma_n]_n^T$, it is replaced with:

$$x_{\sigma_{p,k}} = \frac{\sum_{j=1}^{p-1} \left[x_{\sigma_{p,k}} = x_{\sigma_{p,k}}\right] \cdot Y_{\sigma j} + \beta \cdot P}{\sum_{j=1}^{p-1} \left[x_{\sigma_{p,k}} = x_{\sigma_{p,k}}\right] + \beta} \tag{36}$$

  where the prior value is represented by P and the weight of the value by β. The standard method for pre-calculating regression tasks is using the average label value from the dataset.
- It combines all categorical characteristics into a new combination. CatBoost considers each combination when generating a new split within the tree. For the first split, no combinations are considered, but for the following splits, the CatBoost algorithm considers all the preset combinations of categorical features in the dataset. Each split that is chosen for the tree is considered a category with two values, so it is used as a combination.
- It utilizes unbiased boosting with categorical characteristics, and the TS method converts categorical features into numerical values by creating a different distribution from the original.
- The CatBoost algorithm creates randomly generated permutations of the training data. The algorithm samples a random permutation to obtain gradients, and on its basis creates multiple permutations and increases the robustness of the algorithm. These permutations are similar to the ones used to measure statistics for classification functions. Different permutations are used to train distinct models so that the use of multiple permutations won't cause overfitting.
- CatBoost makes base predictors from oblivious trees. These trees are evenly balanced and, therefore, they are less susceptible to overfitting (Huang, 2019).

Parameters of Key Algorithms		
Function	**XGBoost**	**CatBoost**
Important parameters which control overfitting.	1. learning_rate or eta – optimal values lie between 0.01-0.2 2. max_depth 3. min_child_weight: similar to min_child leaf; default is 1	1. Learning_rate 2. Depth – value can be any integer up to 16. Recommended – [1 to 10] 3. No such feature like min_child_weight 4. l2-leaf-reg: L2 regularization coefficient. Used for leaf value calculation (any positive integer allowed)
Parameters for categorical values	1. Not available	1. cat_features: It denotes the index of categorical features 2. one_hot_max_size: Uses one-hot encoding for all features with number of different values less than or equal to the given parameter value (max – 255)
Parameters for controlling speed	1. colsample_bytree: subsample ratio of columns 2. subsample: subsample ratio of the training instance 3. n_estimators: maximum number of decision trees; high value can lead to overfitting	1. rsm: Random subspace method. The percentage of features to use at each split selection 2. No such parameter to subset data 3. Iterations: maximum number of trees that can be built; high value can lead to overfitting

5.3. Supervised Learning based Highway Safety Studies

Supervised learning has been extensively used in highway safety research. Table 8 provides a list of studies which used different ML algorithms in different highway safety problems.

Table 8. Supervised learning based highway safety studies

Algorithm	Research area	Studies
	Crash Injury Analysis	Li et al. (2012); Iranitalab and Khattak (2017); Zhang et al. (2018); Effati et al. (2015); Assi et al. (2020)
	Real-Time Risk Assessment	Yu and Abdel-Aty (2013)

SVM	Pedestrian Safety	Dollar et al. (2009); Hong Cheng et al. (2005); Ludwig et al. (2011); Severino et al. (2019)
	Bicycle Safety	Cho et al. (2010)
	Truck Safety	He et al. (2019)
	Railroad Safety	Ranganathan and Olson (2010); Toyoda et al. (2017)
	Pipeline Safety	Hou et al. (2014); Wu et al. (2019)
	Intersection Safety	Elhenawy et al. (2015); Aoude et al. (2012)
	Work Zone Safety	Mokhtarimousavi et al. (2019); Wang et al. (2017)
	Roadway Departure Safety	Das et al. (2020)
	Driver Behavior	Tango and Botta (2013); Li et al. (2015); Chen and Chen (2017); Yeo et al. (2009); Ahmadi et al. (2020)
DT	Older Road User	Patel (2019)
	Crash Injury Analysis	Zhang et al. (2018)
	Railroad Safety	Soleimani et al. (2019); Zhou et al. (2020)
	Real-Time Risk Assessment	Theofilatos et al. (2019); Yu and Abdel-Aty (2013)
	Patterns of Contributing Factors in Crashes	López et al. (2014)
	Incident Detection	Lee et al. (2018)
RF	Driver Behavior	Osman et al. (2019); Yao et al. (2019)
	Crash Injury Analysis	Iranitalab and Khattak (2017); Zhang et al. (2018); Müller et al. (2018); Zualkernan et al. (2018)
	Real-Time Risk Assessment	Xu et al. (2013)
	Incident Detection	Dogru and Subasi (2018)
	Motorcycle Safety	Lamb and Lee (2019); Rezapour et al. (2020)
	Railroad Safety	Keramati et al. (2020); Soleimani et al. (2019); Zhou et al. (2020); Xia et al. (2018)
	Intersection Safety	Jahangiri et al. (2016); Elhenawy et al. (2015)
	Work Zone Safety	Chang et al. (2020)
	Roadway Departure Safety	Das et al. (2020)
AdaBoost	Driver Behavior	Osman et al. (2019); Li et al. (2020)
	Older Road User	Mafi et al. (2018)
	Incident Detection	Sivaraman and Trivedi (2009)
	Pedestrian Safety	Broggi et al. (2009); Dollar et al. (2009); Guo et al. (2010)
	Bicycle Safety	Jung et al. (2012)
	Intersection Safety	Yu and Zhou (2019); Elhenawy et al. (2015)

(*Contd.*)

Table 8. (*Contd.*)

Algorithm	Research area	Studies
	Older Road User	Du et al. (2014)
GB	Railroad Safety	Toyoda et al. (2017); Soleimani et al. (2019); Lee et al. (2019); Lu et al. (2020)
KNN	Crash Injury Analysis	Iranitalab and Khattak (2017); Zhang et al. (2018)
SGB	Real-Time Risk Assessment	Ahmed and Abdel-Aty (2013)
XGBoost	Real-Time Risk Assessment	Parsa et al. (2020)
MARS	Crash Frequency Analysis	Abdel-Aty and Haleem (2011)

Resources

Readers can explore the following curated list of machine learning frameworks, libraries and software:
https://github.com/josephmisiti/awesome-machine-learning

Case Study 1

Exposure is important for the precision accuracy of crash prediction models. Show how machine learning models can help in estimating traffic exposures from locations with no count stations.

***Solution*:**

Key information was gathered from the TxDOT roadway inventory database (RHiNO) for the block group level from the 2010 U.S. Census Geographic Information System (GIS) data, and to approximate the number of non-motorized trips from the 2009 NHTS data. The data gathered in this database development task is reviewed in the following sections. For additional details of this study, readers can consult the Dixon et al. (2017) report.

Databases

TxDOT Roadway Inventory Database

Several possible data sources were considered for assessing this information, but in the end RHiNO was chosen for use as one of the main data sources. In TxDOT there are defined criteria for multiple candidate elements that are recognized within this analysis. As an example, bridge reconstruction (shifting barriers from the road), traffic volume, and speed limits are currently impacting the minimum widths of roadway shoulders. These variables were thought of as a starting point for evaluating candidate suitability criteria data elements, and the criteria listed portray the usual shoulder widths as the TxDOT *Roadway Design Manual* recommended and identify existing TxDOT *Roadway Design Manual* recommendations for bicycle usage.

10,357 miles of rural paved roadways were identified for analysis. Rural two-lane roadways make up approximately 56 percent of the total roadways, and their average shoulder width (from a range of observed shoulder widths) ranges from zero to 28 feet. The average shoulder (from a range of observed shoulder widths) width ranges from zero to 32 feet for rural multi-lane roadways. The Texas roadway network for rural multi-lane roadways and rural two-lane roadways is illustrated in Figure 31.

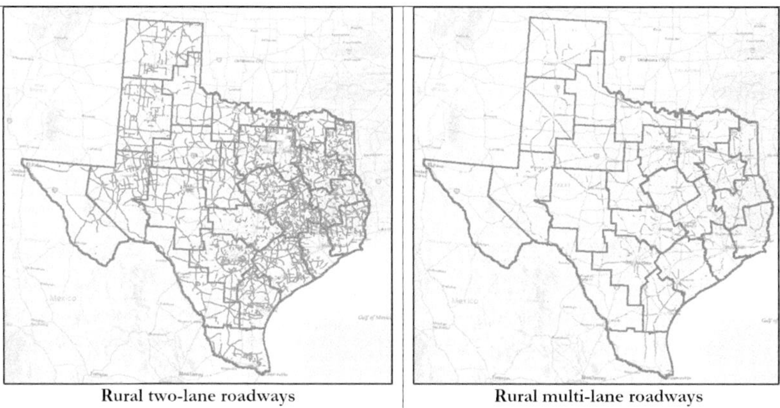

Figure 31. Texas rural two-lane and multi-lane roads of interest.

U.S. Census Data

2010 Census geographic and demographic data was obtained from two different sources: the Topologically Integrated Geographic Encoding and Referencing (TIGER) block shapefiles and the American FactFinder's demographic information. Generally, census data is subdivided into three major units, which are briefly described below:

- The intermediate-level geographic unit, the clusters of blocks and division of tracts, identified as the first digit of the block code, typically defined as containing 600 to 3,000 people, is known as the **block group**.
- The highest-level geographic unit, relatively permanent statistical subdivisions of a region, identified using up to 4 digit integer numbers, typically defined to contain 1,200 to 8,000 people, is known as the **tract**.
- The lowest-level geographic unit, the division of block groups, generally small statistical areas bounded by visible features such as small water bodies, streets, roads, or railroad tracks, is known as the **block**.

Both block group level and tract level Census data for Texas was collected. The geographic unit is the basis for the amount of available economic and demographic data from the census website. At the tract level, more data is easily accessible. The number of data items at the block level is considerably limited, but due to its small spatial size, it has higher data accuracy at the tract level.

National Household Travel Survey (NHTS) Data

Data is limited that is associated with non-motorized travel, but the NHTS database is a primary source for non-motorized trips data that is accessible to transportation professionals. Every five to seven years the NHTS is conducted by the FHWA in order to offer data for different transportation modes on daily travel. The program has expanded from the original 15,000 household samples in 1969 to 150,147 household samples in 2009. 46,423 household samples (out of 150,147) were based in Texas.

Model Development

To aid in prioritizing the selection of potential shoulder widening locations in order to promote pedestrian and bicycle safety, one must figure out the weekly number of predicted non-motorized trips. Locations with more trips of this kind logically ought to be higher ranked than locations that don't have the prospect of any pedestrian or bicycle activity. 9,400 bike trips and 100,400 walk trips were recorded by the 2009 NHTS. 148 households were surveyed for Texas rural roadways, with 1,367 trips. The survey logged 284 bike trips and 1,083 walk trips out of the total trips. The percentages of bike and pedestrian trips per week based on five different trip groups are shown in Table 9 and were generated by using the NHTS data for 148 households in Texas.

Table 9. Non-motorized trips per week from NHTS sample data

Trips Per Week	Pedestrian (percent)	Bicycle (percent)
0-5.00	43.3	64.0
5.01-10.00	36.7	32.0
10.01-15.00	6.7	0.0
15.01-20.00	3.3	0.0
Above 20.00	10.0	4.0

Using the same data, Table 10 recaps the four NHTS block group level rural road variables that were used in this analysis.

To develop the SVR model, five block-group level explanatory variables (household size, population density, urban-rural code, percent renter-occupied housing, and housing units per square mile) were used from the Texas rural roadway NHTS dataset. Models were first separately developed for bicycle and pedestrian trips, and later the bicycle mode share was determined to be very low in comparison to the pedestrian trips. Two different models were developed:

- Model 1: Rural model for weekly pedestrian trips, and
- Model 2: Rural model for weekly non-motorized trips (both pedestrian and bicycle).

A tuning method is performed to select the hyperparameters (cost function (C), $\in$, γ). The final selected C, $\in$, and γ are, respectively, 10, 0.4, and 1. These

Table 10. Summary of four explanatory variables from NHTS sample data

Variable Names	Percentage (%)
Population per sq. mile-Block Group	
0-99	33.6
100-499	28.9
500-999	14.1
1,000-1,999	17.2
2,000-3,999	6.2
Housing units per sq. mile-Block Group	
0-99	44.5
100-499	39.8
500-999	15.7
Percent renter-occupier- Block Group (%)	
0-4	7.8
5-14	37.5
15-24	27.3
25-34	17.2
35-44	5.5
45-54	3.1
55-64	1.6
Household size- Block Group (number of people)	
1	5.5
2	23.4
3	11.7
4	30.5
5	15.6
6	9.4
7	3.9

values' performances are tested on a reduced validation set (10%), and the prediction accuracy of the train set for both models was 90 percent and 68 percent, respectively. Models were also developed for the test set data (40 percent of the main data is considered as a test set). Compared to the train set data, the prediction accuracy of the test set is lower in value (61 percent and 58 percent, respectively). A general framework SVR (where $x < 20\%$, and $a + b = 1$) is shown in Figure 32.

In order to predict the block group using counts of non-motorized trips (using Model 2 - the non-motorized model), the developed models were then utilized. The roadway geometric files were, upon transecting the 2009 NHTS block group

GIS shapefiles with the state roadway inventory shapefile for Texas, in spatial-relation to the block group and their predicted non-motorized trip counts. Using this method, disaggregate-level non-motorized trip counts were determined for certain rural roadways.

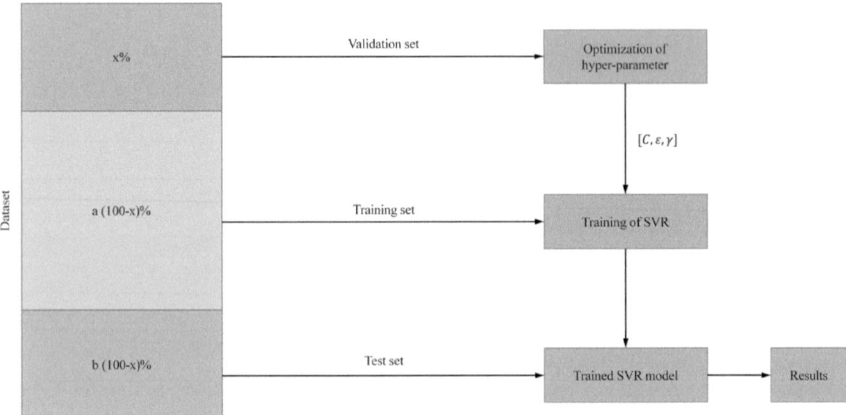

Figure 32. Flowchart of SVR model development.

Although variations accompany the other tested variables, their values drastically differed based on the training set sample size. It isn't practical to repeat the application of this SVR procedure each time to estimate the number of non-motorized trips. To perform this task, variable importance using a random forest algorithm is done using a package with the *R* statistical software (23). Suppose a randomly selected vector of input variables ($X = X_1, \ldots, X_n$) to a random response variable $Y \in Y$ is considered for analysis. The significance of a variable X_k while predicting or estimating Y is found with the Gini index, computed by adding the decrease in impurity according to the following equation:

$$Importance(X_k) = \frac{1}{N_T} \sum_T \sum_{t \in T: v(s_t) = X_k} p(t).d \tag{38}$$

where,

t = node

T = all nodes

$p(t)$ = proportion N_t/N of sample for node t

s_t = split for which all variables are sampled into two major nodes t_L and t_R to maximize the decrease, d

$v(s_t)$ = variable used in split s_t

$d = i(t) - p_L\, i(t_L) - p_R\, i(t_R)$ = decrease

N_T = all variables

Figure 33 shows the variable importance plot for the selected variables, which shows variable importance in descending order.

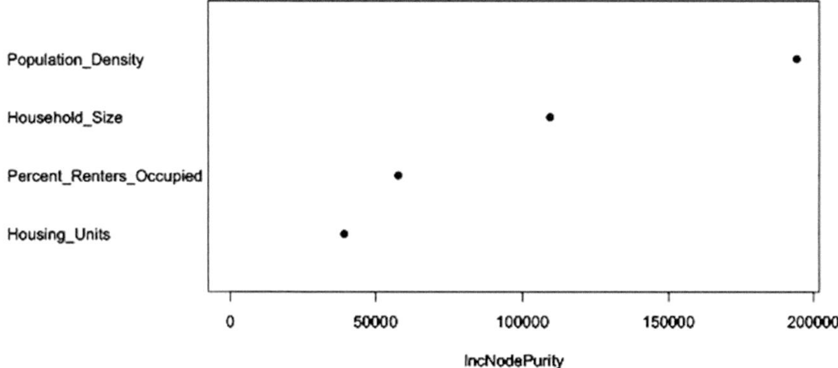

Figure 33. Variable importance plot.

From the variance importance, it is found that population density per square mile is the most significant variable in estimating non-motorized trips per week. Figure 34 shows the distribution of non-motorized trips per week against population density per square mile for the variation of another two key factors: household size per square mile, and percent renters occupied per square mile. Due to the limited frequency above 12,500 people per square mile, the threshold is considered up to 12,500. It clearly shows that non-motorized trips increase against the increase of population density per square mile until hitting a certain threshold for different attributes of these two factors.

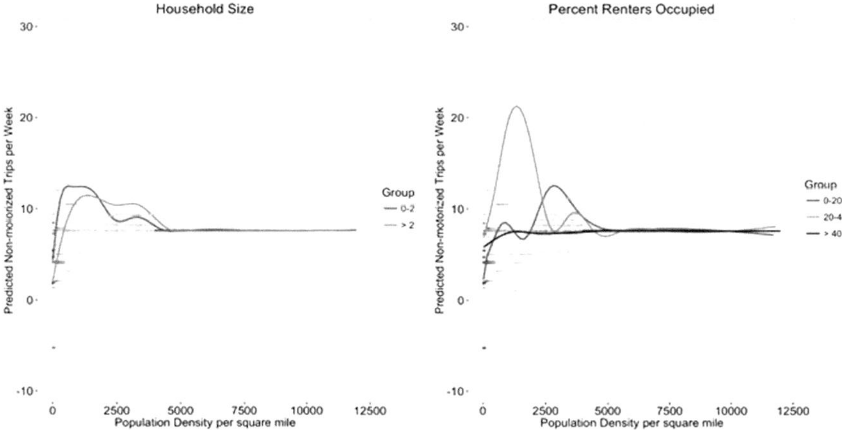

Figure 34. Predicted non-motorized trips per week vs. population density per mile for different household size and percent renters occupied.

The authors also developed a more convenient graphic from the results, shown in Figure 35, in which for rural Texas locations the number of non-motorized trips can be predicted. The key input into this table is the population density- note that for each population density level the 20th percentile and 80th percentile thresholds are shown in order to show this type of data's variable nature.

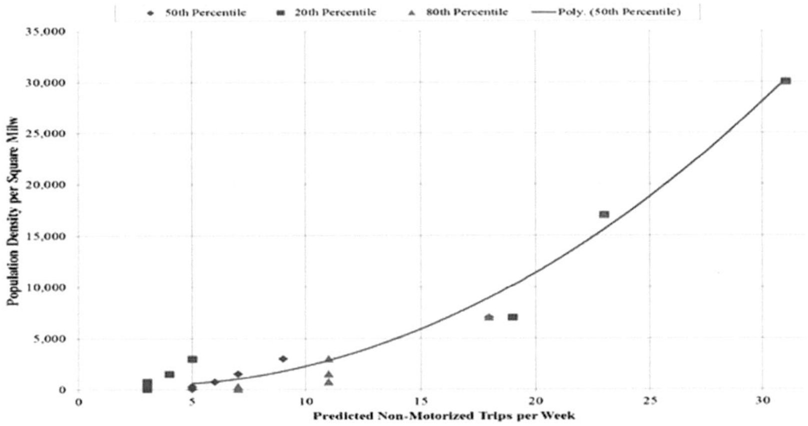

Figure 35. Predicted number of non-motorized trips per week for rural Texas locations.

Case Study 2

Operating speed is a key factor in traffic crashes and crash-related injuries. Show how a decision tree can help in understanding the relationship between operating speed and other key variables.

Solution:

To figure out which variables are most associated with small differences between crowdsourced speed data (i.e., TMCS) and tube speed data, a decision tree approach was used in this evaluation. A decision tree looks like a flow chart wherein the test on a variable (e.g., the number of signals is less than 4) is represented by each node, and the outcomes of that test are represented by the branches. The mean TMCS value for no (there are more than four signals) and yes (there are four or less signals) would be shown by the branches in the example of the number of signals. For additional details of this study, readers can consult the Fitzpatrick and Das (2019) report.

A rule fit method to find hidden rules was adopted for predicting the selected variables from a pool's importance, which contains ranges of the factors using "rule pruning" and "rule generation" algorithms. Large datasets with a mix of variables, ranging from categorical to numeric, can be handled by the rule-based analysis, resulting in easy interpretation. By considering all parameters to be intuitive parameters, rule based-decision trees are derived from the dataset, which eliminates lower significant variables.

To investigate the characteristics that could have affected the results, different subsets of the available variables are used, permitting the opportunity to identify whether a subset of variables could be considered appropriate for estimating an arterial performance *e*. Focusing on the roadway characteristics to explore if those variables could help explain the variations between the speeds measured at the spot location (tube data) and those measured for the corridor (crowdsourced data) was one approach. Number of through lanes, number of signals, median width, the distance between the nearest roundabout or signalized intersection and the tubes, posted speed limit, number of driveways, and segment length were some of the variables considered. Adding in the variables associated with a period, such as light level, type of day (e.g., weekend or weekday), or day of the week was another approach. Adding in the variables that were associated with a 15-min period, such as confidence level, LOS, and vehicle volume per lane for the 15-min period was the third approach.

The results when only considering geometric variables are shown in Figure 36. The number of signals was revealed to be the most influential variable. When there are fewer signals within the corridor, smaller differences between the on-road tube speeds and the crowdsourced speeds are present; segments with less than 4 signals in the corridor had better matches than those with more in this dataset. Signals can introduce delay within the corridor and are associated with large disruptions in travel; subsequently, it is logical that the number of signals would have a noteworthy impact when using crowdsourced data as a representative speed for a specific location. The number of driveways was the next influential geometric variable shown in Figure 36 (DrvUsigSame_BC and DrvUsigOpp_BC). Driveways, like signals, can introduce disruptions or conflicts within the travel stream. The travel time for other vehicles can be increased when a vehicle slows to turn right at a driveway. Although a vehicle that is turning out of a driveway is supposed to wait for a sufficient gap, drivers have been shown to potentially turn out onto the major roadway, anticipating that, in order to avoid a crash, major street drivers will slow down. The likelihood that there will be an additional delay to travel time from one end of the corridor to the other, resulting in a potentially larger difference between speeds measured at a specific location and crowdsourced data, increases with the number of driveways.

Figure 37 shows a decision tree that concentrates on temporal variables like the type of day or the light level. For this analysis all 15-min periods are included; in other words, a range of vehicle volume or level of service is represented. The analysis revealed that the day type was the most influential type of variable; there was a smaller difference between the on-road tube speeds and crowdsourced speeds during the weekend than on week days (i.e., Friday and week days). The next branch in Figure 37 shows the variable of light condition based on time of day. Overall, the dusk light condition on a weekend was associated with the smallest difference between crowdsourced and spot speeds. However, the difference in speeds for both daytime and dusk light conditions on the weekend were very similar to each other.

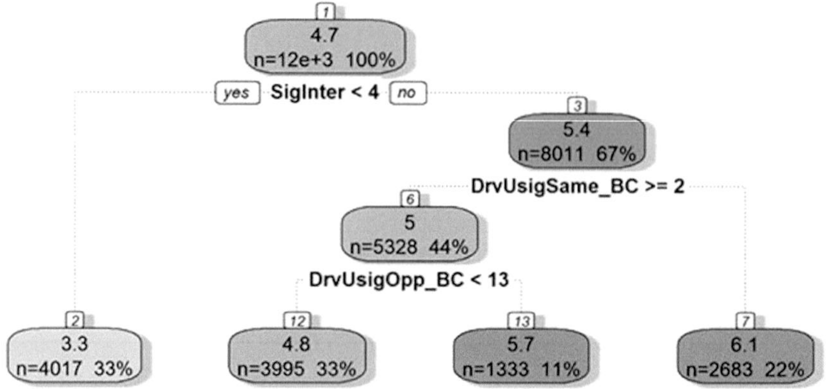

Figure 36. Decision tree for speed difference using only geometric variables.

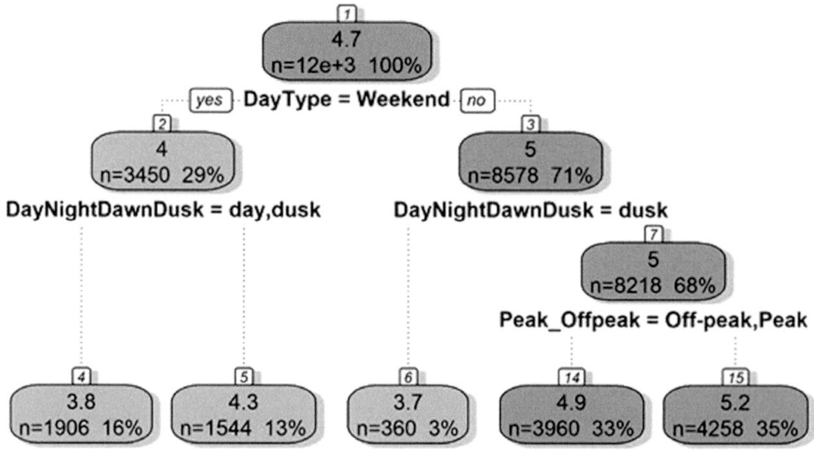

Figure 37. Decision tree for speed difference using only temporal variables.

Figure 38 shows a decision tree that also concentrates on temporal variables like the light level and the day of the week, with the additional restriction of including only the 15-min periods when LOS A, B, or C (as computed from the tube data) are present. Previous research has defined uncongested conditions as being LOS A, B, or C, so those categories were included in this evaluation. This analysis may help with the question of which conditions can be utilized to approximate the speed in uncongested conditions. As shown in Figure 38, the smallest difference between the tube speed and crowdsourced speed was found by the analysis on Saturday and Sunday.

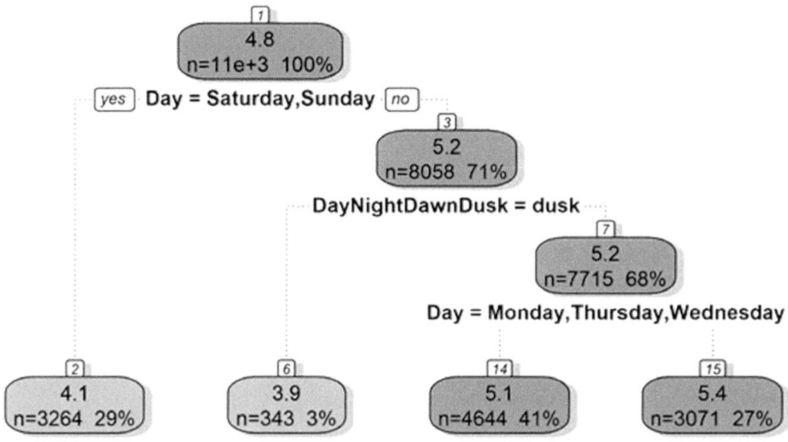

Figure 38. Decision tree for speed difference using temporal variables when only considering those 15-min periods when LOS A, B, or C is present.

Example Problem 1

Show a reproducible example with performance results of different ML algorithm in estimating crash injury types.

***Solution*:**

To perform this analysis, e-scooter crash data from Louisiana has been used. The coding to answer the question is provided in the following code chunks. The code results are not shown (few major plots are shown to explain the results)

Example Problem 1 (Code Chunk 1)

```
## Please check my RPUBS for additional codes: https://rpubs.com/subasish

## Load required packages
library(catboost)
library(caret)
library(data.table)
library(dplyr)
library(kernlab)
library(randomForest)
setwd("~folder_location")

dat1= read.csv("EScotterCr_Fin1.csv")
names(dat1)

dat2=dat1[,-c(1, 2, 3)]
dim(dat2)
```

(*Contd.*)

```
data <- as.data.frame(as.matrix(dat2), stringsAsFactors=TRUE)
dat3=data[,c(1:12, 19)]
head(dat3)

x <- data[,1:12]
y <- data[,19]


grid <- expand.grid(depth = c(4, 6, 8),
                learning_rate = 0.1,
                iterations = 100,
                l2_leaf_reg = 0.1,
                rsm = 0.95,
                border_count = 64)
control <- trainControl(method="repeatedcv", number=10, repeats=3)
model <- train(x, as.factor(make.names(y)),
           method = catboost.caret,
           logging_level = 'Silent', preProc = NULL,
           tuneGrid = grid, trControl = control)

print(model)
importance <- varImp(model, scale = FALSE)
print(importance)

head(predict(model, type = 'prob'))

control <- trainControl(method="repeatedcv", number=10, repeats=3)
# CART
set.seed(7)
fit.cart <- train(SEVERITY_CD~., data=dat3, method="rpart", trControl=control)
# LDA
set.seed(7)
fit.lda <- train(SEVERITY_CD~., data=dat3, method="lda", trControl=control)
# SVM
set.seed(7)
fit.svm <- train(SEVERITY_CD~., data=dat3, method="svmRadial", trControl=control)
# kNN
set.seed(7)
fit.knn <- train(SEVERITY_CD~., data=dat3, method="knn", trControl=control)
# Random Forest
set.seed(7)
fit.rf <- train(SEVERITY_CD~., data=dat3,  method="rf", trControl=control)
# collect resamples
results <- resamples(list(CART=fit.cart, LDA=fit.lda, SVM=fit.svm, KNN=fit.knn,
RF=fit.rf, CB=model))
summary(results)

scales <- list(x=list(relation="free"), y=list(relation="free"))
bwplot(results, scales=scales)
```

Figure 39 shows the accuracy and Kappa measures of different ML algorithms. A box plot is used to show the values. CB is shown to have the highest mean in both accuracy and kappa.

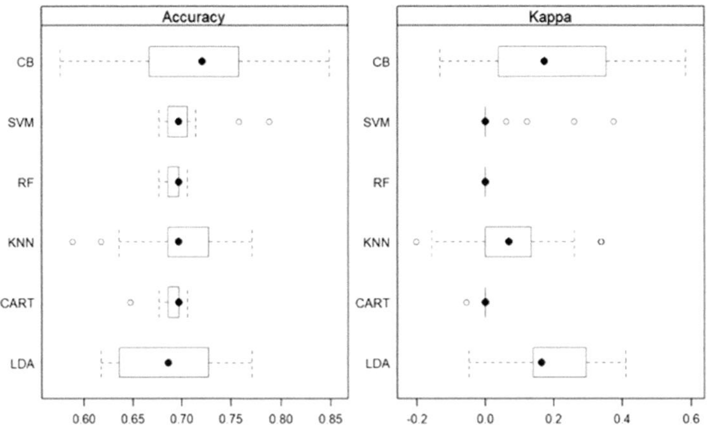

Figure 39. Accuracy and Kappa measures of different ML algorithms.

Coding Help

List all the models in the popular machine learning *R* package ‘caret.’

***Solution*:**

The reader can use the following code chuck to link all ML models in the ‘caret’ package in an interactive table format.

Coding Help

```
## Please check my RPUBS for additional codes: https://rpubs.com/subasish
## Codes are published here: https://rpubs.com/subasish/614171

library(htmltab)
library(DT)

setwd("~folder  location")
caret= read.csv("caret.csv")

datatable(
  caret, extensions = c('Select', 'Buttons'), options = list(
    select = list(style = 'os', items = 'row'),
    dom = 'Blfrtip',
    rowId = 0,
    buttons = c('csv', 'excel')
  ),
  selection = 'none'
)
```

Chapter Conclusion

This chapter provides a brief description of different supervised learning algorithms. Some of the popular models and algorithms discussed in this chapter are logistic regressions, decision trees, support vector machines, random forests, artificial neural networks, naïve bayes classifiers, cubists, XGBoost, and CatBoost. The chapter also provides a list of relevant studies. Example problems and case studies are provided later in this chapter.

Further Reading

Bali, R., Sarkar, D., 2016. R Machine Learning by Example. Packt Publishing Ltd.

Beeley, C., 2013. Web Application Development with R using Shiny. Packt Publishing Ltd.

Bivand, R.S., Pebesma, E. and Gómez-Rubio, V., 2013. Applied Spatial Data Analysis with R. Springer Science & Business Media.

Boehmke, B. and Greenwell, B.M., 2019. Hands-On Machine Learning with R. CRC Press.

Das, S., Dutta, A., Avelar, R., Dixon, K.K., Sun, X., 2019. Supervised association rules mining on pedestrian crashes in urban areas: Identifying patterns for appropriate countermeasures. International Journal of Urban Sciences, 23, pp. 30-48.

Day, G.S. and Schoemaker, P.J.H., 2004. Wharton on Managing Emerging Technologies. John Wiley & Sons.

Dixon, K., Fitzpatrick, K., Avelar, R. and Das, S., 2017. Analysis of the Shoulder Widening Need on the State Highway System. Texas Department of Transportation, Report No. FHWA/TX-15/0-6840-1.

Dorman, M., 2014. Learning R for Geospatial Analysis. Packt Publishing Ltd.

Guomin, H., Wu, L., Ma, X., Zhang, W., Fan, J., et al., 2019 Evaluation of CatBoost method for prediction of reference evapotranspiration in humid regions. Journal of Hydrology, 2019.

Lantz, B., 2019. Machine Learning with R: Expert techniques for predictive modeling, 3rd Edition. Packt Publishing Ltd.

Otero, F., Diego Araneo, D. Zonda, 2020. Wind classification using machine learning algorithms. International Journal of Climatology.

Rezapour, M., Farid, A., Nazneen, S. and Ksaibati, K., 2020. Using machine learning techniques for evaluation of motorcycle injury severity. IATSS Research.

Shalev-Shwartz, S. and Ben-David, S., 2014. Understanding Machine Learning: From Theory to Algorithms. Cambridge University Press.

Zhu, M., Li, Y. and Wang, Y., 2018. Design and experiment verification of a novel analysis framework for recognition of driver injury patterns: From a multi-class classification perspective. Accident Analysis & Prevention, 120, pp. 152–164.

Zopluoglu. C., 2019. Detecting Examinees with Item Preknowledge in Large-Scale Testing Using Extreme Gradient Boosting (XGBoost). Educational and Psychological Measurement.

References

Abdel-Aty, M. and Haleem, K., 2011. Analyzing angle crashes at unsignalized intersections using machine learning techniques. Accident Analysis & Prevention, 43, pp. 461–470.

Ahmadi, A., Jahangiri, A., Berardi, V. and Machiani, S.G., 2020. Crash severity analysis of rear-end crashes in California using statistical and machine learning classification methods. Journal of Highway Safety & Security, 12, pp. 522–546.

Ahmed, M.M. and Abdel-Atz, M., 2013. Application of stochastic gradient boosting technique to enhance reliability of real-time risk assessment: Use of automatic vehicle identification and remote traffic microwave sensor data. Transportation Research Record, 2386, pp. 26–34.

Aoude, G.S., Desaraju, V.R., Stephens, L.H. and How, J.P., 2012. Driver behavior classification at intersections and validation on large naturalistic data set. IEEE Transactions on Intelligent Transportation Systems, 13, pp. 724–736.

Assi, K., Rahman, S.M., Mansoor, U. and Ratrout, N., 2020. Predicting crash injury severity with machine learning algorithm synergized with clustering technique: A promising protocol. International Journal of Environmental Research and Public Health 17, 5497.

Broggi, A., Cerri, P., Ghidoni, S., Grisleri, P., Jung, H.G., et al., 2009. A new approach to urban pedestrian detection for automatic braking. IEEE Transactions on Intelligent Transportation Systems, 10, pp. 594–605.

Chang, Y., Bharadwaj, N., Edara, P. and Sun, C., 2020. Exploring contributing factors of hazardous events in construction zones using naturalistic driving study data. IEEE Transactions on Intelligent Vehicles, 5, pp. 519–527.

Chen, H. and Chen, L., 2017. Support vector machine classification of drunk driving behaviour. International Journal of Environmental Research and Public Health, 14, 108.

Cho, H., Rybski, P.E. and Zhang, W., 2010. Vision-Based Bicycle Detection and Tracking Using a Deformable Part Model and an EKF Algorithm. 13th International IEEE Conference on Intelligent Transportation Systems, 2010, pp. 1875–1880.

Das, S., Sun, X. and Sun, M., 2020. Rule-based safety prediction models for rural two-lane run-off-road crashes. International Journal of Transportation Science and Technology.

Das, S., Storey, B., Shimu, T.H., Mitra, S., Theel, M., et al., 2020. Severity analysis of tree and utility pole crashes: Applying fast and frugal heuristics. IATSS Research, 44, pp. 85–93.

Dogru, N. and Subasi, A., 2018. Traffic accident detection using random forest classifier. *In.* 2018 15th Learning and Technology Conference (L T). Presented at the 2018 15th Learning and Technology Conference (L T), pp. 40–45.

Dollar, P., Wojek, C., Schiele, B. and Perona, P., 2009. Pedestrian detection: A benchmark. *In:* 2009 IEEE Conference on Computer Vision and Pattern Recognition. Presented at the 2009 IEEE Conference on Computer Vision and Pattern Recognition, pp. 304–311.

Du, Y. and Chan, C.-Y., 2014. Transportation Research Board. Older Driver Crash Risk Modeling by AdaBoost. p. 18.

Effati, M., Rajabi, M.A., Hakimpour, F. and Shaban, S., 2015. Prediction of crash severity on two-lane, two-way roads based on fuzzy classification and regression tree using geospatial analysis. Journal of Computing in Civil Engineering, 29, Content ID 04014099.

Elhenawy, M., Jahangiri, A., Rakha, H.A. and El-Shawarby, I., 2015. Modeling driver stop/run behavior at the onset of a yellow indication considering driver run tendency and roadway surface conditions. Accident Analysis & Prevention, 83, pp. 90–100.

Fitzpatrick, K. and Das, S., 2019. Vehicle Operating Speed on Urban Arterial Roadways. SafeD National UTC, Report No. TTI-01-04.

Guo, L., Li, L., Zhao, Y. and Zhang, M., 2010. Study on pedestrian detection and tracking with monocular vision. *In:* 2010 2nd International Conference on Computer Technology and Development. Presented at the 2010 2nd International Conference on Computer Technology and Development, pp. 466–470.

He, P., Wu, A., Huang, X., Scott, J., Rangarajan, A., et al., 2019. Deep learning based geometric features for effective truck selection and classification from highway videos. *In:* 2019 IEEE Intelligent Transportation Systems Conference (ITSC). Presented at the 2019 IEEE Intelligent Transportation Systems Conference (ITSC), pp. 824–830.

Hong Cheng, Nanning Zheng and Junjie Qin, 2005. Pedestrian detection using sparse Gabor filter and support vector machine. *In:* IEEE Proceedings. Intelligent Vehicles Symposium, 2005. Presented at the IEEE Proceedings. Intelligent Vehicles Symposium, 2005, pp. 583–587.

Hou, Q., Jiao, W., Ren, L., Cao, H., Song, G., et al., 2014. Experimental study of leakage detection of natural gas pipeline using FBG based strain sensor and least square support vector machine. Journal of Loss Prevention in the Process Industries, 32, pp. 144–151.

Huang, G., et al., 2019. Evaluation of CatBoost method for prediction of reference evapotranspiration in humid regions. Journal of Hydrology, 574, pp. 1029–1041.

Iranitalab, A. and Khattak, A., 2017. Comparison of four statistical and machine learning methods for crash severity prediction. Accident Analysis & Prevention, 108, pp. 27–36.

Jahangiri, A., Rakha, H. and Dingus, T.A., 2016. Red-light running violation prediction using observational and simulator data. Accident Analysis & Prevention, 96, pp. 316–328.

Jung, H., Ehara, Y., Tan, J.K., Kim, H., Ishikawa, S., et al., 2012. Applying MSC-HOG feature to the detection of a human on a bicycle. *In:* 2012 12th International Conference on Control, Automation and Systems. Presented at the 2012 12th International Conference on Control, Automation and Systems, pp. 514–517.

Keramati, A., Lu, P., Iranitalab, A., Pan, D., Huang, Y., et al., 2020. A crash severity analysis at highway-rail grade crossings: The random survival forest method. Accident Analysis & Prevention, 144, 105683.

Kong, X., Das, S. and Zhang, Y., 2021. Mining patterns of near-crash events with and without secondary tasks. Accident Analysis & Prevention, 157.

Lamb, D.S. and Lee, C., 2019. Measuring changes in the spatiotemporal patterns of motorcycle fatalities in the U.S. Transportation Research Record: Journal of the Transportation Research Board, 2673, pp. 234–243.

Lantz, B., 2013. Machine Learning with R. Packt Publishing Ltd.

Lee, D., Warner, J. and Morgan, C., 2019. Discovering crash severity factors of grade crossing with a machine learning approach. Presented at the 2019 Joint Rail Conference, American Society of Mechanical Engineers Digital Collection.

Lee, Y., Cho, E., Park, M., Kim, H., Choi, K., et al., 2018. A machine learning approach to prediction of passenger injuries on real road situation. *In:* 2018 Joint 10th International

Conference on Soft Computing and Intelligent Systems (SCIS) and 19th International Symposium on Advanced Intelligent Systems (ISIS), pp. 1087–1090.

Li, Z., Jin, X. and Zhao, X., 2015. Drunk driving detection based on classification of multivariate time series. Journal of Safety Research, 54, 61-e29.

Li, Z., Liu, P., Wang, W. and Xu, C., 2012. Using support vector machine models for crash injury severity analysis. Accident Analysis & Prevention, 45, pp. 478–486.

Li, Z., Wang, H., Zhang, Y. and Zhao, X., 2020. Random forest–based feature selection and detection method for drunk driving recognition. International Journal of Distributed Sensor Networks, 16, 1550147720905234.

López, G., Abellán, J., Montella, A. and de Oña, J., 2014. Patterns of single-vehicle crashes on two-lane rural highways in Granada province, Spain in-depth analysis through decision rules. Transportation Research Record, 2432, pp. 133–141.

Lu, P., Zheng, Z., Ren, Y., Zhou, X., Keramati, A., et al., 2020. A gradient boosting crash prediction approach for highway-rail grade crossing crash analysis. Journal of Advanced Transportation, 2020, pp. 1–10.

Ludwig, O., Premebida, C., Nunes, U. and Araujo, R., 2011. Evaluation of boosting-SVM and SRM-SVM cascade classifiers in laser and vision-based pedestrian detection. Institute of Electrical and Electronics Engineers (IEEE), pp. 1574–1579.

Mafi, S., Abdel Razig, Y. and Doczy, R., 2018. Machine learning methods to analyze injury severity of drivers from different age and gender groups. Transportation Research Record: Journal of the Transportation Research Board, 2672, pp. 171–183.

Mokhtarimousavi, S., Anderson, J.C., Azizinamini, A. and Hadi, M., 2019. Improved support vector machine models for work zone crash injury severity prediction and analysis. Transportation Research Record: Journal of the Transportation Research Board, 2673, pp. 680–692.

Müller, M., Botsch, M., Böhmländer, D. and Utschick, W., 2018. Machine learning based prediction of crash severity distributions for mitigation strategies. Journal of Advances in Information Technology, 9.

Osman, O.A., Hajij, M., Karbalaieali, S. and Ishak, S., 2019. A hierarchical machine learning classification approach for secondary task identification from observed driving behavior data. Accident Analysis & Prevention, 123, pp. 274–281.

Parsa, A.B., Movahedi, A., Taghipour, H., Derrible, S., Mohammadian, A. (Kouros), et al., 2020. Toward safer highways, application of XGBoost and SHAP for real-time accident detection and feature analysis. Accident Analysis & Prevention, 136, 105405.

Patel, M.S., 2019. Driver Behavior Analysis of Older Adults at Road Intersections Using Naturalistic Driving Data. M.S. Thesis, The University of Michigan-Dearborn.

Ranganathan, P. and Olson, E., 2010. Automated safety inspection of grade crossings. *In:* 2010 IEEE/RSJ International Conference on Intelligent Robots and Systems. Presented at the 2010 IEEE/RSJ International Conference on Intelligent Robots and Systems, pp. 2149–2154.

Severino, J.V.B., Zimmer, A., Brandmeier, T. and Freire, R.Z., 2019. Pedestrian recognition using micro Doppler effects of radar signals based on machine learning and multi-objective optimization. Expert Systems with Applications, 136, pp. 304–315.

Sivaraman, S. and Trivedi, M.M., 2009. Active learning based robust monocular vehicle detection for on-road safety systems. *In:* 2009 IEEE Intelligent Vehicles Symposium. Presented at the 2009 IEEE Intelligent Vehicles Symposium, pp. 399–404.

Soleimani, S., Mousa, S.R., Codjoe, J. and Leitner, M., 2019. A comprehensive railroad-highway grade crossing consolidation model: A machine learning approach. Accident Analysis & Prevention, 128, pp. 65-77.

Tango, F. and Botta, M., 2013. Real-time detection system of driver distraction using machine learning. IEEE Transactions on Intelligent Transportation Systems, 14, pp. 894–905.

Theofilatos, A., Chen, C. and Antoniou, C., 2019. Comparing machine learning and deep learning methods for real-time crash prediction. Transportation Research Record: Journal of the Transportation Research Board, 2673, pp. 169–178.

Toyoda, M., Yokoyama, D., Komiyama, J. and Itoh, M., 2017. Road safety estimation utilizing big and heterogeneous vehicle recorder data. *In:* 2017 IEEE International Conference on Big Data (Big Data). Presented at the 2017 IEEE International Conference on Big Data (Big Data), pp. 4841–4842.

Wang, S., Sharma, A. and Knickerbocker, S., 2017. Analyzing and improving the performance of dynamic message sign reporting work zone–related congestion. Transportation Research Record: Journal of the Transportation Research Board, 2617(1), pp. 71–77.

Wu, H., Chen, J., Liu, X., Xiao, Y., Wang, M., et al., 2019. One-dimensional CNN-based intelligent recognition of vibrations in pipeline monitoring with DAS. J. Lightwave Technol., JLT, 37, pp. 4359–4366.

Xia, T., Song, X., Fan, Z., Kanasugi, H., Chen, Q., et al., 2018. DeepRailway: A deep learning system for forecasting railway traffic. *In:* 2018 IEEE Conference on Multimedia Information Processing and Retrieval (MIPR). Presented at the 2018 IEEE Conference on Multimedia Information Processing and Retrieval (MIPR), pp. 51–56.

Xu, C., Wang, W. and Liu, P., 2013. A genetic programming model for real-time crash prediction on freeways. IEEE Transactions on Intelligent Transportation Systems, 14, pp. 574–586.

Yao, Y., Zhao, X., Du, H., Zhang, Y., Zhang, G., et al., 2019. Classification of fatigued and drunk driving based on decision tree methods: A simulator study. International Journal of Environmental Research and Public Health, 16, 1935.

Yeo, M.V., Li, X., Shen, K. and Wilder-Smith, E.P., 2009. Can SVM be used for automatic EEG detection of drowsiness during car driving? Safety Science, 47, pp. 115–124.

Yu, Q. and Zhou, Y., 2019. Traffic safety analysis on mixed traffic flows at signalized intersection based on Haar-Adaboost algorithm and machine learning. Safety Science, 120, pp. 248–253.

Yu, R. and Abdel-Aty, M., 2013. Utilizing support vector machine in real-time crash risk evaluation. Accident Analysis & Prevention, 51, pp. 252–259.

Zhang, J., Li, Z., Pu, Z. and Xu, C., 2018. Comparing prediction performance for crash injury severity among various machine learning and statistical methods. IEEE Access, 6, pp. 60079–60087.

Zhou, X., Lu, P., Zheng, Z., Tolliver, D., Keramati, A., et al., 2020. Accident prediction accuracy assessment for highway-rail grade crossings using random forest algorithm compared with decision tree. Reliability Engineering & System Safety, 200, 106931.

Zualkernan, I.A., Aloul, F., Basheer, F., Khera, G. and Srinivasan, S., et al., 2018. Intelligent accident detection classification using mobile phones. *In:* 2018 International Conference on Information Networking (ICOIN). Presented at the 2018 International Conference on Information Networking (ICOIN), pp. 504–509.

CHAPTER

6

Unsupervised Learning

6.1. Introduction

This chapter provides brief descriptions of the popular unsupervised learning algorithms used in highway safety research.

6.2. Popular Algorithms

6.2.1. *K*-Means

The k-means clustering algorithm operates as follows. First, the analysts must select k, which is the number of clusters. Next, they will randomly place k feature vectors, or centroids, in space 1. Then, using a metric, such as the Euclidean distance, they compute the difference between each example x and each centroid c. Next, the closest centroid is assigned to each example, and the average feature vector for each centroid is labeled. The new positions of the centroids are based on the average feature vectors. One can recalculate the distance between each example and centroid to alter the assignment and then repeat the process until the assignments remain the same. The model is the list of examples and the centroid IDs that are assigned to each one. The final positions are influenced by the initial position of the centroids, so two trials of k-means can potentially produce two different models.

One can recompute the distance from each example to each centroid, modify the assignment, and repeat the procedure until the assignments don't change after the centroid locations were recomputed. The model is the list of assignments of centroids ID to the examples. The initial position of centroids influences the final positions, so two runs of k-means can result in two different models. One run of the k-means algorithm results in different background colors representing regions in which all points belong to the same cluster. The value of k, the number of clusters, is a hyperparameter that has to be tuned by the data analyst. There are some techniques for selecting k. None of them have been proven to be optimal. Most of them require the analyst to make an "educated guess" by looking at some metrics or by examining cluster assignments visually. Later in this chapter, one considers a technique that allows choosing a reasonably good value for k without looking at the data and making guesses.

6.2.2. *K*-Nearest Neighbors

K-Nearest Neighbors (kNN) is a type of non-parametric learning algorithm. Unlike learning algorithms that permit the training data to be thrown out after the model is developed, kNN stores all training examples in its memory. The kNN algorithm seeks k training examples nearest to x once a new example x is presented and presents either the average label or the majority label in case of classification or regression, respectively.

A distance function can be utilized to determine two points' closeness. The Euclidean distance given above is often used in practice. The negative **cosine similarity** is another popular choice for the distance function. Cosine similarity is defined as

$$s(x_i, x_k) \overset{def}{=} cos\left(\angle(x_i, x_k)\right) = \frac{\sum_{j=1}^{D} x_i^{(j)} x_k^{(j)}}{\sqrt{\sum_{j=1}^{D} \left(x_i^{(j)}\right)^2} \sqrt{\sum_{j=1}^{D} \left(x_k^{(j)}\right)^2}} \quad (1)$$

and it is a similarity measure of the direction of two vectors. If the angle is 0 degrees between two vectors, that means the vectors point in the same direction and that cosine similarity is 1. If the vectors are orthogonal, the cosine similarity is 0. The cosine similarity is $\neq 1$ if the vectors point in opposite directions. To use cosine similarity as a distance metric, it must be multiplied by $\neq 1$. The Chebychev distance, Mahalanobis distance, and Hamming distance are examples of other popular metrics. The choices the analyst makes prior to running the algorithm include the distance metric and the value for k; these are the hyperparameters.

The next reasonable step in understanding the algorithm is learning about the cost function. Considering the algorithm's popularity from the early 1960s, it is surprising that the cost function is not more widely studied in the literature. For convenience, one will follow the assumptions of binary classification ($y \in \{0,1\}$) with cosine similarity and normalized feature vectors for the derivation. Under these assumptions, kNN conducts a locally linear classification with the coefficient parameter,

$$w_x = \sum_{(x', y') \in R_k(x)} y' x' w_x + \frac{1}{2} \| w \|^2 \quad (2)$$

where $R_k(x)$ represents the set of the nearest neighbors of k to the input example x. The equation above states that one excludes the vectors with a label 0 in order to take the sum of all nearest neighbor feature vectors to some input vector x. The classification judgment is made by specifying a threshold on the dot-product w_x x that is equal to the cosine similarity between w_x and x in the case of normalized feature vectors.

Now, one can define the cost function as such

$$L = -\sum_{(x', y') \in R_k(x)} y' x' w_x + \frac{1}{2} \| w \|^2 \quad (3)$$

and set the right-hand side derivative of the first order to zero, which will yield the coefficient vector formula in Equation 2.

Advantages and Disadvantages of the Key Algorithms

Algorithms	Advantages	Disadvantages
The *k-means* method	• Relatively efficient. • Can process big data.	• Often terminates at a local optimum. • Mean needs to be defined. • Does not work for categorical or nominal data. • Not suitable for noisy datasets. • Not suitable for discovering clusters with non-convex shapes.
k-nearest neighbor (k-NN)	• Nonparametric. • Inexpensive in the learning process. • Classifies any data whenever any given instances of similarity measures are found • Robust to outliers on the predictors	• Computation is costly for big data. • Model interpretation is difficult. • The number of dimensions heavily impacts the performance. • Susceptible to irrelevant features and correlated inputs. • Not suitable for mixed data.

6.3. Dimension Reduction Methods in Highway Safety

Representing Data on Principal Components

A dataset of N d-dimensional vectors $\{x\}$, once translated to have a mean of zero, forms a new dataset $\{m\}$ wherein $m_i = x_i - mean(\{x\})$. $Covmat(\{m\}) = Covmat(\{x\})$ is diagonalized to get

$$U^T Covmat(\{x\}) U = \Lambda \quad (4)$$

and it forms the dataset $\{r\}$, using the rule

$$r_i = U^T m_i = U^T (x_i - mean(\{x\})) \quad (5)$$

This dataset's mean is zero and has a diagonal covariance. In comparison to the majority of high dimensional datasets, many of the covariance matrix's diagonal entries are incredibly small, meaning that it is possible to build on the high dimensional dataset an accurate low dimensional representation.

The covariance matrix of $\{r\}$ is diagonal, and the diagonal has interesting values. It is very common for a small number of large values and a large number of small values in the diagonal to be found in the high dimensional datasets, meaning that the data is a low dimensional blob within a high dimensional space.

Now assume that *Covmat*($\{r\}$) has few large and many small diagonal entries; the data blob denoted by $\{r\}$ admits a low dimensional representation that is accurate. The dataset $\{r\}$ is d-dimensional, but an attempt to represent it with a s-dimensional dataset is made to see what error has occurred. Choose some $s < d$, then choose every data point r_i and replace the last $d - s$ elements with 0 results in data called p_i. It would be beneficial to discern the average error involved in denoting r_i with p_i, and this is

$$\frac{1}{N}\sum_i \left[(r_i - p_i)^T (r_i - p_i)\right] \tag{6}$$

$r_i^{(j)}$ is written for the j' element of r_i, and so on. p_i is zero in the last $d - s$ elements.

The mean error then is

$$\frac{1}{N}\sum_i \left[\sum_{j=s+1}^{j=d} \left(r_i^{(j)}\right)^2\right] \tag{7}$$

This number is known, because it is known that $\{r\}$ has zero mean. The sum of the covariance matrix's diagonal elements from r, r to d, d is the error.

$$\sum_{j=s+1}^{j=d} \left[\frac{1}{N}\sum_i \left(r_i^{(j)}\right)^2\right] = \sum_{j=s+1}^{j=d} var\left(\left\{r^{(j)}\right\}\right) \tag{8}$$

Equivalently, presuming that the eigenvalues are arranged in descending order, writing λ_i for the ith eigenvalue of *Covmat*($\{x\}$), the error is

$$\sum_{j=s+1}^{j=d} \lambda_j \tag{9}$$

If, in comparison to the first s components sum, this sum is small, then a small error results from dropping the last $d - s$ components – the data can be thought of as s-dimensional in this case.

This observation is highly important. Relatively low dimensional blobs are produced by a large amount of high dimensional data. The primary directions of variation can be identified in these blobs, and can be used to represent and understand the dataset.

Representing Data on Principal Components

A new dataset $\{\hat{x}\}$ would be created by reversing the translation and rotation for the predicted dataset $\{p\}$, and the ith element would be given by

$$\hat{x}_i = Up_i + mean(\{x\}) \tag{10}$$

However, this expression states that $\hat{x}_i$ is created by adding *mean*($\{x\}$) to a weighted sum of the first s columns of U (due to the fact that all the other components of p_i are zero). If u_j is written for U's j^{th} column and ω_{ij} for a weight value, then it produces

$$\hat{x}_i = \sum_{j=1}^{s} w_{ij} u_j + mean(\{x\}) \tag{11}$$

As s is typically a lot less than d, which means that the dataset is being represented using a lower-dimensional dataset, this sum is significant. An s-dimensional flat subspace of d-dimensional space was chosen and a point in that subset was used to represent each data item. The u_j are called **loadings** or **principal components** of the dataset; the $r_i^{(j)}$ are usually called **coefficients** but are sometimes known as **scores**. The **principal components analysis** or PCA forms the representation. The weights ω_{ij} are easy to evaluate.

$$w_{ij} = r_i^{(j)} = (x_i - mean(\{x\}))^T u_j \tag{12}$$

The Error in a Low Dimensional Representation

The error is determined easily in approximating $\{x\}$ with $\{\hat{x}\}$. It is also easy to calculate the error in representing $\{r\}$ by $\{p\}$. One has

$$\frac{1}{N}\sum_i \left[(r_i - p_i)^T (r_i - p_i)\right] = \sum_{j=s+1}^{j=d} var(\{r^{(j)}\}) = \sum_{j=s+1}^{j=d} \lambda_j \tag{13}$$

A small error results from dropping the last $d-s$ components if, in comparison to the first s components sum, this sum is small.

It is now easy to get the average error in denoting $\{x\}$ with $\{\hat{x}\}$. Translations and rotations don't change lengths. This means

$$\frac{1}{N}\sum_i \left\|x_i - \hat{x}_i\right\|^2 = \frac{1}{N}\sum_i \left\|r_i - p_i\right\|^2 = \sum_{j=s+1}^{j=d} \lambda_j \tag{14}$$

Since these are the values of the $d-s$ eigenvalues of $Covmat(\{x\})$ that were chosen to be ignored, it is easy to evaluate. s could be chosen by identifying how much error can be tolerated, but it is more typical to plot the covariance matrix's eigenvalues and search for a "knee." It can be seen that the sum of the remaining eigenvalues is small.

Principal Component Analysis

Assume a general dataset x_i consisting of N d-dimensional vectors, then, for the covariance matrix, write $\Sigma = Covmat(\{x\})$. Form U, Λ, such that

$$\Sigma U = U\Lambda$$

These are the eigenvalues and eigenvectors of Σ. The entries of Λ need to be sorted in decreasing order. Choose the number of dimensions that one wishes to represent (r), which is usually done by plotting the eigenvalues and looking for a "knee".

Constructing a Low Dimensional Representation: Write u_i for the ith column of U for $1 \leq j \leq s$. The data point x_i should be represented as

$$\hat{x}_i = mean(\{x\}) + \sum_{j=i}^{s} \left[u_j^T (x_i - mean(\{x\})) \right] u_j$$

The error in this representation is

$$\frac{1}{N} \sum_i \| x_i - \hat{x}_i \|^2 = \sum_{j=s+1}^{j=d} \lambda_j$$

6.4. Categorical Data Analysis

6.4.1. The Singular Value Decomposition

It is possible to obtain a decomposition for any $m \times p$ matrix X.

$$X = U\Sigma V^T, \tag{15}$$

where V is $p \times p$, U is $m \times m$, and Σ is $m \times p$. The diagonal entries of Σ are non-negative, and U and V are both orthonormal (i.e., $UU^T = I$ and $VV^T = I$). This decomposition is called singular value decomposition (SVD).

When the matrix is not square, a diagonal matrix means that all the entries, except for the i, i entries for i in the range of 1 to min(m, p), are zero. If Σ is tall and skinny, then the top square is diagonal and the rest are zero; if Σ is short and broad, the left square is diagonal and the rest are zero. Singular values is the term for what is on the diagonal of Σ. There are methods to accurately and efficiently calculate the SVD on a large scale, but, if the correct function is found, then any computing environment should be able to compute it. More information on this should be given by the manual for a specific environment.

Singular Value Decomposition

Any decent numerical linear algebra package or computing environment will produce a decomposition, given a matrix X, *where*,

$$X = U\Sigma V^T,$$

Σ is the diagonal with non-negative entries, and U and V are both orthonormal. Most environments that can do an SVD can be persuaded to provide the columns of U and rows of V^T corresponding to the k largest singular values.

Since the singular values could be reordered followed by the reordering of U and V, there are many SVDs for a given matrix. It is always assumed that (moving down) the diagonal entries in Σ are arranged from the greatest to the least. Here, the rows of V^T and the columns of U that correspond to non-zero diagonal elements of Σ are distinct.

There's a relationship between diagonalizing a matrix and forming an SVD; particularly, $X^T X$ is symmetric, and is diagonalized as

$$X^T X = \mathrm{V}\Sigma^T \Sigma V^T \tag{16}$$

$$TXX^T = U\Sigma\Sigma^T U \tag{17}$$

Need to know

A SVD decomposes a matrix X as $X = U\Sigma V^T$ where V is $p \times p$, U is $m \times m$, and Σ is $m \times p$ and is diagonal. The diagonal entries of Σ are non-negative and both U and V are orthonormal. The SVD of X yields the diagonalization of XX^T and the diagonalization of $X^T X$.

SVD and PCA

Assume there is a zero mean in a dataset. As is typical, there are N data items, each of which is a d-dimensional column vector. These are arranged into a matrix,

$$X = \left(x_1^T \; x_2^T \cdots x_N^T\right)$$

in which each row is a data vector, and the covariance matrix is

$$Covmat\left(\{X\}\right) = \frac{1}{N} X^T X \tag{18}$$

Remember it has a mean of zero. From the SVD of X, one gets

$$X = U\Sigma V^T \tag{19}$$

However, one has $X^T X = V\Sigma^T \Sigma V^T$ so that

$$Covmat\left(\{X\}\right)V = \frac{1}{N}\left(X^T X\right)V = V\frac{\Sigma^T \Sigma}{N} \tag{20}$$

and $\Sigma^T \Sigma$ is diagonal. *Vs* columns have the principal components of X by pattern matching, and

$$\frac{\Sigma^T \Sigma}{N} \tag{21}$$

are each component's changes, meaning that the principal components of that dataset's SVD can be read without really creating the covariance matrix; the SVD of X is formed, and the principal components are the columns of V. Keep in mind that these are the columns of V, not V^T.

NIPALS is a method of extracting some principal components from a data matrix and is a means of recovering a partial SVD of X. A vector u and a vector w are created by NIPALS so that wu^T is close to X and u is a unit vector. The following is given by pattern matching:

- u^T is V^T's row that corresponds to the largest singular value;
- $\frac{w}{\|w\|}$ is U's column that corresponds to the largest singular value;
- $\|w\|$ is the largest singular value.

If NIPALS is used to extract multiple principal components, several columns of U, several rows of V^T, and several singular values will be obtained, but since numerical errors accumulate, this is not an accurate or efficient way to extract multiple singular values. Specialist packages should be used for a partial SVD that has many singular values.

SVD and Low Rank Approximations

If one wishes to produce X_s such that X_s's rank is s (which is less than d) and such that $\|X - X_s\|^2$ is minimized, and one has X, with rank d an SVD will give X_s. One should take the SVD to get $X = U\Sigma V^T$, then set all except the s largest singular values in Σ to 0 to write Σ_s for the matrix. Given that

$$X_s = U\Sigma_s V^T \tag{22}$$

It is clear X_s has rank s. $\|X - X_s\|^2$ can be minimized by observing,

$$\|X - X_s\|^2 = \|\Sigma - \Sigma_s\|^2. \tag{23}$$

Σ_s has many zeros, which make the majority of U's columns and V^T's rows irrelevant, bringing up a potential source of confusion. Write U_s for the $m \times s$ matrix that consists of the first s columns of U, and so on, and for the $s \times s$ submatrix of Σ_s with non-zero diagonal, write $\Sigma_s^{(s)}$. This gives

$$X_s = U\Sigma_s V^T = U_s \Sigma_s^{(s)} (V_s)^T \tag{24}$$

It is quite common to switch from one representation to the other without comment.

6.5. Correspondence Analysis

6.5.1. Multiple Correspondence Analysis

MCA's mathematical theory development is very complex. It is necessary to construct a matrix that is founded on pairwise cross-tabulation of each variable, but it is not necessary to define dependable and response variables. A way to explain MCA for a table with variables (categorical or qualitative) is selecting an individual record (in a row), i, wherein three columns represent three variables that have three different category indicators (a_1, b_2, and c_3); these three categories can be used to create the spatial distribution of the points in different dimensions. A good comparison for a combination of points is a geographic map with the same distance scale, in all directions. Since a geometric diagram cannot be contracted or strained along a certain dimension, its dimensionality reveals the basic property of any combination of points. A two-dimensional combination is often useful for scrutinizing the points that lie on the plane, and they are generally referred to as the complete combinations' principal dimensions, arranged in descending order of significance. In order to make a combination of groups, MCA aims to use a large dataset.

First it is necessary to think of I as the number of transactions and P as the number of variables; the matrix will appear similar to a table for all the categorical values, "*I multiplied by P*." If variable p's number of categories is T_p, then $T = \sum_{p=1}^{P} T_p$ is the total number of categories for all variables. Another matrix, where each of the variables show all their possible categorical values through several columns, "*I multiplied by T*," is generated.

Now it is necessary to think of category k associates with assorted individual records that can be represented by n_k ($n_k > 0$), wherein $f_k = n_k/n$ = relative frequency of k associated individuals. A row profile is created with the values of f_k. The variables that both have different categories are used to create the distance between two individual records. For variable p, individual record i has category k and individual record i' has category k' (this differs from k). Variable p's part of the squared difference between individual records i' and i is

$$d_p^2(i,i') = \frac{1}{f_k} + \frac{1}{f_{k'}} \tag{25}$$

The overall squared distance between i and i' is,

$$d^2(i,i') = \frac{1}{P} \sum_{p \in P} d_p{}^2(i,i') \tag{26}$$

The individuals' combination of n points in a space is used to determine the set of all distances between individual records. L is the space's dimensionality, where $L \leq K - P$; it is presumed that $n \geq L$. If the mean point of the combination is G and the point representing an individual is denoted by M^i, the squared distance from point M^i to point G is written as

$$(GM^i)^2 = \frac{1}{P} \sum_{k \in K_i} \frac{1}{f_k} \tag{27}$$

Where an individual i's response pattern is K_i; the set of individual records i is associated with P categories.

A weighted combination of K points is the cloud of categories, and category k is written as point M^k with weight n_k. The category points weight sum is n for each variable; subsequently, for the whole set K, the sum is nP. Point M^k's relative weight w_k is $w_k = n_k/(nP) = f_k/P$; the sum of the whole set is 1 as for each variable the sum of the relative weights of category points is $1/P$.

$$w_k = \frac{n_k}{np} = \frac{f_k}{p} \text{ with } \sum_{k \in K_q} w_k = \frac{1}{p} \text{ and } \sum_{k \in K} w_k = 1 \tag{28}$$

The squared distance between $M^{k'}$ and M^k, assuming the number of distinct records with both categories k and k' is denoted by $n_{kk'}$, is,

$$(M^k M^{k'})^2 = \frac{n_k + n_{k'} - 2n_{kk'}}{\frac{n_k n_{k'}}{n}} \tag{29}$$

The number of individual records that are related to either k or k' is the numerator, and the familiar "theoretical frequency" for the cell (k, k') of the $K_p \times K_{p'}$ two-way table for two different variables, p' and p is the denominator.

6.5.2. Taxicab Correspondence Analysis

To explain the extended theory of TCA, a series of papers was used by Choulakian. An overview of TCA is offered in this section. The basis for correspondence analysis (CA) is Euclidean distance, whereas Manhattan, City Block, or Taxicab distance is the basis for Taxicab correspondence analysis (TCA). To evaluate these distances, let $X = (x_1, x_2, \ldots.., x_n)$ and $Y = (y_1, y_2, \ldots.., y_n)$ and a vector $v = (v_1, v_2, \ldots.., v_n)$:

$$\textit{Euclidean Distance} = ED(X, Y) = \sqrt{\sum_{i=1}^{n} (x_i - y_i)^2}$$

$$[\text{with } L_2 \text{ Norm} = \|v\|_2 = \sqrt{\sum_{i=1}^{n} (v_i)^2}] \tag{30}$$

$$\textit{Taxicab Distance} = TD(X, Y) = \sum_{i=1}^{n} |x_1 - y_i|$$

$$[\text{with } L_1 \text{ Norm} = \|v\|_1 = \sum_{i=1}^{n} |v_i|] \tag{31}$$

Singular value decomposition (SVD) is the foundation for both TCA and CA, within which a real matrix A is decomposed as $M\Lambda^{1/2} N'$, with N the matrix of eigenvectors of $A'A$ (with constraints $M'M = I$ and $N'N = I$), M the orthogonal matrix of the corresponding eigenvectors, and Λ the diagonal matrix of the real non-negative eigenvalues of AA'. The SVD theory corresponds to the k-rank matrix reconstruction formula:

$$a_{ij} = \sum_{i=1}^{k} \sqrt{\lambda_\alpha} m_{i\alpha} n_{i\alpha} \tag{32}$$

Finding the first vectors m_1 and n_1 principal components of A to resolve the equivalent optimization problem is the basis of this approach.

$$max \, \|Am\|_2 \text{ subject to } \|m\||_2 = 1$$

$$max \, \|A' n\|_2 \text{ subject to } \|n\|_2 = 1$$

Taxicab Correspondence Analysis considers the table's profiles, respectively $R = D_r^{-1} D$ for the rows and $L = D_l^{-1} D$ for the columns, and is defined as the

Taxicab Singular Value Decomposition of the data table $D = T - rl'$. Unlike CA, the solution is recursive as it considers previous factors' residuals at each step, leading to the reconstruction formula:

$$T = p_r p_c' + \sum_{\alpha=2}^{k} \frac{1}{\lambda_a} B_a C_\alpha' \tag{33}$$

Elementwise the formula becomes

$$t_{ij} = t_{i.} t_{.j} + \sum_{\alpha=2}^{k} \frac{1}{\lambda_\alpha} B_{i\alpha} C_{j\alpha} \tag{34}$$

After transformation

$$n_{ij} = n r_i l_j \left(1 + \sum_{\alpha=2}^{k} \frac{1}{\lambda_\alpha} b_{i\alpha} c_{j\alpha}\right) \tag{35}$$

6.6. Unsupervised Learning, Semi-Supervised, and Reinforcement Learning based Highway safety Studies

Unsupervised learning hasn't been widely used in highway safety analysis. Rule mining and correspondence analysis are the most used algorithms in highway safety research. Usage of semi-supervised and reinforcement learning in highway safety analysis is still limited. Table 11 provides a list of studies which used different ML algorithms in different highway safety problems.

Table 11. Unsupervised, semi-supervised, and reinforcement learning based highway safety studies

Algorithm	Research Area	Studies
	Unsupervised Learning	
Association Rules Mining	Patterns of Contributing Factors in Crashes.	Das et al. (2019); Kong et al. (2020); Kumar and Toshniwal (2016); Liu et al. (1998)
K-means	Patterns of Contributing Factors in Crashes.	Nandurge and Dharwadkar (2017)
	Work Zone Safety.	Wang et al. (2017)
	Children Road Users.	Kwon and Cho (2020)
PCA	Real-Time Risk Assessment.	Ni et al. (2019)
	Pipeline Safety.	Khodayari-Rostamabad et al. (2009)
t-SNE	Work Zone Safety.	Chang et al. (2020)
LDA	Incident Detection.	Nie et al. (2018)
TCA	Patterns of Contributing Factors in Crashes.	Das and Dutta (2020)

(*Contd.*)

Table 11. (*Contd.*)

LCA	Railroad Safety	Zhao et al. (2019)
	Semi-supervised Learning	
Semi-supervised Learning	Driver Behavior.	Wang et al. (2010)
	Route Choice Modelling.	Cao et al. (2020)
Semi-supervised LSTM	Driver Behavior.	Li et al. (2021)
DBNs	Real-Time Risk Assessment.	Ni et al. (2019)
Semi-Supervised Recursively Partitioned Mixture Models	Maritime Safety.	Paolo et al. (2021)
Semi-Supervised Extreme Learning Machine	Driver Distraction Detection.	Liu et al. (2016)
	Reinforcement Learning	
Deep RL	Work Zone Safety.	Ren et al. (2020)
	Roadway Departure Safety.	Mousa et al. (2020)
	AV Safety.	Rasheed et al. (2020)
Multi-Objective RL	Intersection Safety.	Gong et al. (2020)

Resources

Readers can consult the following link for a curated list of unsupervised learning: https://github.com/LongLong-Jing/awesome-unsupervised-learning

Case Study 1

Correspondence analysis is an important tool in categorical data analysis. As crash data have many variables which are categorical in nature, it is important to understand the hidden trends using correspondence analysis. Provide a case study by showing all steps to perform correspondence analysis on a crash event database.

Data Integration

This case study gathered from the Louisiana Department of Transportation and Development (LADOTD) crash data from 2010-2016 (seven years' worth). The dataset has three major files: the crash file, the vehicle file, and the roadway inventory file. The crash file has general information about crash characteristics and circumstances. The roadway inventory file contains information about crash location, roadway type, traffic volume, segment length, and other relevant geometric information. As delivery vehicles are not classified as a specific vehicle type in Louisiana crash data, it is necessary to explore the police-reported crash narrative data to identify which crashes involved delivery vehicles. A set of delivery-related keywords (e.g., delivery, pizza delivery, food delivery, grocery delivery) was used to identify the crash reports associated with delivery-related crashes. A manual effort was made to identify delivery-related crashes using broader vehicle categories (limited to passenger car, light truck, van, and pickups) and manually reading the crash narrative reports. After identifying these events in the 'vehicle' table, a data merging method was conducted to develop a database with crash, roadway, vehicle, and driver information (see Figure 40). The final dataset contains 1,623 unique crashes with 3,015 involved drivers.

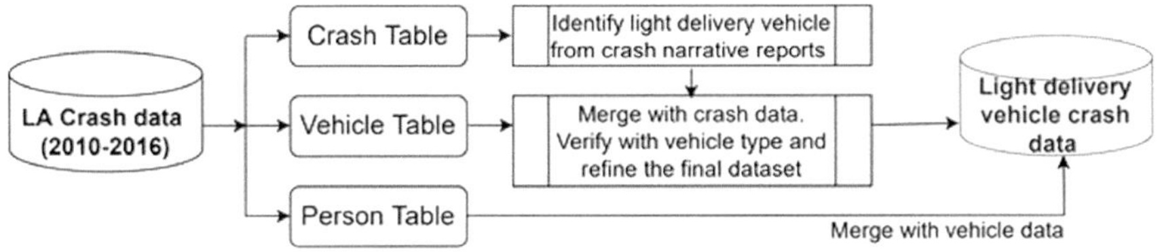

Figure 40. Data preparation flowchart.

Exploratory Data Analysis

It is important to perform a data-driven variable selection method when performing a robust analysis. As the crash dataset contains a wide range of variables (e.g., numerical, integer, nominal or categorical, ordinal), it is important to determine which variables can provide intuitive knowledge about the crash occurrences. After removing redundant variables (e.g., district name, agency name, driver registration) for this study, this study selected a list of 40 variables for preliminary exploration. As the dataset is limited in size, variables with higher than 20% missing data were eliminated. In addition, variables examined in the studies discussed in the literature review were also explored. After performing all quality checks, sixteen variables were selected for the final analysis. The final dataset is conducted at the person level (3,015 drivers), in which each row indicates the driver level information, and each column indicates a selected variable. With one hot encoding, the final matrix was 3,015 by 91. Table 12 lists the distribution of the key variable categories. There were several interesting findings shown in the table. One finding is that the majority of the crashes occurred on straight-aligned roadways. Another finding is that approximately 90% of crashes occurred on city streets, parish roads, and state highways. Two-way undivided roadways are associated with 68% of crashes, and nearly 92% of crashes occurred in business, residential, and mixed localities. Most crashes were multiple vehicle crashes occurring on low posted speed limit roadways, and approximately 70% of the crashes occurred at an intersection. Around 80% of drivers are either white or African American, and most of the drivers involved in delivery-related crashes are between the ages of 25 to 64 years. There are no significant insights in lighting, weather, or day of the week variables. Injury crashes are lower in delivery-related crashes, and there were no fatal crashes during the study period.

Alcohol involvement is also rarely found; in only about 0.40% of cases, the drivers were asked for alcohol tests. Inattention and distraction were associated with approximately 29% of delivery vehicle-related crashes.

Table 12. Descriptive statistics

Category	Perc.	Category	Perc.
Alignment (Align.)		**Posted Speed Limit (PSL)**	
Straight-Level	93.77	30 mph or less	58.79
Straight-Level-Elev.	0.90	35-45 mph	35.04
Curve-Level	2.78	50-60 mph	5.33
Curve-Level-Elev.	0.30	65-70 mph	0.84
Dip, Hump-Straight	0.13	**Number of Vehicles Involved (NVeh)**	
Hillcrest-Curve	0.07	Multi Vehicle	89.21
Hillcrest-Straight	0.57	Single Vehicle	10.75
On Grade-Curve	0.20	Not reported	0.03
On Grade-Straight	0.84	**Intersection Type (Intersec.)**	
Other	0.44	Intersection	70.82
Highway Type (Hwy.)		Segmentation	29.15
City Street	45.46	Not reported	0.03
Parish Road	27.71	**Driver Gender (Gen.)**	
State Hwy	16.28	Female	24.66
U.S. Hwy	7.87	Male	57.39
Interstate	1.74	Unknown	17.82
Toll Road	0.94	**Driver Race (Race)**	
Roadway Type (Road)		White	47.07
2-Way No Sep.	68.27	African American	32.40
2-Way with Sep.	16.08	Others	2.68
One-Way Road	12.76	Asian	0.03
2-Way with Barr.	1.64	Unknown	17.82
Other	1.24	**Driver Age (Age)**	
Locality Type (Locality)		15-24	12.8
Business Cont.	31.69	25-34	20.37
Mixed	33.97	35-44	16.31
Residential	25.76	45-54	15.61
Industrial	2.21	55-64	11.22
Residential Scatt.	3.45	> 65	5.93
Open Country	0.97	**Driver Injury Type (Inj.)**	
School/Playground	0.67	Not reported	17.72
Other	1.27	Incapacitating/Severe	0.50
Lighting Condition (Lighting)		Non-Incapacitating/Moderate	1.64
Daylight	89.15	Possible/Complaint	7.37
Dark – Cont. St. Light	6.16	No Injury	90.49
Dark – No St. Lights	1.68	**Driver Alcohol Test (Alc.)**	

Dark – Int. St.Light	1.04	No Test Given	77.86
Dawn	0.10	Test Given, Bac	0.37
Dusk	1.31	Test Given, Results Pending	0.03
Other	0.57	Not reported	21.61
Weather Type (Weather)		**Driver Condition (Cond.)**	
Clear	75.54	Normal	48.68
Cloudy	17.92	Inattentive	25.56
Rain	5.49	Distracted	3.52
Blowing Sand, Soil, Dirt, Snow	0.07	Drinking Alcohol – Impaired	0.27
Fog/Smoke	0.07	Drinking Alcohol – Not Impaired	0.10
Not reported	0.03	Drug Use – Impaired	0.10
Severe Crosswind	0.03	Apparently Asleep/Blackout	0.23
Sleet/Hail	0.07	Fatigued	0.13
Snow	0.07	Physical Impairment (Eyes, Ear, Limb)	0.07
Other	0.70	Other	21.34
Day of Week (DOW)			
MTWT	71.69		
FSS	28.31		

Cluster Corresponding Analysis

Correspondence analysis (CA) is a frequently used data analysis technique for categorical data analysis. The core idea is to perform dimension reduction from simple multi-way and two-way tables, which contain an association between the columns and rows from a multifaceted dataset. Different variants of CA have been used in transportation studies. Cluster correspondence analysis, a variant of CA, combines both cluster analysis and the dimension reduction method for categorical datasets. The cluster correspondence analysis algorithm assigns individuals to optimal scaling values and variable attributes to clusters to achieve variance maximization objectives. A brief overview of this method is presented here.

First, consider that the data is associated with n individuals (e.g., drivers involved in delivery vehicle-related crashes) for p categorical variables (e.g., roadway alignment). This information can be expressed by super indicator matrix $\boldsymbol{Z}$ with $n \times Q$ dimension, where $Q = \sum_{j=1}^{p} q_j$. An indicator matrix Z_K can be used to develop a tabular format to cross-tabulate cluster memberships with the nominal or categorical variables such as $F = Z'_K Z$, where Z_K is the $n \times K$ indicator matrix indicating cluster membership. The application of the CA framework to this matrix populates optimal scaling values for columns (as categories) and rows (as clusters). The clusters are separated optimally based on the distributions over the categorical variables in the two-dimensional plane. In the same way, the categories that have different distributions over the clusters are separated optimally, which can be expressed as:

$$max\phi_{clusca}(Z_K, B^*) = \frac{1}{p} traceB^{*'} D_z^{-1/2} Z' MZ_K D_Z^{-1} Z'_K MZD_z^{-1/2} B^* \quad (36)$$

Where,

$$M = I_n - 1_n 1'n/n$$

$$B = \sqrt{np} D_z^{-1/2} B^*$$

$D_K = Z'_K Z_K$, is a diagonal matrix with cluster sizes

D_z is a diagonal matrix so that $D_z 1_Q = Z'1_n$

To perform this analysis, an open-source *R* package 'clustrd' was used, and this study utilized the Calinski-Harabasz measure out of several validity measures. This measure, also called the valence ratio criterion, is the ratio of the sum of between-clusters and inter-cluster dispersion for all clusters; the higher the score, the better the performances. This measure is used for the application of *k*-means clustering to complete clustering for different *k* measures.

Results and Discussions

The selection of a suitable number of clusters was one of the critical issues. After performing several tests, this effort finally limited the number of clusters to 6. Due to the nature of the data and unknown information, all the other trials with fewer or more clusters contained more than 50% of the information in cluster 1, which presents a general trend in the overall data. This study determined that a six-cluster, two-dimensional solution would be the most suitable for this analysis. The objective criterion value of the final model is 7.2714. In the framework of CA, the origin designates the mean profile, and all other coordinates show divergences from this mean profile. The locations of the cluster centroids answer research question 1 by indicating that there are cluster or sub-group effects in the light delivery vehicle-related crash databases. Table 13 lists the cluster size, sum of squares, and coordinates of the cluster centroids on two axes or dimensions.

Table 13. Location of the cluster centroids and other measures

Cluster	Size (percentage)	Sum of Squares	Dimension 1	Dimension 2
Cluster 1	1444 (47.4%)	0.0126	-0.0069	-0.0049
Cluster 2	737 (24.7%)	0.0149	-0.0108	0.0022
Cluster 3	524 (17.6%)	0.0217	0.0333	0.0012
Cluster 4	212 (7.1%)	0.0076	0.0051	-0.0021
Cluster 5	73 (2.4%)	0.0141	-0.0081	0.0364
Cluster 6	25 (0.8%)	0.0068	-0.0112	0.0956

Each cluster's 20 characteristics that have the highest standardized residuals (negative or positive) are shown in the six plots of Figures 41 and 42. A positive (or negative) residual means that the attribute has a frequency above (or below) average within the cluster. Characteristics with positive residual means are considered in the following explanation. Cluster-based analysis answers research question 2 by explaining the patterns of the risk factors associated with light delivery vehicle crashes.

Figure 41 goes over the top 20 largest standardized residuals per cluster (clusters 1-3), and Figure 42 goes over the top 20 largest standardized residuals per cluster (clusters 4-6).

Cluster 1

This cluster has seven characteristics with positive residual means: inattentive driver condition, movement due to driver violation, prior movement backing up, male drivers, posted speed limit of 30 mph or less, drivers aged 25-34, and race of the driver as black. This indicates that there is an association between black male drivers aged 25-34 and inattentive driving, driver violations, and a prior movement of backing up on roads with a posted speed limit of 30 mph or less.

Cluster 2

There are ten qualities with positive residual means in this cluster: posted speed limit of 35-45 mph, U.S. highway, state highway, 2-way road with separation, posted speed limit of 50-60 mph, possible injury or complaint, located in a residential scattered area, normal driving conditions, normal movement conditions, and drivers aged 15-24. This indicates that there is an association between possible injuries or complaints from drivers aged 15-24 with normal driver and movement conditions on U.S. highways, state highways, or 2-way roads with separation with a posted speed limit of 35-45 mph or 50-60 mph in residential scattered areas.

Cluster 3

There are eight qualities with positive residual means in this cluster: unknown gender, unknown race, unreported age, other driving condition, properly parked prior condition, other movement condition, other vehicle type, and other prior condition. This indicates that there is an association between drivers with unknown or unreported gender, race, and age and conditions of 'other' for driving condition, movement condition, vehicle type, and prior condition. They are also associated with properly parked as the prior condition.

Cluster 4

There are ten characteristics with positive residual means in this cluster: other movement, other driving condition, other prior condition, other vehicle type, properly parked prior condition, other alignment, black drivers, posted speed limit of 30 mph or less, highway city street, and other weather. This indicates that there is an association between a city street with a posted speed limit of 30 mph or less and 'other' for prior condition, driver condition, movement, weather, vehicle type, and roadway alignment. They were also associated with African American drivers and properly parked as the prior condition.

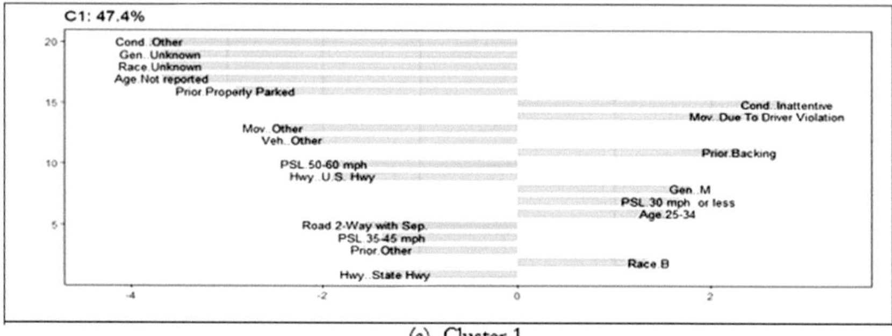

(a) Cluster 1

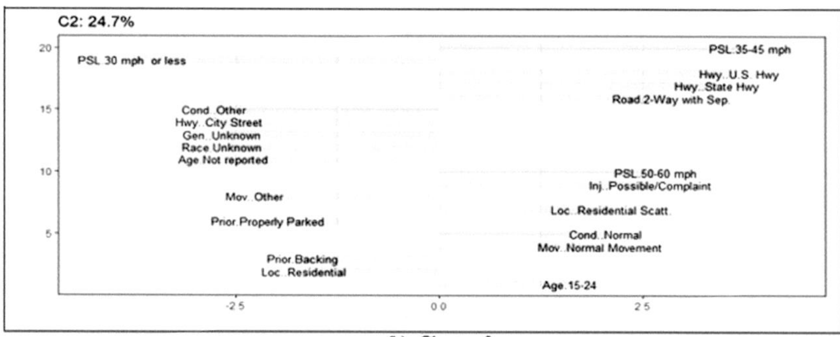

(b) Cluster 2

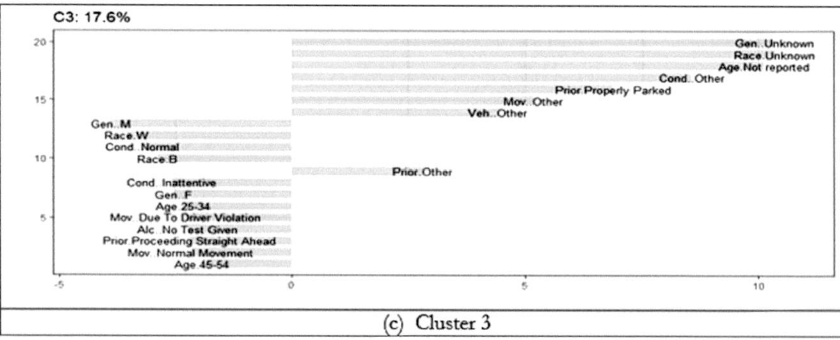

(c) Cluster 3

Figure 41. Top 20 largest standardized residuals per cluster (cluster 1-3).

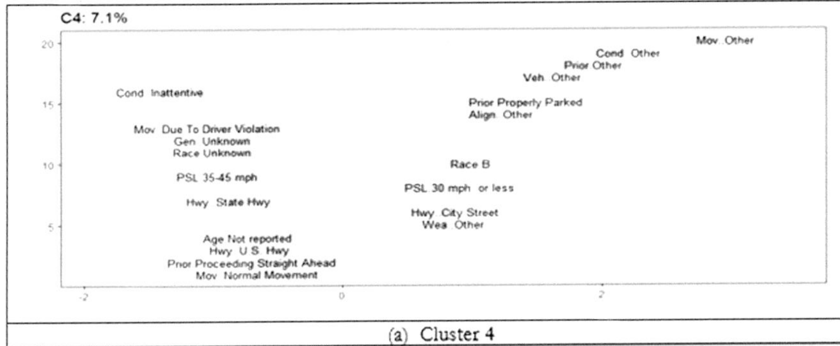

(a) Cluster 4

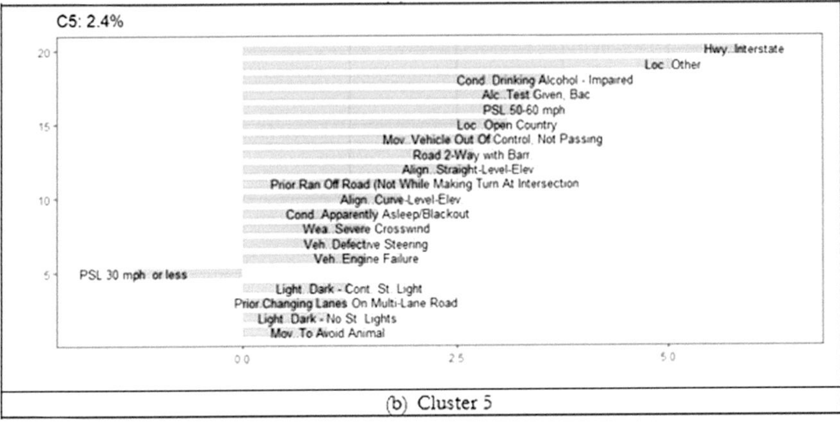

(b) Cluster 5

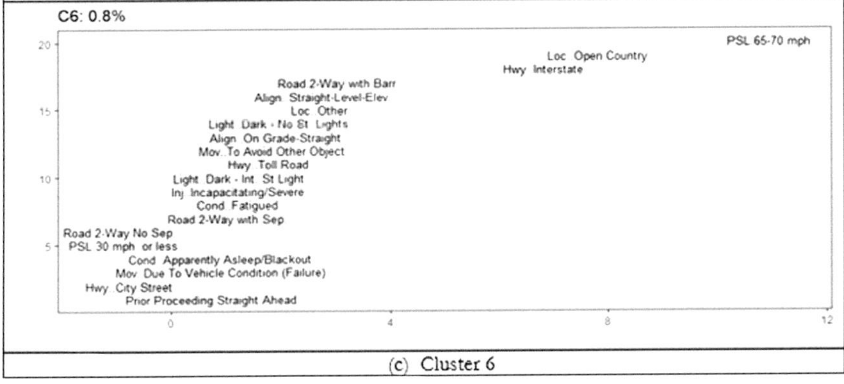

(c) Cluster 6

Figure 42. Top 20 largest standardized residuals per cluster (cluster 4-6).

Cluster 5

There are nineteen qualities with positive residual means in this cluster: interstate highway, other location, driving condition impaired by drinking alcohol, blood alcohol content test given, posted speed limit of 50-60 mph, open country location, movement of vehicle out of control, 2-way road with a barrier, straight-level-elevated alignment, prior condition ran off the road, curve-level-elevated alignment, asleep or blackout driver condition, severe crosswind weather condition, defective steering in the vehicle, engine failure in the vehicle, continuous streetlights, prior condition changing lanes on a multi-lane road, no streetlights, and movement to avoid an animal. This indicates that there is an association between a very large number of variables. Drivers that were asleep or blacked out, impaired by drinking alcohol, and given a blood alcohol content test were associated with out-of-control movements of the vehicle, running off the road, defective steering in the vehicle, engine failure in the vehicle, changing lanes on a multi-lane road, and movement to avoid an animal. They were also associated with interstate highways in open country or other locations with a speed limit of 50-60 mph. The road types associated with this were 2-way roads with a barrier and straight-level-elevated or curve-level-elevated alignment, severe crosswind weather conditions, and either continuous streetlights or no streetlights.

Cluster 6

There are seventeen attributes with positive residual means in this cluster: a posted speed limit of 65-70 mph, open country location, interstate highway, 2-way roads with a barrier, straight-level-elevated alignment, other location, no streetlights, on grade-straight alignment, movement to avoid an object, toll road highway, intermittent streetlights, incapacitating or severe injury, fatigued driver condition, 2-way road with separation, asleep or blackout driver condition, movement due to vehicle condition, and prior movement proceeding straight ahead. This indicates that there is an association between crashes with incapacitating or severe injuries and interstate highways, toll roads, or 2-way roads with a barrier or separation in the open country or another location with intermittent or no streetlights. These were also associated with drivers that were asleep or blacked out and fatigued, as well as a posted speed limit of 65-70 mph, straight-level-elevated or grade-straight alignment, movement to avoid an object, separation movement due to vehicle condition, and prior movement proceeding straight ahead.

One of the major advantages of this analysis is the capability to generate 'proportion odds' for the attributes in each cluster (see Table 14). One general observation is that cluster 5 and cluster 6 have very high odds for a few attributes compared to other clusters. These two clusters are associated with freeway-related crashes, which represent around 3% of the data.

Table 14. Proportion odds of the attributes by clusters

Variable	Category	Cluster 1	Cluster 2	Cluster 3	Cluster 4	Cluster 5	Cluster 6
Align.	Straight-Level	1.05	0.93	1.02	1.00	0.70	0.55
Align.	Straight-Level-Elev.	0.00	1.33	0.44	0.00	15.22	26.67
Align.	Curve-Level	0.29	2.23	0.76	0.86	3.96	2.88
Align.	Curve-Level-Elev.	0.00	1.67	0.67	0.00	18.33	0.00
Align.	Dip, Hump-Straight	0.00	3.08	0.00	0.00	10.77	0.00
Align.	Hillcrest-Curve	1.43	0.00	2.86	0.00	0.00	0.00
Align.	Hillcrest-Straight	0.88	2.46	0.00	0.00	0.00	0.00
Align.	On Grade-Curve	0.50	2.50	0.00	0.00	0.00	0.00
Align.	On Grade-Straight	0.00	2.74	0.00	1.07	3.21	19.05
Align.	Other	0.23	0.00	2.50	6.36	0.00	0.00
Hwy.	City Street	1.16	0.37	1.44	1.38	0.30	0.00
Hwy.	Parish Road	1.27	0.67	0.87	0.99	0.44	0.00
Hwy.	State Hwy	0.62	2.36	0.42	0.35	0.93	0.00
Hwy.	U.S. Hwy	0.23	3.13	0.27	0.24	2.26	0.51
Hwy.	Interstate	0.00	0.06	0.11	0.00	23.62	45.98
Hwy.	Toll Road	0.11	1.60	1.17	2.55	0.00	17.02
Road	2-Way No Sep.	1.14	0.84	0.98	0.97	0.48	0.00
Road	2-Way with Sep.	0.56	2.15	0.53	0.67	1.45	3.23
Road	One-Way Road	0.94	0.39	1.69	1.48	1.94	0.94
Road	2-Way with Barr.	0.00	1.71	0.37	0.55	11.71	21.95
Road	Other	0.89	0.08	2.02	2.66	0.00	0.00
Loc.	Business Cont.	0.95	1.34	0.78	0.95	0.65	0.00
Loc.	Mixed	1.01	0.93	1.17	0.99	0.57	0.12
Loc.	Residential	1.20	0.49	1.20	1.30	0.32	0.00
Loc.	Industrial	1.27	1.04	0.68	0.23	0.63	0.00
Loc.	Residential Scatt.	0.35	2.84	0.38	0.55	1.19	0.00
Loc.	Open Country	0.00	0.00	0.00	0.00	16.91	70.10
Loc.	School/ Playground	0.90	1.04	1.49	0.75	0.00	0.00
Loc.	Other	0.00	0.39	0.79	0.00	23.70	22.05
Light.	Daylight	1.05	0.96	0.95	1.03	0.78	0.72
Light.	Dark – Cont. St. Light	0.67	1.10	1.54	0.76	3.56	0.00
Light.	Dark – No St. Lights	0.00	2.44	0.77	0.30	4.88	14.29
Light.	Dark – Int. St. Light	0.38	2.12	1.06	0.48	0.00	11.54
Light.	Dawn	2.00	0.00	0.00	0.00	0.00	0.00
Light.	Dusk	1.15	0.92	0.84	1.07	0.00	0.00

(Contd.)

Variable	Category	Cluster 1	Cluster 2	Cluster 3	Cluster 4	Cluster 5	Cluster 6
Light.	Other	0.18	0.00	4.39	2.46	0.00	0.00
Wea.	Clear	0.97	1.05	0.99	1.05	0.91	1.11
Wea.	Cloudy	1.17	0.78	0.98	0.69	1.14	0.89
Wea.	Rain	0.95	1.06	0.97	1.04	1.75	0.00
Wea.	Blowing Sand, Soil, Dirt, Snow	1.43	1.43	0.00	0.00	0.00	0.00
Wea.	Fog/Smoke	0.00	0.00	5.71	0.00	0.00	0.00
Wea.	Not reported	0.00	0.00	6.67	0.00	0.00	0.00
Wea.	Severe Crosswind	0.00	0.00	0.00	0.00	46.67	0.00
Wea.	Sleet/Hail	0.00	1.43	2.86	0.00	0.00	0.00
Wea.	Snow	0.00	4.29	0.00	0.00	0.00	0.00
Wea.	Other	0.71	0.00	2.14	4.00	0.00	0.00
DOW	MTWT	1.03	0.97	0.98	0.96	0.82	1.17
DOW	FSS	0.91	1.08	1.04	1.10	1.45	0.57
PSL	30 mph or less	1.26	0.22	1.42	1.35	0.14	0.00
PSL	35-45 mph	0.74	2.04	0.45	0.51	1.25	0.00
PSL	50-60 mph	0.02	2.85	0.19	0.53	8.22	2.25
PSL	65-70 mph	0.00	0.00	0.00	0.00	4.88	104.76
NVeh	Multi Vehicle	0.95	1.05	1.04	1.03	0.97	1.08
NVeh	Single Vehicle	1.39	0.56	0.66	0.79	1.27	0.37
NVeh	Not reported	0.00	0.00	6.67	0.00	0.00	0.00
Intersec	Intersection	0.99	0.91	1.11	1.03	1.14	1.02
Intersec	No-intersection	1.02	1.21	0.72	0.92	0.66	0.96
Intersec	Not reported	0.00	0.00	6.67	0.00	0.00	0.00
Gen.	Female	1.07	1.48	0.02	1.15	1.39	0.81
Gen.	Male	1.28	1.10	0.01	1.15	1.05	1.25
Gen.	Unknown	0.00	0.00	5.52	0.29	0.31	0.45
Race	White	1.18	1.37	0.01	0.87	1.22	1.19
Race	Afrin American (Black)	1.29	0.99	0.02	1.52	1.14	0.86
Race	Others	1.04	1.27	0.22	1.75	0.00	2.99
Race	Asian	3.33	0.00	0.00	0.00	0.00	0.00
Race	Unknown	0.00	0.00	5.52	0.29	0.31	0.45
Age	15-24	1.01	1.73	0.06	0.55	1.28	1.56
Age	25-34	1.41	0.90	0.01	1.20	0.74	0.59
Age	35-44	1.13	1.26	0.08	1.18	1.51	1.96
Age	45-54	1.15	1.24	0.06	1.39	1.14	1.02
Age	55-64	1.28	1.05	0.04	1.27	1.22	0.71
Age	> 65	1.25	1.30	0.03	0.79	0.69	0.67
Age	Not reported	0.00	0.00	5.42	0.48	0.46	0.45
Inj.	Incapacitating/ Severe	0.00	2.80	0.00	1.00	5.40	16.00
Inj.	Non-Incapacitating/ Moderate	0.37	2.80	0.12	0.55	2.50	0.00

Inj.	Possible/ Complaint	0.54	2.54	0.00	0.57	2.42	1.63
Inj.	No Injury	1.05	0.83	1.10	1.04	0.83	0.88
Alc.	No Test Given	1.13	1.15	0.49	0.96	0.69	1.18
Alc.	Test Given, Bac	0.00	0.81	0.00	0.00	29.73	10.81
Alc.	Test Given, Results Pending	0.00	3.33	0.00	0.00	0.00	0.00
Alc.	Test Refused	0.00	0.77	3.08	0.00	10.77	0.00
Alc.	Not reported	0.56	0.44	2.85	1.18	1.58	0.19
Cond.	Normal	1.09	1.48	0.11	0.89	1.10	1.23
Cond.	Inattentive	1.65	0.74	0.02	0.16	0.80	0.31
Cond.	Distracted	0.99	1.88	0.00	0.26	0.40	3.41
Cond.	Drinking Alcohol – Impaired	0.00	0.37	0.00	0.00	35.56	0.00
Cond.	Drinking Alcohol – Not Impaired	1.00	1.00	2.00	0.00	0.00	0.00
Cond.	Drug Use – Impaired	0.00	4.00	0.00	0.00	0.00	0.00
Cond.	Apparently Asleep/Blackout	0.00	1.74	0.00	0.00	17.83	17.39
Cond.	Fatigued	0.00	2.31	1.54	0.00	0.00	30.77
Cond.	Physical Impairment (Eyes, Ear, Limb)	1.43	0.00	0.00	0.00	0.00	0.00
Cond.	Other	0.06	0.05	4.40	2.41	0.52	0.56

The key findings from this table are stated below:

- Cluster 1 does not have drastically high odd measures for any other attributes. The highest odd measures for each of the variables are: alignment (hillcrest-curve = 1.43), highway type (Parish road = 1.27), roadway type (2-way undivided = 1.14), locality (industrial = 1.27), lighting (dawn = 2.00), weather (blowing sand/dirt = 1.43), day of the week (Monday to Thursday = 1.03), posted speed limit (30 mph or less = 1.26), intersection type (non-intersection = 1.02), gender (male = 1.28), race (Asian = 3.33), age (25-34 years = 1.41), injury type (no injury = 1.05), alcohol test (no test given = 1.13), and driver condition (inattentive = 1.65). It should be noted that this cluster comprises around 47% of the overall information. This cluster also shows some odds measures are zero. Based on the values, this cluster is not associated with interstate, open country, and driver impairment.
- Cluster 2 shows higher odds for some key attributes: curve alignment, dark as lighting condition, snow/sleet weather, 35-60 mph posted speed limit, severe and moderate injury, drug-impaired, and distracted driver. This cluster represents around 25% of the data, and it indicates that drug-impaired drivers are associated with delivery-related crashes under certain conditions.
- Cluster 3, with 18% information, mainly presents that there is a significant number of crashes with inadequate information regarding some key variables.

There is a need for additional efforts in the completion of the crash data characteristics, which is at this time out of the scope of this study.

- Cluster 4 represents 7% of the data. For categorical variables, some of the categories and attributes are not well defined. These attributes are clustered together as 'others' to make the number of categories limited. The other attributes with higher odds in this cluster are city streets and roadways with a posted speed limit of 30 mph or less. The other attributes also indicate the trivial nature of the variable attributes.
- Cluster 5 represents alcohol-impaired crashes on interstate roadways in open country localities. Driver condition as apparently asleep/blackout also shows higher odds. Another interesting feature of this cluster is that severe crosswind shows higher odds for this cluster.
- Cluster 6 properties are similar to Cluster 5. However, this cluster is not associated with driver impairment. The driver condition being apparently asleep/blacked out and being fatigued also show higher odds.

Example Problem 1

Provide some use cases of Principal Component Analysis (PCA) and Uniform Manifold Approximation and Projection (UMAP)

***Solution*:**

PCA and UMA are both popular dimension reduction methods for non-categorical data. The following replicable codes show how to use PCA and UMAP in crash data analysis.

Example Problem 1 (Code Chunk 1)

```
## Please check my RPUBS for additional codes: https://rpubs.com/subasish

setwd("~folder location")
library(data.table)
library(embed)
moo= read.csv("new1.csv")
head(moo)
pca_rec <- recipe(~., data = moo) %>%
  update_role(YEAR, SOE, new_role = "id") %>%
  step_normalize(all_predictors()) %>%
  step_pca(all_predictors())

pca_prep <- prep(pca_rec)
pca_prep

tidied_pca <- tidy(pca_prep, 2)
library(tidyverse)
library(tidymodels)
theme_set(theme_bw(base_size = 18))
tidied_pca %>%
```

```
  filter(component %in% paste0("PC", 1:5)) %>%
  mutate(component = fct_inorder(component)) %>%
  ggplot(aes(value, terms, fill = terms)) +
  geom_col(show.legend = FALSE) +
  facet_wrap(~component, nrow = 1) +
  labs(y = NULL)

library(tidytext)

tidied_pca %>%
  filter(component %in% paste0("PC", 1:4)) %>%
  group_by(component) %>%
  top_n(8, abs(value)) %>%
  ungroup() %>%
  mutate(terms = reorder_within(terms, abs(value), component)) %>%
  ggplot(aes(abs(value), terms, fill = value > 0)) +
  geom_col() +
  facet_wrap(~component, scales = "free_y") +
  scale_y_reordered() +
  labs(
   x = "Absolute value of contribution",
    y = NULL, fill = "Positive?"
  )


juice(pca_prep) %>%
  ggplot(aes(PC1, PC2, label = SOE)) +
  geom_point(aes(color =  YEAR ), alpha = 0.7, size = 2) +
  geom_text(check_overlap = TRUE, hjust = "inward", family = "IBMPlexSans") +
  labs(color = NULL)


library(embed)

umap_rec <- recipe(~., data = moo) %>%
  update_role(YEAR, SOE, new_role = "id") %>%
  step_normalize(all_predictors()) %>%
  step_umap(all_predictors())

umap_prep <- prep(umap_rec)
umap_prep

juice(umap_prep) %>%
  ggplot(aes(umap_1, umap_2, label = SOE)) +
  geom_point(aes(color = YEAR), alpha = 0.7, size = 2) +
  geom_text(check_overlap = TRUE, hjust = "inward", family = "IBMPlexSans") +
  labs(color = NULL)
```

Figure 43 and Figure 44 show the PCA plot and UMAP plot, respectively. The clustering patterns of these two methods differ.

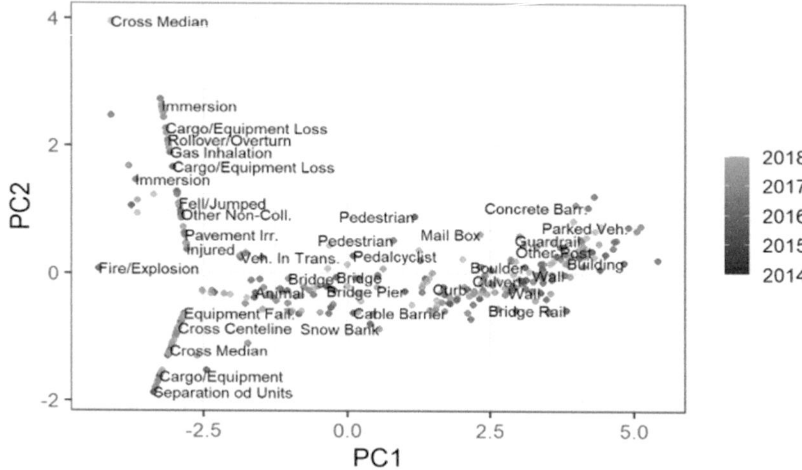

Figure 43. PCA plot.

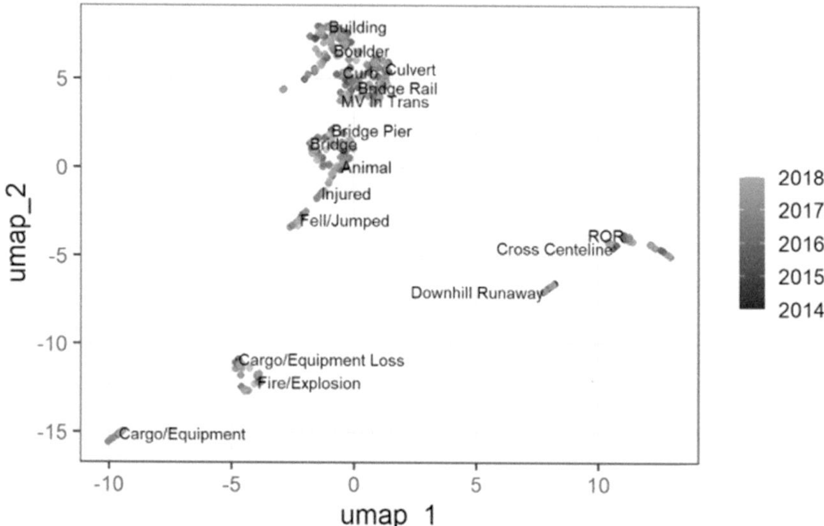

Figure 44. UMAP plot.

Chapter Conclusion

This chapter provides a brief description of different unsupervised learning algorithms. Included are *K*-means, *k*-nearest neighbors, dimension reduction methods, categorical data analysis, and correspondence analysis. The chapter also provides a list of relevant studies. Example problems and case studies are provided later in this chapter.

Further Reading

Bilder, C.R. and Loughin, T.M., 2014. Analysis of Categorical Data with R. CRC Press.

Das, S., 2021. Traffic volume prediction on low-volume roadways: A Cubist approach. Transportation Planning and Technology, 44, pp. 93–110.

Das, S., Kong, X. and Tsapakis, I., 2021. Hit and run crash analysis using association rules mining. Journal of Transportation Safety & Security, 13, pp. 123–142.

Das, S., Kong, X.J., Lavrenz, S.M., Wu, L. and Jalayer, M., 2021. Fatal crashes at highway rail grade crossings: A U.S. based study. International Journal of Transportation Science and Technology.

Das, S., Ashraf, S., Dutta, A. and Tran, L.-N., 2020. Pedestrians Under Influence (PUI) crashes: Patterns from correspondence regression analysis. Journal of Safety Research 75, pp. 14–23.

Das, S., Islam, M., Dutta, A. and Shimu, T.H., 2020. Uncovering deep structure of determinants in large truck fatal crashes. Transportation Research Record: Journal of the Transportation Research Board, 2674, pp. 742–754.

Das, S. and Dutta, A., 2020. Extremely serious crashes on urban roadway networks: Patterns and trends. IATSS Research, 44, pp. 248–252.

Das, S., Jha, K., Fitzpatrick, K., Brewer, M. and Shimu, T.H., 2019. Pattern identification from older bicyclist fatal crashes. Transportation Research Record: Journal of the Transportation Research Board, 2673, pp. 638–649.

Das, S., Kong, X. and Tsapakis, I., 2019. Hit and run crash analysis using association rules mining. Journal of Highway Safety & Security, 1–20.

Das, S., Bibeka, A., Sun, X., Zhou, H. "Tracy" et al., 2019. Elderly pedestrian fatal crash-related contributing factors: Applying empirical bayes geometric mean method. Transportation Research Record: Journal of the Transportation Research Board, 2673, pp. 254–263.

Das, S., Dutta, A., Kong, X. and Sun, X., 2019. Hit and run crashes: Knowledge extraction from bicycle involved crashes using first and frugal tree. International Journal of Transportation Science and Technology, 8, pp. 146–160.

Das, S., Avelar, R., Dixon, K.K. and Sun, X., 2018. Investigation on the wrong way driving crash patterns using multiple correspondence analysis. Accident Analysis & Prevention, 111, pp. 43–55.

Das, S., Brimley, B.K., Lindheimer, T.E. and Zupancich, M., 2018. Association of reduced visibility with crash outcomes. IATSS Research, 42, pp. 143–151.

Das, S., Dutta, A., Jalayer, M., Bibeka, A. and Wu, L., 2018. Factors influencing the patterns of wrong-way driving crashes on freeway exit ramps and median crossovers: Exploration using 'Eclat' Association Rules to promote safety. International Journal of Transportation Science and Technology, 7, pp. 114–123.

Friendly, M., 2000. Visualizing Categorical Data. SAS Institute.

Kong, X., Das, S., Jha, K. and Zhang, Y., 2020. Understanding speeding behavior from naturalistic driving data: Applying classification-based association rule mining. Accident Analysis & Prevention, 144, 105620.

Lovelace, R., Nowosad, J. and Muenchow, J., 2019. Geocomputation with R. CRC Press.

Moraga, P., 2019. Geospatial Health Data: Modeling and Visualization with R-INLA and Shiny. CRC Press.

Müller, A.C. and Guido, S., 2016. Introduction to Machine Learning with Python: A Guide for Data Scientists. O'Reilly Media, Inc.

Murphy, K.P., 2012. Machine Learning: A Probabilistic Perspective. MIT Press.

References

Cao, Q., Ren, G., Li, D., Ma, J. and Li, H., 2020. Semi-supervised route choice modeling with sparse Automatic vehicle identification data. Transportation Research Part C: Emerging Technologies, 121, 102857.

Chang, Y., Bharadwaj, N., Edara, P. and Sun, C., 2020. Exploring contributing factors of hazardous events in construction zones using naturalistic driving study data. IEEE Transactions on Intelligent Vehicles, 5, pp. 519–527.

Das, S. and Dutta, A., 2020. Extremely serious crashes on urban roadway networks: Patterns and trends. IATSS Research, 44, pp. 248–252.

Gong, Y., Abdel-Aty, M., Yuan, J. and Cai, Q., 2020. Multi-objective reinforcement learning approach for improving safety at intersections with adaptive traffic signal control. Accident Analysis & Prevention, 144, 105655.

Khodayari-Rostamabad, A., Reilly, J.P., Nikolova, N.K., Hare, J.R., Pasha, S., et al., 2009. Machine learning techniques for the analysis of magnetic flux leakage images in pipeline inspection. IEEE Transactions on Magnetics, 45, pp. 3073–3084.

Kumar, S. and Toshniwal, D., 2016. A data mining approach to characterize road accident locations. Journal of Modern Transportation, 24, pp. 62–72.

Kwon, J.-H. and Cho, G.-H., 2020. An examination of the intersection environment associated with perceived crash risk among school-aged children: Using street-level imagery and computer vision. Accident Analysis & Prevention, 146, 105716.

Li, P., Abdel-Aty, M. and Islam, Z., 2021. Driving maneuvers detection using semi-supervised long short-term memory and smartphone sensors. Transportation Research Record, 03611981211007483.

Liu, T., Yang, Y., Huang, G.-B., Yeo, Y.K., Lin, Z., et al., 2016. Driver distraction detection using semi-supervised machine learning. IEEE Transactions on Intelligent Transportation Systems, 17, pp. 1108–1120.

Liu, B., Hsu, W. and Ma, Y., 1998. Integrating classification and association rule mining. *In:* KDD, pp. 80–86.

Mousa, S.R., Ishak, S., Mousa, R.M., Codjoe, J., Elhenawy, M., et al., 2020. Deep reinforcement learning agent with varying actions strategy for solving the eco-approach and departure problem at signalized intersections. Transportation Research Record, 2674, pp. 119–131.

Nandurge, P.A. and Dharwadkar, N.V., 2017. Analyzing road accident data using machine learning paradigms. *In:* 2017 International Conference on I-SMAC (IoT in Social,

Mobile, Analytics and Cloud) (I-SMAC). Presented at the 2017 International Conference on I-SMAC (IoT in Social, Mobile, Analytics and Cloud) (I-SMAC), pp. 604–610.

Ni, X., Wang, H., Che, C., Hong, J., Sun, Z., et al., 2019. Civil aviation safety evaluation based on deep belief network and principal component analysis. Safety Science, 112, pp. 90–95.

Nie, Y., Zhao, J., Liu, J. and Ran, R., 2018. Big Data Enabled Vehicle Collision Detection Using Linear Discriminant Analysis. *In:* 2018 10th International Conference on Wireless Communications and Signal Processing (WCSP). Presented at the 2018 10th International Conference on Wireless Communications and Signal Processing (WCSP), pp. 1–5.

Paolo, F., Gianfranco, F., Luca, F., Marco, M., Andrea, M., et al., 2021. Investigating the role of the human element in maritime accidents using semi-supervised hierarchical methods. Transportation Research Procedia, 23rd EURO Working Group on Transportation Meeting, EWGT 2020, 16–18 September 2020, Paphos, Cyprus 52, pp. 252–259.

Rasheed, I., Hu, F. and Zhang, L., 2020. Deep reinforcement learning approach for autonomous vehicle systems for maintaining security and safety using LSTM-GAN. Vehicular Communications, 26, 100266.

Ren, T., Xie, Y. and Jiang, L., 2020. Cooperative highway work zone merge control based on reinforcement learning in a connected and automated environment. Transportation Research Record: Journal of the Transportation Research Board, 2674(10), pp. 361–374.

Wang, J., Zhu, S. and Gong, Y., 2010. Driving safety monitoring using semi supervised learning on time series data. IEEE Transactions on Intelligent Transportation Systems, 11, pp. 728–737.

Wang, S., Sharma, A. and Knickerbocker, S., 2017. Analyzing and improving the performance of dynamic message sign reporting work zone–related congestion. Transportation Research Record: Journal of the Transportation Research Board, 2617(1), pp. 71–77.

Zhao, S., Iranitalab, A. and Khattak, A.J., 2019. A clustering approach to injury severity in pedestrian-train crashes at highway-rail grade crossings. Journal of Highway Safety & Security, 11, pp. 305–322.

CHAPTER

7

Deep Learning

7.1. Introduction

Deep learning has been the most researched area in the past few years. Deep learning algorithms have been used in a multitude of highway safety studies. A brief overview of the most used deep learning algorithms in highway safety analysis is described in this chapter.

7.2. Popular Algorithms

7.2.1. LSTM

The original long short-term memory (LSTM) model was improved by the core contribution of using self-loops to create pathways wherein the gradient is capable of flowing for extended periods of time, and the idea of making the self-loop weights conditioned was pivotal. Controlling the self-loop weight with a hidden unit allows for a dynamic change in the time scale of integration; in this case, due to the fact that the model produces the time constants itself, the time scale of integration for even an LSTM with fixed parameters can change due to the input sequence. There are many applications in which the LSTM has been successful, such as speech recognition, unrestrained handwriting recognition, handwriting generation, image captioning, machine translation, and parsing.

The shallow recurrent network architecture's analogous forward propagation equations are listed below. LSTM recurrent networks contain **LSTM cells** with a self-loop (internal recurrence), along with the outer recurrence of the recurrent neural network (RNN), and have the same outputs and inputs as ordinary recurrent networks, with a unit gating procedure that manages the output of information and more parameters rather than having just one unit apply an elementwise nonlinearity function to the affine transformation of inputs and recurring units.

The state unit, $s_i^{(t)}$, contains a linear self-loop (comparable to the loose units) that is the most crucial part. A forget gate unit, $f_i^{(t)}$ (for time step t and cell i), uses a sigmoid unit to select a weight with a value between 0 and 1 and controls the weight of the self-loop t (or the associated time constant):

$$f_i^{(t)} = \sigma\left(b_i^f + \sum_j U_{i,j}^f x_j^{(t)} + \sum_j W_{i,j}^f h_j^{(t-1)}\right) \quad (1)$$

wherein the current input vector is $x^{(t)}$ and the current hidden layer vector is $h^{(t)}$, with all the LSTM cells outputs, and where $W^{(f)}$, $b^{(f)}$ and $U^{(f)}$ represent the recurrent weights, biases, and input weights for the forget gates, respectively. Then, the LSTM cell's internal state is updated with a conditional self-loop weight $f_i^{(t)}$:

$$s_i^{(t)} = f_i^{(t)} s_i^{(t-1)} + g_i^{(t)} \sigma\left(b_i + \sum_j U_{i,j} x_j^{(t)} + \sum_j W_{i,j}^f h_j^{(t-1)}\right) \quad (2)$$

where W, U, and b represent the recurrent weights, input weights, and biases of the LSTM cell, respectively. The external input gate unit $g_i^{(t)}$ is calculated with a method that is similar to the forget gate (with a sigmoid unit to get a gating value between 0 and 1), but with different constraints:

$$g_i^{(t)} = \sigma\left(b_i^g + \sum_j U_{i,j}^g x_j^{(t)} + \sum_j W_{i,j}^g h_j^{(t-1)}\right) \quad (3)$$

The LSTM cell's output $h_i^{(t)}$ can be turned off through the output gate $q_i^{(t)}$, which additionally employs a sigmoid unit for gating:

$$h_i^{(t)} = \tanh\left(s_i^{(t)}\right) q_i^{(t)}$$

$$q_i^{(t)} = \sigma\left(b_i^o + \sum_j U_{i,j}^o x_j^{(t)} + \sum_j W_{i,j}^o h_j^{(t-1)}\right) \quad (4)$$

which has parameters W^o, U^o, and b^o for its recurrent weights, input weights, and biases, respectively.

The cell state $s_i^{(t)}$ can be used as an additional input (along with its weight) into the i-th unit's gates, but an additional three parameters are required for this.

Need to know

It has been demonstrated that LSTM networks learn long-term dependencies more readily than the simple recurrent architectures. This was first shown in artificial data sets that were created to examine the ability of LTSM networks to learn long-term dependencies, and then on difficult sequence processing tasks in which the performances were state-of-the-art. Many alternatives and variants for the LSTM have been studied and used, which are discussed next.

Autoencoders are neural networks that are trained to duplicate their input into output with an internal hidden layer h that defines a code that is utilized to represent the input. There are essentially two parts to the network: a decoder that produces a reconstruction $r = g(h)$, and an encoder function $h = f(x)$. An autoencoder isn't especially useful if it is able to simply learn to set $g(f(x)) = x$ everywhere, and instead is typically limited in how it is only permitted to make an approximate copy and only a duplicate input that is similar to the training data. The model often learns useful properties of the data because it prioritizes which parts of the input should be duplicated.

The concept of an encoder and a decoder have been generalized by autoencoders' past deterministic functions to stochastic mappings $pencoder(h|x)$

and *pdecoder*($x|h$). The concept of autoencoders has for decades been in the history of neural networks, where they were typically used for feature learning or dimensionality reduction. Autoencoders have recently been brought to the front of generative modeling thanks to theoretical connections between latent variable models and autoencoders. Autoencoders are a distinct case of feedforward networks that can learn using identical methods; recirculation (a learning algorithm that is founded on the comparison of the network activations of the original input to the activations on the reconstructed input), unlike with general feedforward networks, can be used to train autoencoders. AI applications often have used recirculation, but it is considered to be more biologically plausible than back-propagation (see Figure 45).

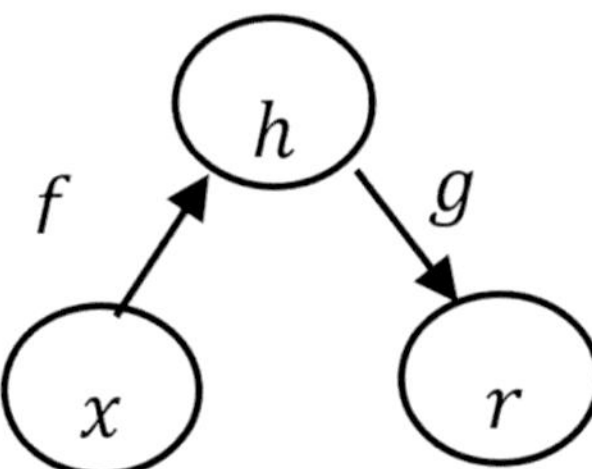

Figure 45. The structure of an autoencoder.

7.2.2. Monte Carlo Sampling

It is possible to approximate a sum or integral when it cannot be exactly computed (e.g., if there is an exponential number of terms in the sum with no known exact simplification) through the use of Monte Carlo sampling. This concept considers the integral or sum to be an expectation under some distribution and by a correspondence average to approximate the expectation. Consider

$$s = \Sigma_x\, p(x) f(x) = E_p[f(x)]$$

$$s = \int p(x) f(x) dx = E_p[f(x)] \tag{5}$$

acts as the integral or sum to be approximated, redrafted as an expected value, with constraint p representing a probability density (for the integral) or probability distribution (for the sum) over random variable x.

S is estimated by taking n samples $x(1), ..., x(n)$ from p, then calculating the empirical average

$$\hat{s}_n = \frac{1}{N} \Sigma_{i=1}^{n} f(x^{(i)}) \tag{6}$$

Different properties justify this approximation. The estimator $\hat{s}$ being unbiased is the first observation, due to the fact that

$$E\left[\hat{s}_n\right] = 1n \Sigma_{i=1}^{n} E\left[f(x^{(i)})\right] = 1n \Sigma_{i=1}^{n} s = s. \tag{7}$$

Along with this, the law of large numbers shows that the mean almost always converges with the anticipated value if the samples $x^{(i)}$ are i.i.d.:

$$\hat{s}_n = s, \tag{8}$$

if the individual terms' variance, $Var\ [f(x^{(i)})]$, is bounded, consider the variance of $\hat{s}_n$ as n increases; so long as $Var\ [f(x^{(i)})], < \infty$, the variance $Var[\hat{s}_n]$ decreases and converges to 0:

$$Var[\hat{S}_n] = \frac{1}{n^2}\sum_{i=1}^{n} Var[f(x)]$$

$$= \frac{Var[f(x)]}{n} \tag{9}$$

7.3. Boltzmann Machines

Boltzmann machines were initially considered to be a general connectionist approach for learning arbitrary probability distributions over binary vectors. This section introduces binary Boltzmann machines.

The definition presented over a d-dimensional binary random vector of the Boltzmann machine is $x \in \{0,1\}^d$. It is an energy-based model, meaning that an energy function can be used to define the joint probability distribution:

$$P(x) = ex(-E(x))Z \tag{10}$$

Z is the partition function and $E(x)$ is the energy function that certifies that $\sum_x P(x) = 1$; the Boltzmann machine's energy function is:

$$E(x) = -x^T Ux - b^T x \tag{11}$$

where b represents the bias parameters vector and U is the "weight" matrix of model parameters.

Generally, a group of training examples (all n-dimensional) is taken from the Boltzmann machine settings. Equation 11 indicates the joint probability distribution over the observed variables. This scenario, even though viable, limits the types of interactions among the variables that are described by the weight matrix with the observed variables, which means that a linear model (logistic regression) produced from the other unit's values provides the probability of one unit being on.

Need to know

The Boltzmann machine increases in power when some variables are not observed. The latent variables are able to act in the likeness of a multi-layer perceptron's hidden units and higher-order interactions among the visible units can be modeled. In the same way that the inclusion of hidden units to convert a logistic regression into a MLP causes it to act as a universal approximator of functions, a Boltzmann machine with hidden units is no longer limited to predicting linear relationships between variables; instead, it acts as a universal approximator over discrete variables of probability mass functions.

The units x are formally decomposed into two subsets: the latent (or hidden) units h and the visible units v. The energy function thus becomes

$$E(x) = -v^T Rv - v^T Wh - h^T Sh - b^T v - c^T h. \tag{12}$$

7.3.1. Boltzmann Machine Learning

The basis for the learning algorithms of Boltzmann machines is usually the maximum likelihood. Shaping of $P_{model}(v)$ and $\widehat{P}_{data}(v)$ $P_{model}(v)$ statistics is aided by the remainder of the network, and knowledge about how the statistics were produced or the rest of the network isn't necessary to update the weight. Subsequently, due to the "local" nature of the learning rule, the Boltzmann machine is biologically possible. If each random variable in a Boltzmann machine is a neuron, the 'dendrites' and 'axons' that connect two random variables can only be taught by discerning the cell firing pattern of the cells with which they have physical contact. Particularly, two units that activate together frequently have a strengthened connection in the positive phase. Despite being among the oldest hypothesized explanations of biological system learning, Hebbian learning rules remain relevant in modern times.

Hypothesizing more machine existence is necessary for other learning algorithms that employ information beyond local statistics (e.g., the brain must retain a secondary communication network to convey gradient information through the network in the backward direction in order to utilize back-propagation in a multilayer perceptron).

7.3.2. Generative Adversarial Networks

Generative adversarial networks (GANs) are a generative modeling method founded on differentiable generator networks. Non-convergence was identified as a problem that could possibly cause GANs to underfit by Goodfellow (2014).

GANs originate from a game theory scenario wherein the generator network competes against an opponent; the generator network yields samples $x = (z; \theta^{(g)})$. The **discriminator network** acts as its opponent to differentiate between samples produced by the generator and samples that are gathered from the training data, and it gives a probability value given by $d = (x; \theta^{(d)})$, which indicates the likelihood that x is an actual training sample rather than a model-produced, fake one.

A zero-sum game, wherein a function $v(\theta^{(d)}, \theta^{(d)})$ determines the payoff of the discriminator, is the easiest method to formulate learning in generative adversarial networks. The generator receives its payoff, $-v(\theta^{(d)}, \theta^{(d)})$. As they learn, the players try to increase their own payoff, so that at the conjunction,

$$g^* = arg\ arg\ v(g, d). \tag{13}$$

The default choice for v is

$$v(\theta^{(g)}, \theta^{(d)} = E_{x \sim P_{data}} \log d(x) + E_{x \sim P_{model}} \log \log (1 - d(x)). \tag{14}$$

Due to this, the discriminator is driven to learn how to accurately identify samples as either fake or real. At the same time, the generator tries to trick the classifier into thinking that the generated samples are real. At the convergence, the generator's samples are indistinguishable from the real data, and the discriminator produces 1 and 2 for all data here. The classifier is unnecessary at this point.

The GAN design's primary motivation is to achieve a learning process that does not require a rough estimate or a partition function gradient estimation. At the point that $max_d\, v(g, d)$ is convex in $\theta^{(g)}$ (i.e., the point of maximization is located directly in the probability density functions), the process is asymptotically consistent and will converge (Goodfellow et al., 2016).

When g and d are represented by neural networks and $max_d\, v(g, d)$ is not convex, learning in GANs can be difficult. In general, it is not guaranteed that concurrent gradient descent on two players' costs will reach equilibrium. Thus, consider the value function $v\ (a, b) = ab$, in which the first player holds a and gains a cost $-ab$, and the second player holds b and gains a cost $-ab$. If both players in the model make infinitesimally small gradient steps, and players aim to reduce their own cost at the cost of the other players, then a and b will be in a stable orbit instead of reaching a point of equilibrium at the origin. The equilibria for minimax games aren't local minima of v, but rather points that have the same minima of time for the costs of both players, meaning that they represent the saddle points of v that are the local minima based on one player's parameters and local maxima based on the other player's parameters. Instead of ending up on the exact saddle point where neither player is able to reduce the cost, both players are able to alternate increasing and then decreasing v endlessly. It is unknown the extent to which this non-convergence problem impacts GANs.

An alternate expression of the payoffs, wherein it is not a zero-sum game, with the same predicted gradient as the maximum likelihood learning with the optimal discriminator, was recognized by Goodfellow (2014). Given enough samples, this new formulation of the GAN game should converge because maximum likelihood training converges. In practice, this alternative formulation, unfortunately, doesn't appear to improve convergence, potentially because of the high variance of the predicted gradient or the suboptimality of the discriminator.

Another formulation that isn't zero-sum or parallel to maximum likelihood is the best-performing formulation of the GAN game in realistic experiments. In this formulation, the generator works to (instead of attempting to lower the log probability that the discriminator makes correct predictions) raise the log probability of the discriminator making a mistake. This reformulation is motivated by the fact that, even in situations where the discriminator rejects all generator samples, the derivative of the generator's cost function according to the discriminator's logits is made to stay big. The stabilization of GAN learning continues to be a problem, but as long as the model architecture and hyperparameters are carefully selected, GAN learning performs well (Goodfellow et al., 2016).

A way to simplify the GAN learning problem is separating the generation process into multiple levels of detail. Training conditional GANs that learn to sample from a distribution $p(x|y)$, instead of just a marginal distribution $p(x)$, is a possibility. LAPGAN generators can confuse both discriminator networks and human observers, with experimental subjects identified as being real data being up to 40% of the outputs of the network (Goodfellow et al., 2016).

Need to know

An unusual capability is that the GAN network can fit probability distributions that assign a zero probability to the training points. The generator net learns to outline a manifold with points that resemble training points instead of specific points that maximize the log probability. This means that the model may allot a log-likelihood of negative infinity to the test set while denoting a manifold that an observer would judge as capturing the essence of the generation task. This is neither an advantage nor a disadvantage, and it could also be guaranteed that adding Gaussian noise to all generated values through the last layer of the generator causes the generator network to allocate non-zero probability to all points. To parametrize the mean of a conditional Gaussian distribution, generator networks that add Gaussian noise in this way use sample points from the same distribution of the generator network.

7.4. Deep Learning Categories

The section below discusses different deep learning architectures, explains their underlying algorithms, and presents an overview of the three primary groups of neural networks- Pretrained Unsupervised Networks, Convolutional Neural Networks, and Recurrent/Recursive Neural Networks (see Figure 46).

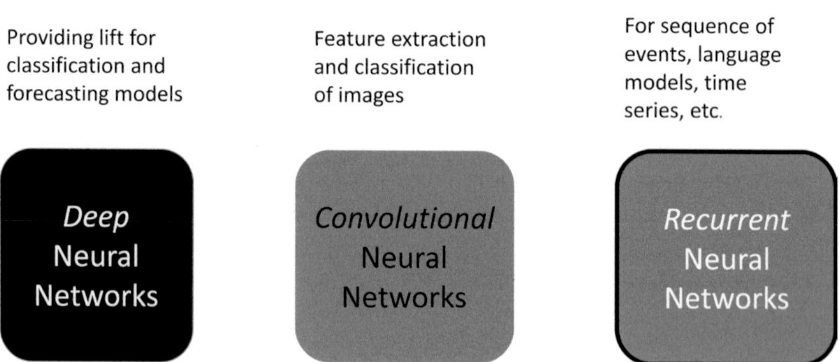

Figure 46. Deep neural network, CNN, and RNN

7.4.1. Convolutional Neural Networks (CNNs)

Biological processes are the inspiration behind CNNs, and, subsequently, they were created to imitate the brain's visual cortex's neural connectivity. They require significantly less data in comparison to conventional image classification algorithms (that need hand-engineered pre-processed filters). CNNs have applications in video and image recognition, medical image analysis, image classification, recommender systems, and natural language processing (NLP).

7.4.2. CNN Structure

In at least one of their layers, CNNs perform convolution rather than standard matrix multiplication (unlike conventional neural networks), and they have two distinct attributes: parameter sharing and sparse interactions. Parameters are generated based on the relationship between each input and output unit and are less efficient in traditional neural networks, and parameter sharing (also called tied weights) involves attaching the weight of one input unit to that of another. This ensures that in image classification scenarios only one set of parameters is learned for every image location. This is different from conventional neural networks, wherein weights are untied and individual parameter sets are learned at each location. Sparse connectivity is attained by reducing the model's kernel size in comparison to the input. There could be millions of pixels that represent a high-resolution image in an image classification application, and the kernel will be configured so that it only captures the features' most revealing image objects (such as contrast and edges). To represent the image when the image in question has fewer pixels, there is a reduction in parameters, which causes the reduction of computational overhead and memory utilization (Goodfellow et al., 2016).

Need to know

There are typically three steps performed in each of the convolutional network's layers. First, the layer generates a set of linear activations by parallelly performing multiple convolutions. The second step (called the detector stage) runs the linear activations through non-linear activation functions to predict a non-linear mapping to the output. The third step is changing the output of a specific location in the net using the nearby outputs' statistical values through a pooling function that further transforms the layer output. This highlights the CNNs convolutional aspect, wherein neighborhood values impact any given node. The operation will change the output value based on the maximum value of its rectangular neighborhood region in max pooling, whereas other pooling functions account for the mean value of the neighborhood region.

Figure 47 shows a diagram of the layers of a CNN from the input layer to the output layer.

Different layers have different weights applied until the network is capable of filtering the data and achieving results; this happens by building feature

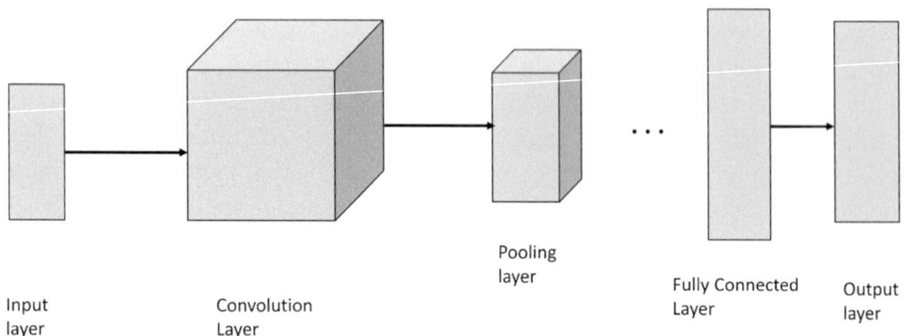

Figure 47. Convolution neural network.

maps using various kernels or filters and pooling the main convolutional layer. These tiers are each completely attached, and they produce an output. Although they are primarily used for visual sorting, CNNs also contain several beneficial applications, including action recognition, object tracking, text and language detection, and other classifications. The CNN forward propagation implemented is illustrated in the equations below, where Ψ is the nonlinearity weight matrix and ω is the $n \times n$ filter.

$$x_{ij}^{l} = \psi\left(\sum_{a-0}^{n-1}\sum_{b-0}^{n-1} \omega_{ab} y_{(i+a)(j+b)}^{l-1}\right) \tag{15}$$

$$\frac{\partial E}{\partial x_{ij}^{l}} = \frac{\partial E}{\partial y_{ij}^{l}}\frac{\partial y_{ij}^{l}}{\partial x_{ij}^{l}} = \frac{\partial E}{\partial y_{ij}^{l}}\frac{\partial y_{ij}^{l}}{\partial x_{ij}^{l}}\left(\psi(x_{ij}^{l})\right) \tag{16}$$

$$\omega_{ab} = J\left(\sum_{a=0}^{n-1}\sum_{b=0}^{n-1} \frac{\partial E}{\partial x_{(i+a)(j+b)}^{l}} \frac{\partial x_{(i+a)(j+b)}^{l}}{\partial y_{ij}^{l-1}}\right) \tag{17}$$

$$J = \left(\sum_{a=0}^{n-1}\sum_{b=0}^{n-1} \frac{\partial E}{\partial x_{(i+a)(j+b)}^{l}}\right)^{-1} \tag{18}$$

7.4.3. CNN Architectures and Applications

Multiple CNN architectures have been developed since their initial creation, such as ResNet, AlexNet, LeNet-5, and GoogLeNet. These networks use the same feature extraction structure with convolutional layers, but differ in feature mapping, the number of layers, and their efficiency. Despite CNN's versatility in different problem spaces, there are limitations in their architectures, and they tend to get stuck at local minima and overfit, resulting in a higher computational time and lower model performance. To help compensate for these limitations, optimization algorithms can be considered.

7.4.4. Forward and Backward Propagation

Once data is put into a neural network, it moves by forward propagation through several layers. The depth of the network is denoted by the number of layers in the network, and it incorporates an input vector, x. Each layer, l, has a size that signifies the number of nodes, and the weight matrix is applied to the activation function. The inbound data, a, is multiplied by a weight, w, and then that result is added to a bias, b. In Equation 19, j is the output node, and it differentiates the jth node from the lth layer; k represents the kth node from the prior layer, $l - 1$,which acts as the input node. Thus, the value w^l_{jk} represents the weight relationship of the nodes from the two layers. The weight matrix and bias (when first set up) are randomly modified through a method called parameter initialization, in which a^0 represents the layer containing the input data vector.

$$z^l_j = \sum_k w^l_{jk} a^{l-1}_k + b^l_j \tag{19}$$

The weighted input of the jth node in the lth layer, z^l_j, is subsequently fed into f, an activation function.

$$a^1_j = f(z^l_j)$$

The purpose of an activation function is the production of a mapping or an output from a real number input to a real number (to figure out if the information in the node is useful, i.e., whether or not to activate the node). The activation function makes the layered design to the neural network, and it works as a neural network layer by executing functions on the initial input data and passing it to the next layer of the neural network (activation function). The type of activation function used determines the values that are made by the activation function. The selection process when developing the network necessitates some experimenting to determine which activation function will have the best results. Below are some common activation functions (Goodfellow et al., 2016).

The sigmoid function (or logistic function) maps to real numbers with values between 0 and 1.

$$f(x) = \sigma(x) = \frac{1}{1+e^{-x}} \tag{21}$$

The hyperbolic tangent (*tanh*) activation function maps to real numbers with values that are between −1 and 1.

$$f(x) = \tanh(x) = \frac{(e^x - e^{-x})}{(e^x + e^{-x})} \tag{22}$$

The Rectified Linear Unit (ReLU) activation function maps to real numbers with values from 0 to ∞.

$$f(x) = \{0 \text{ for } x < 0 \; x \text{ for } x \geq 0\} \tag{23}$$

The Softmax activation function maps to real numbers with values from 0 to 1.

$$fi(\vec{x}) = \frac{e^{x_i}}{\sum_{j=1}^{j} e^{x_j}} \tag{24}$$

The arbitrarily set initialized parameter values are later adjusted during the training of the network. The data is fed forward into the network and an output vector $\hat{y}$ arises from the final result. The output vector is then used to compute the loss.

The forward propagation equation is diminished to the simple vectorized equation

$$A^l = f(W^l A^{l-1} + b^1) \tag{25}$$

The training of a network by reducing the loss computed by the cost function, based on the input on how far the network is from predicting accurately, is called backpropagation. Many cost function types can be utilized, the mean squared error being one.

$$C = \frac{1}{n}\sum_{i=1}^{n}(y_i - \hat{y}_i)^2 \tag{26}$$

Algorithm 1: Forward and Backward propagation in CNN

Input: M-dimensional data, $x = [x_1, \ldots, x_N]T$

where n is the number of data points. The mean of the square of the difference between the actual output given by the network and the desired (or the expected) output is considered to be the mean squared error.

The gradient descent optimization algorithm is utilized in order to minimize loss so as to enhance the cost function, while the errors are backpropagated towards the front of the network. Gradient descent is the negative of the learning rate multiplied by the partial derivative of the cost function with respect to the weights.

$$\Delta w = -\eta \frac{\partial C}{\partial w} \tag{27}$$

Need to know

The chain rule can be used through backpropagation to calculate the gradients all at once (meaning that the gradients are multiplied together to adjust the weights for each node accordingly). Backpropagation, in comparison to forward propagation, is beneficial in that it minimizes the number of calculations necessary to calculate the gradients. Forward propagation suffers from the issue that the cost function must be first computed before computing the partial derivative of the cost function based on each weight, producing an operation that requires a number of parameters, squared, iterations through the network to calculate the gradients. To calculate the gradient for each node, the network must complete an entire forward iteration. However, one propagation to compute the loss and then one backpropagation to update the weights with respect to the loss is the only thing needed to update the network with backpropagation. The pseudo-code in Algorithm 1 can also be used to understand backpropagation.

7.4.5. Pretrained Unsupervised Networks

Due to typically having limited training data, feature extraction and data generation are significant applications in deep learning. Different techniques are employed to supplement the original dataset r and provide a bigger dataset to train the network. Through the use of advanced deep learning architectures (i.e., Autoencoders and Generative Adversarial Networks (GANs)), synthetic data from the original dataset can be generated in order to advance model learning. These architectures both belong to the Pretrained Unsupervised Network (PUN) family, which is a deep learning model that employs unsupervised learning in order to teach each hidden layer in a neural network to produce a better fit for the dataset. To individually train each layer, an unsupervised learning algorithm is independently employed, with the input being the previously trained layer, and a refinement step is conducted throughout the entire network after the pre-training on each layer is conducted with supervised learning. Examples of PUNs include Autoencoders, Generative Adversarial Networks (GAN), and Deep Belief Networks (DBN) (Kelleher, 2019).

7.4.6. Autoencoders

For dimensionality reduction, autoencoders learn a representation in which the input is equal to the output through the use of unsupervised learning. They have three parts: the hidden layer, input, and output. In the hidden layer, the data is compressed and then uncompressed through two primary steps of encoding and decoding the autoencoder algorithm in order to make an output that is close to the input. The mapping function between the input layer and hidden layer is represented by the following:

$$y = f_o(\hat{x}) = s(W\hat{x} + b) \tag{28}$$

wherein the input $\hat{x}$ is mapped to the hidden layer y, W is the weighted matrix, and $\odot$ is the coding parameter. Subsequently, the following would be the decoding function:

$$z = g_{o'}(y) = x(W'y + b') \tag{29}$$

The reconstruction of input x would be z.

A variation of feed-forward neural networks with particular partiality for computing the reconstruction error of the original input is autoencoders, and (post-training) they are utilized as normal feed-forward neural networks for activations. Due to the fact that the neural network only uses the original input to learn weights instead of backpropagation (which has labels), this feature extraction is unsupervised. Autoencoders use unlabeled data in unsupervised learning and create a condensed representation of the input data, and they are taught to reproduce their own input data.

7.4.7. Deep Belief Network

Along with understanding various machine learning networks and their operations, it is useful to look at the ways that different networks are used together. A connection that is built between each network, referred to as the Deep Belief Network (DBN), is able to combine neural networks together in different amalgamations in series with one another. It is structured through a widespread layered connection formed by linking multiple, smaller unsupervised neural networks, which can be better understood by scrutinizing the aspects of a DBN: a Belief Net and a Restricted Boltzmann Machine (Kelleher, 2019).

A Belief Net is made up of randomly generated binary unit layers (ranging from “0” to “1”), with a weight function assigned to each of the connected layers; the bias and weight factor inputs from the other linked units are the basis for the likelihood of having a value of “1.” Layer-by-layer learning allows the determination of how a variable in one level could potentially interrelate with variables in a different layer. After training, the values of variables can be predicted through a bottom-up approach, beginning with a data vector on the bottom layer, and then, in the opposite direction, adding the generative weight function.

A Restricted Boltzmann Machine (RBM) is a stochastic RNN made up of randomly generated binary units, with undefined edges between each unit. Between each of the hidden units, it has restricted connections because scalability is the main limitation of RBM (Goodfellow et al., 2016).

7.4.8. Recurrent and Recursive Neural Networks

Recurrent and Recursive Neural Networks are able to send data over time steps. 4 structures are introduced in this class: Recurrent Neural Network, Recursive Neural Network, Long Short-term Memory (LSTM), and Attention.

Recurrent Neural Network (RNN)

David Rumelhart first introduced RNN in 1986. Image captioning, natural language processing (NLP), video analysis, and music analysis all rely on RNNs. Since they actively gather sequential and time dependencies between data, RNNs differ from standard neural networks (which assume independence between data points). See Figure 48 for more information.

Parameter sharing is a defining attribute of RNNs. Without it, unique parameters are allocated by the model for each data point in a sequence and are thus unable to make predictions about variable-length sequences. This limitation is shown in natural language processing; as an example, the sentences to be decoded are “An incredible cricket player is Sachin Tendulkar” and “Sachin Tendulkar is an incredible cricket player.” A perfect model would be capable of recognizing ‘Sachin Tendulkar’ as the cricket player in both sentences regardless of the words positioning, but a conventional multilayer network would fail in this situation due to the fact that it would interpret the language with respect to the unique weights set for each word in the sentence. RNNs, on the other hand, share weights across time steps (i.e., words in a sentence) and would be better suited for the task, allowing for more accurate sentence comprehension (Kelleher, 2019).

RNNs typically supplement the traditional multilayer network architecture with cycles that connect neighboring time steps or nodes that make up the network’s

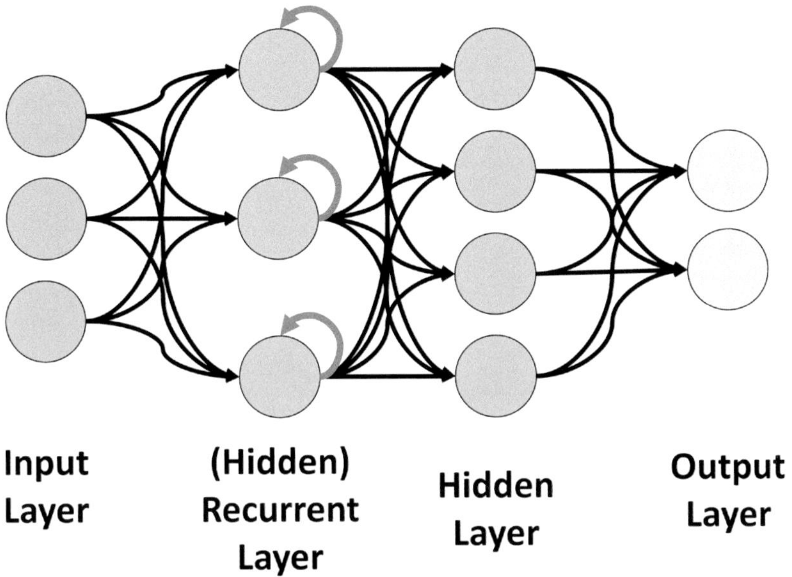

Figure 48. Recurrent neural network.

internal memory (utilized to assess the characteristics of the present data point taken from recent data points). The majority of traditional feedforward neural networks are restricted to one-to-one mappings for input and output, but RNNs are capable of performing many to one (e.g., identifying voice), one to many, and many to many (e.g. translating speech) mappings. The mappings between inputs and outputs and loss are depicted using a computational graph, and a well-defined picture of in-network parameter sharing is given by decomposing the graph into a chain of events. A generalized equation for recurrence relationships is

$$s^{(t)} = f(s^{t-1}) \tag{30}$$

$s^{(t)}$ represents the condition of the system that relies on a prior time-step represented by $t - 1$. This equation can then be rewritten as

$$h^{(t)} = f(h^{t-1}, x^{(t)};) \tag{31}$$

where $h^{(t)}$ is utilized to denote the condition and $x^{(t)}$ represents input from one specific time instance. $h^{(t)}$ is significant because it represents the task-relevant parts of the prior input sequence up to t.

Previous forms of RNN architectures had versatility and promise but still had some limitations; RNN structures can, in theory, retain information for long periods, but not necessarily in practice. Conventional RNN networks (sometimes called Vanilla RNNs) are predisposed to an exploding gradient and a vanishing gradient, phenomena that result from propagation errors that accrue over several steps. RNNs can properly reference pieces of information if the gap between references is not too large, but they start to decline when the gap increases, and RNNs aren't always able to link the data. Variations of traditional RNN architecture that address these concerns include Truncated Backpropagation Through Time (TBPTT) and Long Short-Term Memory (LSTM). TBPTT rectifies exploding gradients by setting a limit for the number of steps through which an error can continue and LSTM counteracts vanishing gradients by utilizing recurrent edges featuring fixed unit weights.

Need to know

Encoder-Decoder Recurrent Neural Networks (EDRNN) and Bidirectional Recurrent Neural Networks (BRNN) are more examples of RNN networks. EDRNN is a framework that permits the RNN to learn how to map an input sequence to output sequences of variable lengths, which can be used to decode speech along with automating responses to speech. BRNNs differ from traditional causal structures used by a majority of other RNN frameworks because they make predictions based on the current data point in a sequence in relation to past and future data points. These predictions are useful in interpreting the meaning of sentences where each word is assessed in the context of all the values of the sentence. By accounting for the words on either side of the current word, many subtle linguistic dependencies are extrapolated, because the context of the sentence can cause words and phrases to have different meanings, and a bidirectional view lets the model be more likely to correctly extrapolate this context. BRNNs are also helpful in handwriting identification and identifying protein sequences from amino acid ordering (proteomics).

Recursive Neural Network

Recursive neural networks (not the same as RNNs) are non-linear adaptive models utilized to analyze data of variable length that feed the state of the network back into itself in a loop and that are capable of processing data structure inputs and are mostly suited for sentence and image deconstruction. Their architecture permits users to both determine the components of input data and quantitatively assess their relationships through a binary tree structure and a shared-weight matrix, which permits the recursive neural network to extrapolate from variable-length sequences of words and images. Recursive networks also have the advantage that for a sequence of length n, the depth (which is given as the number of compositions of nonlinear operations) can be taken from n to $log(n)$, which permits efficient capturing of long-term dependencies. Recursive neural networks typically have a top-down propagation method and a bottom-up feed-forward method. Both these mechanisms make up the propagation through a common structure found in the majority of recursive networks.

Two common types of recursive networks are the semi-supervised recursive autoencoder (used for deconstructing sentences for NLP applications) and the supervised recursive neural tensor (mainly used for computer vision applications).

A disadvantage of the majority of recursive neural networks is significant computational overhead (more than recurrent neural networks). Recursive networks are known for having long training times because they process excessive amounts of data, frequently with millions of parameters. Due to this, optimization techniques are consistently being created for these architectures, and large-scale use of recursive neural networks is enabled through advancements that have been made in parallel computing and the ever-growing advancement of processors.

Attention

The majority of modern neural network architectures use convolution and recurrence mechanisms as well as an encoder-decoder configuration, but an additional "attention" mechanism that's becoming more popular among numerous architectures is employed by attention networks. Attention can be thought of as focusing attention on the task at hand. For example, when fixing paint in a room, attention is placed on the area of the room currently being painted. Attention networks focus at different time steps on specific areas.

Models that use attention show greater prediction accuracy by locating global dependencies between data points and disregarding their distance in output and

Differences between CNN and RNN

CNN	RNN
CNN is applicable for sparse data like images.	RNN is applicable for temporary data and sequential data.
CNN is considered a more powerful tool than RNN.	RNN has fewer features and low capabilities compared to CNN.
The interconnection consumes a limited set of input and generates a limited set of output according to the input.	RNN can allow arbitrary input length and output length.
CNN is a clockwise and feed-forward oriented artificial neural network with a variety of multiple layers of perceptrons which is specially designed to utilize the minimum amount of pre-processing.	RNN works on a loop network which uses its internal memory to handle the arbitrary input sequences.
CNN's are special for video processing and image processing.	RNN works primarily on time series information on the past influence of the consumer. Analyzing if the user is going to talk next or not.
CNN follows interconnectivity patterns between the neurons which are based on the visual cortex of animals, where the neurons are organized so that they are responsible for overlapping areas throughout the visual field.	RNN works primarily on speech analysis and text analysis.

input sequences, and attention mechanisms also make calculations by the neural network more parallelizable. They are usually utilized along with convolution and recurrence, but, in a minimal portion of neural network architectures, attention may take the place of convolution and recurrence schemes. This architecture uses an attention scheme called intra-attention or self-attention, wherein multiple relationships are extrapolated between a data sequence's different positions. Thus, the Transformer's attention mechanism produces a more robust model creation by finding more patterns from input data.

7.5. Deep Learning based Highway Safety Studies

Deep learning has been widely used in highway safety research. Table 15 provides a list of studies which used different deep learning algorithms in different highway safety problems.

Table 15. Deep learning based highway safety studies

Algorithm	Research Area	Studies
DL Model	Patterns of Contributing Factors in Crashes	Dong et al. (2018)
	Crash Injury Analysis	Das et al. (2018)
	Safety Information Narratives	Dabiri and Heaslip (2019)
	Railroad Safety	Sheikh et al. (2004); Xia et al. (2018)
	Pipeline Safety	Mohamed et al. (2015); Layouni et al. (2017); Wu et al. (2017);
	Driver Behavior	Zhu et al. (2018); Kwon and Cho (2020)
CNN	Crash Frequency Analysis	Wu and Hsu (2021)
	Pedestrian Safety	Gauerhof et al. (2020); Li et al. (2020); Pourhomayoun (2020); Billones et al. (2018)
	Truck Safety	Alsanad et al. (2020); Dai et al. (2015); Haj Mosa et al. (2016)
	Pipeline Safety	Wu et al. (2019)
	Intersection Safety	Hu et al. (2020)
	Roadway Departure Safety	Zhang et al. (2018)
	Motorcycle Safety	Siebert and Lin (2020)

R-CNN	Real-Time Risk Assessment	Formosa et al. (2019)
	Incident Detection	Wu et al. (2020)
	Pedestrian Safety	Zhang et al. (2016)
LSTM	Real-Time Risk Assessment	Bao et al. (2019)
	Railroad Safety	Xia et al. (2018)
	Maritime Safety	Liu et al. (2020)
	Driver Behavior	Xie et al. (2019)
Feedforward Neural Network	Crash Injury Analysis	Assi et al. (2020)
MLP	Intersection Safety	Hu et al. (2020)
Deep Neural Network	Work Zone Safety	Chang et al. (2020)
Multilayer Feedforward Neural Network	Work Zone Safety	Chang et al. (2020)

Resources

Readers can consult the following curated lists of deep learning resources:
https://github.com/ChristosChristofidis/awesome-deep-learning
https://github.com/terryum/awesome-deep-learning-papers
https://github.com/endymecy/awesome-deeplearning-resources

Example Problem 1

Show a reproducible example of application of different DL algorithms in a crash count data analysis problem.

Solution: The following code chuck shows the replication code for DL algorithm application in crash count data analysis.

Example Problem 1 (Code Chunk 1)

```
## Please check my RPUBS for additional codes: https://rpubs.com/subasish

setwd("~folder location")
dat= read.csv("TAHIR_rwd1.csv")
table(dat$HwyClass)
head(dat)

dat1= subset(dat, HwyClass=="Rural Two-Lane")
dim(dat1)
```

(*Contd.*)

```
## 75% of the sample size
smp_size <- floor(0.75 * nrow(dat1))

## set the seed to make your partition reproducible
set.seed(123)
train_ind <- sample(seq_len(nrow(dat1)), size = smp_size)

train <- dat1[train_ind, ]
test <- dat1[-train_ind, ]

dim(train)
dim(test)

train_df= train[, c(4, 5, 7:11)]
test_df= test[, c(4, 5, 7:11)]
library(keras)
library(tfdatasets)
library(tensorflow)
library(tidyverse)
library(dplyr)

spec <- feature_spec(train_df, Total_Crash ~ . ) %>%
  step_numeric_column(all_numeric(), normalizer_fn = scaler_standard()) %>%
  fit()

spec

input <- layer_input_from_dataset(train_df %>% select(-Total_Crash))

output <- input %>%
  layer_dense_features(dense_features(spec)) %>%
  layer_dense(units = 64, activation = "relu") %>%
  layer_dense(units = 64, activation = "relu") %>%
  layer_dense(units = 1)

model <- keras_model(input, output)

summary(model)

model %>%
  compile(
    loss = "mse",
    optimizer = optimizer_rmsprop(),
    metrics = list("mean_absolute_error")
  )
  build_model <- function() {
  input <- layer_input_from_dataset(train_df %>% select(-Total_Crash))
```

```
    output <- input %>%
    layer_dense_features(dense_features(spec)) %>%
    layer_dense(units = 64, activation = "relu") %>%
    layer_dense(units = 64, activation = "relu") %>%
    layer_dense(units = 1)

  model <- keras_model(input, output)

  model %>%
    compile(
      loss = "mse",
      optimizer = optimizer_rmsprop(),
      metrics = list("mean_absolute_error")
    )
  model
}

# Display training progress
print_dot_callback <- callback_lambda(
  on_epoch_end = function(epoch, logs) {
    if (epoch %% 80 == 0) cat(„\n“)
    cat(".")
  }
)

model <- build_model()

history <- model %>% fit(
  x = train_df %>% select(-Total_Crash),
  y = train_df$Total_Crash,
  epochs = 200,
  validation_split = 0.2,
  verbose = 0,
  callbacks = list(print_dot_callback)
)
library(ggplot2)
plot(history)+theme_bw(base_size=16)

test_predictions <- model %>% predict(test_df %>% select(-Total_Crash))
test_df$pred= test_predictions[ , 1]
sum(test_df$Total_Crash)
sum(test_df$Total_Crash)

train_predictions <- model %>% predict(train_df %>% select(-Total_Crash))
train_df$pred= train_predictions[ , 1]

sum(train_df$Total_Crash)
sum(train_df$Total_Crash)
```

Figure 49 goes over the performance of training and validation data. The training data has a downward slope for both the graphs of loss and mean_absolute_error, and the validation data has a positive slope for both.

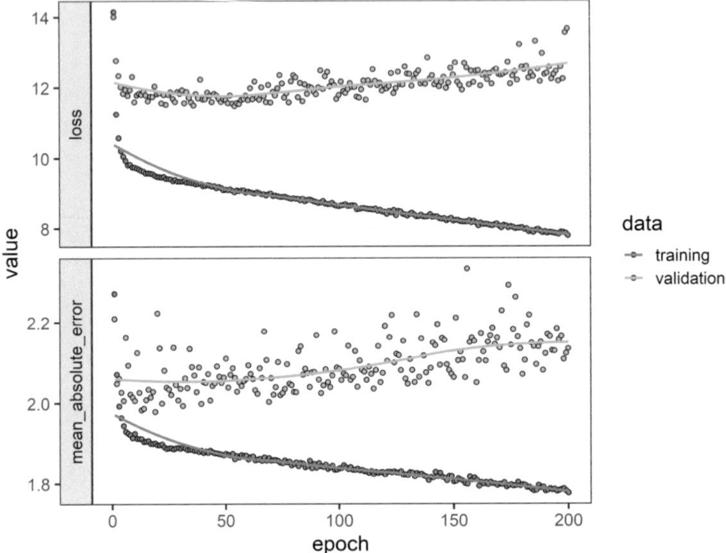

Figure 49. Performance of training and validation data.

Chapter Conclusion

This chapter provides details on some of the core and relevant deep learning algorithms. It documents topics such as LSTM, Monte Carlo sampling, Boltzmann machine learning, generative adversarial networks, and convolutional neural networks. It also provides descriptions on forward and backward propagation, pretrained unsupervised networks, autoencoders, deep belief networks, and recurrent and recursive neural networks. An example problem is also provided at the end of the chapter.

Further Reading

Bengio, Y., 2009. Learning Deep Architectures for AI. Now Publishers Inc.

Buduma, N. and Locascio, N., 2017. Fundamentals of Deep Learning: Designing Next-Generation Machine Intelligence Algorithms. O'Reilly Media, Inc.

Charniak, E., 2019. Introduction to Deep Learning. MIT Press.

Das, H., Pradhan, C. and Dey, N., 2020. Deep Learning for Data Analytics: Foundations, Biomedical Applications, and Challenges. Academic Press.

Das, S., Dutta, A., Dixon, K., Minjares-Kyle, L. and Gillette, G., 2018. Using deep learning in severity analysis of at-fault motorcycle rider crashes. Transportation Research Record: Journal of the Transportation Research Board, 2672, pp. 122–134.

Delen, D., Sharda, R. and Bessonov, M., 2006. Identifying significant predictors of injury severity in traffic accidents using a series of artificial neural networks. Accident Analysis & Prevention, 38, pp. 434–444.

Dogru, N. and Subasi, A., 2018. Traffic accident detection using random forest classifier. *In:* 2018 15th Learning and Technology Conference (L T). Presented at the 2018 15th Learning and Technology Conference (L T), pp. 40–45.

Dutta, A. and Das, S., 2020. Tweets about self driving cars: Deep Sentiment Analysis using Long Short-Term Memory network (LSTM). International Conference on Innovative Computing and Communications, pp. 515–523.

Foster, D., 2019. Generative Deep Learning: Teaching Machines to Paint, Write, Compose, and Play. O'Reilly Media, Inc.

Fullan, M., Quinn, J. and McEachen, J., 2017. Deep Learning: Engage the World Change the World. Corwin Press.

Goodfellow, I., Bengio, Y. and Courville, A., 2016. Deep Learning. MIT Press.

Hosseini, M., Lu, S., Kamaraj, K., Slowikowski, A., Venkatesh, H., et al. Chapter 1 Deep Learning Architectures, Springer Science and Business Media LLC, 2020.

Huang, H., Zeng, Q., Pei, X., Wong, S.C. and Xu, P., 2016. Predicting crash frequency using an optimised radial basis function neural network model. Transportmetrica A: Transport Science, 12, pp. 330–345.

Kelleher, J.D., 2019. Deep Learning. MIT Press.

Krizhevsky, A., I, Sutskever and G. Hilton, 2012. ImageNet Classification with Deep Convolutional Neural Networks. NIPS.

Krohn, J., Beyleveld, G. and Bassens, A., 2019. Deep Learning Illustrated: A Visual, Interactive Guide to Artificial Intelligence. Addison-Wesley Professional.

Li, G., Yang, Y. and Qu, X., 2020. Deep learning approaches on pedestrian detection in hazy weather. IEEE Transactions on Industrial Electronics, 67, pp. 8889–8899.

Patterson, J. and Gibson, A., 2017. Deep Learning: A Practitioner's Approach. O'Reilly Media, Inc.

Perrotta, P., 2020. Programming Machine Learning: From Coding to Deep Learning. Pragmatic Bookshelf.

Quinn, J., McEachen, J., Fullan, M., Gardner, M. and Drummy, M., 2019. Dive into Deep Learning: Tools for Engagement. Corwin Press.

Sejnowski, T.J., 2018. The Deep Learning Revolution. MIT Press.

Shanmugamani, R., 2018. Deep Learning for Computer Vision: Expert Techniques to Train Advanced Neural Networks Using TensorFlow and Keras. Packt Publishing Ltd.

Skansi, S., 2018. Introduction to Deep Learning: From Logical Calculus to Artificial Intelligence. Springer.

Szegedy, C., et al., 2014. Going Deeper with Convolutions. https://arxiv.org/abs/1409.4842

References

Alsanad, H.R., Ucan, O.N., Ilyas, M., Khan, A.U.R., Bayat, O., et al., 2020. Real-time fuel truck detection algorithm based on deep convolutional neural network. IEEE Access, 8, pp. 118808–118817.

Assi, K., Rahman, S.M., Mansoor, U. and Ratrout, N., 2020. Predicting crash injury severity with machine learning algorithm synergized with clustering technique: A promising protocol. International Journal of Environmental Research and Public Health, 17, 5497.

Bao, J., Liu, P. and Ukkusuri, S.V., 2019. A spatiotemporal deep learning approach for citywide short-term crash risk prediction with multi-source data. Transportation Research Board, p. 8.

Billones, R.K.C., Bandala, A.A., Lim, L.A.G., Culaba, A.B., Vicerra, R.R.P., et al., 2018. Vehicle-pedestrian classification with road context recognition using convolutional neural networks. *In:* 2018 IEEE 10th International Conference on Humanoid, Nanotechnology, Information Technology, Communication and Control, Environment and Management (HNICEM), pp. 1–6.

Chang, Y., Bharadwaj, N., Edara, P. and Sun, C., 2020. Exploring contributing factors of hazardous events in construction zones using naturalistic driving study data. IEEE Transactions on Intelligent Vehicles, 5, pp. 519–527.

Dabiri, S. and Heaslip, K., 2019. Developing a Twitter-based traffic event detection model using deep learning architectures. Expert Systems with Applications, 118, pp. 425–439.

Dai, F., Park, M.-W., Sandidge, M. and Brilakis, I., 2015. A vision-based method for on-road truck height measurement in proactive prevention of collision with overpasses and tunnels. Automation in Construction, 50, pp. 29–39.

Das, S., Dutta, A., Dixon, K., Minjares-Kyle, L., Gillette, G., et al., 2018. Using deep learning in severity analysis of at-fault motorcycle rider crashes. Transportation Research Record: Journal of the Transportation Research Board, 2672, pp. 122-134.

Dong, C., Shao, C., Li, J. and Xiong, Z., 2018. An improved deep learning model for traffic crash prediction. Journal of Advanced Transportation, 2018, p. 13.

Formosa, N., Quddus, M. and Ison, S., 2019. Predicting real-time traffic conflicts using deep learning. Transportation Research Board, p. 7.

Gauerhof, L., Hawkins, R., Picardi, C., Paterson, C., Hagiwara, Y., et al., 2020. Assuring the safety of machine learning for pedestrian detection at crossings. *In:* Casimiro, A., Ortmeier, F., Bitsch, F., Ferreira, P. (Eds.), Computer Safety, Reliability, and Security, Lecture Notes in Computer Science. Springer International Publishing, Cham, pp. 197–212.

Goodfellow, I., et al. 2014. Generative Adversarial Networks. Proceedings of the International Conference on Neural Information Processing Systems (NIPS 2014). pp. 2672–2680.

Haj Mosa, A., Kyamakya, K., Junghans, R., Ali, M., Al Machot, F., et al., 2016. Soft Radial Basis Cellular Neural Network (SRB-CNN) based robust low-cost truck detection using a single presence detection sensor. Transportation Research Part C: Emerging Technologies, 73, pp. 105–127.

Hu, J., Huang, M.-C. and Yu, X., 2020. Efficient mapping of crash risk at intersections with connected vehicle data and deep learning models. Accident Analysis & Prevention, 144, 105665.

Kwon, J.-H. and Cho, G.-H., 2020. An Examination of the intersection environment associated with perceived crash risk among school-aged children: Using street-level imagery and computer vision. Accident Analysis & Prevention, 146, 105716.

Layouni, M., Hamdi, M.S. and Tahar, S., 2017. Detection and sizing of metal-loss defects in oil and gas pipelines using pattern-adapted wavelets and machine learning. Applied Soft Computing, 52, pp. 247–261.

Liu, Y., Duan, W., Huang, L., Duan, S. and Ma, X., 2020. The input vector space optimization for LSTM deep learning model in real-time prediction of ship motions. Ocean Engineering, 213, 107681.

Mohamed, A., Hamdi, M.S. and Tahar, S., 2015. A machine learning approach for big data in oil and gas pipelines. *In:* 2015 3rd International Conference on Future Internet of Things and Cloud. Presented at the 2015 3rd International Conference on Future Internet of Things and Cloud, pp. 585–590.

Pourhomayoun, M., 2020. Automatic Traffic Monitoring and Management for Pedestrian and Cyclist Safety Using Deep Learning and Artificial Intelligence. Mineta Transportation Institute Publications.

Sheikh, Y., Zhai, Y., Shafique, K. and Shah, M., 2004. Visual monitoring of railroad grade crossing. Proceedings of SPIE – The International Society for Optical Engineering 5403.

Siebert, F.W. and Lin, H., 2020. Detecting Motorcycle Helmet Use with Deep Learning. Accident Analysis & Prevention, 134.

Wu, H., Qian, Y., Zhang, W. and Tang, C., 2017. Feature extraction and identification in distributed optical-fiber vibration sensing system for oil pipeline safety monitoring. Photonic Sens, 7, pp. 305–310.

Wu, H., Chen, J., Liu, X., Xiao, Y., Wang, M., et al., 2019. One-dimensional CNN-based intelligent recognition of vibrations in pipeline monitoring with DAS. J. Lightwave Technol., JLT, 37, pp. 4359–4366.

Wu, Y., Abdel-Aty, M., Zheng, O., Cai, Q., Zhang, S., et al., 2020. Automated Safety Diagnosis Based on Unmanned Aerial Vehicle Video and Deep Learning Algorithm: Transportation Research Record.

Wu, Y.-W. and Hsu, T.-P., 2021. Mid-term prediction of at-fault crash driver frequency using fusion deep learning with city-level traffic violation data. Accident Analysis & Prevention, 150, 105910.

Xia, T., Song, X., Fan, Z., Kanasugi, H., Chen, Q., et al., 2018. DeepRailway: A deep learning system for forecasting railway traffic. *In:* 2018 IEEE Conference on Multimedia Information Processing and Retrieval (MIPR). Presented at the 2018 IEEE Conference on Multimedia Information Processing and Retrieval (MIPR), pp. 51–56.

Xie, D.-F., Fang, Z.-Z., Jia, B. and He, Z., 2019. A data-driven lane-changing model based on deep learning. Transportation Research Part C: Emerging Technologies, 106, pp. 41–60.

Zhang, L., Lin, L., Liang, X. and He, K., 2016. Is faster R-CNN doing well for pedestrian detection? | SpringerLink, *In:* European Conference on Computer Vision. Presented at the European Conference on Computer Vision.

Zhang, X., Yang, W., Tang, X. and Wang, Y., 2018. Lateral distance detection model based on convolutional neural network. IET Intelligent Transport Systems, 13, pp. 31–39.

Zhu, M., Li, Y. and Wang, Y., 2018. Design and experiment verification of a novel analysis framework for recognition of driver injury patterns: From a multi-class classification perspective. Accident Analysis & Prevention, 120, pp. 152–164.

CHAPTER

8

Natural Language Processing

8.1. Introduction

The most frequently used data is text, and it makes up over 50% of unstructured data. Some examples are chat conversations, news, tweets or posts on social media, reviews of products or services, blogs and articles, and patient records in the health care sector. A relatively new example is the speech of voice-activated bots such as Siri and Alexa. Natural Language Processing should be utilized to gain noteworthy and actionable insights from text data and to discover its potential, along with deep learning and machine learning. However, what, exactly, is Natural Language Processing (NLP)? Machines/algorithms are not able to comprehend text or characters, so it is imperative to translate it into a machine-understandable format (i.e., numbers or binary) in order to complete any kind of text data analysis. Natural language processing allows machines to understand and interpret human language (in the form of text data).

Structured data is usually organized in databases, particularly relational databases. The high-level organization, typically represented by tables, enables easy and efficient processing, for instance, searching or filtering. Text data is usually considered to be unstructured. A newspaper article, e-mail, SMS, or a recipe in a cookbook definitely do not look like a table. However, because the texts are normally generated using the grammar of a natural language and rules of a certain linguistic style, they have some kind of structure. There exists another form of data between the structured and unstructured. It is the data that has some structure, but this structure does not conform to what is normally expected from structured data. It means that this structure cannot be directly converted to the structure of a relational database (tables). This data is known as semi-unstructured. Textual documents, especially those on the web, are a typical representation of this. In the semi-structured form, the structure is usually expressed by using some tags or other marks which identify and separate pieces of data and, thus, enable the creation of some data records and their relationships, which is often hierarchical (a tree of elements).

8.2. Text Mining

Finding useful knowledge in a collection of text documents involves many different steps. To arrange them into a meaningful order, one might look at the general text mining process. It includes these steps:

- ***Defining the problem*:** This step is actually independent of any actions which may subsequently be taken. Here, the problem domain needs to be understood and the questions to be answered need to be defined.
- ***Collecting the necessary data*:** The sources of texts containing the desired information need to be identified and the documents collected. The texts can come from within a company (internal database or archive) or from external sources – for example, from the web. In this case, web scrapers need to be frequently implemented to directly grab the content of the web pages. Alternatively, the API of some web-based systems can be used to retrieve the data. After retrieval, texts are stored so that they are ready for further analysis.
- ***Defining features*:** Features that well characterize the texts and are suitable for the given task need to be defined. The features are typically based on the content of the documents. A very simple approach, bag-of-words with binary attribute weighting, takes every word as a Boolean feature. Its value indicates whether or not the word is in a document. Other methods might use more complicated weighting schemes or features that are derived from the words (modified words, combinations of words).
- ***Analyzing the data*:** This is the process of finding patterns in the data. According to the type of task to be solved (e.g., classification), a specific model or algorithm is selected, and its properties and parameters are defined. Then, the model can be applied to the data and the solved problem's solution can be found. To answer a specific problem, more models are usually available. The choice is not explicitly given in advance. The models have different characteristics that influence the data mining process and its result. The model can be (white box) or does not have to be (black box) well interpretable by a human. Some models have higher computational complexity than others. According to the utilization of the model, fast creation can be preferred over fast application or vice versa. The suitability of a model is often strongly dependent on the data. The same model can provide excellent results for one data set while it can completely fail for another. Thus, selecting a proper model, finding the right structure for it, and tuning the parameters often requires a lot of experimental effort.
- ***Interpreting the results*:** Here, some results are obtained from the analysis. There is a need to carefully look at them and relate them to the problem one wanted to solve. This phase might include verification and validation steps in order to increase the reliability of the results.

Some of the words that are too common do not usually contribute (or contribute only negligibly) to achieving a certain goal. For example, in the query 'Find a hotel in Dhaka' (in Bangladesh) submitted to a web search engine, the word 'a' does not influence what will be retrieved by the search engine. The retrieved results will be the same no matter if 'a' is or is not in the query. The reason is simple – almost all documents written in English contain at least one occurrence of the word '*a*.' On the other hand, the word Dhaka is very important because without it the search engine would return information about hotels in many other locations.

Need to know

Tokenization is the process of splitting a document into pieces of text known as tokens. These tokens are often the words contained in the text. In most European languages where the words are space delimited, the task seems to be quite simple – split the text at the places where there are white spaces. In some other languages, like Chinese, where there are no spaces between words, the text needs to be analyzed in greater depth.

A word is the smallest lexical unit that can be used in isolation. A morpheme is the smallest unit of a word that carries some semantic or grammatical meaning. Morphemes typically include prefixes, suffixes, and a root. For example, the word unexpected consists of three morphemes: a prefix un-, a root expects, and a suffix -ed. Some morphemes can be used in a language by themselves (expect), while the others can't (un, ed). The former is known as free forms, the latter as bound forms.

Stems are parts of words that carry the basic meaning. When a stem consists of a single morpheme, it is identical to the root. Free stems can occur alone whereas bound stems cannot. Words are formed in a word-formation process using several rules. Inflection never changes the category of a word (e.g., a noun will be still a noun after adding a suffix) while derivation can change the category (a noun can become an adjective after adding a suffix).

It is obvious that the semantic meaning of some words, when created from the same stem, is very close. When a newspaper article contains one of the words sport, sports, sporting, sported, or sporty, it is quite likely to be an article from the sports category. However, for a computer, all five words are different, and to assign an article correctly to the category, all five words need to be connected to it – for example, in a classification rule.

The goal of syntactic parsing is to find out whether an input sentence is in a given language or to assign the structure to the input text. In order to assign the structure, the grammar of a language is needed. Since it is generally not possible to define rules that would create a parse for any sentence, statistical or machine learning parsers are very important. Complete parsing is a very complicated problem because ambiguities often exist. In many situations, it is enough to identify only unambiguous parts of texts. These parts are known as chunks, and they are found using a chunker or shallow parser. Shallow parsing (chunking) is thus a process of finding non-overlapping groups of words in the text that have a clear structure. Figure 50 illustrates the steps of NLP analysis, and Figure 51 shows examples of stemming and lemmatization.

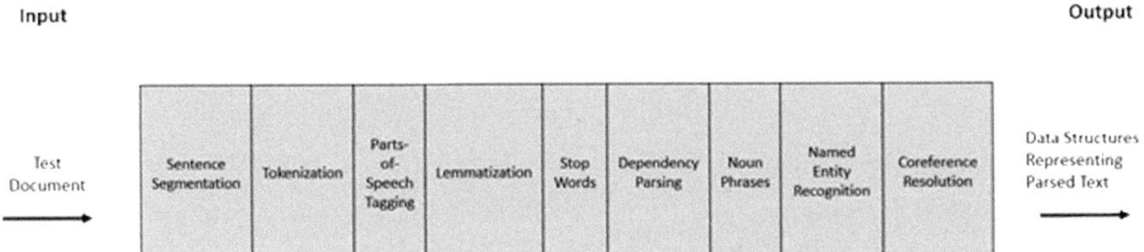

Figure 50. Steps of NLP analysis.

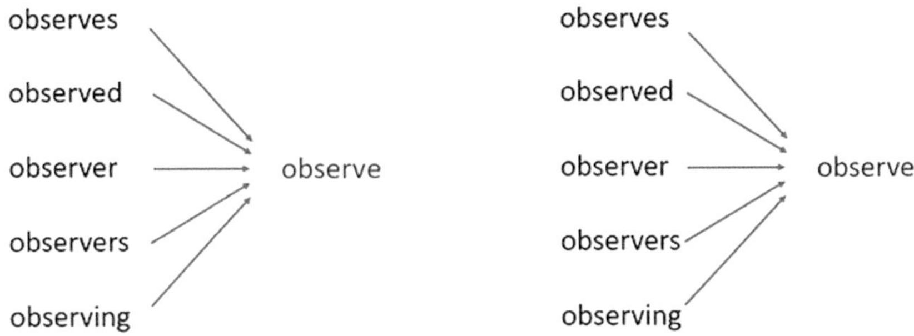

Figure 51. Stemming and lemmatization.

8.3. Topic Modeling

8.3.1. Latent Dirichlet Allocation

The latent Dirichlet allocation (LDA) model was created by Blei et al. (2003) to address issues of the probabilistic latent semantic analysis (PLSI) model, and it has since become a very popular topic model. The LDA model uses a K-dimensional latent random variable, which follows the Dirichlet distribution in order to show the topic mixture ratio of the document, to improve upon the PLSI model.

The LDA model is better able than other models to match the semantic conditions due to it having greater descriptive power. The LDA model's parameter space is simpler than the PLSI model, and the said space isn't pertinent to LDA's number of training documents. Subsequently, it is a hierarchical model with a stable structure that avoids any overfitting scenario. Due to this, the LDA model is viewed as a complete probability generative model.

Let V be the set of distinct words that appear at least once in a bag of words D_u for a user $u \in U$, and let U and D_u represent the set of users and the bag of words created by a user $u \in U$, respectively. Z is utilized by the user to represent the set of latent topics in which a parameter is how the number of topics is given. Each user u has unique preferences for the topics denoted by a probabilistic distribution $\overrightarrow{\theta_u}$, which is a multinomial distribution over Z in the generative process of LDA. Also, $\overrightarrow{\phi_z}$ denotes each topic z which has a multinomial distribution over V.

The visual representation of the LDA model is shown in Figure 52. The LDA generative process can be defined as:

- Consider a multinomial distribution $\phi_z \sim Dir(\vec{\beta})$ for every topic $z \in Z$.
- Consider a multinomial distribution $\phi_u \sim Dir(\vec{\alpha})$ for every user $u \in U$.
- For every word $w \in D_u$,
  - consider a topic z~*Multinomial* $\overrightarrow{\theta_u}$, .
  - consider a word w~*Multinomial* $(\overrightarrow{\phi_u})$.

The LDA model presumes that the multinomial distributions $\overrightarrow{\phi_z}$ and $\overrightarrow{\theta_z}$ are drawn from Dirichlet distributions (conjugate prior distributions), whose parameters are respectively given as $\vec{\beta}$ and $\vec{\alpha}$. Each word w in D_u is assumed to be selected by first drawing a topic z with following the topic preference distribution $\overrightarrow{\theta_u}$ and then choosing a word w from the corresponding distribution $\overrightarrow{\theta_z}$ of the chosen topic z. The probability of a word w being generated by a user u according to the LDA model is estimated as:

$$\int Dir(\theta_u; \alpha)\left(\Sigma_{z=1}^{|Z|}\ \theta_{uz}\phi_{zw}\right)d\theta_u, \tag{1}$$

8.3.2. Structural Topic Model (STM)

The STM is typically used to conduct textual analysis in linguistics and political science. STM and LDA are both Bayesian generative topic models that presume that each document is a mix of corpus-wide topics and that all topics are a distribution over words. STM advantages include document-level structure information presented to impact topic content (the distribution in topics of the keywords) and topical prevalence (i.e., topic proportions by document frequency). The STM highlights the suitability determination of studying how covariates impact text content (Hu et al., 2019).

The technical variations between the frameworks of the LDA and STM models are presented in Figure 52. Each node is signified by a variable that is marked by the role it plays in the data generating method. Shaded nodes are observed variables; the rectangles indicate replication. Unshaded nodes are hidden variables: $k \in \{1, 2,..., K\}$ catalogs each topic based on the user-selected number of topics, K $n \in \{1, 2, ..., N\}$ catalogs words in a document, and $d \in \{1, 2, ..., D\}$ represents the document indexes. Figure 52 also shows that in LDA and STM only node w (i.e., document's words) can be observed. The purpose of these two models is to identify the hidden topic information from the observed words, W, and output two critical matrices, topic-word distributions, β, and per-document topic proportions, θ. Additionally, it shows that LDA and STM have similar frameworks with three components: topical prevalence parameters, the core language model, and consideration of topical content parameters. LDA and STM have the same components of the core language model, where θ_d and $\beta_{d,k,v}$ represent the hidden per-document topic proportions and per-corpus topic-word distributions, respectively. $w_{d,n}$ represents the observed term, which is concluded from words indexed by $v \in \{1, 2, \ldots, V\}$. $z_{d,n}$ represents the hidden topic assignment of each observed term. The two-step generative method for each document d in the corpus is followed by the core language model of STM and LDA.

- **Step 1:** Randomly select a distribution for document d over topics θ_d.
- **Step 2:** In the document d for each word w_n, (1) from the distribution of topics θ_d in Step 1, select a random topic $z_{d,n}$, and (2) randomly select a word w_n from the matching distribution of the vocabulary $\beta_{d,k,v}$, where $k = z_{d,n}$.

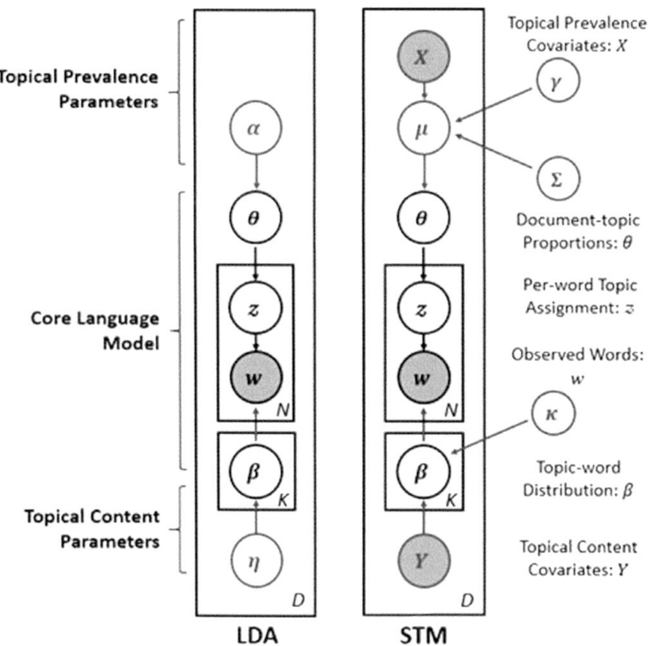

Figure 52. LDA and STM frameworks.

The topical prevalence parameters (i.e., those that impact document-topic proportions θ_d) and topical content parameters (i.e., those that impact topic-word distributions $\beta_{d,k,v}$) distinguish STM from LDA. Previous structures defined by generalized linear models parameterized by document-specific covariates $X(Y)$ replace the topical prevalence (content) parameters of STM, whereas those of LDA are specific shared prior Dirichlet parameters $\alpha(\eta)$ (Hu et al., 2019).

8.3.3. Keyword Assisted Topic Model

Suppose there are a total of D documents, and that all d documents have N_d words and contain a total of V unique words; in document d, where $W_d = \{w_{d_1}, w_{d_2}, \ldots, w_{dN_d}\}$ denotes the set of all words utilized in document d, let the ith word be represented by w_{di}. The topic of interest is recognizing the topics underlying each document. Two groups of topics are considered: *keyword topics*, which are the main topics of interest to researchers, and *no-keyword topics*, or topics with no keywords. Assume there is K number of topics, and that the first $\tilde{K}$ of them are keyword topics (i.e., $\tilde{K} \leq K$), and that for every keyword topic k, a set of L_k keywords, represented by $V_k = \{v_{k1}, v_{k2}, ..., v_{kLk}\}$ is given. The same keywords can be utilized for multiple keyword topics. Keywords are part of a total V distinctive words.

Need to know

Differences in STM compared to LDA are uncovered by the preceding algorithm differences, ensuring that, in theory, STM is more applicable in many research areas. STM pushes for document-level covariates (e.g., if reviews are negative or positive) to be added to the topical prevalence parameters which impact document-topic proportions, it encourages the addition of document-level covariates to the topic content parameters which impact the topic-word distributions, and it is an expansion of the associated topic model (wherein topics can be associated with each other) which allows the correlations among topics to be examined easily

---

The following data generation process is the basis for this model. For every word i in document d, the latent topic variable $z_{di} \in \{1, 2, ..., K\}$ must be drawn out of the document's topic distribution,

$$z_{di} \sim indepCategorical(\theta_d)$$

where θ_d is a K-dimensional vector of topic probabilities for the document d with $\Sigma_{k=1}^{K} \theta_{dk} = 1$. The document-topic distribution θ_d is depicted by the relative ratio of each topic in document d.

If a no-keyword topic is the sampled topic, then one draws the word w_{di} from the associated topic word distribution,

$$w_{di} \mid z_{di} = k \sim indep\ \ Categorical(\Phi_k) \ \text{ for } k \in \{\tilde{K}+1, \tilde{K}+2, ..., K\}$$

where for topic k with $\Sigma_{v=1}^{V} \ \Phi_{kv} = 1$, Φ_k is a V-dimensional vector of word probabilities. The relative frequency of each word within topic k is represented by this probability vector.

If there are keywords in the sampled topic, however, one first draws a Bernoulli random variable s_{di} with success probability π_k for word i in document d. If the said variable equals 1, then from the set of keywords word w_{di} is drawn for the topic using probability vector $\tilde{\Phi}_k$. If the variable equals 0, however, then one samples the word from the standard topic-word distribution

$$s_{di} \mid z_{di} = k \sim indep\ Bernoulli(\pi_k) \text{ for } k \in \{1, 2, ..., \tilde{K}\}$$

$$w_{di} \mid s_{di}, z_{di} = k \sim indep\ \{Categorical(\Phi_k) \text{ if}$$

$$s_{di} = 0\ Categorical(\tilde{\Phi}_k) \text{ if } s_{di} = 1 \text{ for } k \in \{1, 2, ..., \tilde{K}\}$$

where π_k is the likelihood of sampling from the set of keywords and $\tilde{\Phi}_k$ is a V dimensional vector of word probabilities for the set of keywords of topic k, i.e., V_k. Subsequently, L_k of V elements in $\tilde{\Phi}_k$ have positive values and the others are 0 (Das, 2021).

A mixture of two distributions is the foundation of the keyATM, one that has positive probabilities for all words and one that has positive probabilities for keywords only. This structure produces the previous means for the frequency of user-selected keywords given a topic larger than those of non-keywords in the same topic, and the previous variance is also greater for the frequency of keywords given a topic than it is for non-keywords, encouraging the keyATM to place greater importance on keywords, a priority while helping the model learn about the exact degree to which keywords are important for any particular topic from the data.

8.3.4. Text Summarization

Text summarization is the procedure of automatically creating a condensed version of a text with information that is useful to the user. The user's needs determine the information content of a summary.

Sentence's simple heuristic features (like their overall word frequency, their position in the text, or some significant phrases that indicate the sentences' importance) are the basis for early research on extractive summarization. The inverse document frequency, or IDF, is a measure that is frequently utilized to evaluate the significance of the words within a sentence, and is defined by the formula:

$$idf_i = log\ log\left(\frac{N}{n_i}\right) \tag{2}$$

Where n_i is the number of documents in which word i occurs and N is the total number of the documents in a collection. The words likely to occur in almost all of the documents (e.g., articles "the" and "a") have *idf* values closer to zero, whereas rarer words (e.g., proper nouns, medical terms) tend to have higher *idf* values.

More innovative techniques use anaphora resolution or synonyms of the words to consider the relationship between the discourse structure or sentences. As more training data becomes available and more features are proposed, researchers have attempted to integrate machine learning into summarization. The summarization approach evaluates the *centrality* of each sentence within a cluster and extracts the summary from the most central ones.

8.4. Sentence Centrality and Centroid-based Summarization

The centrality of the words contained in a sentence is frequently defined by the centrality of a sentence. A method that is often used to assess word centrality looks at the center of the document cluster in a vector space. The center of a cluster is a pseudo-document consisting of words with $tf \times idf$ scores that are over a previously defined threshold, wherein the frequency of a word in the cluster is *tf*, and *idf* values are generally calculated over a similar genre and a significantly larger data set.

8.5. Centrality-based Sentence Salience

A cluster of documents can be looked at as a network of related sentences.

The cosine between two corresponding vectors is how two sentences' similarity is defined:

$$idf\text{-}modified\text{-}cosine(x, y) = \frac{\Sigma_{w\in x,y}\ tf_{w,x}tf_{w,y}(idf_w)^2}{\sqrt{\Sigma_{xi\in x}\ (tf_{x_i,x}idf_{x_i})^2} \times \sqrt{\Sigma_{y_i\in y}\ (tf_{y_i,y}idf_{y_i})^2}} \tag{3}$$

in which $tf_{w,s}$ is the number of occurrences of the word w in the sentence s.

8.5.1. Eigenvector Centrality and LexRank

Each edge has been treated as a *vote* to figure out the overall centrality value of each node when computing degree centrality.

The quality of the summaries may be negatively impacted by degree centrality in some instances, wherein multiple undesirable sentences vote for each other and therefore raise their centrality.

This idea is formulated by considering how every node has a centrality value and distributing this centrality to its neighbors. This can be expressed by the equation

$$p(u) = \sum_{v\in adj[u]} \frac{p(v)}{\deg(v)} \tag{4}$$

where the set of nodes adjacent to u is $adj[u]$, the centrality of node u is $p(u)$, and $deg(v)$ is the degree of the node v. Equation 4 can be written in matrix notation as

$$p = B^T p \tag{5}$$

or

$${}^T B = p^T \tag{6}$$

where the adjacency matrix of the similarity graph is employed to obtain matrix B by dividing each component by the equivalent row sum:

$$B(i,j) = \frac{A(i, j)}{\Sigma_k\ A(i, k)} \tag{7}$$

A row sum equals the degree of the corresponding node; all row sums are nonzero since every sentence is similar at least to itself. p^T being the left eigenvector of the matrix B with the corresponding eigenvalue of 1 is stated in Equation 7. Some mathematical foundations are necessary to ensure that an eigenvector such as this exists and can be identified and computed.

8.5.2. Continuous LexRank

Using the *strength* of the similarity links shows one improvement over LexRank. If the cosine values are directly used to build the similarity graph, there is typically a much denser but weighted graph. The corresponding transition matrix's row sums can be normalized to give a stochastic matrix, and the subsequent equation is a modified version of LexRank for weighted graphs:

$$p(u) = \frac{d}{N} + (1-d) \sum_{v \in adj[u]} \frac{idf - modified\ - cosine(u, v)}{\Sigma_{z \in adj[v]}\ idf\ - modified\ - cosine(z, v)} p(v) \quad (8)$$

8.6. NLP Based Highway Safety Studies

NLP has been widely used in highway safety research. Table 16 provides a list of studies which used different NLP algorithms in different highway safety problems.

Table 16. NLP based highway safety studies

Algorithm	Research Area	Studies
Heuristic Method	Crash Record Text Mining	Nouioua (2008)
Rudimentary NLP Techniques	Railway Safety	Hughes et al. (2016)
CNN and RNN	Twitter-based Traffic Incident Detection	Dabiri and Heaslip (2019)
Topic Modelling	Driver Behavior	McLaurin et al. (2018)
	Motorcycle Safety	Das et al. (2021)
Speech Recognition	Airline Safety	Sun and Tang (2021)
	Airline Safety	Sun and Tang (2021)
Text Mining	Traffic Safety Culture	Sujon and Dai (2020)
	Public Opinion of Autonomous Vehicles	Das et al. (2019)
Content Analysis	Sustainability Analysis	Serna et al. (2017)

Resources

Julia Silge's blog is an excellent place to get some real training on text mining: https://juliasilge.com/blog/
Her book (Text Mining with R) is also a great resource: https://www.tidytextmining.com/

Case Study 1

It is anticipated that racism is a critical issue in tourism related reviews. Apply NLP tools to identify trends and patterns from these reviews.

***Solution*:**

The data has been collected from a Li et al. study (2020). For this case study, U.S. based comments and reviews were selected. A total of 1,333 reviews (with the highest number of reviews from Nevada, i.e., 294) were included in the dataset. Heatmaps of the states by the number of reviews/comments for four different timelines: 1) 2007-2015, 2) 2016, 3) 2017, and 4) 2017-2018 are shown in Figure 53. Nevada was the state with the most participants in each of the time periods; from 2007-2015 Nevada had approximately 150 reviews, in both 2016 and 2017 it had approximately 40 reviews, and from 2018-2019 the state had approximately 60 reviews. New York (98 reviews), California (83 reviews), Texas (76 reviews), Georgia (75 reviews), and Tennessee (70 reviews) also had a large number of reviews. The number of participants increased in the other states from the first time period (2007-2015) to the most recent time period (2018-2019) in several states, including Alabama, California, Florida, New York, Tennesee, and Texas.

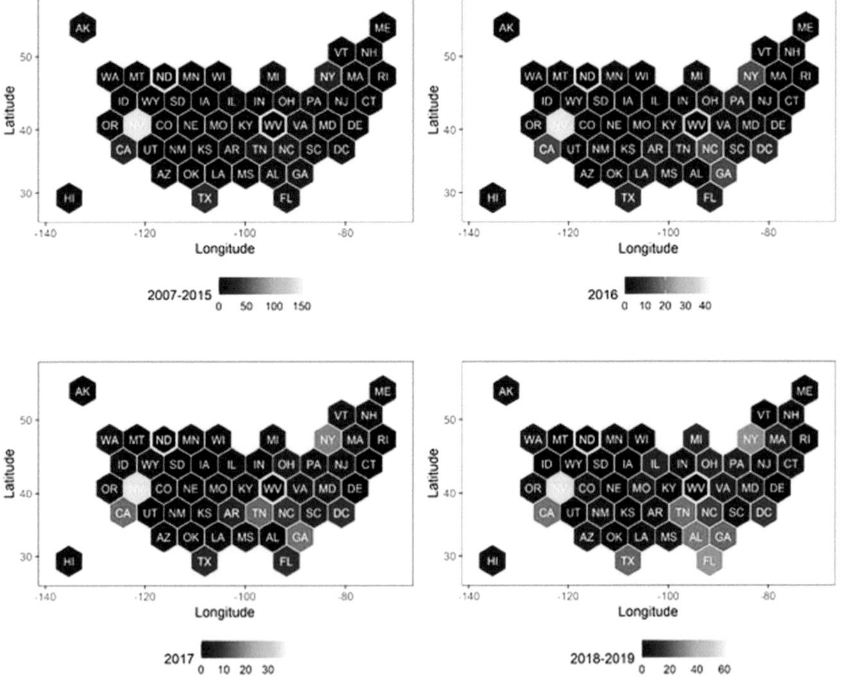

Figure 53. Number of reviews by state.

Three venues were the basis for the reviews: attraction (855 reviews), restaurant (309 reviews), and hotel (169 reviews). The top three states for the number of reviews by attraction are Nevada (288 reviews), New York (75 reviews), and Tennessee (56 reviews). The top three states for hotel-related and restaurant-related reviews, respectively, are Florida (25 reviews), California (24 reviews), and Texas (18 reviews) and California (36 reviews), Texas (28 reviews), and Florida (25 reviews). It is difficult to show this information in a single visualization. Alluvial plots could be suitable to show in between and within the distribution of the categorical information; the height of the black bars indicates the within proportions, and it clearly shows that Nevada and attraction are two major contributors in the state and venue type variables. The in-between proportions of the state and venue type are shown by the links and the width of the links.

Co-occurrence Analysis

An importation step of network analysis is co-occurrence analysis. The co-occurrence of the words in network visualization is shown in Figure 54. There are nine different clusters that contain a wide array of topics, with three visible major clusters (cluster 1 is related to Las Vegas (Nevada)-related trip reviews; cluster 2 is associated with 'museum'-related trip reviews; cluster 3 is mostly associated with the experience-related reviews and comments and some of the racism-related keywords, e.g., black guy, crude humor, dirty joke, racist humor, and racial humor). Several race/racial related topics are in cluster 3; these keywords, however, are generated based on the black history museum-related reviews and include keywords such as racial equality, mass incarceration, Nazi, Hitler, pain, genocide, enslavement, death, bigot, lynching, and victim.

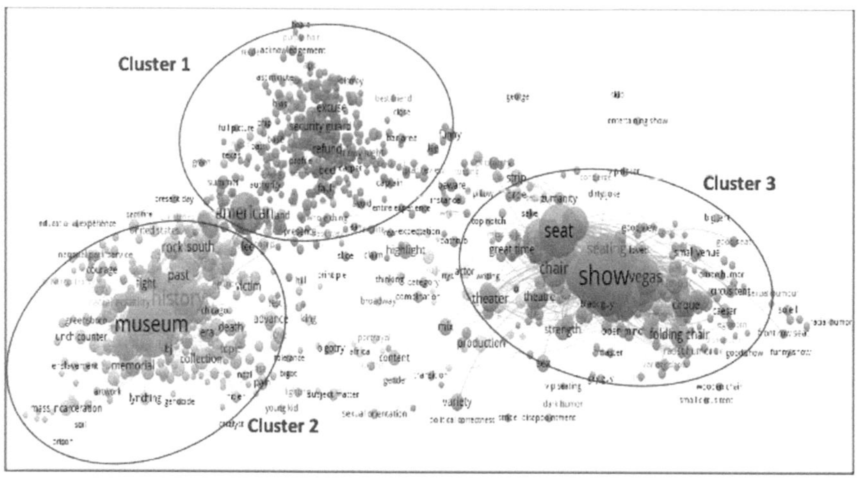

Figure 54. Co-occurrence of the words in the review documents.

Figure 53 is used to generate Figure 54 by using clusters to show the keyword distribution. The co-occurrence of the keywords and their association patterns is better understood through the use of these plots.

Emotion Mining

An initial analysis of corpus-level (a set of texts or documents) emotion mining was first conducted by this study. The NRC Emotion Lexicon contains eight basic emotions (anticipation, surprise, joy, trust, anger, disgust, fear, and sadness) as well as a list of words and their positive and negative sentiment associations based on three prominent studies. The *R* package 'sentimentr,' with the functionality of producing proportional measures by 16 emotion clusters (eight basic emotions and eight negated emotions), was used in this study to perform emotion mining. Figure 55 shows this package's distribution of the emotion patterns by 16 clusters. In comparison to the six other emotion types, joy and trust show higher emotional propensities. This study (based on the proportional emotion measures) ranked the reviews based on two emotion groups: 1) anger-disgust and 2) fear-sadness. The topic models were developed by the top 500 reviews, which the next section discusses.

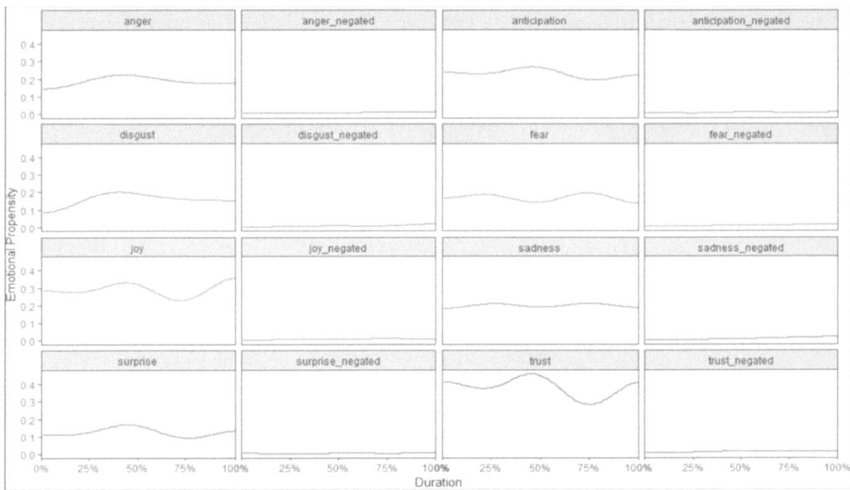

Figure 55. Distribution of the topics based on eight sentiments and their negations.

Anger Disgust Corpora

Value w denotes a vector of N words in document i (considering a total of M documents) in LDA. Each document is a configuration of topics represented by some topic distribution θ over the document i due to the fact that a topic z is assigned to each word w_j of a document i. Low α values indicate that the topics are sparsely distributed in the documents while high α values indicate that each document has a relatively even distribution of the topics. Similarly, low β values signify a sparse distribution of words in each topic while a high β value represents that topics are relatively distributed in the vocabulary of words.

Six topic models based on the 'anger disgust' corpora are shown in Figure 56. Topic 1 and Topic 4 are hotel and food quality-related. The rest of the topics involve some form of 'racist/racism.' Topic 2, Topic 3, and Topic 5 include the term 'museum.' Topic 2 and Topic 3 represent that these topics are related to 'black history' and 'museum.' The usage of racism and slurs in hotels, restaurants, and other places is represented in Topic 5. The usage of racist terms or jokes in tourism-related reviews is also shown in Topic 6.

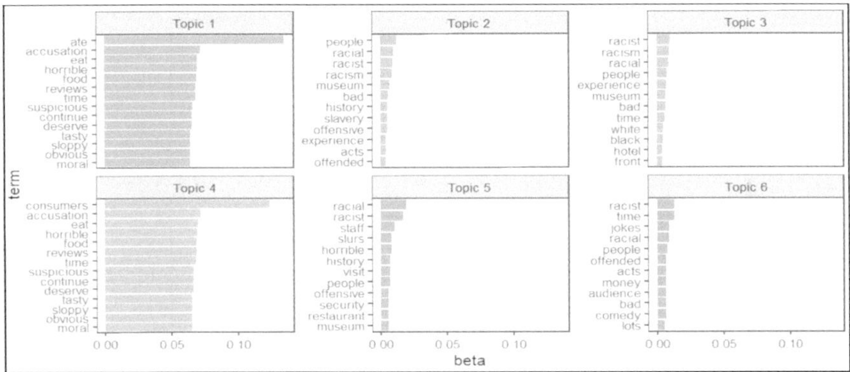

Figure 56. Topic models from 'anger-disgust' corpora.

Fear Sadness Corpora

Six topic models based on the 'fear sadness' corpora are shown in Figure 57. Topic 3, Topic 4, and Topic 5 are related to 'museum.' The usage of 'racist' terms in 'attraction' (e.g., music festival)-related reviews is represented in Topic 1. Hotel-related terms are in Topic 2. The usage of 'racism'-related terms in the reviews associated with different sectors of tourism is displayed in Topic 6.

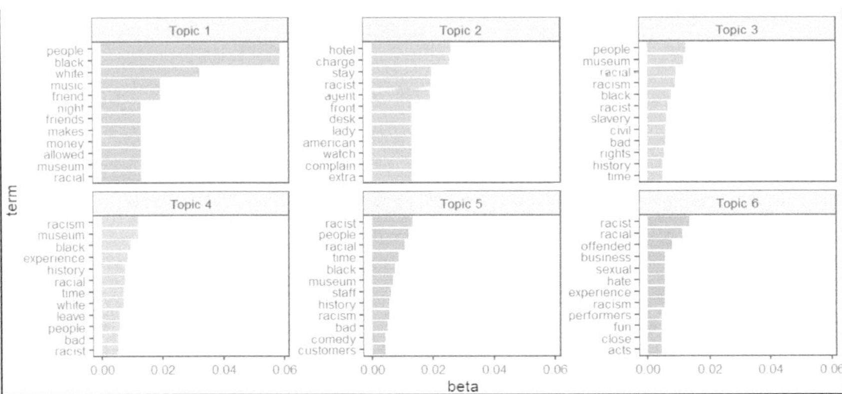

Figure 57. Topic models from 'fear-sadness' corpora.

Interactive Topic Model Visualization

A basic compact technique that is thorough is interactivity. It is an important technique for creating LDA visualizations to account for various challenges. The 'LDAvis' package was utilized in this study to create interactive LDA models based on two highlighted topics (museum and racism) which are displayed in Figure 58 and Figure 59. A weblink was developed in this study to demonstrate these interactive plots. Two sections are contained in the plots:

- A worldwide perspective of the topic model (shown in circles) in a two-dimensional space is represented in the left section. The space between topics and their projections of the inter-topic distances onto two dimensions using multidimensional scaling is the basis for the centroids of the topics. In order to organize the topics by decreasing prevalence, the areas of the circles are used to encode each topic's overall prevalence. The nearer the distance is, the higher the relevance. For example, topic 3, topic 11, and topic 16 are related to the 'museum' topic, and topic 1, topic 2, topic 4, topic 5, topic 7, topic 9, and topic 17 are 'racism' specific topics.
- A horizontal bar chart highlighting the top 30 most significant terms for a specific topic (based on hovering over the circles) is highlighted in the right section. To understand the meaning of each topic by looking at the main terms in it, one must pinpoint what the most important terms are in the topic. The corpus-wide occurrence of a particular term and its topic-specific occurrence are exemplified by a pair of overlaid bars.

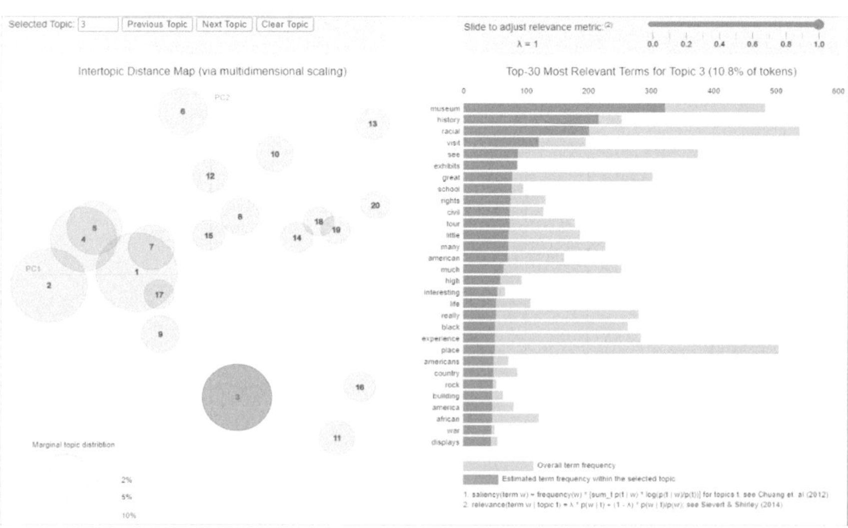

Figure 58. 20 topic models in two-dimensional space (3, 11, 16 topic models are 'museum' specific topics).

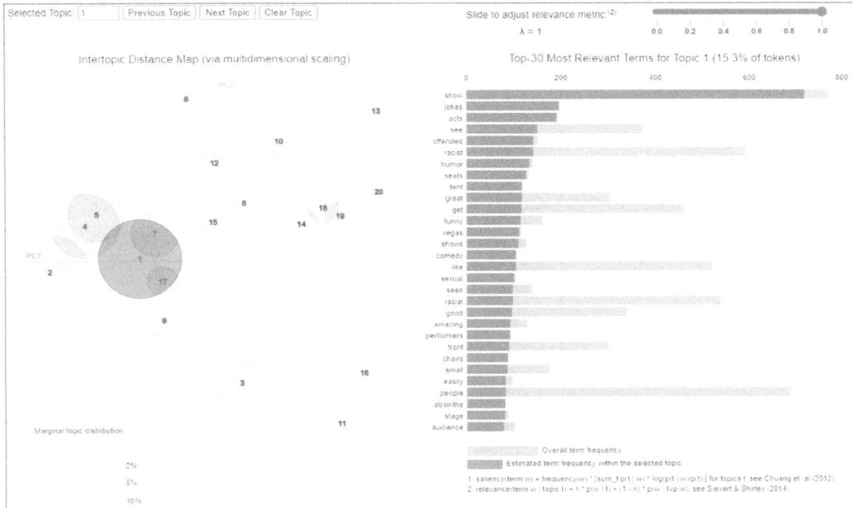

Figure 59. 20 topic models in two-dimensional space (1, 2, 4, 5, 7, 9, and 17 are 'racism' specific topics).

- The segments of this visualization are inter-connected. The visualization emphasizes the most helpful terms (on the right) for understanding the topic selected by the user (on the left). Additionally, the conditional distribution over topics (on the left) is revealed by picking a term (on the right). These capabilities allow for users to efficiently examine many topic-term relationships.

Case Study 2

YouTube is an important source of conflict data. Provide an example by showing how YouTube data can be used to understand a transportation safety issue.

***Solution*:**

To collect the 'bicycle hitting pedestrian'-related videos in YouTube, the following terms were used to develop a detailed list of keywords: "*walking biking collision*," "*biker hits ped*," "*bicyclist hit pedestrian*," "*pedestrian bike crash or incident or accident*," "*pedestrian bicyclist crash or incident or accident*." "Tuber," an open-source *R* software package, was employed to automate the data collection (extraction of the video information along with related comments) process. Another online YouTube comment scrapper has also been used. To perform this analysis, several open-source *R* software packages were used. Figure 60 shows a flowchart of data collection and analysis.

Table 17 gives the top ten most viewed video descriptive statistics. 26,122 was the final number of comments after the removal of non-English and redundant comments. One video in the top ten videos had an earlier release (in 2010). The total views for all the videos was 6,799,938 (mean: 679,994, standard deviation:

1,098,276). On all videos, the number of likes was higher than dislikes (55,482 vs. 7,670). The number of comments was 26,122 (mean: 2,612; standard deviation: 4,901). In these videos, participants also replied to the comments. The replies to the comments were also collected and analyzed in this study. The corpora have around 2,000 replies, based on all replies.

Table 17. Clusters of top-viewed 10 YouTube videos on 'bicyclists hitting pedestrians'

Video Id	Title	Publish Date	Duration (min.)	Views	Likes	Dislikes	Comments
zR4Okh23Zlo	Cyclist hits pedestrian	11-Aug-13	2:06	3,099,255	31,000	2,700	14,737
sYWPHHo0fPU	Pedestrian gets hit, cyclists talk, cops	26-Oct-16	6:33	2,255,886	12,000	4,300	7,939
Wq6rpVMcyas	Cyclist crashes into man full video	12-Nov-17	0:59	748,883	8,300	187	1,424
G4K8AjNIVPA	Angry pedestrian blocks cyclist as he races through zebra crossing	28-Sep-16	0:27	401,683	2,500	146	1,429
0Lm9TPym9A4	Man gets hit by bike	14-Aug-10	0:37	250,312	1,500	288	371
5Qurlf05YYI	Pedestrian and bicycle accident on Venice Beach	1-Apr-13	0:39	20,050	58	15	77
dnkErN9N8KY	Pedestrian hit by bicycle in San Francisco	15-Mar-17	1:44	9,989	51	7	41
uRoU826ywjw	Cyclist hits pedestrian	18-May-15	0:44	6,138	25	23	55
dXpmxmFW164	Accident on the bicycle lane	6-Apr-15	1:50	4,585	26	6`	23
s-PuD8fSI-I	Pedestrian almost hit by cyclist	15-Jul-14	0:34	3,157	22	4	26

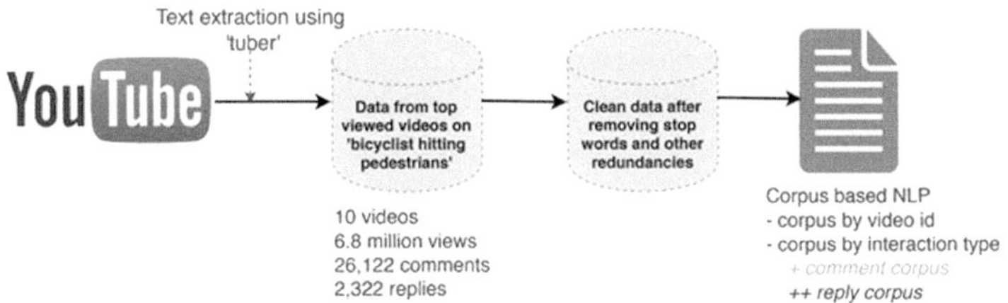

Figure 60. Flowchart of data collection and analysis.

Methodology

Term Frequency-Inverse Document Frequency

Rather than utilizing the frequencies of a word or word group, we can look at the inverse document frequency (IDF) of a term. This concept was introduced by Spark Jones in 1972. One comment for a video *id* can be considered as a document. A compilation of comments based on video *ids* or any other specific clusters can be considered as a corpus. It considers the database term distribution and the database size; for frequently used words, it decreases the weight, and for words that are not commonly used, it increases the weight. For any given term, the *IDF* is given as:

$$DF(term) = ln\left(\frac{N}{d_i}\right) \tag{9}$$

Where,

The total number of documents in the database is N

The number of documents in the database containing the word i is d_i

This is joined with the term frequency to compute a term's $TF - IDF$ (which are the two quantities multiplied together, $TF \times IDF$). This parameter is usually used to identify the significant words within each document's content. It does so by minimizing the weight of words that are often used and increasing the weight of not frequently used words in a corpus of the document. Calculating $TF - IDF$ aims to discover words that are significant in a text but not very frequent in all documents. The final parameter weight, w_i, for $TF - IDF$ is written as:

$$TF - IDF(w_i) = f_i \times \log\left(\frac{N}{d_i}\right) \tag{10}$$

Where,

f_i = the word i's frequency in the document.

Table 18 displays the $TF - IDF$ values for the two categories based on interaction types. All comments or replies for each of these videos are combined by video *ids* for determining $TF - IDF$ measures. As unigrams are not suitable in explaining the intent of the topics, bigrams are considered in this analysis. A threshold of 200 counts is considered as the baseline for comment corpora. For the reply corpora, this threshold was 20. The majority of the bigrams overlap in both categories. Intersection, signal phases, bike lanes, and lighting conditions are the most common bigrams in both categories. The bigrams 'the crosswalk' and 'parents' fault' are present in the comment category analysis. In the reply categories, two unique bigrams are 'walk on' and 'walk in.'

Table 18. TF-IDF of the top bigrams from comment and reply corpora

VID	Bigram	TF	IDF	TF-IDF
Comments				
sYWPHHo0fPU	the light	0.00331	1.20397	0.00398
zR4Okh23Zlo	bike lane	0.00567	0.69315	0.00393
sYWPHHo0fPU	the intersection	0.00197	1.60944	0.00317
sYWPHHo0fPU	yellow light	0.00124	2.30259	0.00286
sYWPHHo0fPU	red light	0.00232	1.20397	0.00279
sYWPHHo0fPU	light was	0.00152	1.60944	0.00245
zR4Okh23Zlo	bike path	0.00218	0.91629	0.002
zR4Okh23Zlo	parents fault	0.0007	2.30259	0.00162
sYWPHHo0fPU	the crosswalk	0.00146	0.91629	0.00134
sYWPHHo0fPU	slow down	0.00177	0.69315	0.00123
Replies				
sYWPHHo0fPU	the light	0.004216	1.504077	0.006342
zR4Okh23Zlo	walk on	0.001681	2.197225	0.003694
zR4Okh23Zlo	bike path	0.001639	2.197225	0.003602
sYWPHHo0fPU	the intersection	0.00233	1.504077	0.003505
sYWPHHo0fPU	light was	0.001498	2.197225	0.003291
sYWPHHo0fPU	was red	0.001387	2.197225	0.003047
zR4Okh23Zlo	cycle lane	0.001303	2.197225	0.002863
sYWPHHo0fPU	red light	0.002441	1.098612	0.002682
zR4Okh23Zlo	walk in	0.001177	2.197225	0.002586
sYWPHHo0fPU	slow down	0.002164	1.098612	0.002377

Sentiment Analysis

Subjective text mining on texts that contain opinions or sentiments allows us to comprehend the perception towards a product. Essentially, the aim of sentiment analysis is to figure out which sentences and words express which feelings, opinions, and sentiments. The sentiment score can be easily calculated by using the number of positive words or sentences minus the number of negative words or sentences. This case study used 'udpipe' inbuilt functions to determine the sentiment scores. Boxplot boxes (shown in Figure 61) represent the 25th percentile, the median, and the 75th percentile. Boxplot whiskers represent the 5th percentile and the 95th percentile. The individual sentiment scores are overlaid on the boxplot as the dot-plot format. The values show that the median of the majority of the video comment groups is below zero, which indicates the nature of higher negative sentiments in these videos.

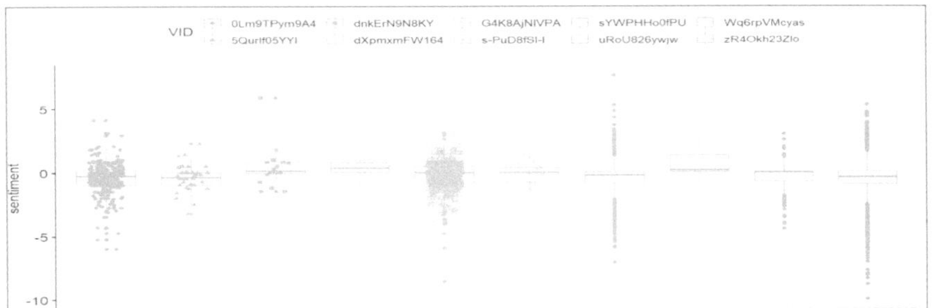

Figure 61. Boxplot of individual sentiment scores by video *id*.

The descriptive statistics of the sentiment scores by the video *ids* are shown in Table 19. Each video identification number (VID) is listed with the minimum, maximum, mean, and standard deviation of each comment and reply. The video with the highest comment average is dnkErN9N8KY (Pedestrian hit by a bicycle in San Francisco) with 0.39. It also has the highest maximum, minimum, and standard deviation.

Table 19. Descriptive statistics of sentiment scores by videos

VID	Max		Min		Mean		STD	
	Comment	Reply	Comment	Reply	Comment	Reply	Comment	Reply
0Lm9TPym9A4	4.10	0.80	–6.00	–2.65	–0.43	–0.71	1.22	0.88
5Qurlf05YYI	2.25	2.80	–3.25	–0.75	–0.41	0.75	1.01	1.20
dnkErN9N8KY	5.85	5.85	–1.50	–2.50	0.39	–0.03	1.53	1.72
dXpmxmFW164	1.05	0.80	–1.00	–1.00	0.26	–0.07	0.75	0.90
G4K8AjNIVPA	3.10	3.10	–8.60	–4.85	–0.28	–0.30	1.13	1.22
s-PuD8fSI-I	1.40	1.40	–1.75	–1.40	–0.13	–0.04	0.84	0.89
sYWPHHo0fPU	7.60	–	–7.15	–	–0.37	–	1.06	–
uRoU826ywjw	2.80	4.80	–0.75	–7.15	0.68	–0.32	1.15	1.27
Wq6rpVMcyas	3.00	1.00	–4.50	–4.10	-0.33	–0.38	0.85	0.84
zR4Okh23Zlo	5.30	5.30	–10.00	–6.45	–0.49	–0.42	1.15	1.32

Emotion Mining

For the emotion mining tasks, this study considers eight major emotion types and their negations. The trends of the emotions are shown at the sentence level (shown in Figure 62). This method uses sentiment lexicons to find emotion-related words and then computes the emotion propensity per sentence (34). The x-axis indicates the number of documents in percentage form. For example, if the analysis is conducted on 100 documents, 25% will indicate the 25th document, and if the vertical line is drawn on 25%, the intersecting points will be the emotion propensity score for that particular sentence. This visualization helps in understanding the overall trends of the emotions expressed by the participants. The general finding is that the negated terms are less in propensity scores than the main emotion-related words. Sadness and anger are the top two emotions in the 'comment' category. For the 'reply' category, anger shows the highest propensity. Sadness shows a declining trend over the duration of the sentences.

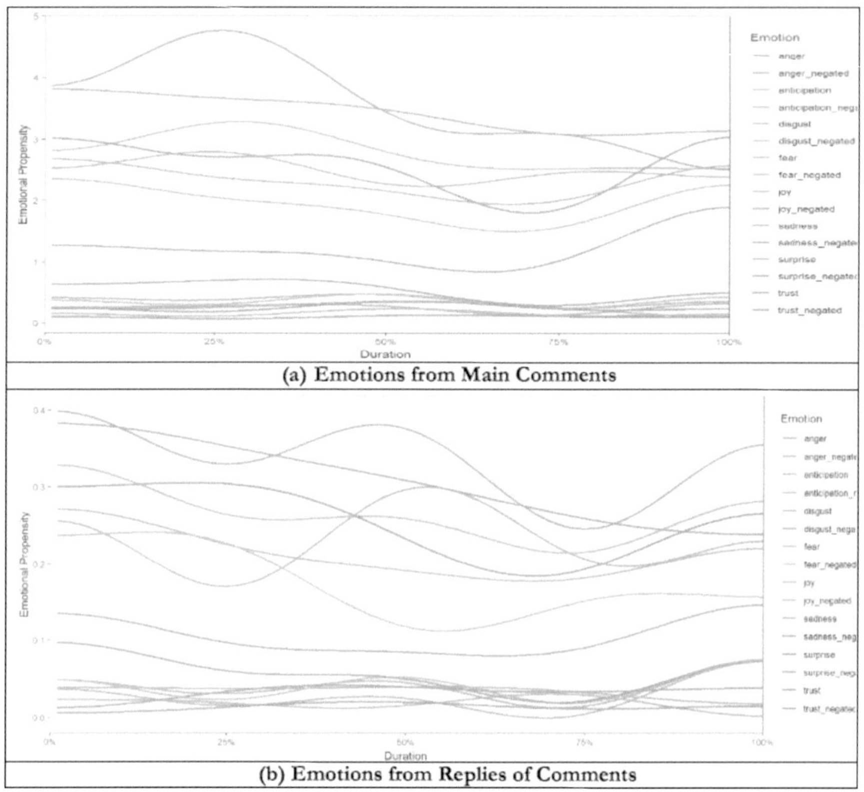

(a) Emotions from Main Comments

(b) Emotions from Replies of Comments

Figure 62. Individual *tf-idf* for texts categorized by content type.

Valence Shift Word Graphs

Dodds and Danforth (2009) provided the importance of the 'Valence Shift Word Graph.' Take into consideration two texts T_{ref} (for reference) and T_{comp} (for comparison) with sentiment scores $s_{mean}^{(ref)}$ and $s_{mean}^{(comp)}$. Comparison of T_{comp} relative to T_{ref} can be expressed as:

$$s_{mean}^{(comp)} - s_{mean}^{(ref)} = \sum_{i=1}^{N} s_{mean}(w_i)\left[p_i^{(comp)} - p_i^{(ref)}\right] \tag{11}$$

$$= \sum_{i=1}^{N} \left[s_{mean}(w_i) - s_{mean}^{(ref)}\right]\left[p_i^{(comp)} - p_i^{(ref)}\right]$$

where,

p_i = the i –th unique word's normalized occurrence frequency and which one interprets as a probability, and

$$\Sigma_{i=1}^{N} s_{mean}^{(ref)}\left[p_i^{(comp)} - p_i^{(ref)}\right] = s_{mean}^{(ref)}\,\Sigma_{i=1}^{N}\left[p_i^{(comp)} - p_i^{(ref)}\right]$$

$$= s_{mean}^{(ref)}(1-1) = 0, \qquad (12)$$

w_i denotes the word i in comparison text, and p_i denotes the percentage of word i in the comparison text.

By introducing the term $-s_{mean}^{(ref)}$, the contribution of the ith word to the difference $s_{mean}^{(comp)} - s_{mean}^{(ref)}$ can be clear. Two major pieces in determining the sign of the ith word's contribution to the sentiment score are considered:

- Whether the ith word is, on average, more positive than text T_{ref}'s average, $s_{mean}^{(ref)}$.
- Whether the ith word is relatively more abundant in text T_{comp} than in text T_{ref}.

A word's sentiment is signified relative to text T_{ref} by + (positive sentiment) and – (negative sentiment), and its relative abundance in text T_{comp} versus text T_{ref} with ↑ (more prevalent) and ↓ (less prevalent). The combination of these two binary possibilities leads to four cases:

- +↑: Increased use of relatively positive words– if a word is happier than text T_{ref} (+) and appears relatively more often in text T_{comp} (↑), then the contribution to the difference $s_{mean}^{(comp)} - s_{mean}^{(ref)}$ is positive.
- –↓: Decreased use of relatively negative words– if a word is less happy than text T_{ref} (–) and appears relatively less often in text T_{comp} (↓), then the contribution to the difference $s_{mean}^{(comp)} - s_{mean}^{(ref)}$ is also positive.
- +↓: Decreased use of relatively positive words– if a word is happier than text T_{ref} (+) and appears relatively less often in text T_{comp} (↓), then the contribution to the difference $s_{mean}^{(comp)} - s_{mean}^{(ref)}$ is negative.
- –↑: Increased use of relatively negative words– if a word is less happy than text T_{ref} (–) and appears relatively more often in text T_{comp} (↑), then the contribution to the difference $s_{mean}^{(comp)} - s_{mean}^{(ref)}$ is also negative.

The normalization of Equation 12 and the conversion to percentages becomes:

$$\delta s_{mean,i} = \frac{100}{\left|s_{mean}^{(comp)} - s_{mean}^{(ref)}\right|}\left[S_{mean}(w_i) - s_{mean}^{(ref)}\right]_{\smile} +/-\left[p_i^{(comp)} - p_i^{(ref)}\right]_{,\smile\uparrow/\downarrow} \qquad (13)$$

Where $\sum_i \delta s_{mean,i} = \pm 100$, depending on the sign of the difference in sentiment between the two texts, $s_{mean}^{(comp)} - s_{mean}^{(ref)}$, and the terms to which the symbols +/– and ↑/↓ apply have been indicated. The $\delta s_{mean,i}$ is referred to as the per word sentiment shift of the ith word. Figure 63 is interpreted as follows:

- A greater frequency of positive emotions is shown by words on the right.
- Negative emotions being used less is denoted by a yellow bar with a down arrow on the right.
- Positive emotion being used more is denoted by a purple bar with an up arrow on the right.
- A decrease in position emotions in the corpus is denoted by words on the left.
- Negative emotions being used more is denoted by a yellow bar with an up arrow on the left.
- Positive emotions being used less is denoted by a purple bar with a down arrow on the left.

The word shift plots are not significantly different between the corpora (plural of corpus) developed for comments and replies. However, the degree of negative emotions is less used in the replies. Some of the terms, such as bike, are considered as positive emotions due to the use of conventional sentiment lexicons. There is a need to develop a highway safety-related sentiment-lexicon to precisely capture the domain-specific sentiments and emotions, which is outside the parameters of the present study.

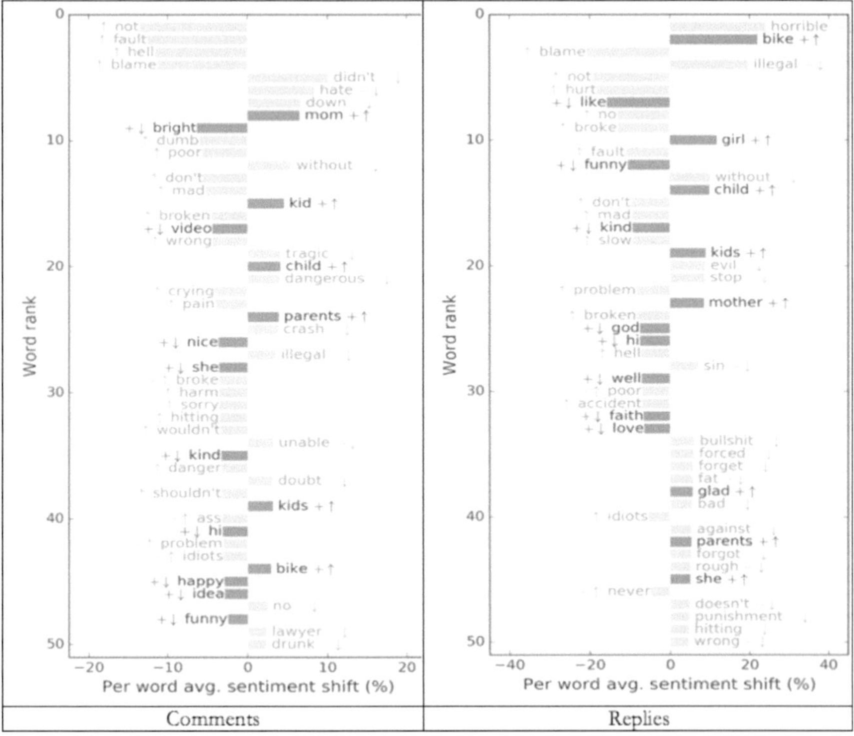

Figure 63. Valence shift word graphs based on comments and replies.

Co-occurrence of Negative Terms

The majority of the sentiment analysis and emotion mining studies perform only *n*-gram related studies to determine the sentiments and emotions over the corpus, document, or sentence level. One area that is less explored is the investigation on determining the relation of other words with the negative sentiments and emotions. This approach will help answer what is causing a negative sentiment or negative emotion. The Stanford Dependencies (SD) representation was initially created as an applied representation of English syntax, directed at natural language understanding (NLU) applications. This is deeply associated with grammatical relation-based syntactic concepts. The dependency relationship output of 'udpipe' was used to figure out which words are linked to negative words from the 'udpipe' sentiment dictionary. Out of several parameters, this study used mainly the parameters associated with adjectives that modify a noun. Before conducting the dependency parsing, this study used the conventional NLP annotation (tokenization, lemmatization, and parts of speech tagging). The lemma values of the negative words and the lemma values of the parent word are used to calculate the co-occurrence. The words' co-occurrence relationships for the datasets of comments and replies are shown in Figure 64.

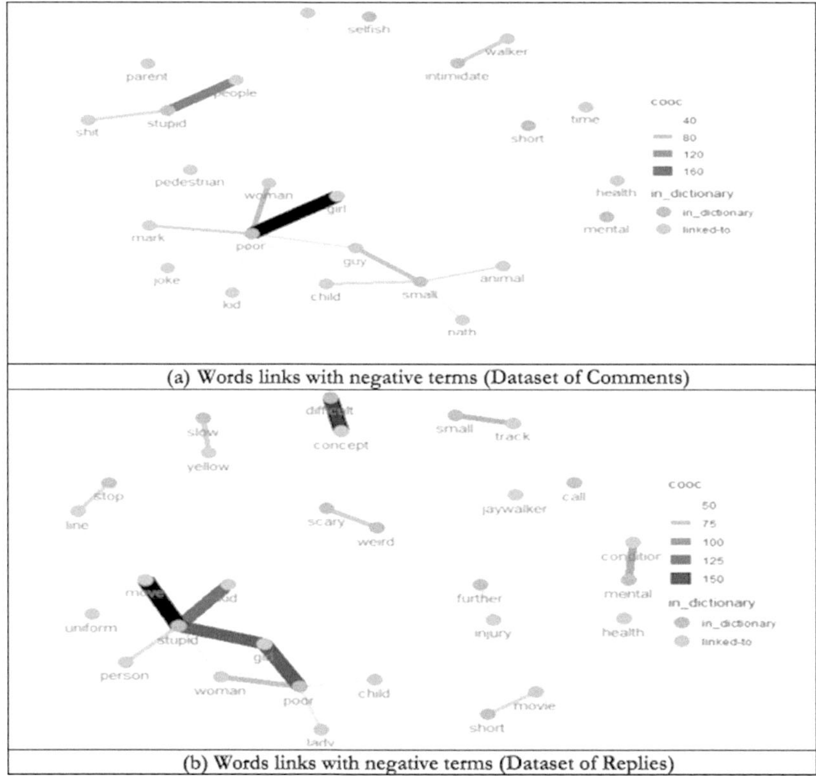

(a) Words links with negative terms (Dataset of Comments)

(b) Words links with negative terms (Dataset of Replies)

Figure 64. Co-occurrences of the negative terms.

Case Study 3

State transportation agencies use their official accounts to inform their followers about traffic crash or road closure information. Show how this data can be collected and used to understand the information shared by the agencies.

***Solution*:**

More general scientific research known as knowledge discovery or data mining has led to the applied method of text mining. Knowledge discovery is the non-trivial process of recognizing useful, valid, and easy to interpret patterns in data. Text mining, or knowledge discovery in the text (KDT), is considered a multi-stage process that makes up all activities, including document collection and knowledge extraction, and that utilizes approaches like supervised and unsupervised machine learning, information retrieval, data mining, and natural language processing (NLP). Identifying contributing factors in associated tasks can aid in the extraction of quick and useful information from data resources through pattern recognition. Massive collections of unstructured textual data can be handled by text mining algorithms. A flowchart of text mining from select Twitter handles is shown in Figure 65.

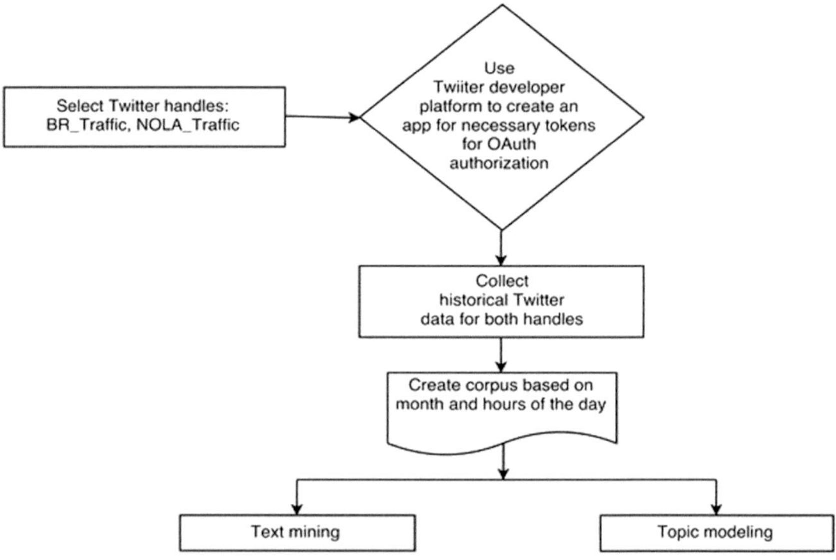

Figure 65. Flowchart of text mining.

In information retrieval approaches, it is presumed that keywords denote condensed information from the documents. Keyword extraction utilizes a NLP method to recognize particular words or terms; this method is combined with supervised or unsupervised machine learning algorithms. Moreover, calculations on the co-occurrence of certain terms and phrases would be a point of interest in various research. As an example, a high frequency of 'congestion,' without any co-occurrence, wouldn't always suggest the nature of the document's particular interest. If the use of the term 'congestion' with another term 'minimal' is high, it would signify a different nature of the document. Corpus denotes a collection of text documents in text mining; it is an abstract concept, and several applications can exist in parallel. After developing a corpus, users are able to easily modify the documents in it: stemming, stop word removal, numbers, particular parts of speech, and redundant words are all examples of this. Figure 65 shows the flowchart of the developed Twitter mining approach.

Twitter is a comparatively new social media that is used for microblogging. The 'tweets' (posts of the user) don't exceed 140 characters; it reflects opinions in real-time and disseminates information. In various aspects, some of the information and unfiltered opinions can be very sensitive. A large amount of textual content is generated daily by Twitter. Text mining, natural language processing, information retrieval, and other methods can be used to study textual content. There is an open debate that if Twitter stratifies the necessary representative sample data for the outside world, important insights may be provided by giving context to the social media data through appropriate means. Several factors, like target specification, appropriate algorithm, and responsiveness of the post, impact the keys to the success of Twitter mining. The terms used in Twitter are briefly described below:

- ***Tweet***: A short message from a Twitter account holder, spanning a maximum of 140 characters. A Twitter handle is the account holder's name.
- ***Reply***: Replies help in responding to a tweet. This syntax automatically inserts the originator's user name.
- ***Hashtag***: Represented by a '#' symbol followed by a word or phrase (e.g., #NOLA_Traffic). Users use this in front of a keyword or phrase (with no spaces in between) in tweets to classify them so they can appear more readily in Twitter Search.
- ***Mention***: Mentions acknowledge a user with the '@' symbol without replying to a specific tweet feature (e.g. @NOLA_Traffic).
- ***Retweet***: Retweeting forwards a tweet from users to their own followers.

Methodology

Three different text analytic approaches were used to study the contents of the official tweets of the government transportation agencies of two major cities in Louisiana: a cluster of the contents by topic modeling, content exploratory analysis by text mining, and perception of the public on different countermeasures by sentimental analysis.

Official Twitter Accounts of DOTD

Sixteen official Twitter accounts are maintained by Louisiana DOTD. The most dominant ones in the number of tweets and followers among them are the Twitter handles for Baton Rouge and New Orleans (see Table 20). Tweets were collected from both these Twitter handles (NOLA_Traffic and BR_Traffic). January 2009 was when both official accounts were created. The number of official tweets and followers of these official Twitter handles in two different time periods (before: July 2015, after: July 2016) are listed in Table 20. The percentage increase of tweets ranges from 25% to 101%, and the range of percentage increase in followers is 25% to 184%. The average growth of followers is nearly 48% for the official Twitter handles in two major cities (Baton Rouge and New Orleans) of Louisiana, indicating that these two Twitter handles are giving followers helpful updates.

Table 20. Official Twitter accounts of DOTD

City	Official Twitter Handle	July, 2015		July, 2016		Percentage Increase	
		Tweets	Followers	Tweets	Followers	Tweets	Followers
New Orleans	NOLA_Traffic	34,700	21,300	45,451	29,445	31%	38%
Baton Rouge	BR_Traffic	26,200	27,900	32,859	43,272	25%	55%
Shreveport	Shreveport_Traf	5,389	2,464	6,883	3,108	28%	26%
North Shore	NS_Traffic	3,340	1,657	5,222	2,802	56%	69%
Houma	Houma_Traffic	2,568	1,776	3,260	2,220	27%	25%
Lafayette	Laf_Traffic	1,862	1,292	3,058	2,718	64%	110%
Lake Charles	LC_Traffic	1,385	373	2,788	1063	101%	185%
Monroe	Monroe_Traffic	432	264	867	469	101%	78%
Alexandria	Alex_Traffic	117	178	187	398	60%	124%
	Total	75,993	57,204	100,575	85,495	32%	49%

Data Collection

The newest version of Twitter currently has two types of authentications, both of which leverage open standards for authorizations (OAuth) still. The two forms are application-user authentication, the most frequently used form of resource authentication in Twitter's OAuth 1.0A implementation to date, and application-only, a form of authentication wherein user application makes API requests without a user context on its own behalf. The one-time tweet extraction limit from a Twitter handle is 3,200.

The authors used popular data mining *R* packages "twitteR" and "tm" to extract tweets from the user timeline of two official DOTD Twitter handles and semantic analysis respectively. The total number of tweets analyzed in this research is nearly nine thousand. The official tweets were retweeted by their followers nearly 36,500 times. Figure 66 shows the tweets and retweets generated from these accounts. In terms of the number of retweets, the followers of

NOLA_Traffic retweeted nearly twice that of the BR_Traffic followers. The peak of the retweets from both handles is visible on January 25, 2014, when the interstates were closed due to severe icy conditions. Both of the Twitter handles shared the most recent status by tweeting real-time information. The followers retweeted those tweets to inform their own followers. This event clearly shows the necessity of using Twitter for information dissemination and sharing by the transportation authorities. Spatial and temporal (in hours) distribution of the tweets and retweets would provide more insight on the circulation of emergency transportation information, which is not done in the current study. Figure 66 shows examples of results.

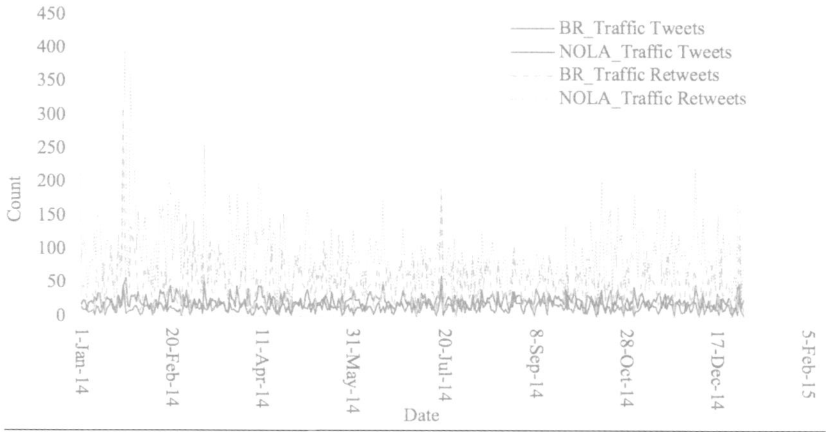

Figure 66. Examples of results.

Text Mining

Two major strategies were taken to make the corpus: month wise and hour wise. At first, the tweets were divided into twelve different documents or corpora per Twitter handle based on the months. Figure 67 shows the heat map of the frequency of the terms in different months. Both of the Twitter handles exhibit high frequency in similar terms (lane closure information, congestion, and blockage).

Another division was done based on the hours of the day. The division was based on the time stamp hour of the tweets: 12AM-6AM, 6AM-12PM, 12PM-6PM, and 6PM-12AM. Both of the Twitter handles exhibit high frequency in similar terms (lane closure information, congestion, and blockage), as shown in Figure 68. It is also inevitable that more tweets were posted in the daytime than nighttime.

Additional statistics on both handles are listed in Table 21. The final analysis was performed on the hourly-based tweets. There were 570 unique terms used in the tweets on average. It is required to eliminate sparse terms (terms occurring only in very few documents) as term-document matrices typically become big enough for normal-sized data sets.

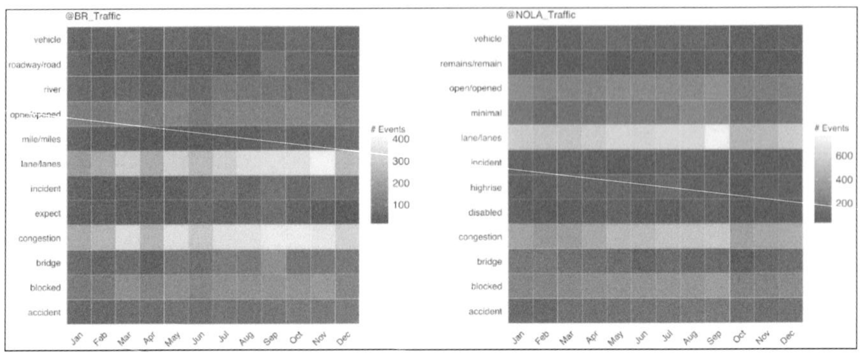

Figure 67. Frequency of terms per month.

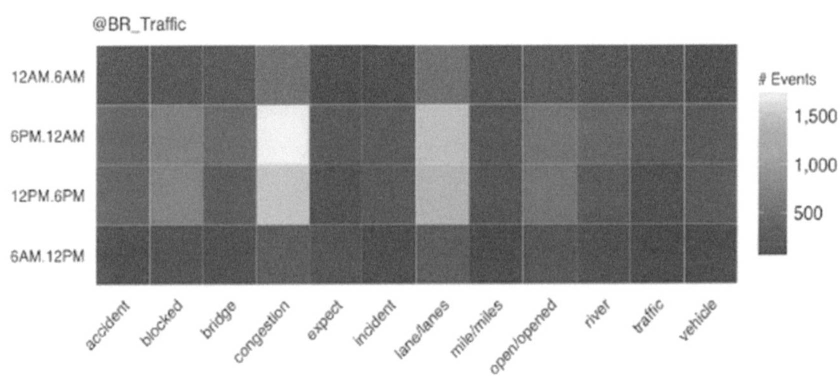

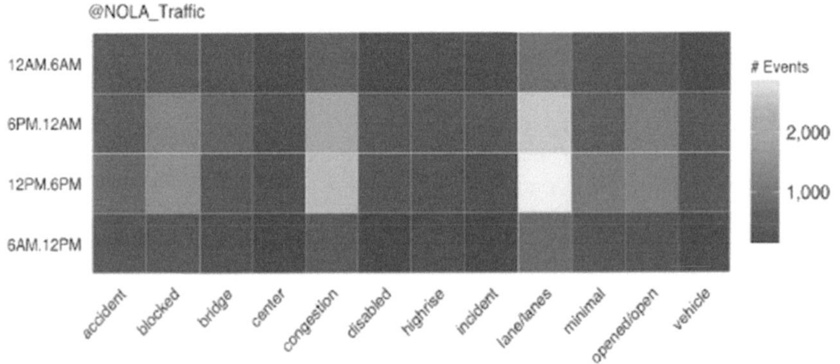

Figure 68. Frequency of terms per hour.

The threshold of relative document frequency for a term is referred to as sparsity. The term will be removed from analysis if it is above this threshold; the sparsity of the terms generated from all tweets was nearly 50 percent. The matrix is reduced dramatically by removing the sparse terms while preserving significant relations that are inherent to the matrix. To make the document noiseless, 25% of sparse elements were removed. The sparsity of the document was reduced to 0% after removing the sparse terms. The highest frequency terms are selected, excluding the redundant terms (combined frequency lower than 100, numbers, specific parts of speech, names of the streets, article and more). In NOLA_Traffic, the top five highly frequent terms are lane/lanes, congestion, open, blocked, and minimal (it refers to minimum congestion on roadways). In BR_Traffic, the top five highly frequent terms are lane/lanes, congestion, blocked, open, accident/accidents.

Table 21. Descriptive statistics

	Baton Rouge	**New Orleans**
Official Twitter Handle	BR_Traffic	NOLA_Traffic
Analyzed Tweets	3304	5605
	Hour of the Day	
12AM- 6AM	15.56%	13.95%
6AM-12PM	13.01%	17.47%
12PM-6PM	35.71%	38.93%
6PM- 12AM	35.71%	29.65%
	All Tweets	
Terms	569	571
Sparsity	49%	48%
Maximal Term length	21	21
	After Removing Sparse Terms (0.25)	
Terms	109	116
Sparsity	0%	0%
Maximal Term length	12	16

Table 22 lists findings obtained from the tweet content analysis. The presence of a particular term will be more intuitive if one knows what most correlated terms it comes with. It lists the correlation ratio for the terms associated with three important terms, 'congestion,' 'blocked,' and 'accident.' This study uses the least correlation factor of 0.97. When 'congestion' is associated with 'minimal,' it implies a less congested phase. The term 'minimal' is highly correlated with 'congestion' in the NOLA_Traffic handle, while it is less correlated with 'congestion' in the BR_Traffic handle. This particular case implies the congestion situations for both of the cities.

Table 22. Correlations between terms

Baton Rouge		New Orleans	
Congestion		**Congestion**	
Lane	1.00	Blocked	1.00
Open	1.00	Connection	1.00
Vehicle	1.00	Lane	1.00
Blocked	0.99	Veterans	1.00
Lanes	0.99	City	0.99
Blocked		**Blocked**	
Port	1.00	Congestion	1.00
Vehicle	1.00	Connection	1.00
Congestion	0.99	Lane	1.00
Hwy	0.99	Center	0.99
Accident		**Accident**	
Clear	1.00	Remains	1.00
Overpass	1.00	Causeway	0.99
Vehicle	0.99	Shoulder	0.99
Blocked	0.98	Split	0.99
Center	0.98	Vehicle	0.99
Current	0.97	Through	0.97

The findings from the text mining part of this study are:

- Government transportation information through tweets is getting popular.
- Social media helps in improving public service during bad weather. Real-time information on roadway blockage and other travel problems would be economically beneficial to the traveling public.
- Text mining shows that most of the tweets were associated with terms like 'congestion,' 'blocked,' 'accidents,' 'lane/lanes,' and 'open.' Real-time utilization of these terms would lessen highway mileage and would be environmentally and economically beneficial. The current research will help in future research on building a transportation information-related real-time Twitterbot.
- The hour-based heat map implies the percentage of terms present used in different documents. The findings are similar to the research analyzing peak-hour traffics.
- The tweets related to Baton Rouge Traffic inform more about congestion, while it is highly associated with the term 'minimal' in the tweets of New Orleans traffic.

The limitation of this study is the usage of limited data (one year of Twitter data). The complete analysis of the tweets since January 2009 is a potential analytic approach to extract knowledge from the data.

Topic Modeling

Latent Dirichlet Allocation (LDA)

LDA is the most popular topic model used for extracting trends of topics from textual data. A detailed introduction of LDA can be found in the Blei et al. (2003) study. A very short introduction of LDA is described here. Suppose there is a group of documents $D = \{d^{(1)}, d^{(2)}, \ldots, d^{(N)}\}$. A particular topic t is a discrete distribution over words with vector ϕ_t. A Dirichlet prior can be placed over $\Phi = \{\phi_1, \ldots \phi_T\}$. This prior is assumed to be symmetric with parameter β:

$$P(\Phi)\prod_t Dir(\phi_{t;\beta\varsigma}) = \prod_t \frac{r(\beta)}{\prod_d r\left(\frac{\beta}{D}\right)} \prod_d \phi_{d/t}^{\frac{\beta}{D}-1} \tau\left(\Sigma_d \phi_{d/t} - 1\right) \quad (14)$$

Here, it is considered that each document, indexed by n, has a document-specific distribution over topics θ_n. The prior over $\Theta = \{\theta_1, \ldots \theta_N\}$ is also assumed to be a symmetric Dirichlet, with parameter α. The tokens in each document $d^{(k)} = \left\{d_k^{(n)}\right\}_{k=1}^{K_n}$ are associated with corresponding topic assignments $y^{(k)} = \left\{y_k^{(n)}\right\}_{k=1}^{K_n}$ and are drawn from the topics' distributions over words Φ:

$$P(y^n \mid \theta_n) = \prod_k \theta_{yk}^{(n)} \mid n \quad (15)$$

$$P(d^{(n)} \mid y^{(n)}, \phi) = \prod_k \phi_{d_k}^{(n)} \mid y_k^{(n)} \quad (16)$$

The authors used textual data from both Baton Rouge and New Orleans to develop topic models for each dataset. Table 23 lists the top five topic models developed from these two datasets. By exploring the terms in the top five topics in both Twitter handles, it is found that most of the tweets are related to congestion, crash, roadway blockage, and after crash/incident status. Real-time alerts based on these tweets would be beneficial for roadway users.

Table 23. Topic models form Twitter handles of two major cities

Topic Models from Tweets from BR_Traffic
Topic 1: congestion, lane, blocked, open, accident
Topic 2: delays, blocked, accident, normal, open
Topic 3: congestion, lane, closed, open, river
Topic 4: accident, incident, delay, blocked, open
Topic 5: congestion, bridge, open, Mississippi, blocked
Topic Models from Tweets from NOLA_Traffic
Topic 1: congestion, lane, open, lane, bridge
Topic 2: minimal, congestion, accident, blocked, lane
Topic 3: congestion, lane, blocked, minimal, open
Topic 4: accident, delay, incident, blocked, lane
Topic 5: congestion, bridge, blocked, lane, disabled

8.6.1. Sentiment Analysis

Sentiments are necessary for most activities and they influence human behaviors. Most beliefs and perceptions of humankind depend on how the world is seen and evaluated by others. Because of this, in order to make better decisions, humans tend to seek out the sentiments of others. This is true for various organizations and programs, not just individuals. Sentiment analysis studies sentiments, attitudes, evaluations, opinions, and emotions. Sentiment analysis of specific tweets gives opportunities to the authorities to understand people's opinions quickly compared to conventional survey methods.

It is essential to note that there are domain-specific sentiment values for the sentiment lexicons. Subsequently, the sentiment classification performance of a given text may differ according to the calculation process of its sentiment. To assist in the identification of negative and positive annotations in the mining-ready texts, assorted sentiment lexicons with different formats and research focuses have been created. Both diversification and similarity were observed while comparing the listed words along with their ratings. To address the classification challenge of sentiment analysis it is necessary to develop a domain-specific sentiment lexicon. Researchers are currently creating a sentiment lexicon that is appropriate for transportation-related tweets, and this area is still a potential research topic. A list of negative and positive sentiment words in English were used in this study to complete the sentiment analysis on the tweets.

For example, mining the Twitter data related to "@NOLA_Traffic" and "#NOLA_Traffic" will provide interesting insights into the sentiment of the New Orleans roadway users. A sentiment score function was developed to mine each tweet with the negative and positive word lexicons and calculated a score that is negative, positive, or zero. A tweet that has a "+2" score means that the tweet has two positive words by hashtagging or mentioning "NOLA_Traffic." A tweet with a negative score designates that negative words were used.

This case study collected tweets related to four search terms: workzone, redlight camera, seatbelt, and pavement marks. The terms workzone and pavement marks show higher trends in positive scores while terms like redlight camera and seatbelt process more inclination towards negative scores. Figure 69 illustrates these scores.

The results demonstrate very positive reactions to the DOTD workzone and pavement markers and negative reactions to automatic red-light enforcement and seatbelt, which is not entirely surprising. Louisiana is one of the states with the lowest seatbelt usage in the country and had some bad publicity over red-light camera usage in a few locations. To improve seatbelt usage and promote automatic red-light safety programs, it is important to change public perceptions of these programs through effective actions.

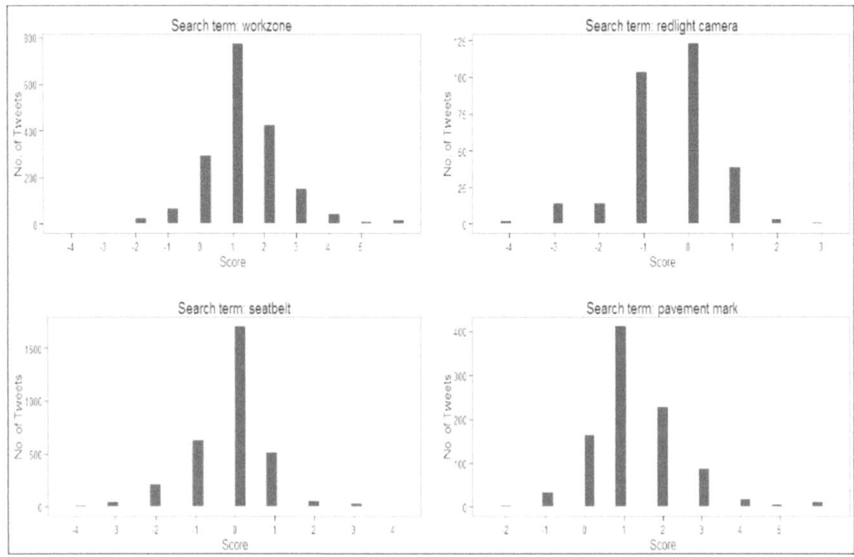

Figure 69. Sentiment scores of four countermeasures.

Example Problem 1

Develop reproducible Python scripts for Topic Model Word clouds.

***Solution*:**

The data is collected from the Motorcycle Crash Causation Study (MCCS). Figure 70 shows eight topic model-based word clouds. The coding to answer the question is shown in the following code chunk. The code results are not shown (few major plots are shown to explain the results).

Example Problem 1 (Code Chunk 1) (Python Code)

```
import os
import codecs
import pandas as pd
import numpy as np
from sklearn.feature_extraction.text import TfidfVectorizer, CountVectorizer
from sklearn.decomposition import NMF, LatentDirichletAllocation
import matplotlib.pyplot as plt
import math
import wordcloud
%matplotlib inline

import string
printable = set(string.printable)
def clean_sentence(s):
    return ''.join(filter(lambda x: x in printable, s))
```

(Contd.)

```
n_topics = 8
n_top_words = 50
data   =   pd.read_csv('~folder_location/MCSS_CrashNarr_02132019FatalNarr.csv',
encoding="ISO-8859-1")
data = data.dropna(subset=['text'])
sentences =  data.text.apply(clean_sentence)

from sklearn.feature_extraction import text
my_words=set(['trbam', 'trb2010', 'nasemtrb', 'trb2011', 'trb2012', 'trbofna','10', 'http',
'ly', 'rt', 'bit', 'trb', 'meeting',
          '20', 'annual', 'ow', '30', '2011', '2012', 'com', 'transport', 'transportation', '.com',
'twitter', 'trb2013',
                'trb2014', 'trb2015', 'trb2016', 'trb2017', 'trb2018', 'trb2019', 'trb2020',
'transportgooru', 'register',
          'registration', 'shana', 'johnson', 'year', 'www', 'pic', '2015', '2016', '2017', '2018',
'2019', '2020', '2013',
             '2014', 'dc', 'shana_johnson', 'org', '.org', 'meetings', 'pdf', 'en', '000', 'crash',
'crashes', 'rider', 'road',
          'vehicle', 'vehicles', 'car', 'cars', 'roadway','roadways'])
my_stop_words=text.ENGLISH_STOP_WORDS.union(my_words)
tf_vectorizer = CountVectorizer(input='content',
¬¬stop_words=set(my_stop_words))
tf = tf_vectorizer.fit_transform(sentences)

lda = LatentDirichletAllocation(n_components = n_topics, max_iter=5,
                                learning_method='online',
                                learning_offset=50.,
                                random_state=0)
lda.fit(tf)
tf_feature_names = tf_vectorizer.get_feature_names()

import os
os.chdir("~folder location")

import re
a = plt.figure(figsize=(20,16))
regex = re.compile("[A-Za-z0-9]+")

import csv
f = open('aFatalNarr.csv', 'w', newline='') #new added rows
writer = csv.writer(f)
writer.writerow(['topic','word', 'count'])


for i in range (0, n_topics):
    print(lda.components_[i])
   termsInTopic = lda.components_[i].argsort()[:-50-1:-1]
```

```
    print(termsInTopic)
    termsAndCounts = {}
    title_str = 'Topic{}'.format(i+1)
    for term in termsInTopic:
        if (str(tf_feature_names[term].strip()) == 'https'): # remove https from the plot
            continue
#           if not bool(re.fullmatch(regex, str(tf_feature_names[term].strip()))):# remove
illegal characters
#           continue
        termsAndCounts[str(tf_feature_names[term].strip())] = math.ceil(lda.components_
[i][term]*1000)
            writer.writerow([i+1,tf_feature_names[term], termsAndCounts[str(tf_feature_
names[term].strip())]])## new added code
    print(termsAndCounts)
    cloud = wordcloud.WordCloud(background_color="white")
    cloud.generate_from_frequencies(termsAndCounts)
    plt.subplot(5, 4, i+1)
    plt.imshow(cloud, interpolation='bilinear')
    plt.axis("off")
    plt.title(title_str)

a.savefig('aFatalNarr.png', dpi=300, bbox_inches='tight')
```

Figure 70. Topic model-based word clouds.

Example Problem 2

Show a reproducible example of 'Structural Topic Model.'

***Solution*:**

The data is collected from the TRID (https://trid.trb.org/). Figure 71 shows the trends of the developed topic models. The following code chunk shows the coding to answer the question. The code results are not shown (few major plots are shown to explain the results).

Example Problem 2 (Code Chunk 1) (Structural topic model)

```
## Please check my RPUBS for additional codes: https://rpubs.com/subasish

setwd("~folder name")
```

(*Contd.*)

```
setwd("~folder name")

library(readxl)
dat <- read_excel("ALL_TRR1.xlsx", sheet="JournalArticle2")
names(dat)
dat$ID1 <- 1:nrow(dat)
dat$ID <- paste0("A","_", dat$ID1)
names(dat)

companyRDF <- data.frame(Doc.id = unique(dat$`Publication Year`),
                textdata = tapply(dat$Title, dat$`Publication Year`, paste, collapse = ' '))
str(companyRDF)
str(companyRDF)
dim(companyRDF)


library("quanteda")
library("stm")

uncorpus.dfm <- dfm(companyRDF$textdata, remove_numbers = TRUE, remove_
punct = TRUE, remove_symbols = TRUE, remove = stopwords("english"))
uncorpus.dfm
uncorpus.dfm.trim <- dfm_trim(uncorpus.dfm, min_docfreq = 0.090, max_docfreq =
0.90, docfreq_type = "prop") # min 7.5% / max 95%
uncorpus.dfm.trim

topic.count <- 12
dfm2stm <- convert(uncorpus.dfm.trim, to = "stm", docvars =companyRDF)
model.stm <- stm(dfm2stm$documents, dfm2stm$vocab, K = topic.count, data =
dfm2stm$meta, init.type = "Spectral")
data.frame(t(labelTopics(model.stm, n = 20)$prob))
#plot(model.stm, type = "summary", text.cex = 0.5)
#plot(model.stm, type = "hist", topics = sample(1:topic.count, size = 12))

model.stm.labels <- labelTopics(model.stm, 1:topic.count)
dfm2stm$meta$datum <- as.numeric(dfm2stm$meta$Doc.id)
model.stm.ee <- estimateEffect(1:topic.count ~ s(Doc.id), model.stm, meta =
dfm2stm$meta)


par(mfrow=c(3,3))

for (i in seq_along(sample(1:topic.count, size = 6)))
{
  plot(model.stm.ee, "Doc.id", method = "continuous", topics = i, main = paste0(model.
stm.labels$prob[i,1:4], collapse = ", "), printlegend = F)
}
```

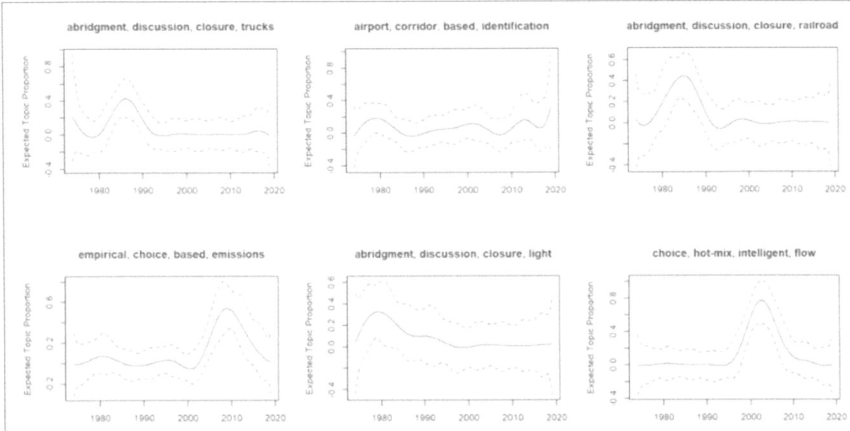

Figure 71. Trends of the topic models.

Chapter Conclusion

This chapter provides some required information on NLP. Topics such as text mining, topic modeling, sentence centrality, centroid-based summarization, centrality-based sentence salience, and NLP-based highway safety studies are covered. Several case studies and example problems are also provided at the end of this chapter.

Further Reading

Blei, D., Ng, A. and Jordan, M., 2003. Latent Dirichlet Allocation. Journal of Machine Learning Research, pp. 993-1022.

Das, S. and Griffin, G.P., 2020. Investigating the Role of Big Data in Transportation Safety. Transportation Research Record: Journal of the Transportation Research Board 2674, pp. 244-252.

Das, S., Mudgal, A., Dutta, A. and Geedipally, S.R., 2018. Vehicle Consumer Complaint Reports Involving Severe Incidents: Mining Large Contingency Tables. Transportation Research Record: Journal of the Transportation Research Board 2672, pp. 72-82.

Das, S., Sun, X. and Dutta, A., 2016. Text Mining and Topic Modeling of Compendiums of Papers from Transportation Research Board Annual Meetings. Transportation Research Record: Journal of the Transportation Research Board, pp. 48–56.

Dodds, P. and C. Danforth, 2009. Measuring the Happiness of Large-Scale Written Expression: Songs, Blogs, and Presidents. J. Happiness Stud.

Eisenstein, J., 2019. Introduction to Natural Language Processing. MIT Press.

Goldberg, Y., 2017. Neural Network Methods in Natural Language Processing. Morgan & Claypool Publishers.

Kulkarni, K. and Shivananda, A., 2019. Natural Language Processing Recipes. Springer Science and Business Media LLC.

Li, S., Li, G., Law, R. and Paradies, Y., 2020. Racism in Tourism Reviews. Tourism Management, Vol. 80, p. 104100. https://doi.org/10.1016/j.tourman.2020.104100.

Silge, J. and Robinson, D., 2017. Text Mining with R: A Tidy Approach. O'Reilly Media, Inc.

References

Dabiri, S. and Heaslip, K., 2019. Developing a Twitter-based traffic event detection model using deep learning architectures. Expert Systems with Applications, 118, pp. 425-439.

Das, S. and Dutta, A., 2020. Characterizing public emotions and sentiments in COVID-19 environment: A case study of India. Journal of Human Behavior in the Social Environment, 31(1-4), pp 154–167.

Das, S., Dutta, A., Lindheimer, T., Jalayer, M. and Elgart, Z., 2019. YouTube as a Source of Information in Understanding Autonomous Vehicle Consumers: Natural Language Processing Study. Transportation Research Record 2673, pp. 242-253.

Das, S., Dutta, A. and Tsapakis, I., 2021. Topic Models from Crash Narrative Reports of Motorcycle Crash Causation Study. Transportation Research Record 03611981211002523.

Das, S., 2021. Exploratory Analysis of Unmanned Aircraft Sightings using Text Mining. Transportation Research Record: Journal of the Transportation Research Board.

Das, S., 2021. Data Dive into Transportation Research Record Articles: Authors, Coauthorships, and Research Trends. TR News, pp. 25-31.

Das, S., 2019. #TRBAM: Social Media Interactions from Transportation's Largest Conference. TR News, pp. 18-23.

Das, S., Dixon, K.K., Sun, X., Dutta, A., Zupancich, M., et al., 2017b. Trends in Transportation Research: Exploring Content Analysis in Topics. Transportation Research Record: Journal of the Transportation Research Board, pp. 27-38.

Das, S., Dutta, A., Lindheimer, T., Jalayer, M., Elgart, Z., et al., 2019. YouTube as a Source of Information in Understanding Autonomous Vehicle Consumers: Natural Language Processing Study. Transportation Research Record: Journal of the Transportation Research Board 2673, pp. 242-253.

Das, S., Dutta, A., Medina, G., Minjares-Kyle, L., Elgart, Z., et al., 2019. Extracting patterns from Twitter to promote biking. IATSS Research, 43, pp. 51-59.

Hu, N., Zhang, T., Gao, B. and Bose, I. 2019. What do hotel customers complain about? Text analysis using structural topic model. Tourism Management.

Hughes, P., Figueres-Esteban, M. and van Gulijk, C., 2016. Learning from text-based close call data. Safety and Reliability, 36, pp. 184-198.

McLaurin, E.J., Lee, J.D., McDonald, A.D., Aksan, N., Dawson, et al., 2018. Using topic modeling to develop multi-level descriptions of naturalistic driving data from drivers with and without sleep apnea. Transportation Research Part F: Traffic Psychology and Behaviour, 58, pp. 25-38.

Nouioua, F., 2008. A Heuristic Approach to Order Events in Narrative Texts. *In:* 2008 15th International Symposium on Temporal Representation and Reasoning. IEEE, pp. 67-71.

Serna, A., Gerrikagoitia, J.K., Bernabé, U. and Ruiz, T., 2017. Sustainability analysis on Urban Mobility based on Social Media content. Transportation Research Procedia, 3rd Conference on Sustainable Urban Mobility, 3rd CSUM 2016, 26-27 May 2016, Volos, Greece 24, pp. 1–8.

Sujon, M. and Dai, F., 2020. Understanding Traffic Safety Culture in Washington Using Twitter Mining, pp. 201-209.

Sun, Z. and Tang, P., 2021. Automatic Communication Error Detection Using Speech Recognition and Linguistic Analysis for Proactive Control of Loss of Separation. Transportation Research Record 03611981209830004.

CHAPTER
9

Explainable AI

9.1. Introduction

Neural networks are an example of explicit AI models, as their deep variants lead areas of computer vision along with other fields and sub-fields. Although these models are very effective in making precise predictions, they are limited in their interpretability and explainability. So, their current practice as models lack the ability to say much about:

- Interpretability: how does the model structure explain its functioning?
- Explainability: what is the rationale behind the decision made?

If one hopes to advance learning machines and incorporate them into decision support systems that involve human supervision, explainability/interpretability capabilities are necessary, despite the fact that a good performance is a crucial requirement for learning machines. To mitigate the crucial gap in interpretation and causality determination, the explainability of the AI models has turned into a robust research trend within the machine learning and computer vision communities. In fact, many recent works have recently been committed to defining interpretability and explainability in the context of models and how to assess these factors. Researchers have been developing innovative mechanisms for explaining suggested models and their structures.

Interpretation means to present or explain in comprehensible terms. One emphasizes providing an explanation to humans in the context of AI systems; that is, to present or explain to a human in understandable terms. One must still answer what an explanation is, even if it is a more intuitive term than interpretability. People look at psychology to answer this, since a formal definition of an explanation is still unknown.

How does the algorithm create the model?

How a model is learned from the data by the algorithm and what kind of relationships it is able to learn is referred to as algorithm transparency. One is able to explain that using convolutional neural networks to classify images is an explanation of how the algorithm works, as opposed to how individual predictions are made or how the algorithm learns filters and edge detectors on the lowest layers. Only knowledge of the algorithm rather than of the learned model or the data is necessary for algorithm transparency. Here, model interpretability rather than algorithm transparency is focused on. Algorithms like the least squares method for linear models are understood well and subsequently have higher transparency. Deep learning methods are not as well understood, and ongoing research is concentrated on the inner workings, so they subsequently are considered to be less transparent.

How does the trained model make predictions?

If one is able to understand the entire model at once, the model can be considered to be interpretable. To describe the global model output, knowledge of the algorithm, the trained model, and the data is necessary. This interpretability level is about understanding how, based off of a comprehensive look at its characteristics and learned elements (such as other parameters, weights, and structures), decisions are made by the model. What kind of interactions take place between features and which of these are important? Understanding the distribution of target outcomes based on the characteristics is aided by global model interpretability, but is in practice incredibly difficult to carry out. A model that surpasses several weights or parameters is not likely to fit into an average human's short-term memory. A person is not capable of imagining a linear model that has five features, as it would necessitate a mental image of the estimated hyperplane in a 5-dimensional space, and humans are unable to comprehend any feature space that has more than three dimensions. People usually consider only parts of a model when they try to comprehend it, like the weights in linear models.

9.1.1. Partial Dependence Plot (PDP)

The marginal effects of one or two features on the predicted measures of an AI algorithm-based model can be described by the partial dependence plot (PDP or PD plot for short). A PDP is able to show that the association between the target and a characteristic is monotonic, linear, or more complex. As an example, partial dependence plots always display a linear relationship when applied to a linear regression model.

To compute PDPs, the partial dependence function at a given feature value depicts the average prediction, if one forces all data points to assume that feature value. The idea of PDPs typically is quickly understood by lay people. If the feature that the PDP is being computed for is not correlated with the other features, then how the prediction on average is influenced by the feature is perfectly represented by the PDP. The interpretation is clear in the uncorrelated case: the partial dependence plot shows how the average prediction in a dataset changes when the j-th feature is changed. When features are correlated, it is more complicated (see also drawbacks).

Two is the maximum credible number of characteristics in a partial dependence function, due to its 2-dimensional representation and people's discomfort in envisioning more than 3 dimensions. Feature distribution is not shown in some PD plots. It can be misleading to omit the distribution, because regions that have almost no data may be over interpreted. This problem can be resolved by displaying a histogram or a rug (indicators for data points on the x-axis). The largest problem with PD plots is the assumption of independence. It is assumed that other features are not correlated with the features that the partial dependence is calculated for.

9.1.2. Individual Conditional Expectation (ICE)

How the prediction of the instance alters when a feature is altered is shown through Individual Conditional Expectation (ICE) plots. These show one line per instance.

The average effect of a feature's partial dependence plot is a universal method due to the fact that it focuses on an overall average rather than specific instances. Individual conditional expectation (ICE) plots are parallel to a PDP for individual data instances; they separately display the dependence of the prediction on a feature for each case, which results in one line per case, as opposed to the partial dependence plots that show one line overall (which is an average of the ICE plot's lines). By keeping all other features constant and making these newly generated instances' predictions with the black box model along with variations of this occurrence by substituting the feature's value with values from a grid, the values for a line are computed. This results in a set of points for an occurrence with the respective predictions and the feature value from the grid.

Compared to partial dependence plots, ICE curves are naturally easier to understand due to the fact that the inferences for one instance are represented by one line if the feature of interest is varied. ICE curves can uncover heterogeneous relationships, unlike partial dependence plots.

Due to the fact that two features would necessitate creating several overlaying surfaces, it would be impossible to understand anything in the plot, since ICE curves are only able to meaningfully display one feature. According to the joint feature distribution, some of the lines' points could be invalid if the feature of interest is associated with the other features. The plot can get overcrowded if too many ICE curves are drawn, meaning that one will be unable to see anything. It may not be easy to see the average in ICE plots.

9.1.3. Accumulated Local Effects (ALE) Plot

Accumulated local effects (ALE) are able to explain how the prediction of a machine learning model on average is influenced by the features. In comparison to PDPs, ALE plots are unbiased and faster. ALE plots still work when features are correlated (as they are unbiased). Since partial dependence plots marginalize over impossible or unlikely combinations of feature values, they fail in this scenario. ALE plots are quicker to calculate than PDPs.

With a large number of intervals, ALE plots sometimes end up having multiple minor issues. The estimate becomes more stable with a reduction in the number of intervals, but it also smooths out and conceals some of the true complexity of the predicted model. There is no perfect solution for picking the interval number: if the number is too high, the curve can become shaky, and if too small, the ALE plots could be inaccurate.

9.1.4. Local Surrogate (LIME)

Individual estimates of black box machine learning models can be described by local surrogate models. A definite implementation of local surrogate models can be narrated as local interpretable model-agnostic explanations (LIME). The estimates of the underlying black box model are approximated by surrogate models that were trained for this purpose. LIME emphasizes training local surrogate models to justify individual predictions instead of training a global surrogate model.

The idea of LIME is instinctive. First, one forgets about the training data and imagines that it has only the black box model in which it can input data points and gets the prediction measures of the model. One is able to utilize the box as often as wanted. The goal is to comprehend why a certain prediction is made by the machine learning model. LIME tests what occurs to the estimates when variations of data are given to the machine learning model, and it then creates a new dataset that consists of perturbed samples and the corresponding predictions of the black box model, wherein an interpretable model weighted by the proximity of the instance of interest to the sampled instances is then trained. The learned model doesn't have to be a good global estimation, but it ought to be a good approximation of the machine learning model predictions locally.

9.1.5. Shapley Value

A feature's contribution to the payout, weighted and summed over all possible feature value combinations, is the Shapley value of a feature value. It is the only attribution method that fulfills the properties of symmetry, dummy, efficiency, and additivity, which can be thought of together as a definition of a fair payout.

The efficiency property of Shapley values differentiates the Shapley value from other methods such as LIME. It is the difference between the prediction and the average prediction which is distributed fairly among the feature values of the instance. Since the Shapley value may be the only method that delivers a complete explanation, it may be the only proper compliant method in situations wherein explainability is required by the law that a solid theory is its basis and it distributes the effects fairly.

A lot of computing time is necessary for the Shapley value; only the approximate solution is feasible in real-world problems 99.9% of the time. Due to the fact that there are 2 potential combinations of the feature values and random instances must be drawn to replicate the "absence" of a feature (increasing the variance for the estimate of the Shapley values estimation), an exact calculation of the Shapley value is computationally expensive. An exponential number of coalitions is handled by the limitation of the number of iterations of M and sampling coalitions. Decreasing M lowers the time needed for computing, but it increases variance. There is no perfect rule for the number of iterations M; it ought to be small enough to conduct the calculation in reasonable time, but large enough to estimate the Shapley values accurately. It ought to be possible to use Chernoff bounds to choose M, but there is a lack of papers evidencing that fact.

9.1.6. SHAP (SHapley Additive exPlanations)

A method to describe individual predictions based on the game theory optimal Shapley Values is called SHAP (SHapley Additive exPlanations). SHAP is not a part of Shapley values, partially because SHAP comes with a multitude of global interpretation methods based on combinations of Shapley values. Secondly, two SHAP values, TreeSHAP (an efficient estimation approach for tree-based models) and KernelSHAP (an alternative, kernel-based estimation approach for Shapley values that was inspired by local surrogate models), were suggested in this method.

SHAP has a **solid theoretical foundation** in game theory. The prediction is **fairly distributed** among the feature values, and one gets **contrastive explanations** that compare the average prediction with the prediction.

SHAP correlates with both LIME and Shapley values. It additionally aids in unifying the field of interpretable machine learning. One of the reasons for SHAP's popularity is that it has a **fast implementation for tree-based models**. Computing Shapley values for multiple instances is necessary for all global SHAP methods, like SHAP feature importance. However, if features are dependent (e.g., correlated), too much weight may be placed on unlikely data points. The TreeSHAP algorithm resolves this issue by modeling the conditional expected prediction explicitly so unintuitive feature attributions can be produced by TreeSHAP. TreeSHAP also has limitations; it alters the value function by relying on the conditional expected prediction.

Resources

Christoph Molnar's book 'Interpretable Machine Learning: A Guide for Making Black Box Models Explainable' is an excellent resource for XAI:
https://christophm.github.io/interpretable-ml-book/
Readers can explore the following curable list of XAI:
https://github.com/wangyongjie-ntu/Awesome-explainable-AI

Example Problem 1

Show a step-by-step method of using explainable AI in crash severity analysis.

Solution: For this analysis, e-scooter-related crash data from Louisiana is collected. The following code chunks are reproducible.

Example Problem 1 (Code Chunk 1)

```
## Please check my RPUBS for additional codes: https://rpubs.com/subasish

library("Numero")
library("DALEX")
library("ranger")
library(data.table)

setwd("~folder location")
it01 <- read.csv("EScotter_Fin2.csv", header=T, na.strings=c("","NA"))
names(it01)
str(it01)
mn01 <- it01[, c("SEVERITY_CD", "DAY_OF_WK", "LIGHTING_CD", "HWY_
TYPE_CD", "WEATHER_CD", "CR_HOUR",
 "NUM_VEH")]
mn02= mn01[complete.cases(mn01),]
dim(mn02)
head(mn02)
mn02$SEVERITY_CD= as.factor(mn02$SEVERITY_CD)
# prepare model
library("randomForest")
model_titanic_rf <- randomForest(SEVERITY_CD == "A" ~ ., data = mn02)
model_titanic_rf

explain_titanic_rf <- explain(model_titanic_rf,
 data = mn02[,-1],
 y = mn02$SEVERITY_CD == "A",
 label = "Random Forest v7",
 colorize = FALSE)
vi_rf <- variable_importance(explain_titanic_rf)
head(vi_rf)
plot(vi_rf)

vr_age <- variable_effect(explain_titanic_rf, variables = "CR_HOUR")
head(vr_age)
plot(vr_age)

vr_class <- variable_effect(explain_titanic_rf, variables = "DAY_OF_WK")
plot(vr_class)

vr_fare <- variable_effect(explain_titanic_rf, variables = "NUM_VEH")
plot(vr_fare)

library("rms")
model_titanic_lmr <- lrm(SEVERITY_CD == "A" ~ ., data = mn02)
explain_titanic_lmr <- explain(model_titanic_lmr, data = mn02,
 y = mn02$SEVERITY_CD == "A",
predict_function = function(m,x) predict(m, x, type="fitted"),
```

(*Contd.*)

```
 label = "Logistic regression")

library("gbm")
model_titanic_gbm <- gbm(SEVERITY_CD == "A" ~ ., data = mn02, n.trees = 1500)
explain_titanic_gbm <- explain(model_titanic_gbm, data = mn02,
 y = mn02$SEVERITY_CD == "A",
 predict_function = function(m,x) predict(m, x, n.trees = 15000, type = "response"),
 label = "Generalized Boosted Models",
 colorize = FALSE)
library("e1071")
model_titanic_svm <- svm(SEVERITY_CD == "A" ~ ., data = mn02,
 type = "C-classification", probability = TRUE)
explain_titanic_svm <- explain(model_titanic_svm, data = mn02,
 y = mn02$SEVERITY_CD == "A",
 label = "Support Vector Machines",
 colorize = FALSE)

vi_rf <- variable_importance(explain_titanic_rf)
vi_lmr <- variable_importance(explain_titanic_lmr)
vi_svm <- variable_importance(explain_titanic_svm)

plot(vi_rf, vi_lmr, vi_svm, bar_width = 4)

vr_age_rf <- variable_effect(explain_titanic_rf, variables = "CR_HOUR")
vr_age_lmr <- variable_effect(explain_titanic_lmr, variables = "CR_HOUR")
vr_age_svm <- variable_effect(explain_titanic_svm, variables = "CR_HOUR")
plot(vr_age_rf, vr_age_lmr, vr_age_svm)
```

Figure 72 goes over the drop-out loss for random forest v7, logistic regression, and support vector machines. Logistic regression is shown to have the highest

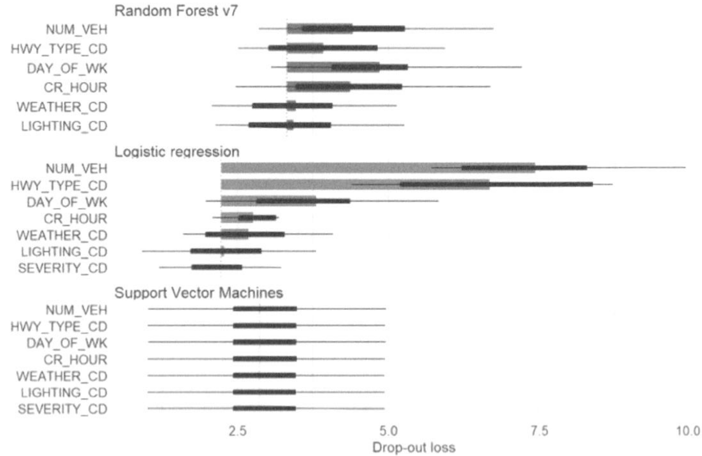

Figure 72. Drop-out loss for three algorithms.

amount of drop-out loss, and support vector machines are shown to have the lowest. Figure 73 illustrates predictions for a particular variable of these three algorithms. Logistic regression has the highest average prediction.

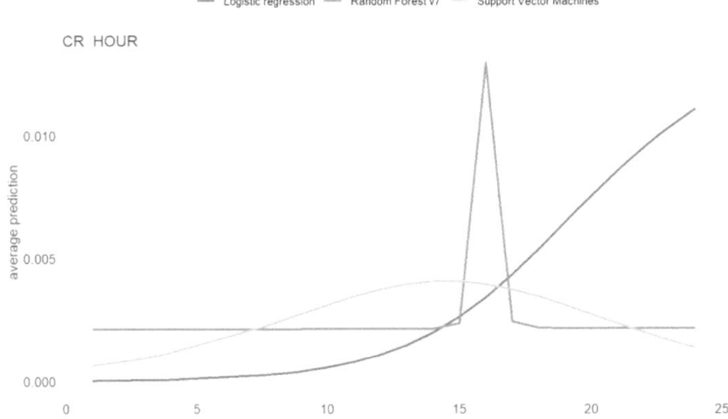

Figure 73. Prediction for a particular variable measure for three algorithms.

Example Problem 2

It is anticipated that racism is a critical issue in tourism-related reviews. Apply NLP tools to identify trends and patterns from these reviews.

Solution: The following code chunks show the coding to answer the question. The code results are not shown (few major plots are shown to explain the results).

Example problem 2 (Code Chunk 1)

```
# load the required packages

library("Numero")
library("DALEX")
library("ranger")
library(data.table)
library("DALEX")
library("h2o")
setwd("~folder location")

it01 <- fread("IT_aadtMaster.csv")
mn= subset(it01, State=="MN")
dim(mn)
## [1] 11498 86
mn01 <- mn[, c("Default_AADT", "FC_RU", "HU", "Pop", "WAC", "RAC", "Agg_
Inc", "Agg_Veh", "Empl")]
mn02= na.omit(mn01)
```

(*Contd.*)

```
custom_predict <- function(model, newdata) {
 newdata_h2o <- as.h2o(newdata)
 res <- as.data.frame(h2o.predict(model, newdata_h2o))
 return(as.numeric(res$predict))
}

h2o.init()
h2o.no_progress()

apartments_hf <- as.h2o(mn02)
model_h2o_glm <- h2o.glm(y = "Default_AADT", training_frame = apartments_hf)
model_h2o_gbm <- h2o.gbm(y = "Default_AADT", training_frame = apartments_hf)
###model_h2o_automl <- h2o.automl(y = "Default_AADT", training_frame =
apartments_hf, max_models = 10)

explainer_h2o_glm <- explain(model = model_h2o_glm,
 data = mn02[,2:8],
 y = mn02$Default_AADT,
 predict_function = custom_predict,
 label = "h2o glm",
 colorize = FALSE)

explainer_h2o_gbm <- explain(model = model_h2o_gbm,
 data = mn02[,2:8],
 y = mn02$Default_AADT,
 predict_function = custom_predict,
 label = "h2o gbm",
 colorize = FALSE)

mp_h2o_glm <- model_performance(explainer_h2o_glm)
mp_h2o_gbm <- model_performance(explainer_h2o_gbm)
plot(mp_h2o_glm, mp_h2o_gbm)
plot(mp_h2o_glm, mp_h2o_gbm, geom = "boxplot")


vi_h2o_glm <- variable_importance(explainer_h2o_glm)
vi_h2o_gbm <- variable_importance(explainer_h2o_gbm)
plot(vi_h2o_glm, vi_h2o_gbm)


pdp_h2o_glm <- variable_effect(explainer_h2o_glm, variable = "WAC")
pdp_h2o_gbm <- variable_effect(explainer_h2o_gbm, variable = "WAC")
plot(pdp_h2o_glm, pdp_h2o_gbm)
```

Figure 74 shows drop-out loss measures for GLM and BGM using H_2O, and Figure 75 shows predictions for a particular variable measure for three algorithms.

Example Problem 3

Show a reproducible example of SHAP value usage using crash count data.

Solution: The following code chunks show the coding to answer the question. The code results are not shown (few major plots are shown to explain the results).

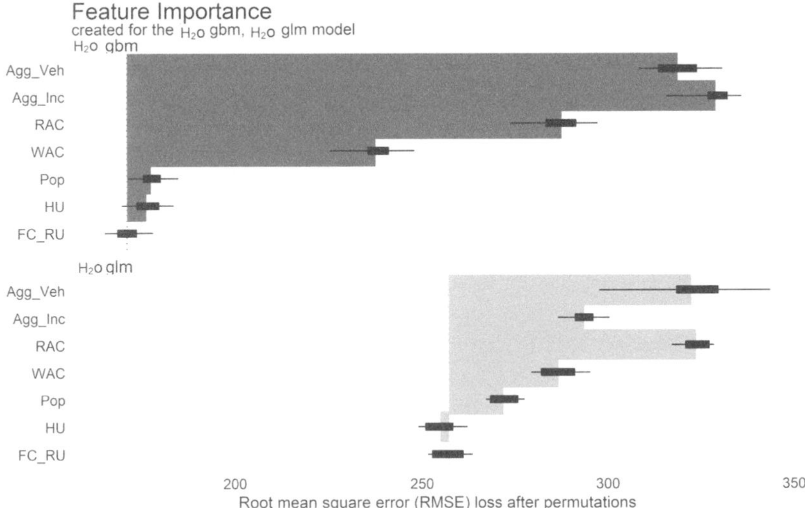

Figure 74. Drop-out loss measures for GLM and GBM using H_20.

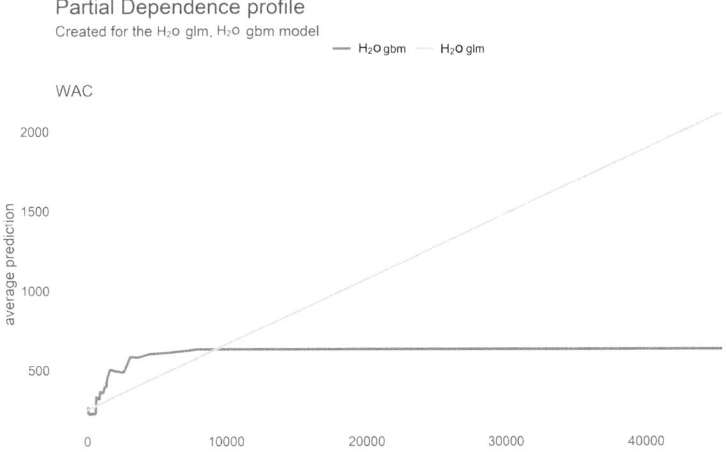

Figure 75. Prediction for a particular variable measure for three algorithms.

Example problem 3 (Code Chunk 1)

```
## Please check my RPUBS for additional codes: https://rpubs.com/subasish

setwd("~your folder")
dat= read.csv("TAHIR_rwd1.csv")
table(dat$HwyClass)
head(dat)

dat= subset(dat, HwyClass=="Rural Two-Lane")
dim(dat)

## 75% of the sample size
smp_size <- floor(0.75 * nrow(dat))

## set the seed to make your partition reproducible
set.seed(123)
train_ind <- sample(seq_len(nrow(dat)), size = smp_size)

train <- dat[train_ind, ]
test <- dat[-train_ind, ]

dim(train)
dim(test)

train_df= train[, c(4, 5, 7:11)]
test_df= test[, c(4, 5, 7:11)]

library(keras)
library(tfdatasets)
library(tensorflow)
library(tidyverse)
library(dplyr)
require(xgboost)
require(Matrix)
require(data.table)
require(vcd)

germanvar<-train_df[,1:6]
label <- as.numeric(train_df$Total_Crash)
data <- as.matrix(germanvar)
mode(data) <- 'double'

param_dart <- list(objective = "reg:linear",
 nrounds = 366,
 eta = 0.018,
max_depth = 10,
 gamma = 0.009,
```

```
subsample = 0.98,
colsample_bytree = 0.86)

mod <- xgboost(data = data, label = label,
 xgb_param = param_dart, nrounds = param_dart$nrounds,
 verbose = FALSE, nthread = parallel::detectCores() - 2,
 early_stopping_rounds = 8)

library("SHAPforxgboost")
shap_values <- shap.values(xgb_model = mod, X_train = data)
shap_values$mean_shap_score

shap_long <- shap.prep(xgb_model = mod, X_train = data)
# is the same as: using given shap_contrib
shap_long <- shap.prep(shap_contrib = shap_values$shap_score, X_train = data)

shap.plot.summary(shap_long)
```

Figure 76 shows SHAP values for the key variables, and Figure 77 shows feature values for the key variables.

Example Problem 3 (Code Chunk 2)

```
shap.plot.dependence(data_long = shap_long, x= "AADT",
color_feature = "MinPSL")
```

Example Problem 3 (Code Chunk 3)

```
fig_list = lapply(names(shap_values$mean_shap_score)[1:6], shap.plot.dependence,
 data_long = shap_long, dilute = 5)
gridExtra::grid.arrange(grobs = fig_list, ncol = 2)
```

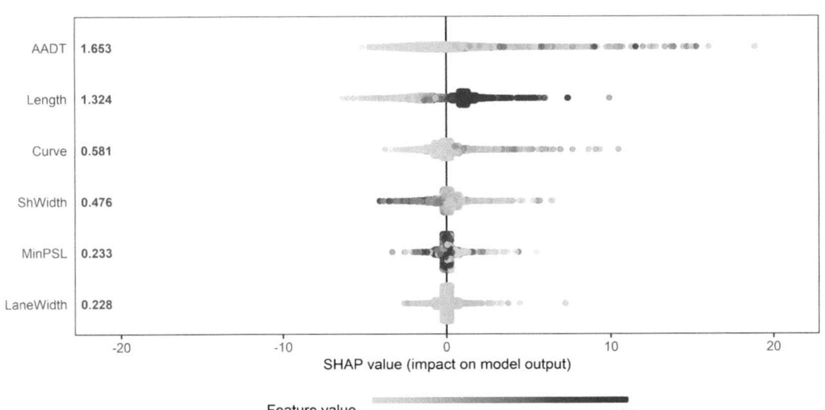

Figure 76. SHAP values for the key variables.

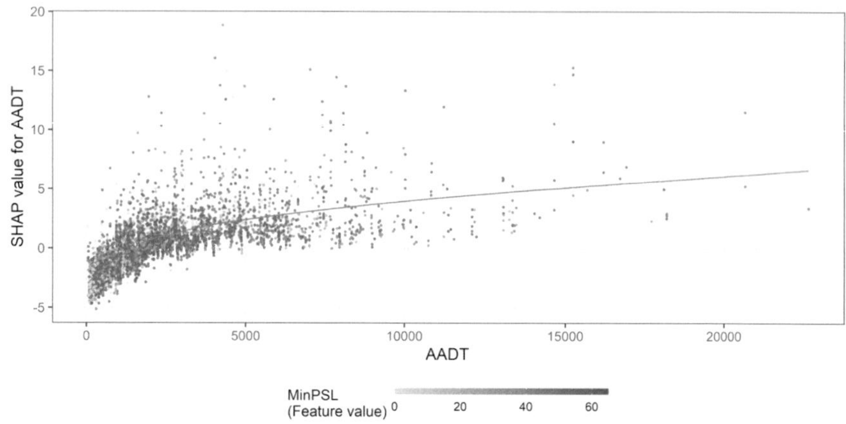

Figure 77. Feature value for two variables.

Figure 78 shows dependence plots. AADT and length both have upward slopes, whereas the others have more variable slopes. ShWidth has a large decline and then increases.

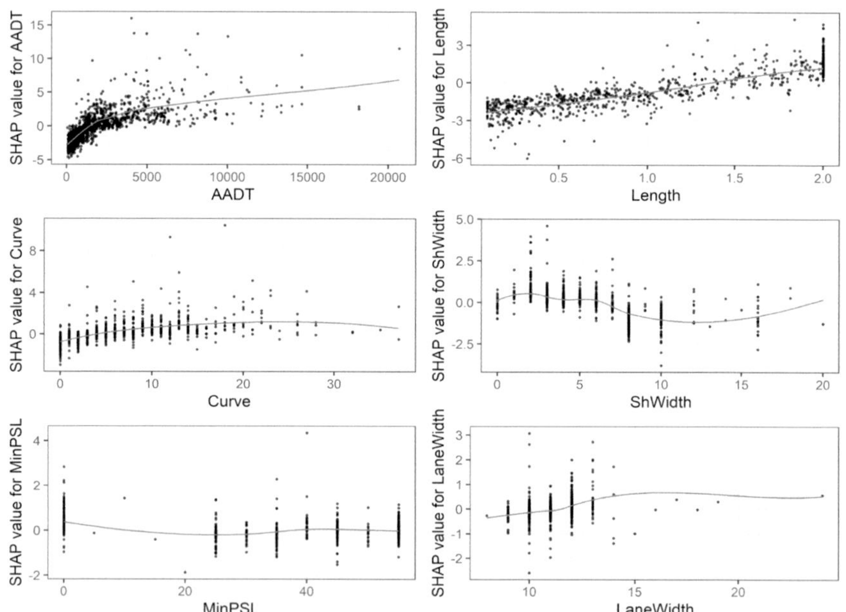

Figure 78. Dependence plots.

Example Problem 3 (Code Chunk 4)

```
plot_data <- shap.prep.stack.data(shap_contrib = shap_values$shap_score,
 top_n = 4, n_groups = 6)


shap.plot.force_plot(plot_data, zoom_in_location = 500, y_parent_limit = c(-1,1))
shap.plot.force_plot_bygroup(plot_data)
```

Figure 79 shows the first six observations of AADT, length, curve, ShWidth, and rest_variables.

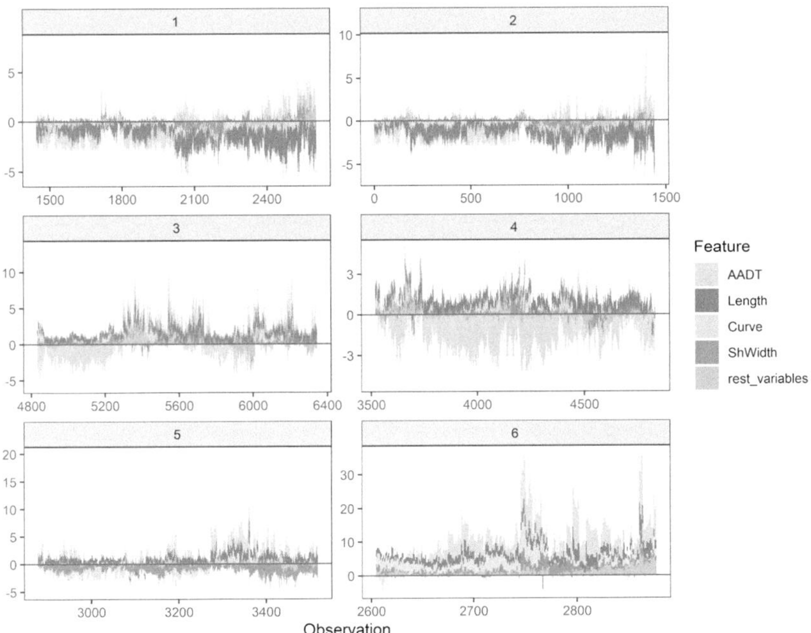

Figure 79. First six observations.

Chapter Conclusion

This chapter provides a brief introduction of explainable AI and its application in highway safety studies. Some of the key topics included in this chapter are partial dependence plots, individual conditional expectation plots, accumulated local effects plots, local surrogates, Shapley values, and SHAP values. A few example problems are provided at the end of this chapter.

Further Reading

Das, S. and Tsapakis, I., 2020. Interpretable machine learning approach in estimating traffic volume on low-volume roadways. International Journal of Transportation Science and Technology, 9, pp. 76-88.

Das, S., Dutta, A., Dey, K., Jalayer, M. and Mudgal, A., 2020. Vehicle involvements in hydroplaning crashes: Applying interpretable machine learning. Transportation Research Interdisciplinary Perspectives, 6, 100176.

Das, S., Datta, S., Zubaidi, H.A. and Obaid, I.A., 2021. Applying interpretable machine learning to classify tree and utility pole related crash injury types. IATSS Research.

Escalante, H.J., Escalera, S., Guyon, I., Baró, X., Güçlütürk, Y., Güçlü, U. and Gerven, M. van, 2018. Explainable and Interpretable Models in Computer Vision and Machine Learning. Springer.

Gianfagna, L., 2021. Explainable AI with Python. Springer Nature.

Kalatian, A. and Farooq, B., 2021. Decoding pedestrian and automated vehicle interactions using immersive virtual reality and interpretable deep learning. Transportation Research Part C: Emerging Technologies, 124, 102962.

Kim, E.-J., 2021. Analysis of travel mode choice in Seoul using an interpretable machine learning approach. Journal of Advanced Transportation, 2021, e6685004.

Molnar, C., 2020. Interpretable Machine Learning. Lulu.com.

Rothman, D., 2020. Hands-On Explainable AI (XAI) with Python: Interpret, visualize, explain, and integrate reliable AI for fair, secure, and trustworthy AI apps. Packt Publishing Ltd.

Samek, W., Montavon, G., Vedaldi, A., Hansen, L.K. and Müller, K.-R., 2019. Explainable AI: Interpreting, Explaining and Visualizing Deep Learning. Springer Nature.

CHAPTER

10

Disruptive and Emerging Technologies in Highway Safety

10.1. Introduction

Everyday life relies on the transportation of people and goods. Behaviors and the expectations of transportation customers, stakeholders, partners, and employees worldwide are being changed by the arrival of the 4th industrial revolution and the rapid development and fusion of multiple emerging and disruptive technologies, such as artificial intelligence, big data and digitization, next generation wireless technologies (5G), the Internet of Things (IoT), connected and automated vehicles (CAV) technologies, Mobility as a Service (MaaS)/Mobility on Demand (MOD), on-demand ride-sharing services, additive manufacturing, and others. A technological revolution that is already altering the way people work, live, and relate to one another is being brought about by the fusion of these technologies. The transformation is outpacing governmental entities in its scope, scale, and

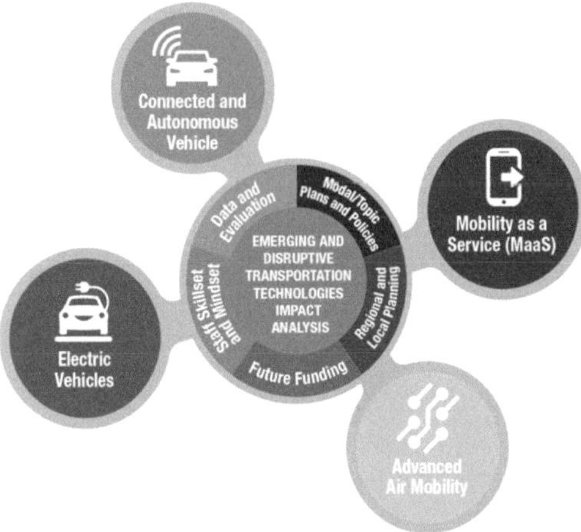

Figure 80. Impact analysis of emerging and disruptive technologies.

complexity. To build an adaptable and competent workforce, there is a need to continually train the transportation workforce for new technologies. The rapid advancement and rise in technologies, along with the increased demand for technical personnel in data-related fields, calls for an increasing emphasis on multi-disciplinary technical skills and core competencies related to emergency and disruptive technologies.

Emerging technologies bring about several possible challenges to state Departments of Transportation (DOTs) and other agencies that the existing infrastructure is owned/managed by. Uncertainty about changes that could be probable and where the most significant impacts could be is substantial and hampers an effective national alignment in approach and policy. The risks related to the emerging and disruptive technologies can include those to the agency (e.g., budget, workforce, data governance, tort liability, and changes in mission or role) and the public (e.g., privacy, safety, inclusion, security, mobility, equity, public health, and acceptance). Figure 80 shows the impact of these technologies.

The production of a guidance document for state Departments of Transportation (DOTs) and other transportation planning agencies in order to help them respond to and manage the potential risks associated with the disruptive and emerging technologies on their organizational performance is this study's objective. Empirical research is necessary to identify proactive practices and strategies for mitigating risks.

10.2. Risks Associated with Emerging and Disruptive Technologies

The current project is limited to four broad emerging and disruptive technologies, such as CAVs, EVs, MaaS/MOD, and AAM. This section provides some highlights on the key risks associated with each of the four major emerging and disruptive technologies.

10.2.1. Connected and Autonomous Vehicles

Connected and autonomous vehicles (CAVs) are approaching their market release soon and are one of the most disruptive and emerging technologies. CAVs affect their environments and vice versa, increasing the risk of exploitation of security vulnerabilities by malicious actors and the size of the cyberattack surface.

10.2.2. Electric Vehicles

The use of CAVs and electromobility is promoted by the proliferation of next-generation mobility. It makes novel attack surfaces for high impact cyberattacks that affect society. A multi-faceted and proactive approach that combines techniques arising from various domains of Information and Communications Technology (ICT) is necessary to address the risk-associated challenges introduced by electric vehicles. New potential risk issues and challenges in the next generation mobility ecosystem are introduced by emerging technologies such as LiDAR, 5G, novel in-vehicle and roadside sensors, and smart charging, which electric cars utilize.

10.2.3. Mobility as a Service/Mobility on Demand

There is an increasing demand for smart mobility solutions to lower negative environmental, social, and economic externalities of private automobile travel. Mobility-as-a-Service (MaaS) is an integrated system that allows commuters to use a single online interface to book, plan, and pay for trips with a range of mobility providers. MaaS uniquely provides a system wherein traditional transportation modes can be integrated with new service options, making it a possible alternative for private vehicle ownership and a way to overcome some negative externalities of automobile dependency. Many cities have implemented—or are working on implementing—MaaS trials to understand better how this service will function in cities, in order to realize this potential. A systematic literature review was utilized to extract insights and develop a conceptual framework to detect risks and barriers related to MaaS adoption in cities. Supply strongly impacts transport demand, especially with shared transport services where availability is frequently limited. Since observed demand can't be higher than available supply, historical transport data generally shows a biased, or censored, version of the actual underlying demand pattern. The paradigm of Mobility on Demand (MOD) has been emerging with good potential for providing convenient individual mobility. Increasing the occupancy rate of MOD by ridesharing (companies such as Uber, Lyft, Ridecell, Bird, Lime, Capital Bikeshare) is considered a necessary prerequisite for sustainable future mobility. However, both MaaS and MOD have risks and vulnerabilities, such as security issues, privacy distortion, and roadway safety issues (i.e., child-seat usage during Uber or Lyft rides).

10.2.4. Advanced Air Mobility

Advanced air mobility (AAM) seeks to renovate everyday commute and is expected to operate in the near future. It is in the form of a taxi service and functions as an aerial on-demand transport for either a small group of riders or a single passenger. This unfamiliar area is expected to allow consumers to bypass urban road network's traffic congestion. AAM could operate from sky ports retrofitted onto building rooftops by implementing an electric vertical takeoff and landing concept (eVTOL), subsequently gaining an advantage from an implementation standpoint.

10.3. Studies on Emerging and Disruptive Technologies

Table 24 lists computer vision-based highway safety studies, Table 25 lists robotics-based highway safety studies, Table 26 lists CAV-related highway safety studies, Table 27 provides a list of EV-related transportation studies, Table 28

Table 24. Computer vision-based highway safety studies

Algorithm	Research Area	Studies
YOLO	Incident Detection	C. Wang et al. (2020)
	Pedestrian Safety	Kohli and Chadha (2020); G. Li et al. (2020)
	Truck Safety	Alsanad et al. (2020)
	Pipeline Safety	Meng et al. (2020)
	Railroad Safety	Guo et al. (2021)
Temporal-Spatial-Semantic Analysis	Incident Detection	Zhu et al. (2019)
Scene Segmentation	Children Road User Safety	Kwon and Cho (2020)
	Pedestrian Safety	Bustos et al. (2021)
	Real-time Risk Assessment	Li et al. (2021)
Face Detection	Driver Behavior	Alshaqaqi et al. (2013)
	Railroad Safety	Avizzano et al. (2021)
DFF-Net	Railroad Safety	Ye et al. (2021)
Object Detection	Maritime Safety	Prasad et al. (2020)

Table 25. Robotics-based highway safety studies

Algorithm	Research Area	Studies
UAV	Bridge Defect Inspection	Potenza et al. (2020)
Mobile Robotics Platform	Bridge Defect Inspection	McLaughlin et al. (2020)
Underwater Robotics	Maritime Technology	Casalino et al. (2016); Vukić and Mišković+ (2016)
Design Schemata	Off-road Robotics Design	Schafer et al. (2013)

Table 26. CAV related highway safety studies

Algorithm	Research Area	Studies
LSTM	Trajectory Prediction	Lin et al. (2021)
Deep RL	Path Tracking	Chen and Chan (2021)
	Security and Safety	Rasheed et al. (2020)
	Lane Keeping Assistant	Q. Wang et al. (2020)
Gaussian Process	Vehicle Control	Su et al. (2018)
CNN	Intersection Safety	Hu et al. (2020)
SVM	Vehicle Reidentification	Miao et al. (2018)
RF	Aggressive Driving Identification	Jahangiri et al. (2018)

Table 27. EV related highway safety studies

Algorithm	Research Area	Studies
NN	Driving Cycle Recognition	Krithika and Subramani (2021)
Probabilistic Bayesian ML	Routing	Basso et al. (2021)
RL	Ride Hailing	Shi et al. (2020)
	Energy Management	Xu et al. (2020); Mittal et al. (2020); Wang and Northrop (2020); Li et al. (2019); Xu et al. (2019); Chiş et al. (2017)
SVM	Driver Behavior	Lee and Wu (2019)
	Energy Management	Goebel and Plötz (2019)
	Driving Cycle Recognition	Shi et al. (2018)
LSTM	Transportation System	Khan and Byun (2020)
Transfer Learning	Energy Management	Fukushima et al. (2018)
SOM	Driver Behavior	Yang et al. (2018)
Q-Learning	Energy Management	Qi et al. (2015)

Table 28. Air mobility related highway safety studies

Algorithm	Research Area	Studies
Heuristic Algorithms	Network Design	Willey and Salmon (2021)

Table 29. Ridesharing related highway safety studies

Algorithm	Research Area	Studies
Bayesian Supervised Learning	Ridesharing Pattern Analysis	Zhu et al. (2021)
P-PPM	Ridesharing Group Recommendation	Tang et al. (2021)
Transit-Based Ridesharing Matching Algorithm	Ridesharing Scheduling	Kumar and Khani (2021)
Path-Based Equilibrium Model	Ridesharing Matching	Li et al. (2020)
Doubly Dynamical Approach	Ridesharing Modelling	Wei et al. (2020)

lists air mobility-related highway safety studies, and Table 29 provides a list of ridesharing-related highway safety studies.

Resources

1. It is worthy to follow Gartner's Hype Chart to understand the emerging and disruptive technologies:
   https://www.gartner.com/smarterwithgartner/5-trends-drive-the-gartner-hype-cycle-for-emerging-technologies-2020/
2. An ongoing project NCHRP 23-15 (Guidance on Risks Related to Emerging and Disruptive Transportation Technologies) will be a good resource for emerging and disruptive transportation technologies and associated risks:
   https://apps.trb.org/cmsfeed/TRBNetProjectDisplay.asp?ProjectID=5000

Chapter Conclusion

This chapter provides a brief overview of emerging and disruptive technologies in transportation safety-related issues. Additionally, some state-of-the-art applied algorithms and their applications are briefly introduced.

Further Reading

Anderson, J.M., Nidhi, K., Stanley, K.D., Sorensen, P., Samaras, C. and Oluwatola, O.A., 2014. Autonomous Vehicle Technology: A Guide for Policymakers. Rand Corporation.

Armstrong, P., 2017. Disruptive Technologies: Understand, Evaluate, Respond. Kogan Page Publishers.

Baba, N., Baba, N., Jain, L.C. and Handa, H., 2007. Advanced Intelligent Paradigms in Computer Games, 1st ed. Springer Publishing Company, Incorporated.

Bartoletti, I., Leslie, A. and Millie, S.M., 2020. The AI Book: The Artificial Intelligence Handbook for Investors, Entrepreneurs and FinTech Visionaries. John Wiley & Sons.

Brownlee, J., 2019. Deep Learning for Computer Vision: Image Classification, Object Detection, and Face Recognition in Python. Machine Learning Mastery.

Coletta, C., Evans, L., Heaphy, L. and Kitchin, R., 2018. Creating Smart Cities. Routledge.

Coppola, P. and Esztergár-Kiss, D., 2019. Autonomous Vehicles and Future Mobility. Elsevier.

Géron, A., 2019. Hands-On Machine Learning with Scikit-Learn, Keras, and TensorFlow: Concepts, Tools, and Techniques to Build Intelligent Systems. O'Reilly Media, Inc.

Hennig, N., 2017. Keeping Up with Emerging Technologies: Best Practices for Information Professionals. ABC-CLIO.

Howse, J., 2013. OpenCV Computer Vision with Python. Packt Publishing Ltd.

Hutter, F., Kotthoff, L. and Vanschoren, J., 2019. Automated Machine Learning: Methods, Systems, Challenges. Springer.

Jerald, J., 2015. The VR Book: Human-Centered Design for Virtual Reality. Association for Computing Machinery and Morgan & Claypool.

Kaehler, A. and Bradski, G., 2016. Learning OpenCV 3: Computer Vision in C++ with the OpenCV Library. O'Reilly Media, Inc.
Larminie, J. and Lowry, J., 2012. Electric Vehicle Technology Explained. John Wiley & Sons.
Lian, Y., Zhang, G., Lee, J. and Huang, H., 2020. Review on big data applications in safety research of intelligent transportation systems and connected/automated vehicles, Accident Analysis & Prevention.
Mao, W. and Wang, F.-Y., 2012. Advances in Intelligence and Security Informatics, 1st ed. Academic Press, Inc., USA.
Marchant, G.E., Abbot, K.W. and Allenby, B., 2013. Innovative Governance Models for Emerging Technologies. Edward Elgar Publishing.
Martin, J., 2000. After the Internet: Alien Intelligence. Regnery Publishing, Inc., An Eagle Publishing Company.
Maurer, M., Gerdes, J.C., Lenz, B. and Winner, H., 2016. Autonomous Driving: Technical, Legal and Social Aspects. Springer.
Minker, W., Weber, M., Hagras, H., Callagan, V. and Kameas, A.D., 2009. Advanced Intelligent Environments, 1st ed. Springer Publishing Company, Incorporated.
Murty, M.N. and Biswas, A., 2019. Centrality and Diversity in Search: Roles in A.I., Machine Learning, Social Networks, and Pattern Recognition. Springer.
Nanaki, E.A., 2020. Electric Vehicles for Smart Cities: Trends, Challenges, and Opportunities. Elsevier.
Pistoia, G., 2010. Electric and Hybrid Vehicles: Power Sources, Models, Sustainability, Infrastructure and the Market. Elsevier.
Pohl, K., Broy, M., Daembkes, H. and Hönninger, H., 2016. Advanced Model-Based Engineering of Embedded Systems: Extensions of the SPES 2020 Methodology. Springer.
Prince, S.J.D., 2012. Computer Vision: Models, Learning, and Inference. Cambridge University Press.
Song, H., Srinivasan, R., Sookoor, T. and Jeschke, S., 2017. Smart Cities: Foundations, Principles, and Applications. John Wiley & Sons.
Szeliski, R., 2010. Computer Vision: Algorithms and Applications. Springer Science & Business Media.
Townsend, A.M., 2013. Smart Cities: Big Data, Civic Hackers, and the Quest for a New Utopia. W.W. Norton & Company.
Tsapakis, I., Das, S., Khodadi, A., Lord, D. and Li, E., et al., 2021. Use of Disruptive Technologies to Support Safety Analysis and Meet New Federal Requirements. Safe-D Project Report 04-113.
Turner, S., Martin, M., Griffin, G., Le, M., Das, S., et al., 2020. Exploring Crowdsourced Monitoring Data for Safety. Safety through Disruption University Transportation Center, Texas A&M Transportation Institute, Office of the Assistant Secretary for Research and Technology.

References

Alsanad, H.R., Ucan, O.N., Ilyas, M., Khan, A.U.R., Bayat, O., et al., 2020. Real-time fuel truck detection algorithm based on deep convolutional neural network. IEEE Access, pp. 8.

Alshaqaqi, B., Baquhaizel, A.S., Ouis, M.E.A., Boumehed, M., Ouamri, A., et al., 2013. Vision Based System for Driver Drowsiness Detection. *In:* 11th International Symposium I of Programming and Systems (ISPS). pp. 103–108.

Avizzano, C.A., Tripicchio, P., Ruffaldi, E., Filippeschi, A., Jacinto-Villegas, J.M., et al., 2021. Real-time embedded vision system for the watchfulness analysis of train drivers. IEEE Transactions on Intelligent Transportation Systems, 22, pp. 208–218.

Basso, R., Kulcsár, B. and Sanchez-Diaz, I., 2021. Electric vehicle routing problem with machine learning for energy prediction. Transportation Research Part B: Methodological, 145, 24–55.

Bustos, C., Rhoads, D., Solé-Ribalta, A., Masip, D., Arenas, et al., 2021. Explainable, automated urban interventions to improve pedestrian and vehicle safety. Transportation Research Part C: Emerging Technologies, 125, 103018.

Casalino, G., Caccia, M., Caselli, S., Melchiorri, C., Antonelli, G., et al., 2016. Underwater Intervention Robotics: An Outline of the Italian National Project MARIS. Marine Technology Society Journal, 50, pp. 98–107.

Chen, I.-M. and Chan, C.-Y., 2021. Deep reinforcement learning based path tracking controller for autonomous vehicle. Proceedings of the Institution of Mechanical Engineers, Part D: Journal of Automobile Engineering, 235, pp. 541–551.

Chiş, A., Lundén, J. and Koivunen, V., 2017. Reinforcement learning-based plug-in electric vehicle charging with forecasted price. IEEE Transactions on Vehicular Technology, 66, pp. 3674–3684.

Das, S., 2021. Autonomous vehicle safety: Understanding perceptions of pedestrians and bicyclists. Transportation Research Part F: Traffic Psychology and Behaviour, 81, pp. 41–54.

Das, S., 2022. Impact of COVID-19 on Industries. COVID-19 in the Environment Impact, Concerns, and Management of Coronavirus, Elsevier, Washington.

Das, S., 2022. Challenges and Opportunities of Electric Vehicles: A Short Review. Preprint.

Das, S., Dutta, A., Lindheimer, T., Jalayer, M. and Elgart, Z., 2019. YouTube as a source of information in understanding autonomous vehicle consumers: Natural language processing study. Transportation Research Record: Journal of the Transportation Research Board, 2673, pp. 242–253.

Das, S., Dutta, A. and Tsapakis, I., 2020e. Automated vehicle collisions in California: Applying Bayesian latent class model. IATSS Research, 44, pp. 300–308.

Fukushima, A., Yano, T., Imahara, S., Aisu, H., Shimokawa, Y., et al., 2018. Prediction of energy consumption for new electric vehicle models by machine learning. IET Intelligent Transport Systems, 12, pp. 1174–1180.

Goebel, D. and Plötz, P., 2019. Machine learning estimates of plug-in hybrid electric vehicle utility factors. Transportation Research Part D: Transport and Environment, 72, pp. 36–46.

Guo, F., Qian, Y. and Shi, Y., 2021. Real-time railroad track components inspection based on the improved YOLOv4 framework. Automation in Construction, 125, 103596.

Hu, J., Huang, M.-C. and Yu, X., 2020. Efficient mapping of crash risk at intersections with connected vehicle data and deep learning models. Accident Analysis & Prevention, 144, pp. 105665.

Jahangiri, A., Berardi, V.J. and Ghanipoor Machiani, S., 2018. Application of real field connected vehicle data for aggressive driving identification on horizontal curves. IEEE Transactions on Intelligent Transportation Systems, 19, pp. 2316–2324.

Jalayer, M., O'Connell, M., Zhou, H., Szary, P. and Das, S., 2019a. Application of unmanned aerial vehicles to inspect and inventory interchange assets to mitigate wrong-way entries. ITE Journal, 89, pp. 36–42.
Khan, P.W. and Byun, Y.-C., 2020. Smart contract centric inference engine for intelligent electric vehicle transportation system. Sensors, 20, 4252.
Kohli, P. and Chadha, A., 2020. Enabling pedestrian safety using computer vision techniques: A case study of the 2018 Uber Inc. Self-driving Car Crash. *In:* Arai, K. and Bhatia, R. (Eds.), Advances in Information and Communication. Lecture Notes in Networks and Systems. Presented at the Advances in Information and Communication, Cham, pp. 261–279.
Krithika, V. and Subramani, C., 2021. Neural network based drive cycle analysis for parallel hybrid electric vehicle. J. Test. Eval., 49, 20200233.
Kumar, P. and Khani, A., 2021. An algorithm for integrating peer-to-peer ridesharing and schedule-based transit system for first mile/last mile access. Transportation Research Part C: Emerging Technologies, 122, 102891.
Kutela, B., Das, S. and Dadashova, B., 2021. Mining patterns of autonomous vehicle crashes involving vulnerable road users to understand the associated factors. Accident Analysis & Prevention, 106473.
Kwon, J.-H. and Cho, G.-H., 2020. An examination of the intersection environment associated with perceived crash risk among school-aged children: Using street-level imagery and computer vision. Accident Analysis & Prevention, 146, 105716.
Lee, C.-H. and Wu, C.-H., 2019. Learning to recognize driving patterns for collectively characterizing electric vehicle driving behaviors. Int. J Automot. Technol., 20, pp. 1263–1276.
Li, G., Yang, Y. and Qu, X., 2020. Deep learning approaches on pedestrian detection in hazy weather. IEEE Transactions on Industrial Electronics, 67, pp. 8889–8899.
Li, Y., He, H., Peng, J. and Wang, H., 2019. Deep reinforcement learning-based energy management for a series hybrid electric vehicle enabled by history cumulative trip information. IEEE Transactions on Vehicular Technology, 68, pp. 7416–7430.
Li, Y., Karim, M.M., Qin, R., Sun, Z., Wang, Z., et al., 2021. Crash report data analysis for creating scenario-wise, spatio-temporal attention guidance to support computer vision-based perception of fatal crash risks. Accident Analysis & Prevention, 151, 105962.
Li, Y., Liu, Y. and Xie, J., 2020. A path-based equilibrium model for ridesharing matching. Transportation Research Part B: Methodological, 138, pp. 373–405.
Lin, L., Gong, S., Peeta, S. and Wu, X., 2021. Long short-term memory-based human-driven vehicle longitudinal trajectory prediction in a connected and autonomous vehicle environment. Transportation Research Record 0361198121993471.
McLaughlin, E., Charron, N. and Narasimhan, S., 2020. Automated defect quantification in concrete bridges using robotics and deep learning. Journal of Computing in Civil Engineering, 34, 04020029.
Meng, L., Peng, Z., Zhou, J., Zhang, J., Lu, Z., et al., 2020. Real-time detection of ground objects based on unmanned aerial vehicle remote sensing with deep learning: Application in excavator detection for pipeline safety. Remote Sensing, 12, pp. 182.
Miao, Z., Head, K.L. and Beak, B., 2018. Vehicle reidentification in a connected vehicle environment using machine learning algorithms. Transportation Research Record, 2672, pp. 160–172.

Mittal, N., Pundlikrao Bhagat, A., Bhide, S., Acharya, B., Xu, B., et al., 2020. Optimization of Energy Management Strategy for Range-Extended Electric Vehicle Using Reinforcement Learning and Neural Network. Presented at the WCX SAE World Congress Experience, 2020-01-1190.

Potenza, F., Rinaldi, C., Ottaviano, E. and Gattulli, V., 2020. A robotics and computer-aided procedure for defect evaluation in bridge inspection. J. Civil Struct. Health Monit, 10, pp. 471–484.

Prasad, D.K., Dong, H., Rajan, D. and Quek, C., 2020. Are object detection assessment criteria ready for maritime computer vision? IEEE Transactions on Intelligent Transportation Systems, 21, pp. 5295–5304.

Qi, X., Wu, G., Boriboonsomsin, K. and Barth, M.J., 2015. A novel blended real-time energy management strategy for plug-in hybrid electric vehicle commute trips. *In:* 2015 IEEE 18th International Conference on Intelligent Transportation Systems. Presented at the 2015 IEEE 18th International Conference on Intelligent Transportation Systems, pp. 1002–1007.

Rahman, M.T., Dey, K., Das, S. and Sherfinski, M., 2021. Sharing the road with autonomous vehicles: A qualitative analysis of the perceptions of pedestrians and bicyclists. Transportation Research Part F: Traffic Psychology and Behaviour, 78, pp. 433–445.

Rasheed, I., Hu, F. and Zhang, L., 2020. Deep reinforcement learning approach for autonomous vehicle systems for maintaining security and safety using LSTM-GAN. Vehicular Communications, 26, 100266.

Schafer, B.-H., Armbrust, C., Fohst, T. and Berns, K., 2013. The application of design schemata in off-road robotics. IEEE Intelligent Transportation Systems Magazine, 5, pp. 4–27.

Shi, J., Gao, Y., Wang, W., Yu, N. and Ioannou, P.A., 2020. Operating Electric Vehicle Fleet for Ride-Hailing Services with Reinforcement Learning. IEEE Transactions on Intelligent Transportation Systems, 21, pp. 4822–4834.

Shi, Q., Qiu, D., He, L., Wu, B., Li, Y., et al., 2018. Support vector machine–based driving cycle recognition for dynamic equivalent fuel consumption minimization strategy with hybrid electric vehicle. Advances in Mechanical Engineering, 10, 1687814018811020.

Su, J., Wu, J., Cheng, P. and Chen, J., 2018. Autonomous vehicle control through the dynamics and controller learning. IEEE Transactions on Vehicular Technology, 67, pp. 5650–5657.

Tang, L., Duan, Z., Zhu, Y., Ma, J., Liu, Z., et al., 2021. Recommendation for ridesharing groups through destination prediction on trajectory data. IEEE Transactions on Intelligent Transportation Systems, 22, pp. 1320–1333.

Tsapakis, I., Das, S., Khodadadi, A., Lord, D., Morris, J. and Li, E., 2020. Use of Disruptive Technologies to Support Safety Analysis and Meet New Federal Requirements. SafeD UTC Project Report, Washington DC.

Vukić, Z. and Mišković, N., 2016. State and Perspectives of Underwater Robotics – Role of Laboratory for Underwater Systems and Technologies. Pomorski Zbornik Special edition, pp. 15–27.

Wang, C., Dai, Y., Zhou, W. and Geng, Y., 2020. A vision-based video crash detection framework for mixed traffic flow environment considering low-visibility condition. Journal of Advanced Transportation, 2020, pp. 1–11.

Wang, P. and Northrop, W., 2020. Data-driven framework for fuel efficiency improvement in extended range electric vehicle used in package delivery applications. Presented at the WCX SAE World Congress Experience, 2020-01-0589.

Wang, Q., Zhuang, W., Wang, L. and Ju, F., 2020. Lane keeping assist for an autonomous vehicle based on deep reinforcement learning. Presented at the WCX SAE World Congress Experience, 2020-01–0728.

Wei, B., Saberi, M., Zhang, F., Liu, W., Waller, S.T., et al., 2020. Modeling and managing ridesharing in a multi-modal network with an aggregate traffic representation: A doubly dynamical approach. Transportation Research Part C: Emerging Technologies 117, 102670.

Willey, L.C. and Salmon, J.L., 2021. A method for urban air mobility network design using hub location and subgraph isomorphism. Transportation Research Part C: Emerging Technologies, 125, 102997.

Xu, B., Hu, X., Tang, X., Lin, X., Li, H., Rathod, et al., 2020. Ensemble reinforcement learning-based supervisory control of hybrid electric vehicle for fuel economy improvement. IEEE Transactions on Transportation electrification 6, pp. 717–727.

Xu, B., Malmir, F., Rathod, D., Filipi, Z., et al., 2019. Real-time reinforcement learning optimized energy management for a 48v mild hybrid electric vehicle. Presented at the WCX SAE World Congress Experience, 2019-01–1208.

Yang, J., Dong, J., Zhang, Q., Liu, Z., Wang, W., et al., 2018. An investigation of battery electric vehicle driving and charging behaviors using vehicle usage data collected in Shanghai, China. Transportation Research Record, 2672, pp. 20–30.

Ye, T., Zhang, X., Zhang, Y. and Liu, J., 2021. Railway traffic object detection using differential feature fusion convolution neural network. IEEE Transactions on Intelligent Transportation Systems, 22, pp. 1375–1387.

Zhu, R., Fang, J., Xu, H. and Xue, J., 2019. Progressive temporal-spatial-semantic analysis of driving anomaly detection and recounting. Sensors, 19, 5098.

Zhu, Z., Sun, L., Chen, X. and Yang, H., 2021. Integrating probabilistic tensor factorization with Bayesian supervised learning for dynamic ridesharing pattern analysis. Transportation Research Part C: Emerging Technologies, 124, 102916.

CHAPTER

11

Conclusions and Future Needs

11.1. Introduction

With the rise of AI applications, more and more research has begun to apply AI techniques to address highway safety problems. Traditional ways of solving highway safety-related problems always involve statistical and mathematical models. However, in order to perform an unbiased analysis, a large amount of data is needed from various sources. Moreover, when it is difficult to collect traffic data, video data can serve as an alternative. As such, traditional methods cannot address the needs of these data. Compared to traditional methods, AI can perform analyses on big data more efficiently and provide more accurate results. Moreover, computer vision (CV) techniques can help to analyze video footage, which traditional methods are unable to do.

11.2. Highway Safety AI 101

There is an urgent need for the Highway Safety AI 101 framework. The framework will provide a big picture overview of the existing AI applications in highway safety, potential precise solutions, adaptability in emerging and disruptive technologies, and justifiable contexts of ethical issues.

11.3. Ethics in Highway Safety AI

AI has many benefits. However, the everyday application of artificial intelligence in different emerging and disruptive technologies raises ethical concerns. Here is an example. Should automated vehicles have in-built ethical thresholds? If so, what are these thresholds, and how should they be determined? If an automated vehicle gets into a situation where it must choose between driving into a child or an animal or a fixed object to save lives who are outside of the vehicle, what decision will it make? Who is controlling these decisions? And what are the consequences or responsibilities of these events? If the decision-making process and the algorithm are not bias-free, AI can thus increase bias and discrimination.

11.3.1. Ethics and Regulation

Given the ethical problems with AI, there is a need for regulation. In today's world, most AI policy initiatives include AI ethics. It is important to note that a straightforward regulation is not available and there is a need to determine what precise course of action should be taken. For example, many agencies do not know how to deal with transparency of bias given the technologies, as there is existing bias in society and divergent views on justice and fairness. Figure 81 shows a diagram of ethics in AI, including bias & fairness, interpretability, and robustness & security.

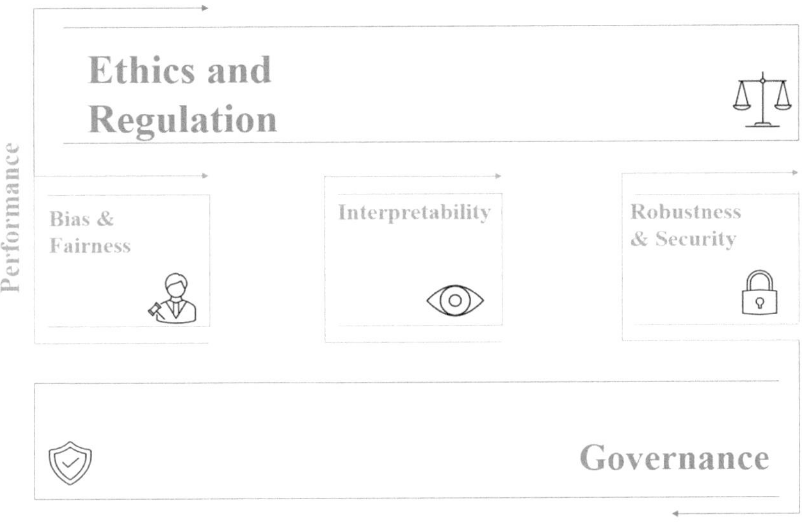

Figure 81. Ethics in AI.

11.3.2. Bias, Fairness, Interpretability, Robustness, and Security

The need for ethical AI is recognized by many companies; Google, for instance, has published ethical principles for AI, such as avoiding creating or reinforcing unfair bias, enforcing safety, maintaining accountability, promoting scientific excellence, providing social benefit, maintaining privacy design, and limiting potentially abusive or harmful applications (i.e., weapons/technologies that violate international law and human rights). These ethics of AI are about changes in technology and how it impacts human lives, but it is also about changes in the economy and society. A goal shared by many policymakers is that AI has societal "Explainable AI," which is indicated by the issues of discrimination and bias that already exist. Something going wrong is always a risk. Should safety ethics become a matter of trade-offs? Security is another issue that existed before AI, but now deserves even more attention; every electronic software or device can be invaded, hacked, and manipulated by people with malicious intentions while in a networked world. While some people are more vulnerable to issues than others, all are vulnerable due to technologies such as AI, because as their agency increases and more tasks are delegated to them, humanity becomes more dependent on them.

11.3.3. Governance

Responsible innovation necessitates taking the opinions and interests of stakeholders into account, not simply embedding ethics into the design. Public debate, broad stakeholder involvement, and early societal intervention in innovation and research are entailed in inclusive governance. The applied ethics of most policy documents (which are typically more abstract and top-down) are in conflict with this more bottom-up responsible innovation approach. Policies are often created, without the input of stakeholders, by experts, and even principles that are endorsed, such as ethics by design, tend to be too vague when it comes to the meaning of the implications of their application in practice. It remains a huge challenge to build a bridge between the practices of technology development and their use in particular contexts, the technologies, and the voices of those who are part of these practices and work in these contexts and high-level ethical and legal, abstract principles in order to make AI work. Covering this bridging work is left to the addressees of these proposals. At the earlier stage of policymaking, should/can more be done? More work on the "how" is at least required alongside the "what": the procedures, methods, and institutions necessary for making AI ethics work in practice. More attention must be paid to this process.

11.4. AI based Highway Safety Guidances

The first version and the upcoming second version of the HSM are more focused on statistical modeling techniques. There is a need for a future AI Highway Safety Manual (AiHSM) which will incorporate AI solutions in solving highway safety problems. There are three ongoing national or National Cooperative Highway Research Program (NCHRP) projects which have focused on the potential of AI in solving transportation research problems. These projects are:

- NCHRP 17-100: Leveraging Big Data and Artificial Intelligence to Streamline Safety Data Analyses
- NCHRP 23-12: Artificial Intelligence Opportunities for State and Local DOTs – A Research Roadmap
- NCHRP 23-16: Implementing and Leveraging Machine Learning at State Departments of Transportation

These projects indicate that the interest in 'AI in Highway Safety' has increased significantly in recent years. The newly adopted Safe System Approach (SSA) by the USDOT will gain significant interest from the researchers throughout the world. Inclusion of AI in SSA can initiate a new domain like AI-based SSA (AiSSA). Approaches such as the Artificial Intelligence Road Assessment Program (AiRAP) have been gaining advancement in data fusion using data from LIDAR, telematics, cell phone, probe, and other data sources to deliver AI analytic-based critical information for road safety improvement. Wider and real-life usage of AI tools will show the importance of AiHSM, AiSSA, and AiRAP in the upcoming days.

Chapter Conclusion

This chapter provides conclusions and future needs. It reviews highway safety and AI, ethics in highway safety AI, and the need for AI based tools such as AiRAP, AiSSA, and AiHSM.

Further Reading

Boddington, P., 2017. Towards a Code of Ethics for Artificial Intelligence. Springer.
Dubber, M.D., Pasquale, F. and Das, S., 2020. The Oxford Handbook of Ethics of AI. Oxford University Press.
Hongladarom, S., 2020. The Ethics of AI and Robotics: A Buddhist Viewpoint. Rowman & Littlefield.
Kearns, M. and Roth, A., 2019. The Ethical Algorithm: The Science of Socially Aware Algorithm Design. Oxford University Press.
Liao, S.M., 2020. Ethics of Artificial Intelligence. Oxford University Press.
Wallach, W. and Allen, C., 2010. Moral Machines: Teaching Robots Right from Wrong. Oxford University Press.

Appendix A

Case Study of Exploratory Data Analysis

Problem Statement

Exploratory data analysis is a critical part of analyzing data. This case study shows the steps of an exploratory data analysis by exploring the differences of crash characteristics by different generations.

Data Description

This case study collected traffic fatality data from FARS covering 2010-2018 (nine years). All three levels of data (crash, vehicle, and person) were merged together at the person level. The person age variables have been converted into seven generations based on the birth year calculated from the person age data and year of fatality occurrences. There are a limited number of cases with missing information about the person age. These entries were removed. Table 30 shows the frequencies of traffic fatalities by year and generation. The counts clearly show that Gen X, Millennial, and Gen Z are the three generations with a large number of traffic fatalities. Millennial is the generation that has the highest number of traffic fatalities (98,810 fatalities in nine years).

Before starting the analysis of generation-based information, it is important to show the overall fatality rates of the states in the U.S. Figure 82 represents traffic fatalities by year for every state. The number of fatalities is represented by a color gradient for easy visual interpretation. Overall, states like California (CA), Texas (TX), and Florida (FL) have large numbers of traffic fatalities relative to other states. California and Texas are the top states with the highest number of traffic fatalities every year. From 2010 to 2018, the trends of traffic fatalities are usually in decreasing order for all the states except for a few, such as New York and Pennsylvania.

Table 30. Traffic fatalities by American generations

Year	Greatest	Silent	Boomers	Gen X	Millennial	Gen Z	Post-Z	Yearly Total
2010	1,402	4,122	8,632	7,465	10,269	1,063	0	32,953
2011	1,120	3,998	8,446	7,213	10,511	1,139	0	32,427
2012	952	4,014	8,806	7,450	11,138	1,372	0	33,732
2013	791	3,924	8,483	7,264	10,741	1,578	57	32,838
2014	683	3,770	8,389	6,925	10,837	1,940	119	32,663
2015	599	3,827	8,993	7,685	11,404	2,665	231	35,404
2016	547	3,989	9,299	8,054	11,927	3,549	321	37,686
2017	387	4,019	9,023	8,187	11,258	4,072	404	37,350
2018	288	3,711	8,846	7,951	10,725	4,491	416	36,428
Generation Total	6,769	35,374	78,917	68,194	98,810	21,869	1,548	311,481

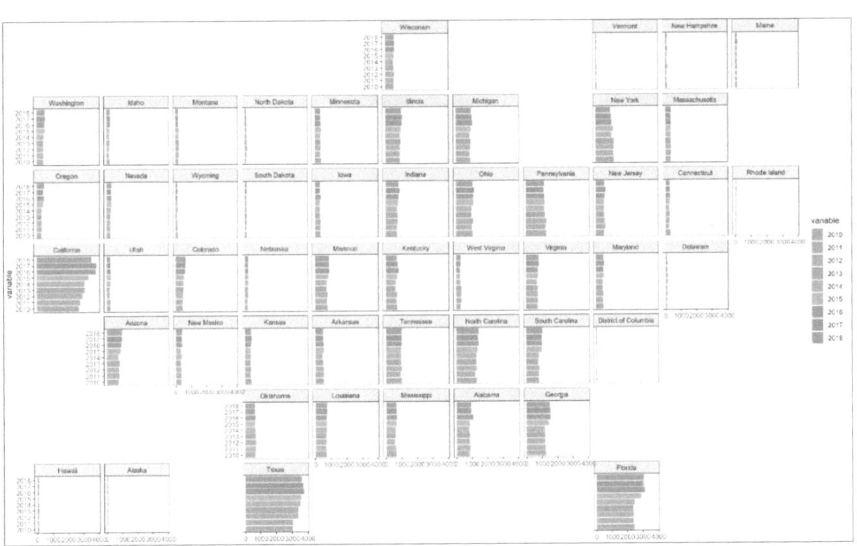

Figure 82. Traffic fatalities by state (2010-2018).

Exploratory Data Analysis

Figure 83 represents traffic fatalities by American generations for every state. The frequencies are denoted by a color gradient with dark indicative of a more populous state and light of a lower population. Overall, states like California (CA), Texas (TX), and Florida (FL) have large fatality counts relative to other states. Since Florida is known to be the "retirement" state, the presence of Silent and Boomer populations, along with the number of fatality counts, is higher than other American generations. The trends of fatalities by generation are similar for Texas except for the Greatest generation. Similarly, the trends are slightly low for Post-Z in Florida and California. For the northern states, the fatalities of the Silent and Boomer generations are slightly higher.

Figure 84 displays the population and traffic fatalities by American generations. The graph on the left represents the population of each categorized

Figure 83. Traffic fatalities in the U.S. states by generations.

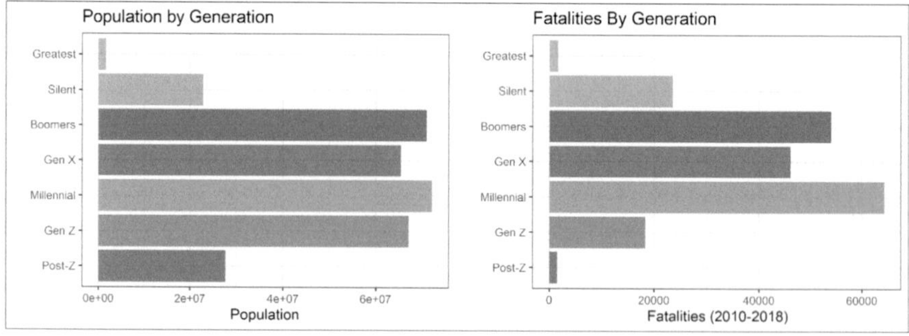

Figure 84. Population and fatalities by American generations.

generation. The graph on the right represents the fatalities from 2010-2018 with the number of fatalities from each categorized generation. In comparison to the population, there is a significantly lower proportional number of fatalities for Gen Z and Post-Z populations. This is mostly due to the smaller number of drivers in these two groups. A majority of these fatalities are associated with either occupants or non-motorists. Gen X and Boomers show a slight decrease in proportional fatalities. There are slight increases in proportional fatalities for the Millennial and Silent generations.

Race is another critical aspect that requires more attention. Table 31 lists the traffic fatalities in nine years by American generations and their races. White Americans are disproportionately high in traffic fatalities (62%) compared to African Americans and Hispanics in terms of total fatality counts. It is important to know that White Americans represent 73% of the U.S. population (according to the U.S. Census). The fatalities of African Americans and Hispanics are 12.8% and 12.9%, respectively. African Americans make up 13.4% of the U.S. population, and Hispanics represent 18.5%. Based on the population-fatality percentage distribution, African Americans are represented disproportionately high in traffic fatalities.

Table 31. Fatality counts by generation and race

Race	Greatest	Silent	Boomers	Gen X	Millennial	Gen Z	Post-Z
White Alone	5320	26164	53423	40979	54964	11368	626
Black Alone	250	2274	9224	9856	14361	3555	379
Hispanic	291	2222	6838	9283	16980	4246	332
Asian Alone	170	1091	1651	1142	1847	406	36
American Indian	19	238	950	1296	2080	436	44
Two or More Races	717	3361	6759	5546	8386	1811	129
Native Hawaiian Alone	1	19	52	59	119	39	2
Guamanian/ Samoan	1	5	20	33	73	8	0

Crash and fatality data are complex in nature. Crash data has a significant amount of categorical information. Alluvial plots are great data visualization tools to show complex interactions between multiple categories in a two-dimensional space. The black bars indicate the ratios of the categories in each variable. These bars are sorted in descending order of the proportions in each variable. The width of the links between the variables indicates the in between proportions. Figure 85 shows alluvial plots by considering several key factors in two groups: 1) generation, person type, drinking, and drug, and 2) generation, race, gender, and work injury. These two plots can be explained in detail. Currently, only a few observations are described here. In pedestrian and bicyclist groups, Boomers are higher in frequencies than other generations. Drivers and pedestrians are the two groups that show high alcohol impairment compared to other person types. Compared to the Greatest and Silent generations, the fatalities among non-Americans are higher in other generations. Males are disproportionately higher in fatalities compared to females. The majority of the fatalities are not work-related. Males are represented disproportionately higher in work-related injuries compared to females. Findings from this section answer research question 1.

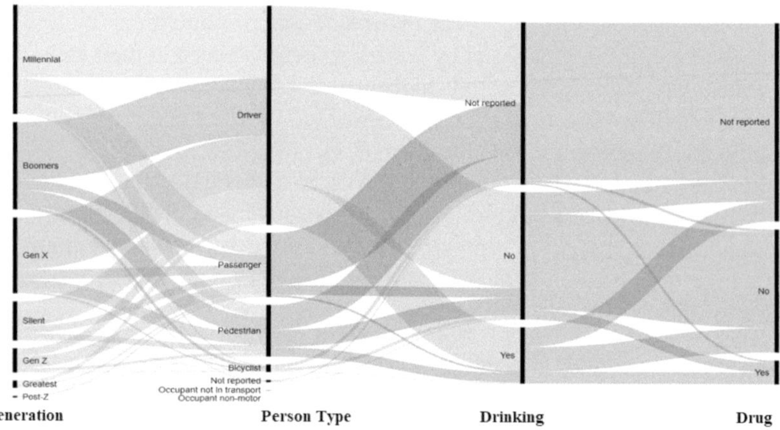

(a) Generation, person type, drinking, and drug

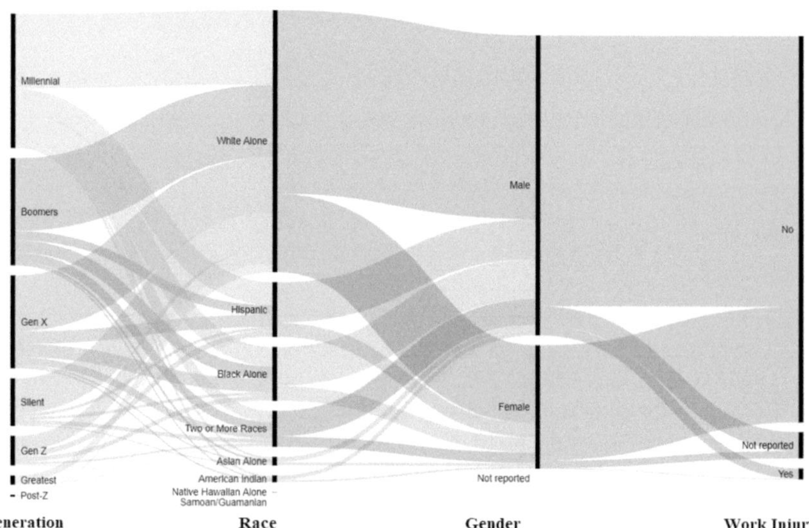

(b) Generation, race, gender, and work-related injury

Figure 85. Alluvial plots on factor interactions.

Results and Discussions

Statistical analyses were performed using *R* (version 3.6.0) with the package 'compareGroups' for descriptive tables. This study defined statistical significance as p-value < 0.05. Table 32 lists the comparisons of person fatalities by five American generations. Eight key person-level variables (sex or gender, person type, race, alcohol impairment, drug impairment, seat-belt usage, location of death, and work-related injury) were considered for analysis. These person-level variables were selected based on their variable importance measures. The generations used in this table include Silent, Boomers, Gen X, Millennial, and Gen Z. In the United States, males played a major role in traffic fatalities in all five American generations (Boomers=72.8%, Gen X=73.7%, Gen Z=62.4%, Millennial=73.5%, and Silent=61.6%). In Silent and Gen Z generations, females are represented disproportionately higher compared to the other three generations. The fatalities of the White Americans show a downward trend from the Silent generation to Gen Z. The opposite is visible for African Americans. The proportions show that drivers are the most likely of all person types to be involved in a traffic fatality except in Gen Z, which is obvious. Passengers are the most likely to be involved in traffic fatalities for Gen Z, with 47.5%. As Gen Z are the youngest among these five generations, the majority of the Gen Z population are occupants or passengers. In seat-belt usage, the Silent generation shows disproportionately high proportions in both lap and shoulder belt usage. To compute the count and percentages of variable categories by groups (i.e., five generations in this case), it is important to test whether the distribution of the variables differs between groups. As all the variables of interest in this group are categorical in nature, a Chi-square test was performed. As this study design contains more than two groups, there is a need for performing overall association assessment, as well as pairwise comparisons. This study conducted pairwise tests and displayed p-values. From Table 32, all the variables significantly differ by generations.

As Baby Boomers, Millennials, and Gen X represent a high number of fatalities, it is intuitive to make comparisons between these generations. As Baby Boomers are an aging group among these three generations, the comparisons were done with this group: Baby Boomers vs Millennials and Baby Boomers vs Gen X. Table 33 lists the comparisons of person fatalities between Baby Boomers and Millennials. Consider for a given data matrix with the response and predictor variables that the mean parameter vector is $\underline{\beta}$. Using the odds of the combination x, $Odd(\underline{\beta}x) = \dfrac{\pi(\underline{\beta}x)}{1-\pi(\underline{\beta}x)} = e^{(x'\underline{\beta})}$. The odds ratio (*OR*) can be expressed as:

$$OR(\underline{\beta}x_1x_2) = \frac{Odd(\underline{\beta}x_1)}{Odd(\underline{\beta}x_2)} = e^{(x_1'\underline{\beta} - x_2'\underline{\beta})} \quad (1)$$

Male, drivers, White Americans, no alcohol impairment, no drug impairment, shoulder and lap belt usage, death at scene, and non-work-related injury are the dominant categories in the listed variables of interest for both groups. The

Table 32. Comparison between five generations

Variable Categories	Silent N=35,374	Baby Boomers N=78,917	Gen X N=68,194	Millennial N=98,810	Gen Z N=21,869	p-value
SEX (Gender)						**0.000***
Female	13,561 (38.3%)	21,470 (27.2%)	17,932 (26.3%)	26,113 (26.4%)	8,220 (37.6%)	
Male	21,807 (61.6%)	57,430 (72.8%)	50,248 (73.7%)	72,670 (73.5%)	13,642 (62.4%)	
Not reported	6 (0.02%)	17 (0.02%)	14 (0.02%)	27 (0.03%)	7(0.03%)	
PER_TYP (Person Type)						**0.000***
Driver	22,041 (62.3%)	51,989 (65.9%)	46,739 (68.5%)	65,820 (66.6%)	7,308 (33.4%)	
Passenger	6,507 (18.4%)	8,840 (11.2%)	8,799 (12.9%)	20,064 (20.3%)	10,377 (47.5%)	
Pedestrian	5,898 (16.7%)	14,838 (18.8%)	10,770 (15.8%)	10,937 (11.1%)	3,072 (14.0%)	
Bicyclist	579 (1.64%)	2,588 (3.28%)	1,510 (2.21%)	1,339 (1.36%)	717 (3.28%)	
Occupant non-motor	12 (0.03%)	39 (0.05%)	26 (0.04%)	37 (0.04%)	43 (0.20%)	
Occupant not in transport	31 (0.09%)	101 (0.13%)	75 (0.11%)	91 (0.09%)	38 (0.17%)	
Not reported	306 (0.87%)	522 (0.66%)	275 (0.40%)	522 (0.53%)	314 (1.44%)	
RACE (Race)						**0.000***
White Alone	26,164 (74.0%)	53,423 (67.7%)	40,979 (60.1%)	54,964 (55.6%)	11,368 (52.0%)	
Black Alone	2,274 (6.43%)	9,224 (11.7%)	9,856 (14.5%)	14,361 (14.5%)	3,555 (16.3%)	
Hispanic	2,222 (6.28%)	6,838 (8.66%)	9,283 (13.6%)	16,980 (17.2%)	4,246 (19.4%)	
Asian Alone	1,091 (3.08%)	1,651 (2.09%)	1,142 (1.67%)	1,847 (1.87%)	406 (1.86%)	
Two or More Races	3,361 (9.50%)	6,759 (8.56%)	5,546 (8.13%)	8,386 (8.49%)	1,811 (8.28%)	

American Indian	238 (0.67%)	950 (1.20%)	1,296 (1.90%)	2,080 (2.11%)	436 (1.99%)	
Native Hawaiian Alone	19 (0.05%)	52 (0.07%)	59 (0.09%)	119 (0.12%)	39 (0.18%)	
Samoan/Guamanian	5 (0.01%)	20 (0.03%)	33 (0.05%)	73 (0.07%)	8 (0.04%)	
DRINKING (Alcohol Impairment)						**0.000***
No	18,554 (52.5%)	32,291 (40.9%)	22,105 (32.4%)	29,623 (30.0%)	7,884 (36.1%)	
Yes	1,250 (3.53%)	11,751 (14.9%)	15,177 (22.3%)	21,354 (21.6%)	1,148 (5.25%)	
Not reported	15,570 (44.0%)	34,875 (44.2%)	30,912 (45.3%)	47,833 (48.4%)	12,837 (58.7%)	
DRUGS (Drug Impairment)						**0.000***
No	15,724 (44.5%)	30,912 (39.2%)	23,203 (34.0%)	30,977 (31.4%)	7,008 (32.0%)	
Yes	609 (1.72%)	4,671 (5.92%)	6,164 (9.04%)	9,095 (9.20%)	917 (4.19%)	
Not reported	19,041 (53.8%)	43,334 (54.9%)	38,827 (56.9%)	58,738 (59.4%)	13,944 (63.8%)	
REST_USE (Seat-belt Usage)						**0.000***
Lap and shoulder belt	16,685 (47.2%)	23,068 (29.2%)	16,433 (24.1%)	24,818 (25.1%)	5,676 (26.0%)	
Lap belt only	234 (0.66%)	358 (0.45%)	249 (0.37%)	362 (0.37%)	261 (1.19%)	
Shoulder belt only	94 (0.27%)	176 (0.22%)	163 (0.24%)	230 (0.23%)	38 (0.17%)	
Child/Booster	0 (0.00%)	0 (0.00%)	0 (0.00%)	0 (0.00%)	1,257 (5.75%)	
Helmet	843 (2.38%)	4,995 (6.33%)	4,315 (6.33%)	5,614 (5.68%)	375 (1.71%)	
No helmet	692 (1.96%)	6,458 (8.18%)	6,062 (8.89%)	5,480 (5.55%)	654 (2.99%)	

(Contd.)

Table 32. *(Contd.)*

Variable Categories	Silent N=35,374	Baby Boomers N=78,917	Gen X N=68,194	Millennial N=98,810	Gen Z N=21,869	p-value
Restraint unknown	317 (0.90%)	338 (0.43%)	266 (0.39%)	357 (0.36%)	167 (0.76%)	
None	5,931 (16.8%)	14,538 (18.4%)	16,751 (24.6%)	29,746 (30.1%)	4,116 (18.8%)	
Not reported	10,578 (29.9%)	28,986 (36.7%)	23,955 (35.1%)	32,203 (32.6%)	9,325 (42.6%)	
DOA (Death Location)						**0.000***
Died at scene	13,419 (37.9%)	41,885 (53.1%)	41,864 (61.4%)	62,845 (63.6%)	11,918 (54.5%)	
Died en route	370 (1.05%)	921 (1.17%)	804 (1.18%)	1,035 (1.05%)	216 (0.99%)	
Not applicable	21,559 (60.9%)	36,056 (45.7%)	25,477 (37.4%)	34,848 (35.3%)	9,715 (44.4%)	
Not reported	26 (0.07%)	55 (0.07%)	49 (0.07%)	82 (0.08%)	20 (0.09%)	
WORK_INJ (Work related Injury)						**0.000***
No	32,601 (92.2%)	70,550 (89.4%)	61,111 (89.6%)	91,050 (92.1%)	20,789 (95.1%)	
Yes	528 (1.49%)	3,208 (4.07%)	2,626 (3.85%)	1,694 (1.71%)	82 (0.37%)	
Not reported	2,245 (6.35%)	5,159 (6.54%)	4,457 (6.54%)	6,066 (6.14%)	998 (4.56%)	

Note: Post Z is omitted due to low sample size.

Table 33. Comparison between baby boomers and millennials

Variable Categories	Baby Boomers N=78,917	Millennials N=98,810	OR	p-ratio	p-value
SEX					**0.001***
Female	21,470 (27.2%)	26,113 (26.4%)	Ref.	Ref.	
Male	57,430 (72.8%)	72,670 (73.5%)	1.04 [1.02;1.06]	<0.001	
Not reported	17 (0.02%)	27 (0.03%)	1.30 [0.71;2.44]	0.394	
PER_TYP					**0.000***
Bicyclist	2,588 (3.28%)	1,339 (1.36%)	Ref.	Ref.	
Driver	51,989 (65.9%)	65,820 (66.6%)	2.45 [2.29;2.62]	0.000	
Passenger	8,840 (11.2%)	20,064 (20.3%)	4.39 [4.09;4.71]	0.000	
Pedestrian	14,838 (18.8%)	10,937 (11.1%)	1.42 [1.33;1.53]	0.000	
Occupant non-motor	39 (0.05%)	37 (0.04%)	1.83 [1.16;2.90]	0.010	
Occupant not in transport	101 (0.13%)	91 (0.09%)	1.74 [1.30;2.33]	<0.001	
Not reported	522 (0.66%)	522 (0.53%)	1.93 [1.68;2.22]	0.000	
RACE					**0.000***
American Indian	950 (1.20%)	2080 (2.11%)	Ref.	Ref.	
White Alone	53,423 (67.7%)	54,964 (55.6%)	0.47 [0.43;0.51]	0.000	
Black Alone	9,224 (11.7%)	14,361 (14.5%)	0.71 [0.66;0.77]	0.000	
Hispanic	6,838 (8.66%)	16,980 (17.2%)	1.13 [1.04;1.23]	0.003	

(Contd.)

Table 33. *(Contd.)*

Variable Categories	Baby Boomers N=78,917	Millennials N=98,810	OR	p-ratio	p-value
Asian Alone	1,651 (2.09%)	1,847 (1.87%)	0.51 [0.46;0.57]	0.000	
Two or More Races	6,759 (8.56%)	8,386 (8.49%)	0.57 [0.52;0.62]	0.000	
Native Hawaiian Alone	52 (0.07%)	119 (0.12%)	1.04 [0.75;1.47]	0.803	
Samoan/Guamanian	20 (0.03%)	73 (0.07%)	1.66 [1.02;2.81]	0.040	
DRINKING					**0.000***
No	32,291 (40.9%)	29,623 (30.0%)	Ref.	Ref.	
Yes	11,751 (14.9%)	21,354 (21.6%)	1.98 [1.93;2.04]	0.000	
Not reported	34,875 (44.2%)	47,833 (48.4%)	1.50 [1.46;1.53]	0.000	
DRUGS					**0.000***
No	30,912 (39.2%)	30,977 (31.4%)	Ref.	Ref.	
Yes	4,671 (5.92%)	9,095 (9.20%)	1.94 [1.87;2.02]	0.000	
Not reported	43,334 (54.9%)	58,738 (59.4%)	1.35 [1.33;1.38]	0.000	
REST_USE					**0.000***
Helmet	4,995 (6.33%)	5,614 (5.68%)	Ref.	Ref.	
No helmet	6,458 (8.18%)	5,480 (5.55%)	0.76 [0.72;0.80]	0.000	
Lap and shoulder belt	23,068 (29.2%)	24,818 (25.1%)	0.96 [0.92;1.00]	0.042	
Lap belt only	358 (0.45%)	362 (0.37%)	0.90 [0.77;1.05]	0.170	

Shoulder belt only	176 (0.22%)	230 (0.23%)	1.16 [0.95;1.42]	0.139	
Restraint unknown	338 (0.43%)	357 (0.36%)	0.94 [0.81;1.10]	0.428	
None	1,4538 (18.4%)	29,746 (30.1%)	1.82 [1.74;1.90]	0.000	
Not reported	28,986 (36.7%)	32,203 (32.6%)	0.99 [0.95;1.03]	0.583	
DOA					**0.000***
Died at scene	41,885 (53.1%)	62,845 (63.6%)	Ref.	Ref.	
Died en route	921 (1.17%)	1,035 (1.05%)	0.75 [0.68;0.82]	<0.001	
Not applicable	36,056 (45.7%)	34,848 (35.3%)	0.64 [0.63;0.66]	0.000	
Not reported	55 (0.07%)	82 (0.08%)	0.99 [0.71;1.40]	0.966	
WORK_INJ					**<0.001***
No	70,550 (89.4%)	91,050 (92.1%)	Ref.	Ref.	
Yes	3,208 (4.07%)	1,694 (1.71%)	0.41 [0.39;0.43]	0.000	
Not reported	5,159 (6.54%)	6,066 (6.14%)	0.91 [0.88;0.95]	<0.001	

difference of all variables between these two generations is statistically significant (see Table 33). For each of the variables, the first category is considered as the 'reference' category. Male Millennials have higher odds for traffic fatalities (Odds Ratio or OR=1.04, 95% C.I.=1.02-1.06). Compared to the bicyclists, other person types show higher odds for the Millennials. For alcohol and drug impairment-related traffic fatalities, odds are higher for the Millennials. For lap and shoulder belt usage, odds measures are not statistically significant. For shoulder belt only and unknown restraint type, the odds are not statistically significant. For work-related injuries, Millennials show lower odds. For Baby Boomers, the higher odds are associated with some of the key attributes such as no helmet, lap and shoulder belt, lap belt only, died en route, and work-related injuries. The 'no helmet' issue clearly indicates that aging motorcyclists and bicyclists are vulnerable to collisions. The seat belt issues indicate that proper seat belts are also not sufficient when the aging population is involved in crashes. The 'died en route' scenario also indicates the vulnerability of this aging group. Work-related fatalities indicate that the aging population is mostly associated with work-related trips, which may end up in crashes and related consequences.

Table 34 lists the comparisons of person fatalities between Baby Boomers and Gen X. Work-related injury is a not factor for the high likelihood of Gen X traffic fatalities. The odds of three-person types (occupant non-motor, occupant not in transport, and unknown person type) are not statistically significant between Baby Boomers and Gen X. Similarly, the odds of three races (Hispanic, Native Hawaiian Alone, and Samoan/Guamanian) are not statistically significant between Baby Boomers and Gen X. For lap and shoulder belt usage, Gen X show lowers odds (OR: 0.82, 95% C.I.: 0.79- 0.86). For alcohol and drug impairment-related traffic fatalities, odds are higher for Gen X. For Baby Boomers, the higher odds are associated with some of the key attributes such as no helmet, lap and shoulder belt, lap belt only, died en route, and work-related injuries. The interpretations are similar to the previous section. The findings from this section answer the second research question (RQ2).

Table 34. Comparison between baby boomers and Gen X

	Baby Boomers N=78917	**Gen X N=68194**	**OR**	**p-ratio**	**p-value**
GENDER					**<0.001***
Female	21,470 (27.2%)	17,932 (26.3%)	Ref.	Ref.	
Male	57,430 (72.8%)	50,248 (73.7%)	1.05 [1.02;1.07]	<0.001	
Not reported	17 (0.02%)	14 (0.02%)	0.99 [0.48;2.01]	0.974	
PER_TYP					**<0.001***
Bicyclist	2,588 (3.28%)	1,510 (2.21%)	Ref.	Ref.	
Driver	51,989 (65.9%)	46,739 (68.5%)	1.54 [1.44;1.64]	0.000	

Passenger	8,840 (11.2%)	8,799 (12.9%)	1.71 [1.59;1.83]	0.000	
Pedestrian	14,838 (18.8%)	10,770 (15.8%)	1.24 [1.16;1.33]	<0.001	
Occupant non-motor	39 (0.05%)	26 (0.04%)	1.14 [0.69;1.88]	0.599	
Occupant not in transport	101 (0.13%)	75 (0.11%)	1.27 [0.94;1.73]	0.124	
Not reported	522 (0.66%)	275 (0.40%)	0.90 [0.77;1.06]	0.208	
RACE					**0.000***
American Indian	950 (1.20%)	1,296 (1.90%)	Ref.	Ref.	
White Alone	53,423 (67.7%)	40,979 (60.1%)	0.56 [0.52;0.61]	0.000	
Black Alone	9,224 (11.7%)	9,856 (14.5%)	0.78 [0.72;0.86]	<0.001	
Hispanic	6,838 (8.66%)	9,283 (13.6%)	1.00 [0.91;1.09]	0.915	
Asian Alone	1,651 (2.09%)	1,142 (1.67%)	0.51 [0.45;0.57]	0.000	
Two or More Races	6,759 (8.56%)	5,546 (8.13%)	0.60 [0.55;0.66]	0.000	
Native Hawaiian Alone	52 (0.07%)	59 (0.09%)	0.83 [0.57;1.22]	0.346	
Samoan/ Guamanian	20 (0.03%)	33 (0.05%)	1.21 [0.69;2.15]	0.513	
REST_USE					**<0.001***
Helmet	4,995 (6.33%)	4,315 (6.33%)	Ref.	Ref.	
No helmet	6,458 (8.18%)	6,062 (8.89%)	1.09 [1.03;1.15]	0.002	
Lap and shoulder belt	23,068 (29.2%)	16,433 (24.1%)	0.82 [0.79;0.86]	0.000	
Lap belt only	358 (0.45%)	249 (0.37%)	0.81 [0.68;0.95]	0.011	
Shoulder belt only	176 (0.22%)	163 (0.24%)	1.07 [0.86;1.33]	0.530	
Restraint unknown	338 (0.43%)	266 (0.39%)	0.91 [0.77;1.08]	0.271	
None	1,4538 (18.4%)	1,6751 (24.6%)	1.33 [1.27;1.40]	0.000	
Not reported	28,986 (36.7%)	23,955 (35.1%)	0.96 [0.92;1.00]	0.050	
DRINKING					**0.000***
No	32,291 (40.9%)	22,105 (32.4%)	Ref.	Ref.	
Yes	11,751 (14.9%)	15,177 (22.3%)	1.89 [1.83;1.94]	0.000	
Not reported	34,875 (44.2%)	30,912 (45.3%)	1.29 [1.27;1.32]	0.000	
DRUGS					**<0.001***
No	30,912 (39.2%)	23,203 (34.0%)	Ref.	Ref.	

(*Contd.*)

Table 34. (*Contd.*)

	Baby Boomers N=78917	Gen X N=68194	OR	p-ratio	p-value
Yes	4,671 (5.92%)	6,164 (9.04%)	1.76 [1.69;1.83]	0.000	
Not reported	43,334 (54.9%)	38,827 (56.9%)	1.19 [1.17;1.22]	0.000	
DOA					**<0.001***
Died at scene	41,885 (53.1%)	41,864 (61.4%)	Ref.	Ref.	
Died en route	921 (1.17%)	804 (1.18%)	0.87 [0.79;0.96]	0.005	
Not applicable	36,056 (45.7%)	25,477 (37.4%)	0.71 [0.69;0.72]	0.000	
Not reported	55 (0.07%)	49 (0.07%)	0.89 [0.60;1.31]	0.560	
WORK_INJ					**0.109**
No	70,550 (89.4%)	61,111 (89.6%)	Ref.	Ref.	
Yes	3,208 (4.07%)	2,626 (3.85%)	0.94 [0.90;1.00]	0.035	
Not reported	5,159 (6.54%)	4,457 (6.54%)	1.00 [0.96;1.04]	0.901	

Appendix B

Steps of Big Data Analysis in Highway Safety

Problem Statement

By the year 2035, Texas is expected to grow from its present population of 26 million to 40 million people according to the Texas State Data Center (see Figure 86). More congestion will occur in urban areas, meaning that road and bridge stress will increase, and greater demand will be placed on rural highways to support travel connections and freight movement between farms, ranches, homes, jobs, and markets due to the population and job growth. These demands keep growing faster than the roadway capacity that is necessary to handle this growth. Exploration of big data and big data management are the future needs for transportation safety professionals. This case study shows the step-by-step methods of big data analysis in highway safety and mobility analysis.

Enterprise Data Analytics Platform

In analyzing big data analysis, there is a need for advanced enterprise cloud data platforms. Figure 87 shows how enterprise data platforms can seamlessly perform data sharing, preparation, analysis, and visualization.

Site Selection

An image of Texas growth and gridlock prior to the occurrence of the COVID-19 pandemic is offered in the 2020 ranking of Texas' most congested roadways. For example, Interstate Highway (IH)-35 through downtown Austin overtook Houston's West Loop (IH-610) as the most gridlocked corridor in the state. Houston's Southwest Freeway (IH-69), Dallas' Woodall Rodgers Freeway (SS-366), and the Eastex Freeway (IH-69) in Houston make up the rest of the top five.

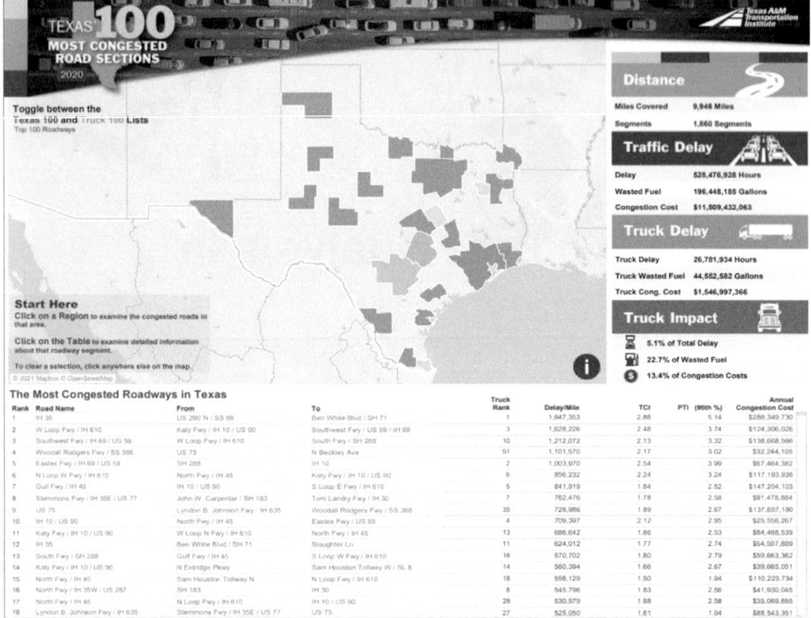

Rank	Road Name	From	To	Truck Rank	Delay/Mile	TCI	PTI (95th %)	Annual Congestion Cost
1	IH 35	US 290 N / SS 69	Ben White Blvd / SH 71	1	1,647,353	2.88	5.14	$288,349,730
2	W Loop Fwy / IH 610	Katy Fwy / IH 10 / US 90	Southwest Fwy / US 59 / IH 69	3	1,628,226	2.48	3.74	$124,306,026
3	Southwest Fwy / IH 69 / US 59	W Loop Fwy / IH 610	South Fwy / SH 288	10	1,212,072	2.13	3.32	$138,668,566
4	Woodall Rodgers Fwy / SS 366	US 75	N Beckley Ave	51	1,101,570	2.17	3.02	$32,244,105
5	Eastex Fwy / IH 69 / US 59	SH 288	IH 10	2	1,003,970	2.54	3.99	$67,464,382
6	N Loop W Fwy / IH 610	North Fwy / IH 45	Katy Fwy / IH 10 / US 90	6	856,232	2.24	3.24	$117,193,926
7	Gulf Fwy / IH 45	IH 10 / US 90	S Loop E Fwy / IH 610	5	841,919	1.84	2.52	$147,204,103
8	Stemmons Fwy / IH 35E / US 77	John W. Carpenter / SH 183	Tom Landry Fwy / IH 30	7	762,476	1.78	2.58	$91,478,884
9	US 75	Lyndon B. Johnson Fwy / IH 635	Woodall Rodgers Fwy / SS 366	35	728,986	1.89	2.67	$137,657,190
10	IH 10 / US 90	North Fwy / IH 45	Eastex Fwy / US 59	4	709,397	2.12	2.95	$25,556,267
11	Katy Fwy / IH 10 / US 90	W Loop N Fwy / IH 610	North Fwy / IH 45	13	686,642	1.86	2.53	$84,468,539
12	IH 35	Ben White Blvd / SH 71	Slaughter Ln	11	624,012	1.77	2.74	$54,507,889
13	South Fwy / SH 288	Gulf Fwy / IH 45	S Loop W Fwy / IH 610	16	570,702	1.80	2.79	$59,663,362
14	Katy Fwy / IH 10 / US 90	N Eldridge Pkwy	Sam Houston Tollway W / SL 8	14	560,394	1.66	2.67	$39,665,051
15	North Fwy / IH 45	Sam Houston Tollway N	N Loop Fwy / IH 610	18	556,129	1.50	1.94	$110,223,734
16	North Fwy / IH 35W / US 287	SH 183	IH 30	8	545,796	1.83	2.56	$41,930,045
17	North Fwy / IH 45	N Loop Fwy / IH 610	IH 10 / US 90	28	530,579	1.88	2.58	$35,069,655
18	Lyndon B. Johnson Fwy / IH 635	Stemmons Fwy / IH 35E / US 77	US 75	27	525,050	1.61	1.94	$88,543,351

Figure 86. Most congested roadways in Texas.

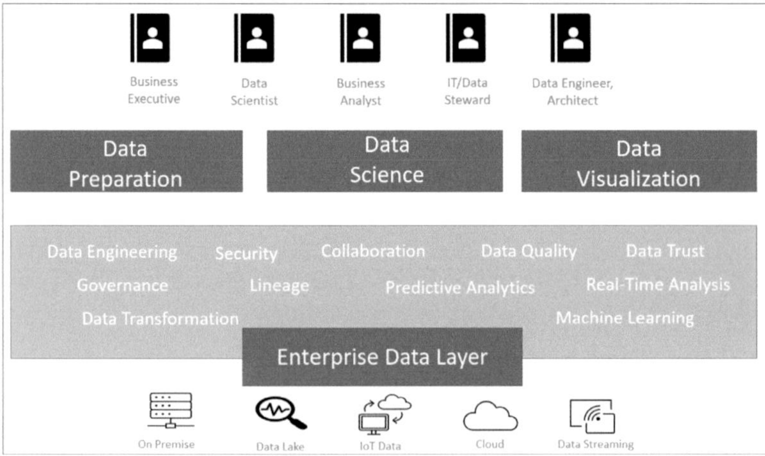

Figure 87. Enterprise data layer.

Identify Commercial Datasets

Travel Time Data

The NPMRDS, the recently released Performance Network from Federal Highway Way Administration (FHWA), and INRIX's XD network (see Figure 88) provide disaggregate level operating speed data. The NPMRDS dataset, procured by

FHWA, is free to state DOT's and Metropolitan Planning Organizations (MPOs) for research. The FHWA Performance Network is a conflation of NPMRDS data back onto states' HPMS submissions. While the NPMRDS and Performance Network data are free, these are limited to covering only the National Highway System (NHS) portion of the state roadway network. Figure 88 shows the difference in coverage between the NPMRDS/ Performance Network and INRIX XD conflated to the Texas roadway network.

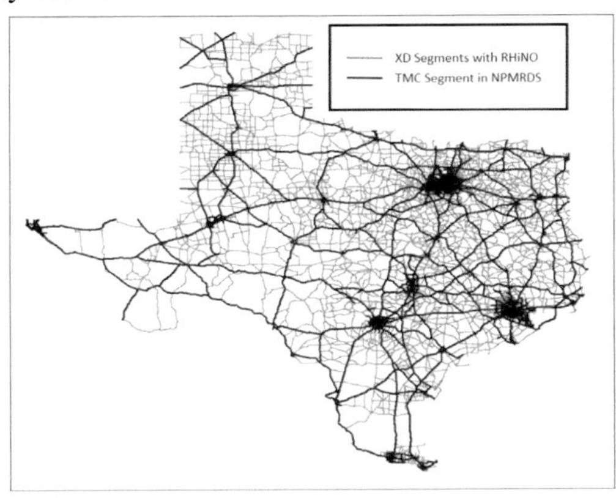

Figure 88. Texas NPMRDS network.

Since July 2013, the FHWA has used NPMRDS (including probe vehicle-based travel time data for both freight and passenger vehicles for all NHS facilities at 5-minute intervals) in order to support its Urban Congestion Report and its Freight Performance Measurement (FPM) programs (Lomax, 2004). The data is supplied by a combination of the American Trucking Research Institute (ATRI) and HERE (the company once known as Traffic.com and later known as NAVTEC). HERE gives the data needed to estimate 'car' vehicle travel times, and ATRI gives the data for 'truck' travel times. HERE formulates the data from these two datasets into one travel time statistic meant to be an estimate of 'average vehicle travel time' for both trucks and cars. NPMRDS travel time is reported based on TMC segments with link length varying from under a mile to multiple miles. NPMRDS is meant for state agencies to measure system performance in reaching new federal performance management requirements. The first version of the NPMRDS is known as "Version 1' or 'HERE NPMRDS,' and the recent version is known as 'Version 2' or 'INRIX NPMRDS,' which gives data from January 1, 2017.

Other Data Sources

Some examples of big enterprise datasets are:

- Vehicle trajectory data or waypoint data: INRIX, Wejo
- Bike volume data: Strava
- Event data: Wejo, WayCare
- Hourly traffic volume: StreetLight Data Inc.
- 1.70 million cases (2016–2019) (every 90 seconds): MapQuest Traffic API
- 0.54 million cases (2016–2019) (every 90 seconds): Bing Map Traffic API
- Uber movement data
- Online social network (OSN) data

For example, Lonestar has a robust Data Archiving Application (DAA). The DAA archives near-real-time data (defined as collected within the last 24 hours) and historical data (defined as older than 24 hours). Within the DAA, the data elements below are known to be archived. Examples of some of the critical data elements are listed below:

- Speed, volume, occupancy data in various temporal archive levels
- Vehicle classification data
- Lane Closures
- Dynamic Message Sign (DMS) status update messages

Identify Existing Datasets

Granular Level Traffic Volume Data: TMAS

State highway and transportation agencies sustain the TMAS, which is a system of traffic count stations that watch roadway usage by gathering vehicle class, volume, and weight information, with traffic monitoring stations that can be permanent or temporarily implemented. Permanent traffic count stations continuously function throughout the year and are called continuous count stations, whereas the short duration, or temporary count stations, are locations where traffic counting is not covered through the entire year. Typically, the short duration portable count time is either 48 or 72 hours.

Roadway Inventory Data: RHiNO

The Texas Department of Transportation (TxDOT) maintains the RHiNO, which is a database with a variety of roadway characteristics and that mainly offers road characteristic information, such as the estimated traffic volume and corridor length, for every road that is known in Texas.

Crash Data: CRIS

CRIS data elements are split into three main groups: crash event, primary person, and vehicle (unit) characteristics. CRIS has over 150 fields that contain data about spatial and temporal characteristics (including, but not limited to, time, date, and geodesic coordinates), roadway characteristics, contributing factors (including, but not limited to, weather, lighting, pavement conditions), manner of collision (including, but not limited to, head-on, rear-end, sideswipe), crash severity, vehicle type, driver characteristics, and passenger characteristics, among others.

Demographic Data: U.S. Census and LEHD

The U.S. Census provides demographic information on various spatial units. This study used the Census block group level demographic data due to its higher relevance to the modeling outcomes. The American Community Survey (ACS) (performed by the U.S. Census Bureau) is a continuous national survey of U.S.

households done to gather a large assortment of information such as a primary travel mode from home to work, and it is an essential tool for tracking travel patterns. The ACS gives estimates for different levels: one (1)-year estimates, three (3)-year estimates, and five (5)-year estimates. Using three (3)-year or five (5)-year ACS estimates is helpful due to the large sample size relative to one (1)-year estimates. The multi-year estimates have benefits of statistical reliability for small population subgroups and less populated areas.

Longitudinal Employer-Household Dynamics (LEHD) data is a part of the Center for Economic Studies at the U.S. Census Bureau, which creates new, public-use, cost-effective, information that combines state, federal, and Census Bureau data on employees and employers with the Local Employment Dynamics Partnership. Additionally, states agree to share with the Census Bureau the Quarterly Census of Employment and Wages data and the unemployment insurance earnings data. The LEHD data provides both home and work Census block data. Home level data is known as Residence Area Characteristic (RAC) data files, and work level data is known as Workplace Area Characteristic (WAC) data files. These files are released at the state level and are totaled by the home Census block and the work Census block, respectively.

Weather Data: NOAA

Normal climate is broadly used to reference a full suite of products issued by the National Oceanic and Atmospheric Administration (NOAA) that explains climatological conditions with 30-year averages and other statistics. Due to its large size, Texas has ten distinct climate regions. This means that weather patterns vary tremendously across the state on any given day. The majority of the state's precipitation happens in the form of rainfall, with little amounts of ice and snow occurring more frequently in the north and west, further away from the moderating effects of the Gulf of Mexico. Figure 89 shows the average precipitation measures across the state over a thirty-year period (1981-2010).

Perform Data Fusion

There is a need to establish a data warehouse to archive selected data elements to be used later for testing different AI techniques and for the development of performance metrics. It is important to set up relational databases and utilize secured Cloud services including, but not limited to, Microsoft Azure or Amazon Web Services. There are also a number of data issues including, but not limited to, negative speeds, unreliable zero speeds, and presence of volumes without speed data. Thus, an efficient relational database is necessary to perform high-level data quality checks such as the ones outlined in FHWA's Using Archived Operations Data for Reliability and Mobility Measurement Report.

Figure 90 illustrates the research framework. The data cleaning from the multisource data, the computational framework, and the AI framework will overlap in several places. Large amounts of data on transportation infrastructure

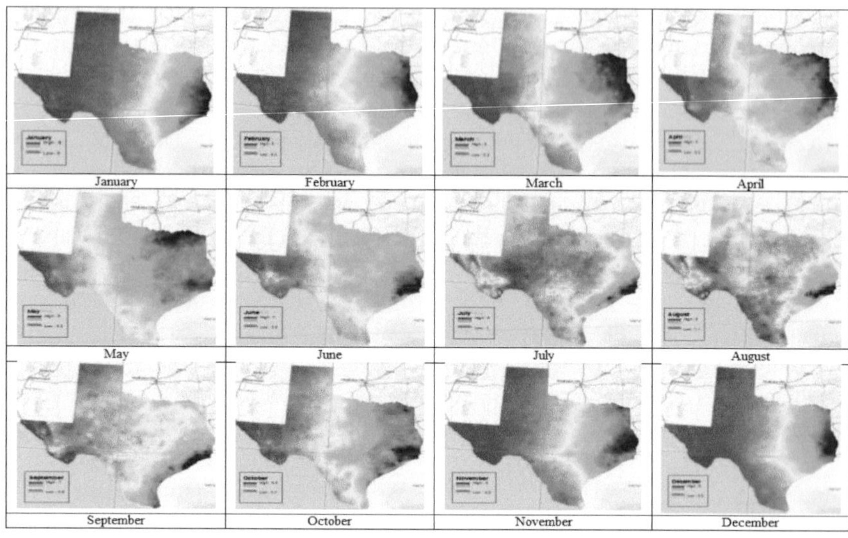

Figure 89. Average monthly precipitation (in.) (1981-2010 NOAA Normal Dataset).

assets are continuously collected at the network level due to advancements in technology and in response to data-driven processes. Advancements in technology have increased the amount of data and data coverage along highway corridors. These vast amounts of new data, combined with existing data, leave practitioners searching for ways to share information intelligently. The transition from data to information identifies underlying causes of poor network health. The data analytics and decision support tool (with dashboard) can provide congestion scenarios on the freeways with the potential design parameters and performance probabilities.

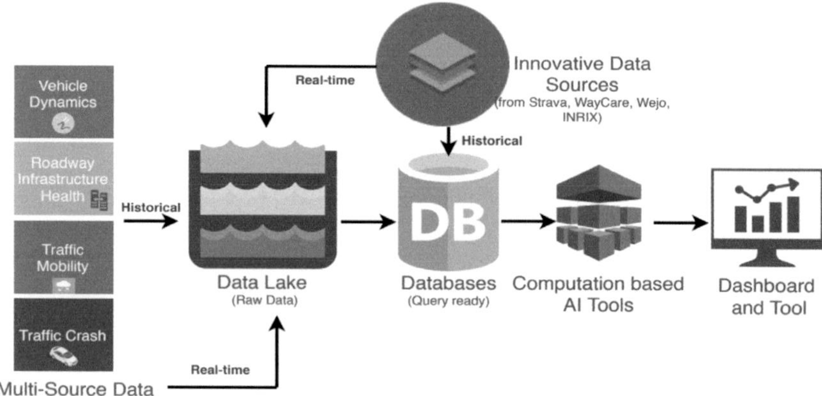

Figure 90. Example data fusion and analysis framework.

Referenced Links

https://npmrds.ritis.org/analytics/help/#npmrds
https://www.fhwa.dot.gov/policyinformation/tables/performancenetwork/
https://www.fhwa.dot.gov/policyinformation/tables/performancenetwork/
https://mobility.tamu.edu/texas-most-congested-roadways/
https://www.mapquest.com/
https://www.bingmapsportal.com/

Further Reading

Lomax, T. et al., Monitoring Urban Roadways in 2002: Using Archived Operations Data for Reliability and Mobility Measurement, FHWA-HOP-04-011, March 2004.

Appendix C

ML Interpretability and Model Selection

Problem Statement

AI models are often tagged as black box models due to having fewer interpretability issues. In recent years, explainable AI has gained much attraction in the research community. The following replicable case study shows the steps to perform crash severity modeling using AI and explains the models with the help of different explainable AI metrics.

Code Chunk 1

```
## Please check my RPUBS for additional codes: https://rpubs.com/subasish

setwd("~your folder")
library(readxl)
aa1= read_excel("Bicycle_10_16a.xlsx", sheet= "Main")
names(aa1)

aa2= aa1[, -c(1, 2, 3, 4, 24)]
names(aa2)
library(tidyverse)
aa2 <- aa2 %>% mutate_if(is.character, as.factor)

detach("package:tidyverse", unload=TRUE)
library(fairmodels)
library(DALEX)
library(ranger)

# train
rf_compas <- ranger(SEVERITY ~., data = aa2, probability = TRUE)

# numeric target values
y_numeric <- as.numeric(aa2$SEVERITY)-1
```

```
# explainer
rf_explainer <- DALEX::explain(rf_compas, data = aa2[,-c(18)],
               y = y_numeric, colorize = FALSE)


fobject <- fairness_check(rf_explainer,                 # explainer
           protected = aa2$LIGHTING,         # protected variable as factor
           privileged = "Daylight",          # level in protected variable, potentially
more privileged
                  cutoff = 0.5,              # cutoff - optional, default = 0.5
                  colorize = FALSE)

print(fobject, colorize = FALSE)
plot(fobject)
```

Figure 91 shows a fairness check using an accuracy equality ratio, an equal opportunity ratio, a predictive equality ration, a predictive parity ratio, and a statistical parity ratio.

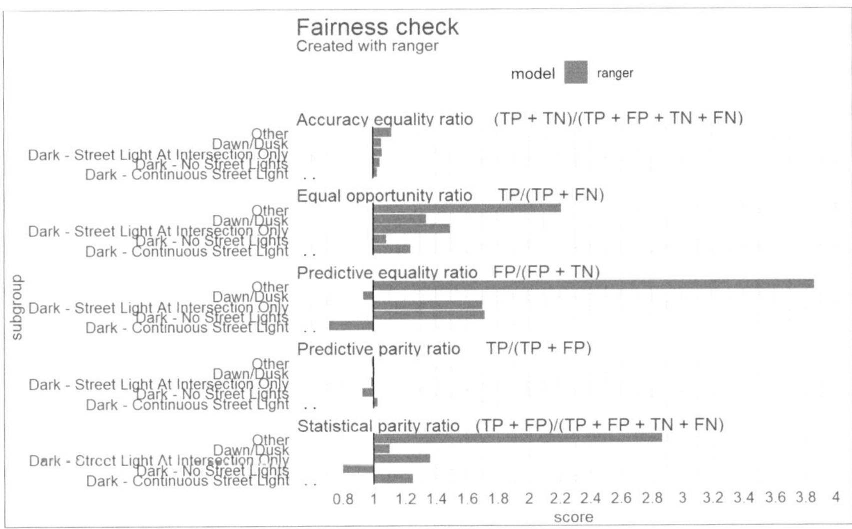

Figure 91. Fairness check.

Code Chunk 2

```
plot_density(fobject)
```

Figure 92 shows a density plot with different protective variables.

Code Chunk 3

```
plot(metric_scores(fobject))
```

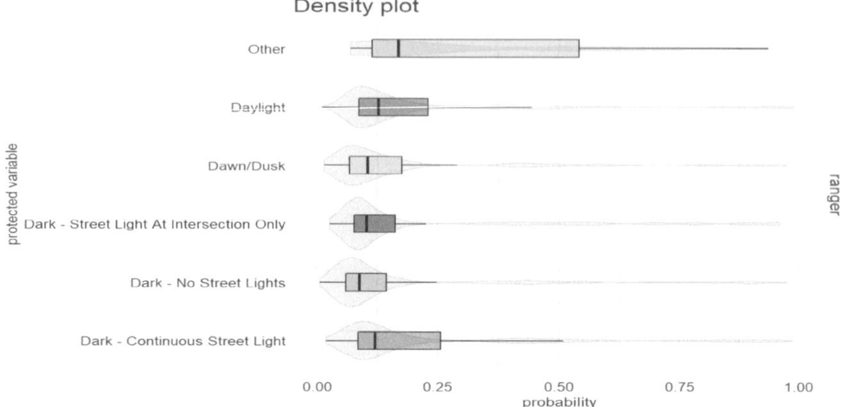

Figure 92. Density plot with probability vs. protected variables.

Figure 93 shows a metric scores plot created with ranger, with some of the protective variables mentioned in Figure 92.

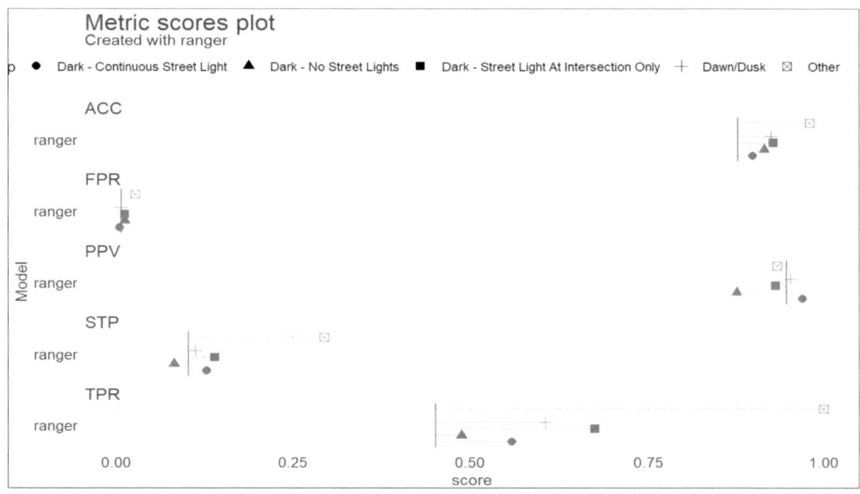

Figure 93. Metric scores plot.

Code Chunk 4

```
library(gbm)
rf_compas_1 <- ranger(SEVERITY
~DR_COND+TRAFF_CNTL+VIOLATIONS+MAN_COLL+LIGHTING,
          data = aa2,
          probability = TRUE)
```

```
lr_compas_1 <- glm(SEVERITY ~., data = aa2,
           family=binomial(link="logit"))

rf_compas_2 <- ranger(SEVERITY ~DR_COND+TRAFF_
CNTL+VIOLATIONS+MAN_COLL+LIGHTING+WEATHER, data = aa2, probability
= TRUE)
rf_compas_3 <- ranger(SEVERITY ~DR_COND+PRIOR_MOVEMENT+TRAFF_
CNTL+MAN_COLL+LIGHTING, data = aa2,
 probability = TRUE)

df <- aa2
df$SEVERITY <- as.numeric(aa2$SEVERITY)-1
gbm_compas_1<- gbm(SEVERITY ~., data = df)


explainer_1 <- DALEX::explain(rf_compas_1,
              data = aa2[-18], y = y_numeric)
explainer_2 <- DALEX::explain(lr_compas_1, data = aa2[,-18],
              y = y_numeric)
explainer_3 <- DALEX::explain(rf_compas_2, data = aa2[-18],
              y = y_numeric, label = "ranger_2")
explainer_4 <- DALEX::explain(rf_compas_3, data= aa2[-18],
              y = y_numeric, label = "ranger_3")

explainer_5 <- DALEX::explain(gbm_compas_1, data = aa2[,-18], y = y_numeric)


fobject <- fairness_check(explainer_1, explainer_2,
              explainer_3, explainer_4,
              explainer_5,
              protected = aa2$LIGHTING, # protected variable as factor
              privileged = "Daylight",
              verbose = FALSE)

fobject$parity_loss_metric_data
fobject$cutoff$ranger
sm <- stack_metrics(fobject)
###plot(sm)
fair_pca <- fairness_pca(fobject)
plot(fair_pca)
```

Figure 94 shows a fairness PCA plot for PC1 and PC2.

Code Chunk 5

```
fheatmap <- fairness_heatmap(fobject)
plot(fheatmap, text_size = 3)
```

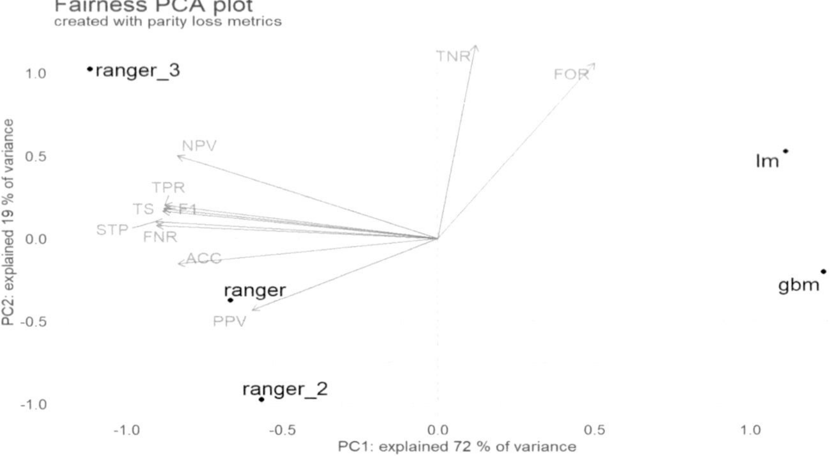

Figure 94. Fairness PCA plot.

Figure 95 shows a heatmap with dendrograms, showing measures of loss metrics for different models.

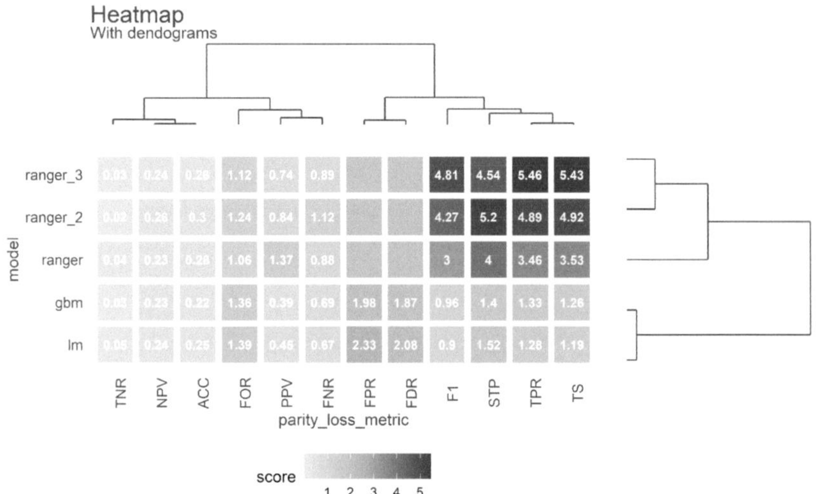

Figure 95. Heatmap with dendrograms.

Appendix D

Develop an Interactive Map

Problem Statement

Geospatial data is one of the most used datasets by transportation safety professionals. Conventionally, proprietary software such as ArcGIS is used for spatial maps. There are many open-source web GIS products such as QGIS, Leaftlet, and different spatial R packages. The following replicable case study shows the steps to plot an interactive map in R by showing crash count differences before and during the COVID-19 pandemic in New York.

Code Chunk 1

```
## Please check my RPUBS for additional codes: https://rpubs.com/subasish

# load required packages
library(maptools)
library(rgdal)
library(sp)
library(sf)
library(tigris)
library(hrbrthemes)
library(tidyverse)
require(spatialEco)
library(maptools)
###library(GISTools)
library(rgdal)

## read crash
setwd("~folder location")
march <- read.csv("NY_March_CrashesLL03.csv")
dim(march)
names(march)

coordinates(march)=~LONGITUDE+LATITUDE
proj4string(march)<- CRS("+proj=longlat +datum=WGS84")
march1 <-spTransform(march,CRS("+proj=longlat"))
```

(Contd.)

```
### NY TaxiZone
st_read("D:/From
Syncplicity/Bulk_Papers/03142019/covid/NY_TrafficCrash/zones.geojson") %>%
    st_set_crs(4326) %>%
    st_transform("+proj=longlat +datum=WGS84 +no_defs") -> ny
plot(ny)

pts_sf = st_as_sf(march1)
p_sf = st_as_sf(ny)

st_crs(p_sf)
p_sf1= st_transform(p_sf, st_crs(pts_sf))

##https://mgimond.github.io/Spatial/index.html
## https://cengel.github.io/R-spatial/spatialops.html
nn= p_sf1 %>%
    st_join(pts_sf) %>%
    group_by(zone, Year) %>%
    summarize(count = n())

nn1=subset(nn, Year==2020)
nn2=subset(nn, Year==2019)
colnames(nn1)[3] <- "2020 Crashes"
p1= plot(nn1["2020 Crashes"])
colnames(nn2)[3] <- "2019 Crashes"
p2= plot(nn2["2019 Crashes"])

#par(mfrow=c(1,2))
#plot(nn1["2020 Crashes"])
#plot(nn2["2019 Crashes"])

library(tmap)

tm_shape(nn) +
    tm_polygons("count", palette = "RdYlBu") +
    tm_facets(by = "Year")

nn1= subset(nn, Year> 2016 & Year < 2021)

tm_shape(nn1) +
    tm_polygons("count", palette = "RdYlBu") +
    tm_facets(by = "Year")

nn1= subset(nn, Year> 2016 & Year < 2021)

tm_shape(nn1) +
    tm_polygons("count", palette = "RdYlBu") +
    tm_facets(by = "Year")
```

```
tmap_mode("view")
tm_basemap("Stamen.Toner") +
   tm_shape(nn1) +
   tm_polygons("count", palette = "YlOrRd") +
   tm_facets(by = "Year")+
   tm_tiles("Stamen.TonerLabels")
```

The above code is reproducible. Figure 96 shows New York traffic crashes from March 2017-2020. The interactive format can be found in: https://rpubs.com/subasish/599855.

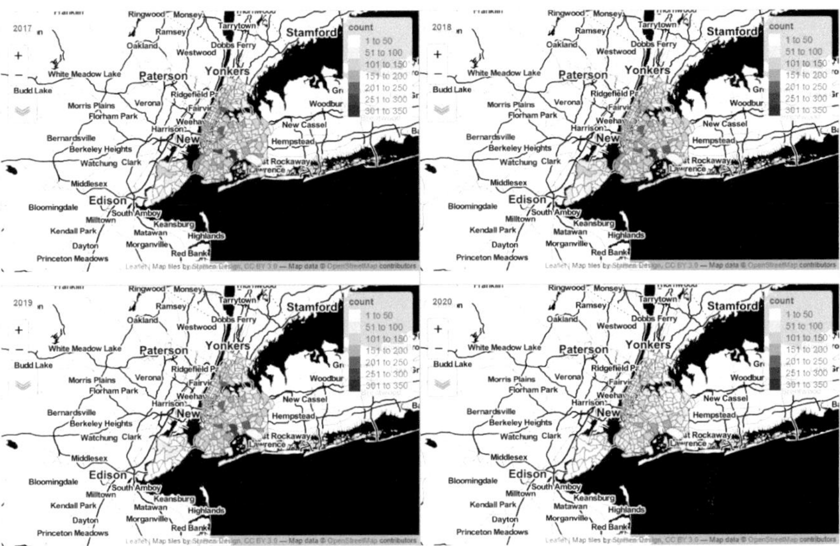

Figure 96. New York traffic crashes in March 2017-2020.

Appendix E

Develop an interactive Shiny App for Highway Safety Analysis with AI Models

Problem Statement

Interactive tools are very useful tools for the users as they can select different drop-down panels to select the right filter to produce a map and relevant information. The following case study provides the code to develop a shiny app that can show the roadway segments with higher crash risks.

Code Chunk 1

```
## Please check my RPUBS for additional codes: https://rpubs.com/subasish

# Load the packages

library(shiny)
library(shinydashboard)
library(shinyjs)
library(sf)
library(leaflet)
library(leaflet.extras)
library(dplyr)
library(DT)
library(htmltools)

# Read State/Counties CSV File
#StateCountyData = read.csv("C:/Subasish/FHWA Rural Speed Safety Project For USDOT SDI/app/www/US_Counties/USCounties.csv")
StateCountyData = read.csv("www/US_Counties/USCounties.csv")

# Create State and Initial County List
StateCountyData$State <- as.character(StateCountyData$State)
StateCountyData$County <- as.character(StateCountyData$County)
```

```
### Temporarily filter for only 3 states - WA, NC, OH
#StateCountyData <- filter(StateCountyData, State == 'WA' | State == 'NC' | State ==
'OH')
StateCountyData <- filter(StateCountyData, State == 'WA' | State == 'OH')
StatesList <- unique(StateCountyData$State)
StateCountyList <- subset(StateCountyData$County, StateCountyData$State == "WA")
StateNameList <- data.frame(
 unique(StateCountyData[c("State","StateID")])
)

# Read WA SHP file
#WA_shp = st_transform(st_read("www/WA_shp/new1.shp"), 4326)
#WA_shp$Fatal_Injury <- WA_shp$Fatal + WA_shp$Injury
WA_shp = st_transform(st_read("www/WA_shp2/WA_TMC_Census.shp"), 4326)

# Read OH SHP file
OH_shp = st_transform(st_read("www/OH_shp2/OH_Fin2.shp"), 4326)

# Read NC SHP file
#NC_shp = st_transform(st_read("www/NC_shp/Final1_NC.shp"), 4326)

# Read Counties SHP file
UScounties_shp = st_transform(st_read("www/US_Counties/tl_2018_us_county.shp"),
4326)


# Start Creating Dashboard layout
header <- dashboardHeader(
 title = "Rural Speed Tool (BETA)"
)

body <- dashboardBody(useShinyjs(),
        tabsetPanel(
            tabPanel(HTML(paste(tags$span(style="font-size:                  18px",
"RuralSpeedSafetyX"))), id="RuralSpeedTool",
                tags$h1(tags$b("Interactive Decision Support Tool to Improve Safety")),
                fluidRow(
                column(width = 8,
                        box(width = NULL, solidHeader = TRUE,
                            leafletOutput("MapOut", height = 500),
                            h2() )
                    ),
                    column(width = 3,
                            box(width = NULL, status = "warning",
                              selectInput("YearInput","Year",choices = list("2015" = 2015),
selected = 2015),
                             selectInput("StateInput","State",choices = StatesList,selected =
'WA'),
```

(*Contd.*)

```
                              selectInput("CountyInput","County",choices = c("All
Counties",StateCountyList)),
                                  selectInput("FacilityInput","Facility",choices =
c("All","Interstate/Freeway/Expressway","Multilane","Two-lane")),
                           radioButtons("Severity", label = "Severity", choices = list("All",
"Fatal and Injury"), inline=TRUE),
                           actionButton(inputId = "RefreshMap", label = "Refresh Map",
class = "butt"),
                               tags$head(tags$style(".butt{background-color:#0000FF;}
.butt{color: white;}")), # background color and font color
                           downloadButton("downloadData",label ="Download Data")
                           )
                        )

                  ),
                  DT::dataTableOutput('outputDT'),
                  h2(),tags$br(),
                  h2(),tags$br()


                )
            )
)

# Put them together into a dashboardPage
ui <- dashboardPage(
   #header,
   dashboardHeader(disable = TRUE),
   dashboardSidebar(disable = TRUE),
   body
)

server <- function(input, output, session) {

StateCountyList <- eventReactive(input$StateInput, {
   subset(StateCountyData$County, StateCountyData$State == input$StateInput)
})
observeEvent(input$StateInput,
        updateSelectInput(session, "CountyInput","County",
                choices = c("All Counties",
                        subset(StateCountyData$County,    StateCountyData$State    ==
input$StateInput)))
)
observeEvent(input$StateInput,
        updateSelectInput(session, "FacilityInput","Facility",
                  choices = c("All","Interstate/Freeway/Expressway","Multilane","Two-
lane"))
 )
```

```
output$MapOut <- renderLeaflet({
  leaflet() %>%
        addTiles(urlTemplate = "//cartodb-basemaps-{s}.global.ssl.fastly.net/dark_all/
{z}/{x}/{y}{r}.png", layerId = 'Carto DB Dark Matter') %>%
    setView(lng = -95.7129, lat = 37.0902, zoom = 4)
    #setView(lng = -120.740135, lat = 47.376903, zoom = 7)
 })

observeEvent(input$RefreshMap, {

STATEFPin <- switch(input$StateInput,
        "NC"= 37,
        "OH" = 39,
        "WA" = 53
        )
 COUNTYin = input$CountyInput
 if (COUNTYin != "All Counties"){
  Countyin_Code <- select(filter(filter(StateCountyData, StateID == STATEFPin),
(County == COUNTYin)), StateCounty)
} else {
    Countyin_Code <- 0
 }
 FacilityIn = input$FacilityInput
 if (FacilityIn == "Interstate/Freeway/Expressway"){
   FacilityIn_Code <- "Interstate"
 } else {
   FacilityIn_Code <- FacilityIn
 }

 ### Will need to change MapOutputData switch to include other states
 #MapOutputData <- WA_shp
 MapOutputData <- switch(input$StateInput,
            "NC"= WA_shp,
            "OH" = OH_shp,
            "WA" = WA_shp
 )

 if (Countyin_Code == 0){
   MapOutputDataTempCounty <- MapOutputData

   UScounties_shp_selected <- st_as_sf(filter(as.data.frame(UScounties_shp),
STATEFP == STATEFPin))
    LATzoom <- switch(input$StateInput,
            "NC"= 35.782169,
            "OH" = 40.367474,
            "WA" = 47.376903
 )
```

(*Contd.*)

```
LONzoom <- switch(input$StateInput,
          "NC"= -80.793457,
          "OH" = -82.996216,
          "WA" = -120.740135
)
  zoomLevel <- 6
} else {
  MapOutputDataTempCounty <- st_as_sf(filter(as.data.frame(MapOutputData),
COUNTYFP == sprintf('%03d', as.integer(Countyin_Code) %% 1000)))

  UScounties_shp_selected <- st_as_sf(filter(filter(as.data.frame(UScounties_shp),
STATEFP == STATEFPin), COUNTYFP == sprintf('%03d', as.integer(Countyin_Code)
%% 1000)))

  LATzoomTemp <- select(as.data.frame(UScounties_shp_selected), INTPTLAT)
  LONzoomTemp <- select(as.data.frame(UScounties_shp_selected), INTPTLON)

  LATzoom <- as.numeric(as.character(unlist(LATzoomTemp[[1]])))
  LONzoom <- as.numeric(as.character(unlist(LONzoomTemp[[1]])))

 zoomLevel <- 8
}

if (FacilityIn_Code == 'All'){
  MapOutputDataFinal <- MapOutputDataTempCounty
} else {
  MapOutputDataFinal <- st_as_sf(filter(as.data.frame(MapOutputDataTempCounty),
Facility == FacilityIn_Code))
}

DataForPal <- switch(input$Severity,
          "All" = MapOutputDataFinal$Total_Exp,
          "Fatal and Injury" = MapOutputDataFinal$FI_Exp)

pal_Total <- colorNumeric("YlOrRd", DataForPal)
labelOut <- as.list(paste0('TMC: ', MapOutputDataFinal$TMC, "<br>",
             'Road: ', MapOutputDataFinal$ROAD_NUMBE, "<br>",
             'State: ', input$StateInput, "<br>",
          'County: ', input$CountyInput, "<br>",
          'Facility: ', MapOutputDataFinal$Facility, "<br>",
          'Total Expected: ', MapOutputDataFinal$Total_Exp, "<br>",
          'Fatal, Injury Expected: ', MapOutputDataFinal$FI_Exp, "<br>",
          'AADT: ', round(MapOutputDataFinal$AADT, 0), "<br>",
          #'Freeflow Speed: ', round(MapOutputDataFinal$SpdFF, 2), "<br>",
          'Speed Variance 1: ', round(MapOutputDataFinal$SpdVarr1, 2), "<br>"
))
popupOut <- paste0('TMC: ', MapOutputDataFinal$TMC, "<br>",
          'Road: ',MapOutputDataFinal$ROAD_NUMBE, "<br>",
```

```
            'State: ', input$StateInput, "<br>",
            'County: ', input$CountyInput, "<br>",
            'Facility: ', MapOutputDataFinal$Facility, "<br>",
          'Total Expected: ', MapOutputDataFinal$Total_Exp, "<br>",
          'Fatal, Injury Expected: ', MapOutputDataFinal$FI_Exp, "<br>",
          'AADT: ', round(MapOutputDataFinal$AADT, 0), "<br>",
          #'Freeflow Speed: ', round(MapOutputDataFinal$SpdFF, 2), "<br>",
          'Speed Variance 1: ', round(MapOutputDataFinal$SpdVarr1, 2), "<br>"
)

 leafletProxy("MapOut") %>% clearPopups() %>% clearGroup("Total/Fata/Injury")
%>% clearGroup("CountiesSHP") %>% clearControls() %>%
   ###setView(lng = -120.740135, lat = 47.376903, zoom = 7) %>%
   setView(lng = LONzoom, lat = LATzoom, zoom = zoomLevel) %>%
   addPolylines(data=MapOutputDataFinal,
       color=~pal_Total(
       switch(input$Severity,
             "All" = MapOutputDataFinal$Total_Exp,
             "Fatal and Injury" = MapOutputDataFinal$FI_Exp)
          ),
          group="Total/Fata/Injury",
          popup = popupOut,
          label = lapply(labelOut, HTML)) %>%
 addPolylines(data=UScounties_shp_selected,
          color='green',
          group="CountiesSHP",
          weight = 1) %>%
 addLegend("bottomright", pal = pal_Total,
          values = switch(input$Severity,
                "All" = MapOutputDataFinal$Total_Exp,
                "Fatal and Injury" = MapOutputDataFinal$FI_Exp),
             title = paste0(input$Severity, " Crashes")
             )
if (nrow(as.data.frame(MapOutputDataFinal)) > 0){
  MapOutputDataFinalDTtemp <- cbind(input$StateInput,input$CountyInput,
             select(as.data.frame(MapOutputDataFinal),
                c('TMC',
                  #'ADMIN_LE_1',
                  #'ADMIN_LE_2',
                  'ROAD_NUMBE',
                  'Facility',
                  'DISTANCE',
                  'Population',
                  'Household',
                  'AADT',
                  'NO_LANES',
                  'SPD_LIMT',
```

(Contd.)

```
                  'OptSpd',
                  #'SpdFF',
                  'SpdVarr1',
                  'Total_Exp',
                  'FI_Exp'
                )
            )
)
 MapOutputDataFinalDTtemp <- distinct(MapOutputDataFinalDTtemp, TMC, .keep_
all = TRUE)
} else {
 MapOutputDataFinalDTtemp <- cbind(input$StateInput,
                input$CountyInput,
                'None',
                #'None',
                #'None',
                'None',
                'None',
                'None',
                'None',
                'None',
                'None',
                'None',
                'None',
                'None',
                'None',
                'None',
                #'None',
                'None'
 )

}

 MapOutputDataFinalDT <- datatable(MapOutputDataFinalDTtemp,
                class = 'cell-border stripe',
                 colnames = c('State',
                    'County',
                    'TMC',
                    #'State',
                    #'County',
                    'Road',
                    'Facility',
                    'Segment Length',
                    'Population',
                    'Household',
                    'AADT',
                    'Number of Lanes',
                    'Speed Limit',
```

```
                    'Avg. Ope. Speed - Yearly',
                    #'Freeflow Speed',
                    'Std. Dev. of Ope. Speed - Hourly',
                    'Total - Expected',
                    'Fatal and Injury - Expected'
               )
  )
  output$outputDT = DT::renderDataTable(MapOutputDataFinalDT, options =
list(lengthChange = FALSE))

  outputDTdowload <- MapOutputDataFinalDTtemp
  names(outputDTdowload) <- c('State',
               'County',
               'TMC',
               #'State',
               #'County',
               'Road',
               'Facility',
               'Segment Length',
               'Population',
               'Household',
               'AADT',
               'Number of Lanes',
               'Speed Limit',
               'Avg. Ope. Speed - Yearly',
               #'Freeflow Speed',
               'Std. Dev. of Ope. Speed - Hourly',
               'Total - Expected',
               'Fatal and Injury - Expected'
)

output$downloadData <- downloadHandler(
  #filename = function() {paste("test.csv")},
  #filename = function() {gsub("" "",paste(input$StateInput,"_",input$CountyInput,"_
",input$YearInput,".csv"))},
filename = function() {gsub(" ","",paste(input$StateInput,"_",
                    input$CountyInput,"_",
                    switch(input$FacilityInput,
                      "All"= "All",
                    "Interstate/Freeway/Expressway" = "IntFwayExpway",
                    "Multilane" = "Multilane",
                    "Two-lane" = "Twolane"
                  ),
                  "_",input$YearInput,".csv"))},
content = function(file) {
  write.csv(outputDTdowload,file, row.names=FALSE)
```

(Contd.)

```
    })
})


}

shinyApp(ui, server)
```

Figure 97 shows the interface of RuralSpeedSafetyX. The above code is reproducible.

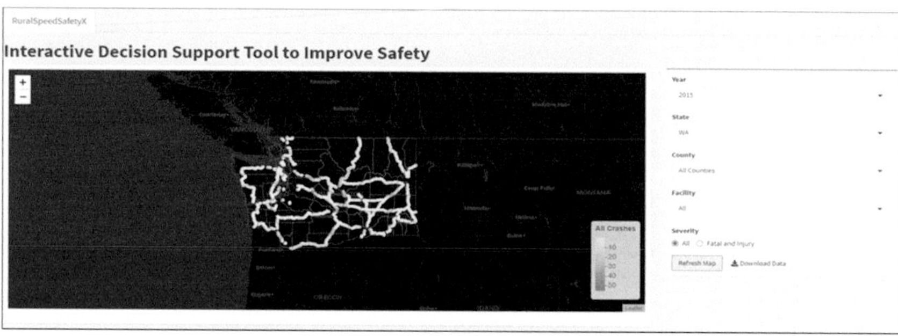

Figure 97. Interface of Rural Speed Safety X.

Supportive Information

- The Shiny Tool
  https://ruralspeedsafety.shinyapps.io/rss_sdi/
- Similar Tool with more functions
  https://ruralspeedsafety.shinyapps.io/0_7051Tool_v2/
- GitHub Page
  https://github.com/subasish/RuralSpeedSafetyX
- Presentation
  http://subasish.github.io/pages/BigDataGoesCountry
- USDOT Page on Rural Speed Safety Project
  http://subasish.github.io/pages/FHWA_Rural_Speed_T4_1/
- Feature
  https://tti.tamu.edu/researcher/big-data-goes-country-integrating-speed-and-weather-measures-to-study-rural-roadway-safety/

Peer Reviewed Journal Articles

- Das, S., S. Geedipally, and K. Fitzpatrick. Inclusion of speed and weather measures in safety performance functions for rural roadways. IATSS Research, 2020.
  https://www.sciencedirect.com/science/article/pii/S0386111220300583
- Das, S. and L. White. RuralSpeedSafetyX: Interactive decision support tool to improve safety. SoftwareX. 2020.
  https://www.sciencedirect.com/science/article/pii/S2352711019303553
- Das, S., and S. Geedipally. Rural Speed Safety Project for USDOT Safety Data Initiative: Findings and Outcomes. ITE Journal. September, 2020
  https://www.nxtbook.com/ygsreprints/ITE/ITE_Sept2020/index.php#/p/38

Appendix F

Develop an Interactive Shiny App with Application Programming Interface (API) based Queries

Problem Statement

For safety analysis of vulnerable roadway users (VRUs) such as pedestrians and bicyclists, it is important to determine the exposure measures of VRUs. The following code chunk shows how to develop a shiny tool by calling queries using U.S. Census API to acquire VRU exposure data. The live tool can be found at: https://subasish.shinyapps.io/ScRAM/. Figure 98 shows the interface of the tool.

Code Chunk 1

```
#install.packages("acs")
#install.packages("DT")
library(shiny)
library(shinydashboard)
library(leaflet)
library(DT)
library(shinyjs)
# START from code_SEERTOOL.R - SD
require(dplyr)
require(maptools) # required for rgdal to work correctly
require(tigris)
require(acs)
require(stringr) # to pad FIPS codes
require(leaflet)
library(acs)
# END from code_SEERTOOL.R - SD


# Read CSV files
#StateCountyData = read.csv("C:/SEER_ACS_Explorer_Dashboard/Data/USCounties.
csv")
```

```
#bg_land = read.csv("C:/SEER_ACS_Explorer_Dashboard/Data/BG_land.csv")
#state_land = read.csv("C:/SEER_ACS_Explorer_Dashboard/Data/state_land.csv")
#tract_land = read.csv("C:/SEER_ACS_Explorer_Dashboard/Data/tract_land.csv")
#StateNonMotorPM = read.csv("C:/SEER_ACS_Explorer/Data/State_NonMooto_
Performance_Measure1_GeoID.csv")
StateCountyData = read.csv("Data/USCounties1.csv")
bg_land = read.csv("Data/BG_land.csv")
state_land = read.csv("Data/state_land.csv")
tract_land = read.csv("Data/tract_land.csv")
StateNonMotorPM = read.csv("Data/State_NonMooto_Performance_Measure1_
GeoID.csv")

# Create State and Initial County List
StatesList <- unique(StateCountyData$State)
StateCountyList <- subset(StateCountyData$County, StateCountyData$State == "AL")
StateCountyData$County <- as.character(StateCountyData$County)
StateNameList <- data.frame(
 unique(StateCountyData[c("State","StateID")])
)

# Set land data
bg_land$GEOID <- substr(bg_land$GEOID_Data, 8, 19)
bg_L <- bg_land[c(18, 17)]
names(state_land)[names(state_land) == 'GEOID'] <- 'GEOIDin'
state_land$GEOID <- substr(state_land$GEOID_Data, 8, 9)
state_L <- state_land[c(20, 19)]
tract_land$GEOID <- substr(tract_land$GEOID_Data, 8, 18)
tract_L <- tract_land[c(18, 17)]

# Start Creating Dashboard layout
header <- dashboardHeader(
 title = "SEER ACS Explorer"
)

body <- dashboardBody(useShinyjs(),
        tabsetPanel(
         tabPanel(HTML(paste(tags$span(style="font-size: 18px", "Introduction"))),
                tags$br(),
                tags$h1(tags$b("Scalable Risk Assessment Methods for Pedestrians and
Bicyclists")),
                h2(),
                div(style = "font-size: 18px;", HTML("The FHWA Office of Safety
has initiated the Scalable Risk Assessment project to develop approaches to estimate
pedestrian and ",
                                "bicyclist risk, as well as the associated exposure to risk, at
several different geographic scales.
```

```
            h2(),
            div(style = "font-size: 18px;", HTML("The <b >Scalable Non-Motorized
Exposure Tool</b> provided here in <b >BETA VERSION </b> is intended to make it
easy for practitioners to obtain and ",
            "summarize nationwide travel survey data to estimate pedestrian and
bicyclist exposure to risk at ",
                        "several different areawide geographic scales.")),
            h2(),
            tags$h3(tags$b("Statewide Non-Motorized Exposure - All Trips
(BETA)")),
            h2(),
            div(style = "font-size: 18px;", HTML("The <b >Statewide</b> tab
provides a simplified query tool to obtain statewide pedestrian and bicyclist exposure
estimates for each year ",
                        "between 2009 and 2015. Three statewide exposure measures
are reported separately for pedestrian and bicyclist trips:")),
            h2(),
            tags$span(style="font-size: 18px", tags$ul(
             tags$li("Total estimated annual trips"),
             tags$li("Total estimated annual miles traveled"),
             tags$li("Total estimated annual hours traveled")
            )
            ),
            h2(),
            div(style = "font-size: 18px;", HTML("The statewide exposure estimates
are based on a combination of the U.S. Census Bureau's American Community Survey
(ACS) and FHWA's",
                        "2009 National Household Travel Survey (NHTS). The ACS
records primary commute trips only on an annual basis, whereas NHTS records all",
                        "trips about once a decade. Therefore, the NHTS total trips
are adjusted to represent better the selected analysis year by using the",
                        "more current ACS population and commute travel estimates.
The adjustment factors account for change in both population and the number",
                        "of commute trips per mode over time. The NHTS average
trip lengths and average trip durations per state are then applied to the total",
                        "trips to estimate the number of miles and hours traveled
annually per mode for each state. The exposure estimates are graphically",
                        "displayed in a color-coded map and are available for
download in CSV format.")),
            h2(),
            tags$h3(tags$b("FHWA Rural Speed Project Decision Support Tool
(Beta)")),
```

(Contd.)

```
            h2(),
            div(style = "font-size: 18px;", HTML("The <b >Scalable</b> tab offers
more query options and provides exposure estimates at more detailed geographic scales,
such as county, census tract,",
                          "or census block group. Because these more detailed
geographic scales are provided, the exposure estimates are based on the ACS",
                          "only (i.e., the NHTS estimates are not considered
statistically reliable at these detailed geographic scales). The query tool",

                          "provides options for one-, three-, and five-year estimates
for pedestrian and bicyclist commute trips (the recommended exposure measure), total
commute trips, and",
                          "total population. Note that this query tool does not perform
any adjustments to the ACS trip information-it simply queries the",
                          "available ACS database. The estimates are graphically
displayed in a color-coded map and are available for download in CSV format.")),
                  tags$h3(tags$b("Acknowledgments")),
                  h2(),
                  div(style = "font-size: 18px;", HTML("xxx")),
                  h2(),
                  div(style = "font-size: 18px;", HTML("xxx.")),
                  h2(),
                  div(style = "font-size: 18px;", HTML("xxx")),
                  tags$br(),
                  tags$br()
            ),
            tabPanel(HTML(paste(tags$span(style="font-size: 18px", "Statewide
(BETA)"))), id="StNmPM",
                  tags$h1(tags$b("FHWA Rural Speed Project Decision Support
Tool (Beta)")),
                  fluidRow(
                  column(width = 9,
                     box(width = NULL, solidHeader = TRUE,
                         leafletOutput("StNmPMmap", height = 600),
                         h2(),
                         DT::dataTableOutput('acsDTStNmPM'),
                         h2(),tags$br(),
                         h2(),tags$br() )
                     ),
                     column(width = 3,
                          box(width = NULL, status = "warning",
                            selectInput("YearInputStNmPM","ACS Estimate
Years",choices = list("2015" = 2015, "2014" = 2014, "2013" = 2013, "2012" = 2012,
"2011" = 2011, "2010" = 2010, "2009" = 2009), selected = 2015),
                            radioButtons("ModeInputStNmPM", label = "Mode",
choices = list("Bike", "Walk"), inline=TRUE),
```

```
                              h2(),
                              radioButtons("MapDataSelectionStNmPM",    label    =
"Map Data Selection:", choices = list('Estimated Annual Trips','Estimated Annual Miles
Traveled',
                                                  'Estimated Annual Hours Traveled'),
                                  selected = 'Estimated Annual Trips', inline=FALSE),
                              h2(),
                              actionButton(inputId = "RefreshMapStNmPM", label =
"Refresh Map", class = "butt"),
                               tags$head(tags$style(".butt{background-
color:#0000FF;} .butt{color: white;}")), # background color and font color
                               downloadButton("downloadDataStNmPM",label
="Download Data")
                            )
                         )
                      ),
                      h2(),tags$br(),
                      h2(),tags$br()

                  ),
                  tabPanel(HTML(paste(tags$span(style="font-size: 18px", "Scalable
(BETA)"))), id="ACSexplorer",
                      tags$h1(tags$b("FHWA Rural Speed Project Decision Support
Tool (Beta)")),
                      fluidRow(
                      column(width = 9,
                         box(width = NULL, solidHeader = TRUE,
                            leafletOutput("busmap", height = 600),
                            h2(),
                            DT::dataTableOutput('acsDT'),
                            h2(),tags$br(),
                            h2(),tags$br()
                         )
                      ),
                      column(width = 3,
                         box(width = NULL, status = "warning",
                            h2(),
                            selectInput("YearInput","Year",choices   =   list("2015"   =
2015,"2016" = 2014,"2009 - 2013" = 2013,
                             "2008 - 2012" = 2012,"2007 - 2011" = 2011,"2006 - 2010" =
2010), selected = 2015),
                            selectInput("StateInput","State",choices = StatesList),
                            selectInput("CountyInput","County",choices     =     c("All
Counties",StateCountyList)),
                            radioButtons("ModeInput", label = "Severity", choices =
list("All", "Fatal and Injury"), inline=TRUE),
                            actionButton(inputId = "RefreshMap", label = "Refresh Map",
class = "butt"),
```

(Contd.)

```
tags$head(tags$style(".butt{background-color:#0000FF;} .butt{color: white;}")), #
background color and font color
                              downloadButton("downloadData",label ="Download Data")
                           )
                        )


                    ),
                    h2(),tags$br(),
                    h2(),tags$br()


                )
            )
)

# Put them together into a dashboardPage
ui <- dashboardPage(
    #header,
    dashboardHeader(disable = TRUE),
    dashboardSidebar(disable = TRUE),
    body
)
server <- function(input, output, session) {

 observeEvent(input$TimeSpan,
        if(input$TimeSpan==1){
           updateSelectInput(session, "YearInput","ACS Estimate Years",choices =
list("2013" = 2013, "2012" = 2012), selected = 2013)
        }else{
           if(input$TimeSpan==3){
           updateSelectInput(session, "YearInput","ACS Estimate Years",choices =
list("2011 - 2013" = 2013, "2010 - 2012" = 2012), selected = 2013)
        }else{
          updateSelectInput(session, "YearInput","ACS Estimate Years",choices =
list("2011 - 2015" = 2015,"2010 - 2014" = 2014,"2009 - 2013" = 2013,
                              "2008 - 2012" = 2012,"2007 - 2011" = 2011,"2006 - 2010" =
2010), selected = 2015)
           }
        }
 )
 observeEvent(input$TimeSpan,
        if(input$TimeSpan==1){
           updateSelectInput(session, "StateInput","State",choices = "All States")
        }else{
        if(input$TimeSpan==3){
           updateSelectInput(session, "StateInput","State",choices = "All States")
        }else{
           updateSelectInput(session, "StateInput","State",choices = StatesList)
```

```
            }
        }
)
observeEvent(input$TimeSpan,
        if(input$TimeSpan==1){
          disable("CountyInput")
        }else{
          if(input$TimeSpan==3){
        disable("CountyInput")
        }else{
           enable("CountyInput")
         }
        }
)


observeEvent(input$StateInput,
         StateCountyList         <-          as.character(subset(StateCountyData$County,
StateCountyData$State == input$StateInput))
)
observeEvent(input$StateInput,
        if(input$StateInput=="All States"){
           updateSelectInput(session, "CountyInput","County",choices = "")
        }else{
           updateSelectInput(session, "CountyInput","County",
                choices = c("All Counties",
                        subset(StateCountyData$County,     StateCountyData$State      ==
input$StateInput)))
        }
)
observeEvent(input$TimeSpan,
        if(input$TimeSpan==1){
           disable("StateInput")
        }else{
        if(input$TimeSpan==3){
           disable("StateInput")
        }else{
           enable("StateInput")
        }
        }
)
observeEvent(input$CountyInput,
        if(input$CountyInput==""){
           updateRadioButtons(session, "SpatialInput", label = "Spatial", choices =
list("State"))
        }else{
        if(input$CountyInput=="All Counties"){
           updateRadioButtons(session, "SpatialInput", label = "Spatial", choices =
list("Tract"))
```

(Contd.)

```
        }else{
          updateRadioButtons(session, "SpatialInput", label = "Spatial", choices =
list("Block Group"))
          }
        }
)

output$ACSinfoMessage <- renderUI({
   HTML("Note: Selection of 5-year ACS is statistically reliable for small spatial units
(tract and block group level).
   Selection of 3-year ACS or 1-year ACS is beneficial for larger spatial units (state).")
})

output$busmap <- renderLeaflet({

leaflet() %>%
   addProviderTiles("CartoDB.Positron") %>%
   setView(-98.35, 39.7, zoom = 4)

})

observeEvent(input$RefreshMap, {

withProgress(message = 'Processing ', value = 0, {

   #StateInput <- "AR"
   #YearInput <- 2015
   TimeSpan <- input$TimeSpan
   YearInput <- input$YearInput
   StateInput <- input$StateInput
   CountyInput <- input$CountyInput
   SpatialInput <- input$SpatialInput
   ModeInput <- input$ModeInput
   CountyCode <- subset(StateCountyData$CountyID, StateCountyData$State ==
StateInput & StateCountyData$County == CountyInput)

   TimeSpanDesc <- ifelse(TimeSpan == 5,"5 Year ACS",ifelse(TimeSpan == 3,"3
Year ACS","1 Year ACS"))
   YearDesc <- if (TimeSpan == 5) {

   ifelse(YearInput == 2015,"2011 - 2015",ifelse(YearInput == 2014,"2010 - 2014",
                  ifelse(YearInput == 2013,"2009 - 2013",
                     ifelse(YearInput == 2012,"2008 - 2012",
                          ifelse(YearInput == 2011,
                             "2007 - 2011","2006 - 2010")
                       )
                  )
)
)
```

```
}else{
   if (TimeSpan == 3) {

       ifelse(YearInput == 2013,"2011 - 2013","2010 - 2012")

}else{

   YearInput
   }
}

TimeYearDesc <- paste(TimeSpanDesc,": ",YearDesc)

if(TimeSpan == 1 || TimeSpan == 3){

incProgress(1/6, detail = paste("Retrieving Geography..."))
states <- states(cb = TRUE)

incProgress(2/6, detail = paste("Retrieving Data..."))
fetched <- acs.fetch(
   geography = geo.make(state="*"),
   endyear = YearInput, span = TimeSpan,# Package only goes to 2013, so end=2012
   table.number = "B08301", # Table showing 'Income'
   key="12c55b28a8b13fd30e88db9e59bee9edd0fa8ce1",
   col.names = "pretty")

### names(attributes(fetched)) # see what's available

### attr(fetched, "acs.colnames") # see column names

incProgress(3/6, detail = paste("Retrieving Data..."))
fetched1 <- acs.fetch(
   geography = geo.make(state="*"),
   endyear = YearInput, span = TimeSpan,# Package only goes to 2013, so end=2012
   table.number = "B01003", # Table showing 'Income'
   key="12c55b28a8b13fd30e88db9e59bee9edd0fa8ce1",
   col.names = "pretty")

incProgress(4/6, detail = paste("Preparing Output..."))
if(ModeInput == "Bike"){
   acs_df <- data.frame(
   paste0(
   str_pad(fetched@geography$state, 2, "left", pad="0"),
   str_pad(fetched@geography$county, 3, "left", pad="0"),
   str_pad(fetched@geography$tract, 6, "left", pad="0")),
  fetched@estimate[,c("Means of Transportation to Work: Total:",
          "Means of Transportation to Work: Bicycle")],
   stringsAsFactors = FALSE)
```

(Contd.)

```
    acs_df <- select(acs_df, 1:3) %>% tbl_df()
    rownames(acs_df) <- 1:nrow(acs_df)
    names(acs_df) <- c("GEOID", "total", "bike")
    acs_df$percent <- round(100*(acs_df$bike/acs_df$total),2)
    acs_df$percent <- replace(acs_df$percent, is.na(acs_df$percent), 0) #### to remove
NaN
    #head(acs_df)

    acs_df1 <- data.frame(
      paste0(
        str_pad(fetched1@geography$state, 2, "left", pad="0"),
        str_pad(fetched1@geography$county, 3, "left", pad="0"),
        str_pad(fetched1@geography$tract, 6, "left", pad="0")),
    fetched1@estimate[,c("Total Population: Total")],
    stringsAsFactors = FALSE)
   acs_df1 <- select(acs_df1, 1:2) %>% tbl_df()
   rownames(acs_df1) <- 1:nrow(acs_df1)
   names(acs_df1) <- c("GEOID", "popu")
   acs_df <- merge(acs_df, acs_df1, by="GEOID")

  df_merged <- geo_join(states, acs_df, "GEOID", "GEOID")
  #head(df_merged)
  df_merged <- df_merged[df_merged$ALAND>0,]
  #head(df_merged)
   df_merged <- df_merged[!(is.na(df_merged$percent)),] ###drop missing (NA)
values

   #popup <- paste0(df_merged$NAME, ", GeoID: ", df_merged$GEOID, "<br>",
"Commuters (16 Yrs and above) used Bicycle (%): ", round(df_merged$percent,2))
   #pal <- colorNumeric(
   # palette = "YlOrRd",
   # domain = df_merged$percent
   #)
   popup <- paste0(df_merged$NAME, ", GeoID: ", df_merged$GEOID, "<br>",
"Estimated Bike/Total Commute Trips (%) - ", round(df_merged$percent,2),
              "<br>","Estimated Total Commute Trips - ", round(df_merged$total,2),"<
br>","Exposure: Estimated Bike Commute Trips - ", round(df_merged$bike,2))
        pal <- colorNumeric(
        palette = "YlOrRd",
        domain = df_merged$bike
   )
   label <- paste0(df_merged$NAME, ", GeoID: ", df_merged$GEOID)

   acsT1 <- acs_df
   acsT1$StateID <- as.numeric(acsT1$GEOID)
   acsT1 <- merge(acsT1, StateNameList, by="StateID")
   acsT1$County <- "All Counties"
   acsT1 <- merge(acsT1, state_L, by="GEOID")
```

```
  acsT2 <- acsT1[c(7,8,1,6,9,5,3,4)]
  acsT2$percent <- round(acsT2$percent, 2)
  acsDTtemp <- datatable(cbind(TimeYearDesc,acsT2), class = 'cell-border stripe', colnames = c('Record No.','Time Period','State', 'County', 'GeoID (State)', 'Population Estimates',
                'Land Area in Square Mile',
                'Estimated Bike/Total Commute Trips (%)',
                'Estimated Total Commute Trips',
                'Exposure: Estimated Bike Commute Trips')
        ) %>% formatRound('percent', 2)
        output$acsDT = DT::renderDataTable(acsDTtemp, options = list(lengthChange = FALSE))

        acsT2dowload <- cbind(TimeYearDesc,acsT2)
        names(acsT2dowload) <- c('Time Period','State', 'County', 'GeoID (State)', 'Population Estimates',
                'Land Area in Square Mile',
                'Estimated Bike/Total Commute Trips (%)',
                'Estimated Total Commute Trips',
                'Exposure: Estimated Bike Commute Trips')

    incProgress(5/6, detail = paste("Writing Output..."))
 }else{
    acs_df <- data.frame(
      paste0(
                str_pad(fetched@geography$state, 2, "left", pad="0"),
                str_pad(fetched@geography$county, 3, "left", pad="0"),
                str_pad(fetched@geography$tract, 6, "left", pad="0")),
                fetched@estimate[,c("Means of Transportation to Work: Total:",
                                "Means of Transportation to Work: Walked")],
                stringsAsFactors = FALSE)

    acs_df <- select(acs_df, 1:3) %>% tbl_df()
    rownames(acs_df) <- 1:nrow(acs_df)
    names(acs_df) <- c("GEOID", "total", "walk")
    acs_df$percent <- round(100*(acs_df$walk/acs_df$total),2)
    acs_df$percent <- replace(acs_df$percent, is.na(acs_df$percent), 0) #### to remove NaN
    ### head(acs_df)

    acs_df1 <- data.frame(
    paste0(
        str_pad(fetched1@geography$state, 2, "left", pad="0"),
        str_pad(fetched1@geography$county, 3, "left", pad="0"),
        str_pad(fetched1@geography$tract, 6, "left", pad="0")),
    fetched1@estimate[,c("Total Population: Total")],
    stringsAsFactors = FALSE)
```

(*Contd.*)

```
    acs_df1 <- select(acs_df1, 1:2) %>% tbl_df()
    rownames(acs_df1) <- 1:nrow(acs_df1)
    names(acs_df1) <- c("GEOID", "popu")
    acs_df <- merge(acs_df, acs_df1, by="GEOID")

    df_merged <- geo_join(states, acs_df, "GEOID", "GEOID")
    #head(df_merged)
    df_merged <- df_merged[df_merged$ALAND>0,]
    #head(df_merged)
    df_merged <- df_merged[!(is.na(df_merged$percent)),] ###drop missing (NA)
values


    #popup <- paste0(df_merged$NAME, ", GeoID: ", df_merged$GEOID, "<br>",
"Commuters (16 Yrs and above) Walked (%): ", round(df_merged$percent,2))
    #pal <- colorNumeric(
    # palette = "YlOrRd",
    # domain = df_merged$percent
    #)
    popup <- paste0(df_merged$NAME, ", GeoID: ", df_merged$GEOID, "<br>",
"Estimated Walk/Total Commute Trips (%) - ", round(df_merged$percent,2),
            "<br>","Estimated Total Commute Trips - ", round(df_merged$total,2),"<br>
","Exposure: Estimated Walk Commute Trips - ", round(df_merged$walk,2))
    pal <- colorNumeric(
      palette = "YlOrRd",
      domain = df_merged$walk
    )
    label <- paste0(df_merged$NAME, ", GeoID: ", df_merged$GEOID)

    acsT1 <- acs_df
    acsT1$StateID <- as.numeric(acsT1$GEOID)
    acsT1 <- merge(acsT1, StateNameList, by="StateID")
    acsT1$County <- "All Counties"
    acsT1 <- merge(acsT1, state_L, by="GEOID")
    acsT2 <- acsT1[c(7,8,1,6,9,5,3,4)]
    acsT2$percent <- round(acsT2$percent, 2)
    acsDTtemp <- datatable(cbind(TimeYearDesc,acsT2), class = 'cell-border stripe',
colnames = c('Record No.','Time Period','State', 'County', 'GeoID (State)', 'Population
Estimates',
                    'Land Area in Square Mile',
                    'Estimated Walk/Total Commute Trips (%)',
                    'Estimated Total Commute Trips',
                    'Exposure: Estimated Walk Commute Trips')
    ) %>% formatRound('percent', 2)
    output$acsDT = DT::renderDataTable(acsDTtemp, options = list(lengthChange =
FALSE))
```

```
    acsT2dowload <- cbind(TimeYearDesc,acsT2)
    names(acsT2dowload) <- c('Time Period','State', 'County', 'GeoID (State)',
'Population Estimates',
                    'Land Area in Square Mile',
                    'Estimated Walk/Total Commute Trips (%)',
                    'Estimated Total Commute Trips',
                    'Exposure: Estimated Walk Commute Trips')

      incProgress(5/6, detail = paste("Writing Output..."))
  }
 }else{
   ### TimeSpan = 5
   if(CountyInput == "All Counties"){

   incProgress(1/6, detail = paste("Retrieving Geography..."))
   tracts <- tracts(state = StateInput, cb=TRUE)

   incProgress(2/6, detail = paste("Retrieving Data..."))
   fetched <- acs.fetch(
      geography = geo.make(state = StateInput, county="*", tract = "*"),
      endyear = YearInput, span = TimeSpan,# Package only goes to 2013, so end=2012
      table.number = "B08301", # Table showing 'Income'
      key="12c55b28a8b13fd30e88db9e59bee9edd0fa8ce1",
      col.names = "pretty") # Gives the full column definitions

      ### head(fetched)
      incProgress(3/6, detail = paste("Retrieving Data..."))
      fetched1 <- acs.fetch(
      geography = geo.make(state = StateInput, county="*", tract = "*"),
      endyear = YearInput, span = TimeSpan,# Package only goes to 2013, so end=2012
      table.number = "B01003", # Table showing 'Income'
      key="12c55b28a8b13fd30e88db9e59bee9edd0fa8ce1",
      col.names = "pretty") # Gives the full column definitions

    ### names(attributes(fetched)) # see what's available

    ### attr(fetched, "acs.colnames") # see column names

    incProgress(4/6, detail = paste("Preparing Output..."))
    if(ModeInput == "Bike"){
      acs_df <- data.frame(
        paste0(
          str_pad(fetched@geography$state, 2, "left", pad="0"),
          str_pad(fetched@geography$county, 3, "left", pad="0"),
          str_pad(fetched@geography$tract, 6, "left", pad="0")),
        fetched@estimate[,c("Means of Transportation to Work: Total:",
                "Means of Transportation to Work: Bicycle")],
        stringsAsFactors = FALSE)
```

(Contd.)

```
### head(acs_df)

###write.csv(acs_df, "Data2.csv")

acs_df <- select(acs_df, 1:3) %>% tbl_df()
rownames(acs_df) <- 1:nrow(acs_df)
names(acs_df) <- c("GEOID", "total", "bike")
acs_df$percent <- 100*(acs_df$bike/acs_df$total)
acs_df$percent <- replace(acs_df$percent, is.na(acs_df$percent), 0) #### to remove
NaN
### head(acs_df)

acs_df1 <- data.frame(
  paste0(
    str_pad(fetched1@geography$state, 2, "left", pad="0"),
    str_pad(fetched1@geography$county, 3, "left", pad="0"),
    str_pad(fetched1@geography$tract, 6, "left", pad="0")),
  fetched1@estimate[,c("Total Population: Total")],
  stringsAsFactors = FALSE)
acs_df1 <- select(acs_df1, 1:2) %>% tbl_df()
rownames(acs_df1) <- 1:nrow(acs_df1)
names(acs_df1) <- c("GEOID", "popu")
acs_df <- merge(acs_df, acs_df1, by="GEOID")
df_merged <- geo_join(tracts, acs_df, "GEOID", "GEOID")
### head(df_merged)

df_merged$StateCounty <- as.numeric(paste0(df_merged$STATEFP, df_
merged$COUNTYFP))
# head(df_merged)

df_merged <- merge(df_merged, StateCountyData, by="StateCounty")

# there are some tracts with no land that we should exclude
df_merged <- df_merged[df_merged$ALAND>0,]
### head(df_merged)

#popup <- paste0(df_merged$NAME, ", GeoID: ", df_merged$GEOID, "<br>",
"Commuters (16 Yrs and above) used Bicycle (%): ", round(df_merged$percent,2))
#pal <- colorNumeric(
# palette = "YlOrRd",
# domain = df_merged$percent
#)
popup <- paste0(df_merged$County, ", GeoID: ", df_merged$GEOID, "<br>",
"Estimated Bike/Total Commute Trips (%) - ", round(df_merged$percent,2),
          "<br>","Estimated Total Commute Trips - ", round(df_merged$total,
2),"<br>","Exposure: Estimated Bike Commute Trips - ", round(df_merged$bike,2))
pal <- colorNumeric(
palette = "YlOrRd",
```

```
    domain = df_merged$bike
   )
   label <- paste0(df_merged$County, ", ", "GeoID: ", df_merged$GEOID)

   acsT1 <- acs_df
   acsT1$StateCounty <- as.numeric(substr(acsT1$GEOID, 1, 5))
   acsT1 <- merge(acsT1, StateCountyData, by="StateCounty")
   acsT1 <- merge(acsT1, tract_L, by="GEOID")
   acsT2 <- acsT1[c(7,10,1,6,11,5,3,4)]
   acsT2$percent <- round(acsT2$percent, 2)
   acsDTtemp <- datatable(cbind(TimeYearDesc,acsT2), class = 'cell-border stripe',
colnames = c('Record No.','Time Period','State', 'County',
                       'GeoID (Tract)', 'Population Estimates',
                       'Land Area in Square Mile',
                       'Estimated Bike/Total Commute Trips (%)',
                       'Estimated Total Commute Trips',
                       'Exposure: Estimated Bike Commute Trips')
   ) %>% formatRound('percent', 2)
   output$acsDT = DT::renderDataTable(acsDTtemp, options = list(lengthChange =
FALSE))

   acsT2dowload <- cbind(TimeYearDesc,acsT2)
   names(acsT2dowload) <- c('Time Period','State', 'County', 'GeoID (Tract)',
'Population Estimates', 'Land Area in Square Mile',
                       'Estimated Bike/Total Commute Trips (%)',
                       'Estimated Total Commute Trips',
                       'Exposure: Estimated Bike Commute Trips')

   incProgress(5/6, detail = paste("Writing Output..."))

 }else{
   acs_df <- data.frame(
     paste0(
       str_pad(fetched@geography$state, 2, "left", pad="0"),
       str_pad(fetched@geography$county, 3, "left", pad="0"),
       str_pad(fetched@geography$tract, 6, "left", pad="0")),
       fetched@estimate[,c("Means of Transportation to Work: Total:",
              "Means of Transportation to Work: Walked")],
    stringsAsFactors = FALSE)

   ### head(acs_df)

   acs_df <- select(acs_df, 1:3) %>% tbl_df()
   rownames(acs_df) <- 1:nrow(acs_df)
   names(acs_df) <- c("GEOID", "total", "walk")
   acs_df$percent <- 100*(acs_df$walk/acs_df$total)
   acs_df$percent <- replace(acs_df$percent, is.na(acs_df$percent), 0) #### to remove
NaN
```

(Contd.)

```
### head(acs_df)

acs_df1 <- data.frame(
 paste0(
   str_pad(fetched1@geography$state, 2, "left", pad="0"),
   str_pad(fetched1@geography$county, 3, "left", pad="0"),
   str_pad(fetched1@geography$tract, 6, "left", pad="0")),
 fetched1@estimate[,c("Total Population: Total")],
 stringsAsFactors = FALSE)
 acs_df1 <- select(acs_df1, 1:2) %>% tbl_df()
 rownames(acs_df1) <- 1:nrow(acs_df1)
 names(acs_df1) <- c("GEOID", "popu")
 acs_df <- merge(acs_df, acs_df1, by="GEOID")

 df_merged <- geo_join(tracts, acs_df, "GEOID", "GEOID")
 ### head(df_merged)

 df_merged$StateCounty <- as.numeric(paste0(df_merged$STATEFP, df_
merged$COUNTYFP))
 # head(df_merged)

 df_merged <- merge(df_merged, StateCountyData, by="StateCounty")


 # there are some tracts with no land that we should exclude
 df_merged <- df_merged[df_merged$ALAND>0,]
 ### head(df_merged)

 #popup <- paste0(df_merged$NAME, ", GeoID: ", df_merged$GEOID, "<br>",
"Commuters (16 Yrs and above) Walked (%): ", round(df_merged$percent,2))
 #pal <- colorNumeric(
 # palette = "YlOrRd",
 # domain = df_merged$percent
 #)
 popup <- paste0(df_merged$County, ", GeoID: ", df_merged$GEOID, "<br>",
"Estimated Walk/Total Commute Trips (%) - ", round(df_merged$percent,2),
            "<br>","Estimated Total Commute Trips - ", round(df_merged$total,2),"<b
r>","Exposure: Estimated Walk Commute Trips - ", round(df_merged$walk,2))
 pal <- colorNumeric(
 palette = "YlOrRd",
 domain = df_merged$walk
)
label <- paste0(df_merged$County, ", ", "GeoID: ", df_merged$GEOID)

acsT1 <- acs_df
acsT1$StateCounty <- as.numeric(substr(acsT1$GEOID, 1, 5))
acsT1 <- merge(acsT1, StateCountyData, by="StateCounty")
acsT1 <- merge(acsT1, tract_L, by="GEOID")
```

```
  acsT2 <- acsT1[c(7,10,1,6,11,5,3,4)]
  acsT2$percent <- round(acsT2$percent, 2)
  acsDTtemp <- datatable(cbind(TimeYearDesc,acsT2), class = 'cell-border stripe',
colnames = c('Record No.','Time Period','State', 'County', 'GeoID (Tract)',
          'Population Estimates', 'Land Area in Square Mile',
          'Estimated Walk/Total Commute Trips (%)',
          'Estimated Total Commute Trips',
          'Exposure: Estimated Walk Commute Trips')
  ) %>% formatRound('percent', 2)
  output$acsDT = DT::renderDataTable(acsDTtemp, options = list(lengthChange =
FALSE))

  acsT2dowload <- cbind(TimeYearDesc,acsT2)
  names(acsT2dowload) <- c('Time Period','State', 'County', 'GeoID (Tract)',
'Population Estimates', 'Land Area in Square Mile',
          'Estimated Walk/Total Commute Trips (%)',
          'Estimated Total Commute Trips',
          'Exposure: Estimated Walk Commute Trips')

   incProgress(4/5, detail = paste("Writing Output..."))

   }

   }else{

   if(ModeInput == "Bike"){

   incProgress(1/6, detail = paste("Retrieving Geography..."))
   bg <- block_groups(StateInput, county=CountyCode, cb=TRUE)
   ### head(bg)


   incProgress(2/6, detail = paste("Retrieving Data..."))
   fetched <- acs.fetch(
   geography = geo.make(state = StateInput, county=CountyCode, tract = "*", block.
group = "*"),
   endyear = YearInput,span=TimeSpan,# Package only goes to 2013, so end=2012
   table.number = "B08301", key="12c55b28a8b13fd30e88db9e59bee9edd0fa8ce1",
   col.names = "pretty")

   ### head(fetched)

   ### names(attributes(fetched)) # see what's available

   ### attr(fetched, "acs.colnames") # see column names

   incProgress(3/6, detail = paste("Retrieving Data..."))
```

(*Contd.*)

```
    fetched1 <- acs.fetch(
    geography = geo.make(state = StateInput, county=CountyCode, tract = "*", block.
group = "*"),
    endyear = YearInput,span=TimeSpan,# Package only goes to 2013, so end=2012
    table.number = "B01003", key="12c55b28a8b13fd30e88db9e59bee9edd0fa8ce1",
    col.names = "pretty")

    incProgress(4/6, detail = paste("Preparing Output..."))
    acs_df <- data.frame(
     paste0(
        str_pad(fetched@geography$state, 2, "left", pad="0"),
        str_pad(fetched@geography$county, 3, "left", pad="0"),
        str_pad(fetched@geography$tract, 6, "left", pad="0"),
        str_pad(fetched@geography$blockgroup, 1, "left", pad="0")),
    fetched@estimate[,c("Means of Transportation to Work: Total:",
             "Means of Transportation to Work: Bicycle")],
    stringsAsFactors = FALSE)

    ### head(acs_df)

    acs_df <- select(acs_df, 1:3) %>% tbl_df()
    rownames(acs_df) <- 1:nrow(acs_df)
    names(acs_df) <- c("GEOID", "total", "bike")
    acs_df$percent <- 100*(acs_df$bike/acs_df$total)
    acs_df$percent <- replace(acs_df$percent, is.na(acs_df$percent), 0) #### to remove
NaN
    ### head(acs_df)

    ###write.csv(acs_df, "Data1.csv")
    acs_df1 <- data.frame(
    paste0(
        str_pad(fetched1@geography$state, 2, "left", pad="0"),
        str_pad(fetched1@geography$county, 3, "left", pad="0"),
        str_pad(fetched1@geography$tract, 6, "left", pad="0"),
        str_pad(fetched1@geography$blockgroup, 1, "left", pad="0")),
    fetched1@estimate[,c("Total Population: Total")],
    stringsAsFactors = FALSE)
    acs_df1 <- select(acs_df1, 1:2) %>% tbl_df()
    rownames(acs_df1) <- 1:nrow(acs_df1)
    names(acs_df1) <- c("GEOID", "popu")
    acs_df <- merge(acs_df, acs_df1, by="GEOID")

    df_merged <- geo_join(bg, acs_df, "GEOID", "GEOID")
    ### head(df_merged)

    df_merged$StateCounty <- as.numeric(paste0(df_merged$STATEFP, df_
merged$COUNTYFP))
```

```
    # head(df_merged)
    df_merged <- merge(df_merged, StateCountyData, by="StateCounty")

    ##there are some tracts with no land that we should exclude
    df_merged2 <- df_merged[df_merged$ALAND>0,]
    ### head(df_merged2)

    #popup <- paste0(df_merged$NAME, ", GeoID: ", df_merged$GEOID, "<br>",
"Commuters (16 Yrs and above) used Bicycle (%): ", round(df_merged$percent,2))
    #pal <- colorNumeric(
    # palette = "YlOrRd",
    # domain = df_merged$percent
    #)
    popup <- paste0(df_merged$County, ", GeoID: ", df_merged$GEOID, "<br>",
"Estimated Bike/Total Commute Trips (%) - ", round(df_merged$percent,2),
            "<br>","Estimated Total Commute Trips - ", round(df_merged$total,2),"<
br>","Exposure: Estimated Bike Commute Trips - ", round(df_merged$bike,2))
    pal <- colorNumeric(
    palette = "YlOrRd",
    domain = df_merged$bike
    )
    label <- paste0(df_merged2$County, ", ", "GeoID: ", df_merged2$GEOID)

    acsT1 <- acs_df
    acsT1$StateCounty <- as.numeric(substr(acsT1$GEOID, 1, 5))
    acsT1 <- merge(acsT1, StateCountyData, by="StateCounty")
    acsT1 <- merge(acsT1, bg_L, by="GEOID")
    acsT2 <- acsT1[c(7,10,1,6,11,5,3,4)]
    acsT2$percent <- round(acsT2$percent, 2)
    acsDTtemp <- datatable(cbind(TimeYearDesc,acsT2), class = 'cell-border stripe',
colnames = c('Record No.','Time Period','State', 'County',
    'GeoID (Block Group)', 'Population Estimates',
            'Land Area in Square Mile',
            'Estimated Bike/Total Commute Trips (%)',
            'Estimated Total Commute Trips',
            'Exposure: Estimated Bike Commute Trips')
    ) %>% formatRound('percent', 2)
    output$acsDT = DT::renderDataTable(acsDTtemp, options = list(lengthChange =
FALSE))

    acsT2dowload <- cbind(TimeYearDesc,acsT2)
    names(acsT2dowload) <- c('Time Period','State', 'County', 'GeoID (Block Group)',
'Population Estimates', 'Land Area in Square Mile',
            'Estimated Bike/Total Commute Trips (%)',
            'Estimated Total Commute Trips',
            'Exposure: Estimated Bike Commute Trips')

    incProgress(4/6, detail = paste("Writing Output..."))
```

(Contd.)

```
    }else{

    incProgress(1/6, detail = paste("Retrieving Geography..."))
    bg <- block_groups(StateInput, county=CountyCode, cb=TRUE)
    ### head(bg)


    incProgress(2/6, detail = paste("Retrieving Data..."))
    fetched <- acs.fetch(
    geography = geo.make(state = StateInput, county=CountyCode, tract = "*", block.
group = "*"),
    endyear = YearInput,span=TimeSpan,# Package only goes to 2013, so end=2012
    table.number = "B08301", key="12c55b28a8b13fd30e88db9e59bee9edd0fa8ce1",
    col.names = "pretty")

    ### head(fetched)

    ### names(attributes(fetched)) # see what's available

    ### attr(fetched, "acs.colnames") # see column names

    incProgress(3/6, detail = paste("Retrieving Data..."))
    fetched1 <- acs.fetch(
    geography = geo.make(state = StateInput, county=CountyCode, tract = "*", block.
group = "*"),
    endyear = YearInput,span=TimeSpan,# Package only goes to 2013, so end=2012
    table.number = "B01003", key="12c55b28a8b13fd30e88db9e59bee9edd0fa8ce1",
    col.names = "pretty")

    incProgress(4/6, detail = paste("Preparing Output..."))
    acs_df <- data.frame(
    paste0(
        str_pad(fetched@geography$state, 2, "left", pad="0"),
        str_pad(fetched@geography$county, 3, "left", pad="0"),
        str_pad(fetched@geography$tract, 6, "left", pad="0"),
        str_pad(fetched@geography$blockgroup, 1, "left", pad="0")),
        fetched@estimate[,c("Means of Transportation to Work: Total:",
                    "Means of Transportation to Work: Walked")],
        stringsAsFactors = FALSE)

        ### head(acs_df)

        acs_df <- select(acs_df, 1:3) %>% tbl_df()
        rownames(acs_df) <- 1:nrow(acs_df)
        names(acs_df) <- c("GEOID", "total", "walk")
        acs_df$percent <- 100*(acs_df$walk/acs_df$total)
        acs_df$percent <- replace(acs_df$percent, is.na(acs_df$percent), 0) #### to
remove NaN
```

```
### head(acs_df)

acs_df1 <- data.frame(
paste0(
str_pad(fetched1@geography$state, 2, "left", pad="0"),
str_pad(fetched1@geography$county, 3, "left", pad="0"),
str_pad(fetched1@geography$tract, 6, "left", pad="0"),
str_pad(fetched1@geography$blockgroup, 1, "left", pad="0")),
fetched1@estimate[,c("Total Population: Total")],
stringsAsFactors = FALSE)
acs_df1 <- select(acs_df1, 1:2) %>% tbl_df()
rownames(acs_df1) <- 1:nrow(acs_df1)
names(acs_df1) <- c("GEOID", "popu")
acs_df <- merge(acs_df, acs_df1, by="GEOID")

df_merged <- geo_join(bg, acs_df, "GEOID", "GEOID")
### head(df_merged)

df_merged$StateCounty <- as.numeric(paste0(df_merged$STATEFP, df_
merged$COUNTYFP))

# head(df_merged)

df_merged <- merge(df_merged, StateCountyData, by="StateCounty")

##there are some tracts with no land that we should exclude
df_merged2 <- df_merged[df_merged$ALAND>0,]
### head(df_merged2)

#popup <- paste0(df_merged$NAME, ", GeoID: ", df_merged$GEOID, "<br>",
"Commuters (16 Yrs and above) Walked (%): ", round(df_merged$percent,2))
#pal <- colorNumeric(
# palette = "YlOrRd",
# domain = df_merged$percent
#)
popup <- paste0(df_merged$County, ", GeoID: ", df_merged$GEOID, "<br>",
"Estimated Walk/Total Commute Trips (%) - ", round(df_merged$percent,2),
"<br>","Estimated Total Commute Trips - ", round(df_merged$total,2),"<br>","
Exposure: Estimated Walk Commute Trips - ", round(df_merged$walk,2))
pal <- colorNumeric(
palette = "YlOrRd",
domain = df_merged$walk
)
label <- paste0(df_merged2$County, ", ", "GeoID: ", df_
merged2$GEOID)

acsT1 <- acs_df
acsT1$StateCounty <- as.numeric(substr(acsT1$GEOID, 1, 5))
```

(Contd.)

```
        acsT1 <- merge(acsT1, StateCountyData, by="StateCounty")
        acsT1 <- merge(acsT1, bg_L, by="GEOID")
        acsT2 <- acsT1[c(7,10,1,6,11,5,3,4)]
        acsT2$percent <- round(acsT2$percent, 2)
        acsDTtemp <- datatable(cbind(TimeYearDesc,acsT2), class = 'cell-border stripe',
colnames = c('Record No.','Time Period','State', 'County',
                        'GeoID (Block Group)', 'Population Estimates',
                        'Land Area in Square Mile',
                        'Estimated Walk/Total Commute Trips (%)',
                        'Estimated Total Commute Trips',
                        'Exposure: Estimated Walk Commute Trips')
        ) %>% formatRound('percent', 2)
        output$acsDT = DT::renderDataTable(acsDTtemp, options = list(lengthChange
= FALSE))

        acsT2dowload <- cbind(TimeYearDesc,acsT2)
        names(acsT2dowload) <- c('Time Period','State', 'County', 'GeoID (Block
Group)', 'Population Estimates', 'Land Area in Square Mile',
                        'Estimated Walk/Total Commute Trips (%)',
                        'Estimated Total Commute Trips',
                        'Exposure: Estimated Walk Commute Trips')

        incProgress(4/5, detail = paste("Writing Output..."))

      }
    }
 }

 output$busmap <- renderLeaflet({

   if(TimeSpan == 1 || TimeSpan == 3){
   if(ModeInput == "Bike"){
        leaflet() %>%
   setView(-98.35, 39.7, zoom = 4) %>%
   addProviderTiles(providers$CartoDB.Positron) %>%
   addPolygons(data = df_merged,
        #fillColor = ~pal(percent),
        fillColor = ~pal(bike),
        color = "#5e6e88", # you need to use hex colors
        fillOpacity = 0.7,
        weight = 1,
        smoothFactor = 0.30,
        popup = popup,
        highlightOptions = highlightOptions(color = "black", weight = 2,
                              bringToFront = TRUE),
        label = label) %>%
    addLegend(pal = pal,
        #values = df_merged$percent,
```

```
        values = df_merged$bike,
        position = "bottomright",
        #title = "Commuters (%) Bike to Work",
        #labFormat = labelFormat(suffix = "%"))
        title = "Commuters Bike to Work")
    }else{
    leaflet() %>%
    setView(-98.35, 39.7, zoom = 4) %>%
     addProviderTiles(providers$CartoDB.Positron) %>%
    addPolygons(data = df_merged,
        #fillColor = ~pal(percent),
        fillColor = ~pal(walk),
        color = "#5e6e88", # you need to use hex colors
        fillOpacity = 0.7,
        weight = 1,
        smoothFactor = 0.30,
        popup = popup,
        highlightOptions = highlightOptions(color = "black", weight = 2,
                                bringToFront = TRUE),
        label = label) %>%

addLegend(pal = pal,
        #values = df_merged$percent,
        values = df_merged$walk,
        position = "bottomright",
        #title = "Commuters (%) Walk to Work",
        #labFormat = labelFormat(suffix = "%"))
        title = "Commuters Walk to Work"
    )
    }
}else{
    ### TimeSpan = 5
    if(CountyInput == "All Counties"){
    if(ModeInput == "Bike"){
     leaflet() %>%
      addProviderTiles("CartoDB.Positron") %>%
      addPolygons(data = df_merged,
        #fillColor = ~pal(percent),
        fillColor = ~pal(bike),
        color = "#b2aeae", # you need to use hex colors
        fillOpacity = 0.7,
        weight = 1,
        smoothFactor = 0.2,
        popup = popup,
        highlightOptions = highlightOptions(color = "black", weight = 2,
                                bringToFront = TRUE),
        label = label) %>%
addLegend(pal = pal,
```

(Contd.)

```
        #values = df_merged$percent,
        values = df_merged$bike,
        position = "bottomright",
        #title = "Commuters (%) Bike to Work (Census Tract)",
        #labFormat = labelFormat(suffix = "%")
        title = "Commuters Bike to Work (Census Tract)"
  )
}else{
  leaflet() %>%
    addProviderTiles("CartoDB.Positron") %>%
   addPolygons(data = df_merged,
        #fillColor = ~pal(percent),
        fillColor = ~pal(walk),
        color = "#b2aeae", # you need to use hex colors
        fillOpacity = 0.7,
        weight = 1,
        smoothFactor = 0.2,
        popup = popup,
        highlightOptions = highlightOptions(color = "black", weight = 2,
                                bringToFront = TRUE),
        label = label) %>%
addLegend(pal = pal,
        #values = df_merged$percent,
        values = df_merged$walk,
        position = "bottomright",
        #title = "Commuters (%) Walk to Work (Census Tract)",
        #labFormat = labelFormat(suffix = "%")
        title = "Commuters Walk to Work (Census Tract)"
  )
 }

}else{

  if(ModeInput == "Bike"){
   leaflet() %>%
   addProviderTiles("CartoDB.Positron") %>%
   addPolygons(data = df_merged2,
        #fillColor = ~pal(percent),
        fillColor = ~pal(bike),
        color = "#b2aeae", # you need to use hex colors
        fillOpacity = 0.7,
        weight = 1,
        smoothFactor = 0.2,
        popup = popup,
        highlightOptions = highlightOptions(color = "black", weight = 2,
                                bringToFront = TRUE),
```

```
        label = label) %>%
addLegend(pal = pal,
        #values = df_merged$percent,
        values = df_merged$bike,
        position = "bottomright",
        title = "Commuters Bike to Work (Census Block group)"
        #title = "Commuters (%) Bike to Work (Census Block group)",
        #labFormat = labelFormat(suffix = "%")
  )


}else{
  leaflet() %>%
   addProviderTiles("CartoDB.Positron") %>%
   addPolygons(data = df_merged,
        #fillColor = ~pal(percent),
        fillColor = ~pal(walk),
        color = "#b2aeae", # you need to use hex colors
        fillOpacity = 0.7,
        weight = 1,
        smoothFactor = 0.2,
        popup = popup,
        highlightOptions = highlightOptions(color = "black", weight = 2,
                              bringToFront = TRUE),
        label = label) %>%
addLegend(pal = pal,
        #values = df_merged$percent,
        values = df_merged$walk,
        position = "bottomright",
        title = "Commuters Walk to Work (Census Block group)"
        #title = "Commuters (%) Walk to Work (Census Block group)",
        #labFormat = labelFormat(suffix = "%")
    )
    }
   }
 }
})
incProgress(6/6, detail = paste("Finished!"))

output$downloadData <- downloadHandler(
  #filename = function() {paste("test.csv")},
  filename = function() {gsub(" ","",paste(StateInput,"_",CountyInput,"_",YearInput,"
                         ",TimeSpan,"yr_",SpatialInput,"_",
                         ModeInput,".csv"))},
  content = function(file) {
   write.csv(acsT2dowload,file, row.names=FALSE)
  })
```

(*Contd.*)

```
 })

})

output$StNmPMmap <- renderLeaflet({

leaflet() %>%
  addProviderTiles("CartoDB.Positron") %>%
  setView(-98.35, 39.7, zoom = 4)

})

observeEvent(input$RefreshMapStNmPM, {
  withProgress(message = 'Processing ', value = 0, {

      YearInputStNmPM <- input$YearInputStNmPM
      ModeInputStNmPM <- input$ModeInputStNmPM

      incProgress(1/3, detail = paste("Retrieving Geography..."))
      StatePerMeasureData <- subset(StateNonMotorPM, StateNonMotorPM$Year ==
YearInputStNmPM )

      StatePerMeasureData <- subset(StatePerMeasureData,
StatePerMeasureData$Mode == ModeInputStNmPM)

      StatePerMeasureData <- StatePerMeasureData[c(1,2,6,7,12,13,14)]
      StatePerMeasureData$GEOID <- str_pad(StatePerMeasureData$GEOID, 2, pad
= "0")

      states <- states(cb = TRUE)
      df_mergedStNmPM <- geo_join(states, StatePerMeasureData, "GEOID",
"GEOID")
      df_mergedStNmPM$Estimated_Annual_Trips_Million <-
replace(df_mergedStNmPM$Estimated_Annual_Trips_Million, is.na(df_
mergedStNmPM$Estimated_Annual_Trips_Million), 0)
      df_mergedStNmPM$Estimated_Annual_MilesTraveled_Million <-
replace(df_mergedStNmPM$Estimated_Annual_MilesTraveled_Million, is.na(df_
mergedStNmPM$Estimated_Annual_MilesTraveled_Million), 0)
      df_mergedStNmPM$Estimated_Annual_HoursTraveled_Million <-
replace(df_mergedStNmPM$Estimated_Annual_HoursTraveled_Million, is.na(df_
mergedStNmPM$Estimated_Annual_HoursTraveled_Million), 0)
      df_mergedStNmPM <- subset(df_mergedStNmPM, !(is.na(df_
mergedStNmPM$State))) ###drop where State is NA (Samoa, etc.)
      df_mergedStNmPM <- subset(df_mergedStNmPM, df_mergedStNmPM$GEOID
!= 72) ###drop Puerto Rico (no NHTS data)
```

```
    popupStNmPM <- paste0(df_mergedStNmPM$State, ", GeoID: ", df_mergedStNmPM$GEOID, "<br>", "Year: ", df_mergedStNmPM$Year, ", Mode: ", df_mergedStNmPM$Mode, "<br>",
          "Estimated Annual Trips (Million): ", df_mergedStNmPM$Estimated_Annual_Trips_Million, "<br>",
          "Estimated Annual Miles Traveled (Million): ", df_mergedStNmPM$Estimated_Annual_MilesTraveled_Million, "<br>",
          "Estimated Annual Hours Traveled (Million): ",df_mergedStNmPM$Estimated_Annual_HoursTraveled_Million)
   labelStNmPM <- paste0(df_mergedStNmPM$State, ", GeoID: ", df_mergedStNmPM$GEOID)
   palStNmPM <- colorNumeric(palette = "YlOrRd", domain = df_mergedStNmPM$Estimated_Annual_Trips_Million)


   incProgress(2/3, detail = paste("Preparing Output..."))
   StatePerMeasureDataNoPuertoRico <- subset(StatePerMeasureData, StatePerMeasureData$GEOID != 72 )
   acsDTtempStNmPM <- datatable(StatePerMeasureDataNoPuertoRico, class = 'cell-border stripe', colnames = c('Record No.','State','GeoID (State)','Mode','Year','Estimated Annual Trips (Million)',
          'Estimated Annual Miles Traveled (Million)','Estimated Annual Hours Traveled (Million)')
 )
   names(StatePerMeasureDataNoPuertoRico) <- c('State','GeoID (State)','Mode','Year','Estimated Annual Trips (Million)',
             'Estimated Annual Miles Traveled (Million)','Estimated Annual Hours Traveled (Million)')

 observe({
   if (input$MapDataSelectionStNmPM == 'Estimated Annual Trips') {
      palStNmPM <- colorNumeric(palette = "YlOrRd", domain = df_mergedStNmPM$Estimated_Annual_Trips_Million)
    leafletProxy("StNmPMmap") %>%
    clearControls() %>%
    clearShapes() %>%
    addProviderTiles(providers$CartoDB.Positron) %>%
    addPolygons(data = df_mergedStNmPM,
       fillColor = ~palStNmPM(Estimated_Annual_Trips_Million),
       color = "#5e6e88", # you need to use hex colors
       fillOpacity = 0.7,
       weight = 1,
       smoothFactor = 0.30,
       popup = popupStNmPM,
       highlightOptions = highlightOptions(color = "black", weight = 2, bringToFront = TRUE),
       label = labelStNmPM) %>%
 addLegend(pal = palStNmPM,
```

(Contd.)

```
        values = df_mergedStNmPM$Estimated_Annual_Trips_Million,
        position = "bottomright",
        title = "Estimated Annual Trips (Million)",
        labFormat = labelFormat(suffix = ""))
 } else {
    if (input$MapDataSelectionStNmPM == 'Estimated Annual Miles Traveled') {
        palStNmPM <- colorNumeric(palette = "YlOrRd", domain = df_
mergedStNmPM$Estimated_Annual_MilesTraveled_Million)
     leafletProxy("StNmPMmap") %>%
     clearControls() %>%
     clearShapes() %>%
     addProviderTiles(providers$CartoDB.Positron) %>%
     addPolygons(data = df_mergedStNmPM,
        fillColor = ~palStNmPM(Estimated_Annual_MilesTraveled_Million),
        color = "#5e6e88", # you need to use hex colors
        fillOpacity = 0.7,
        weight = 1,
        smoothFactor = 0.30,
        popup = popupStNmPM,
        highlightOptions = highlightOptions(color = "black", weight = 2, bringToFront =
TRUE),
        label = labelStNmPM) %>%
        addLegend(pal = palStNmPM,
        values = df_mergedStNmPM$Estimated_Annual_MilesTraveled_Million,
        position = "bottomright",
        title = "Estimated Annual Miles Traveled (Million)",
        labFormat = labelFormat(suffix = ""))
 } else {
        palStNmPM <- colorNumeric(palette = "YlOrRd", domain = df_
mergedStNmPM$Estimated_Annual_HoursTraveled_Million)
    leafletProxy("StNmPMmap") %>%
    clearControls() %>%
    clearShapes() %>%
    addProviderTiles(providers$CartoDB.Positron) %>%
        addPolygons(data = df_mergedStNmPM,
        fillColor = ~palStNmPM(Estimated_Annual_HoursTraveled_Million),
        color = "#5e6e88", # you need to use hex colors
        fillOpacity = 0.7,
        weight = 1,
        smoothFactor = 0.30,
        popup = popupStNmPM,
        highlightOptions = highlightOptions(color = "black", weight = 2, bringToFront =
TRUE),
        label = labelStNmPM) %>%
 addLegend(pal = palStNmPM,
        values = df_mergedStNmPM$Estimated_Annual_HoursTraveled_Million,
        position = "bottomright",
```

```
        title = "Estimated Annual Hours Traveled (Million)",
        labFormat = labelFormat(suffix = ""))
    }
  }
})

 output$acsDTStNmPM = DT::renderDataTable(acsDTtempStNmPM, options =
list(lengthChange = FALSE),
                                         rownames= FALSE)

   output$downloadDataStNmPM <- downloadHandler(
   filename = function() {gsub(" ","",paste("StatewideNmPerfMeas_",YearInputStNm
PM,"_",ModeInputStNmPM,".csv"))},
   content = function(file) {write.csv(StatePerMeasureDataNoPuertoRico,file, row.
names=FALSE)}
   )

    incProgress(3/3, detail = paste("Finished!"))
  })
})


}

shinyApp(ui, server)
```

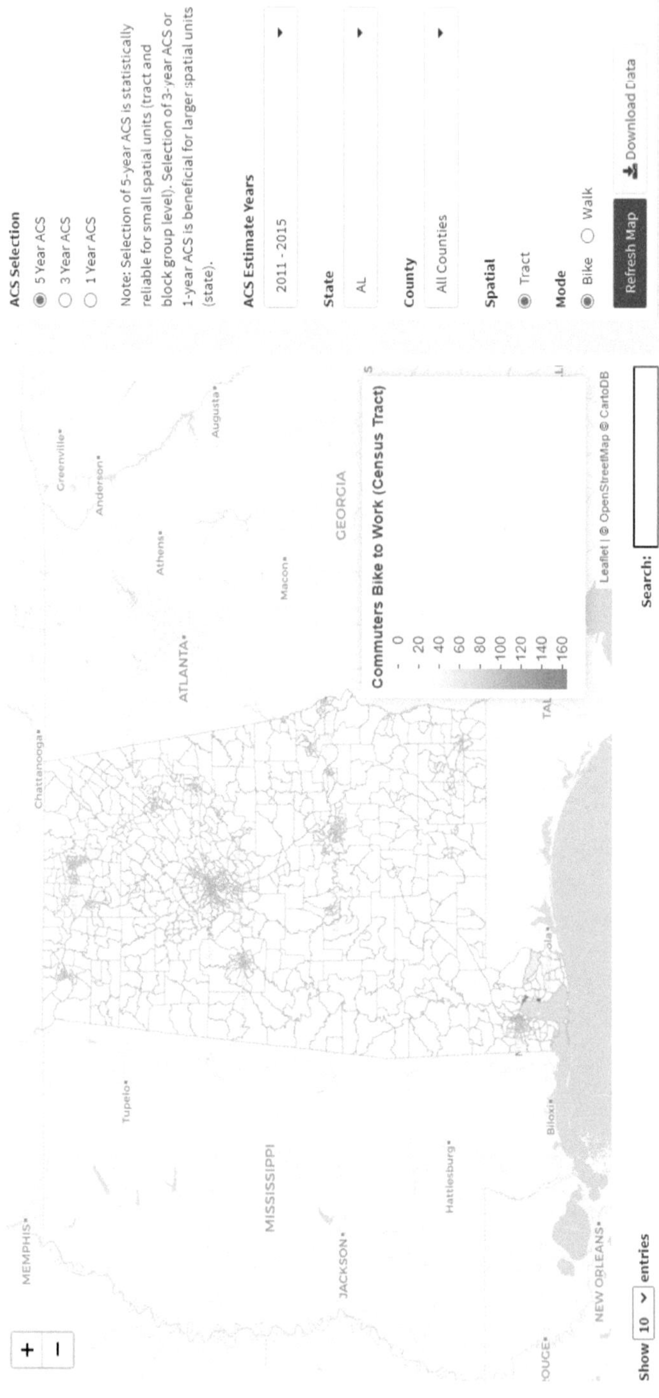

Figure 98. Interface of VRU exposure tool.

Appendix G

Alternative to Crash Tree Tool

Problem Statement

The Data Driven Safety Analysis (DDSA) Crash Tree Tool allows users to generate crash tree diagrams based on the NHTSA Fatality Analysis Reporting System (FARS) or other crash datasets. The Crash Tree Tool is considered a useful tool to perform systematic safety analysis. However, the tool and generated trees are difficult to reproduce with little or no flexibility. The following 'Shiny Tool' can be considered as an alternative. This tool has the following functionalities:

- Updated crash level categorical data in csv format
- Selection of multiple variables to perform the safety diagnostics
- Interactive crash collapsible tree with percentages in each branch

Crash Collapsible Tree Tool (CCTT)

```
## Please check my RPUBS for additional codes: https://rpubs.com/subasish

library(shiny)
library(dplyr)
library(collapsibleTree)
library(data.tree)
#UI
ui <- navbarPage("Crash Collapsible Tree",

 tabPanel("Tree Diagram", fluidPage(
 # Application title
 titlePanel("Tree Diagram"),
sidebarLayout(
  sidebarPanel(
    fileInput('myfileinput', label = 'Select File',
         accept = c(".csv")),
    selectInput("hierarchy",
         "Select variables",
```

```
        choices = 'No choices here yet',
        multiple = TRUE
        ),
 tags$style(type="text/css",
        ".shiny-output-error { visibility: hidden; }",
        ".shiny-output-error:before { visibility: hidden; }"
 ), width=2),
 # Show a tree diagram with the selected root node
 mainPanel(
    collapsibleTreeOutput("plot", height = "800px", width="1200px")
 )))

 ),
 tabPanel("Table", fluidPage(
        DT::dataTableOutput("mytable"))))

#Server
server <- function(input, output, session) {

    observeEvent(input$myfileinput, {

    mytable <- read.csv(input$myfileinput$datapath)
    mytable <- mutate_if(mytable, is.character, as.factor)


 updateSelectInput(session, "hierarchy",
                label = "Select variables",
                choices = colnames(mytable))

 output$mytable = DT::renderDataTable({
 mytable})

output$plot <- renderCollapsibleTree({
 mytable %>%
    group_by(across(all_of(input$hierarchy))) %>%
    summarize(`Count` = n(), `Percentage`=`Count`/nrow(mytable)*100) %>%
   collapsibleTreeSummary(
    attribute= "Percentage", fontSize=16,
    hierarchy = as.character(input$hierarchy))})
 })

 }


shinyApp(ui = ui, server = server)
```

The above code is reproducible. Figure 99 shows the interface of the CCTT. The shiny tool is available here: https://subasish.shinyapps.io/CrashCollapsibleTree/

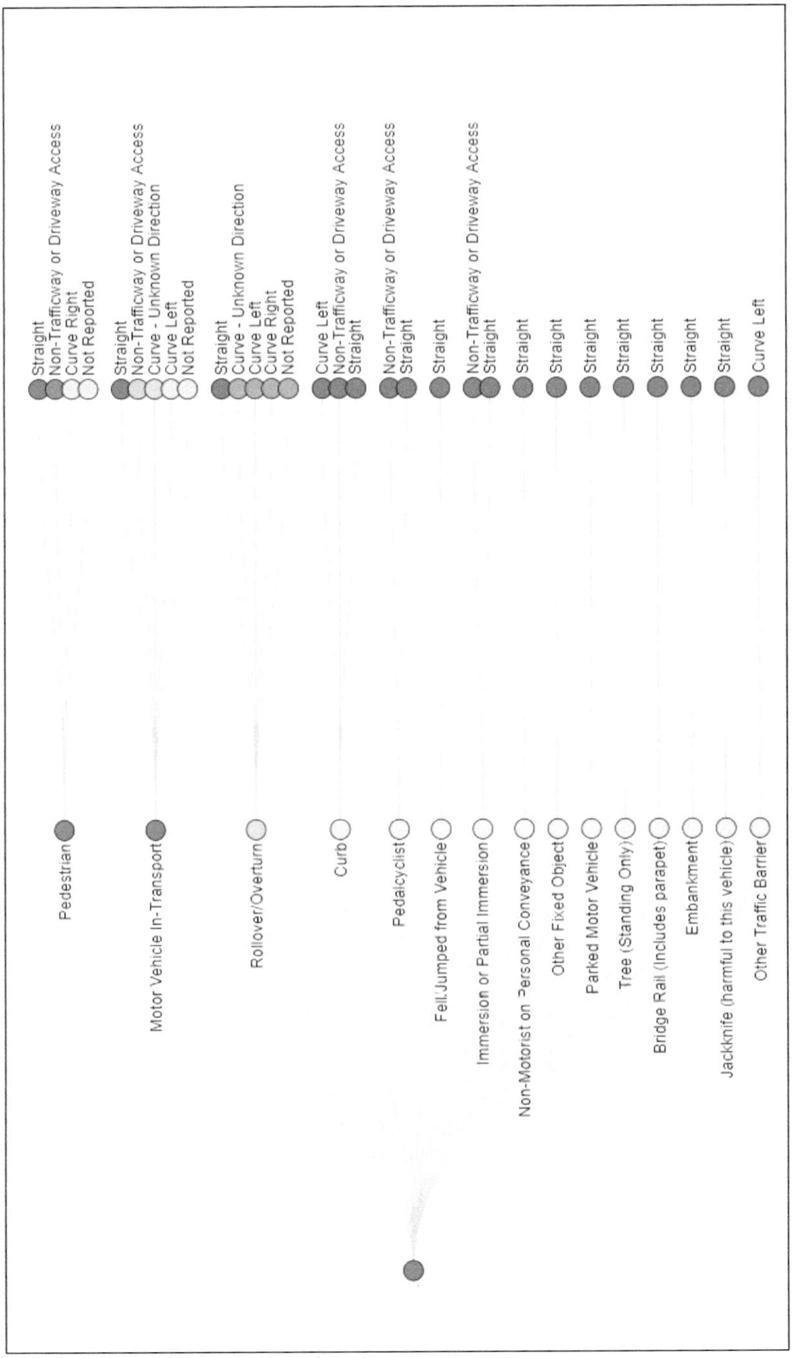

Pedestrian
- Straight
- Non-Trafficway or Driveway Access
- Curve Right
- Not Reported

Motor Vehicle In-Transport
- Straight
- Non-Trafficway or Driveway Access
- Curve - Unknown Direction
- Curve Left
- Not Reported

Rollover/Overturn
- Straight
- Curve - Unknown Direction
- Curve Left
- Curve Right
- Not Reported

Curb
- Curve Left
- Non-Trafficway or Driveway Access
- Straight

Pedalcyclist
- Non-Trafficway or Driveway Access
- Straight

Fell/Jumped from Vehicle
- Straight

Immersion or Partial Immersion
- Non-Trafficway or Driveway Access
- Straight

Non-Motorist on Personal Conveyance
- Straight

Other Fixed Object
- Straight

Parked Motor Vehicle
- Straight

Tree (Standing Only)
- Straight

Bridge Rail (Includes parapet)
- Straight

Embankment
- Straight

Jackknife (harmful to this vehicle)
- Straight

Other Traffic Barrier
- Curve Left

Figure 99. Crash collapsible tree tool (CCTT).

Appendix H

Example of Quick Bibliographic Search

Problem Statement

Researchers need to generate a literature review for many of their ongoing studies. There are many referencing servers such as Web of Science, Scopus, and TRID (https://trid.trb.org/). TRID is sometimes considered to be a better search engine for transportation research due to its backend, which is based on transportation research only. The following example shows how to perform a TRID-based literature search, which can provide some additional bibliometric information. For this work, NLP-based keywords are used to identify the relevant studies.

Code Chunk 1

```
## Please check my RPUBS for additional codes: https://rpubs.com/subasish
library(readxl)
library(DT)
library(dplyr)
library(reshape2)
library(data.table)
library(tidyr)

setwd("~folder location")


dat1 <- read_excel("NLP_032020.xlsx", sheet="fin00") ## generated from TRID
(https://trid.trb.org/) search
dat2 <- dat1[,c("title", "abstract", "year", "serial", "publisher")]
dat2a <- dat2[!duplicated(dat2[,c(1:5)]),]



dat2a$non_na <- 3- apply(dat2a, 1, function(x) sum(is.na(x)))
```

```
# use aggregate to create new data frame with the maxima
dat2b <- aggregate(non_na ~ title, dat2a, max)
# then simply merge with the original
dat2c  <- merge(dat2b, dat2a)
dim(dat2c)

### generated 45 papers
```

Code Chunk 2

```
dat4 <- dat1[,c("title", "term", "subject_area", "author")]
dat4a <- dat4[!duplicated(dat4[,c(1:4)]),]
dat5 = melt(dat4a, id.vars = c("title" ))
dat6 = dat5[complete.cases(dat5), ]
dat7= dat6 %>% group_by(title, variable) %>% mutate(rowind = row_number())

dat2e <- dat1[,c("title", "year")][complete.cases(dat1[,c("title", "year")]), ]
[!duplicated(dat1[,c("title", "year")][complete.cases(dat1[,c("title", "year")]), ]
[,c(1:2)]),]
dat8= left_join(dat7, dat2e, by="title")
```

Code Chunk 3 (by Keywords)

```
dat8a= subset(dat8, variable=="term")
dat8a= subset(dat8a, year > 1990)
dat9 <- dat8a[,c("value", "year")] %>% group_by(value, year) %>% summarise(count
= n()) %>%
   spread(year, count)
dat9[is.na(dat9)] <- 0


dat9$Total=rowSums(dat9[,c(2:11)])
datatable(dat9, extensions = c('Scroller', 'FixedColumns'), options = list(
   deferRender = TRUE,
   scrollY = TRUE,
   scrollX = TRUE,
   fixedColumns = list(leftColumns = 2, rightColumns = 1)
))
```

Table 35 shows the partial display by keywords.

Code Chunk 4 (by Author Numbering)

```
dat8a= subset(dat8, variable=="author")
dat9 <- dat8a[,c("value", "rowind")] %>% group_by(value, rowind) %>%
summarise(count = n()) %>%
   spread(rowind, count)
```

```
dat9[is.na(dat9)] <- 0
datatable(dat9, extensions = c('Scroller', 'FixedColumns'), options = list(
  deferRender = TRUE,
  scrollY = TRUE,
  scrollX = TRUE,
  fixedColumns = list(leftColumns = 2, rightColumns = 1)
))
```

Table 35. Partial display by keywords

Show 10 entries								Search:			
	Value	**2008**	**2009**	**2012**	**2013**	**2014**	**2015**	**2016**	**2017**	**2018**	**Total**
1	Accuracy	0	0	0	0	0	0	0	0	0	1
2	Activities of daily living	0	0	0	0	0	1	0	0	0	1
3	Advanced traveler information system	0	0	0	0	0	0	1	0	0	1
4	Aircraft incidents	0	0	0	0	0	0	0	0	0	1
5	Airlines	0	0	0	0	0	0	2	0	0	1
6	Algorithms	0	1	0	0	1	0	2	1	0	1
7	Apnea	0	0	0	0	0	0	0	0	0	1
8	Artificial intelligence	0	0	0	0	0	0	0	0	0	1

Table 36 shows the partial display by author numbering.

Table 36. Partial display by author numbering

Show 10 entries					Search:			
	Value	**1**	**2**	**3**	**4**	**5**	**6**	**7**
1	Abbasi, Allreza	0	1	0	0	0	0	0
2	Ali Farman	1	0	0	0	0	0	0
3	Alluri Priyanka	0	0	1	0	0	0	0
4	An, Nan	0	0	0	1	0	0	0
5	Belnke, Thies	1	0	0	0	0	0	0

Code Chunk 5 (by Author and Publication Year)

```
dat8a= subset(dat8, variable=="author")
dat8a= subset(dat8a, year > 1990)
```

```
dat9 <- dat8a[,c("value", "year")] %>% group_by(value, year) %>% summarise(count
= n()) %>%
  spread(year, count)
dat9[is.na(dat9)] <- 0
datatable(dat9, extensions = c('Scroller', 'FixedColumns'), options = list(
  deferRender = TRUE,
  scrollY = TRUE,
  scrollX = TRUE,
  fixedColumns = list(leftColumns = 2, rightColumns = 1)
))
```

Table 37 shows the partial display by author and publication year.

Table 37. Partial display by author and publication year

	Value	2008	2009	2012	2013	2014	2015	2016	2017	2018	2019
1	Abbasi, Allreza	0	0	0	0	0	1	0	0	0	0
2	Ali Farman	0	0	0	0	0	0	0	0	0	1
3	Alluri Priyanka	0	0	0	0	0	0	1	0	0	0
4	An, Nan	0	0	0	0	0	0	0	0	0	1
5	Belnke, Thies	0	0	0	0	0	0	0	1	0	0

Code Chunk 6 (by Journal)

```
dat4 <- dat1[,c("title", "serial")]
dat4a <- dat4[!duplicated(dat4[,c(1:2)]),]
dat5 = melt(dat4a, id.vars = c("title" ))

dat6 = dat5[complete.cases(dat5), ]
dat7= dat6 %>% group_by(title, variable) %>% mutate(rowind = row_number())
dat2e <- dat1[,c("title", "year")][complete.cases(dat1[,c("title", "year")]), ]
[!duplicated(dat1[,c("title", "year")][complete.cases(dat1[,c("title", "year")]), ]
[,c(1:2)]),]
dat8= left_join(dat7, dat2e, by="title")
colnames(dat8)[3] <- "serial"
dat9 <- dat8[,c("serial", "year")] %>% group_by(serial, year) %>% summarise(count =
n()) %>%
  spread(year, count)
dat9[is.na(dat9)] <- 0
dat9$Total=rowSums(dat9[,c(2:11)])
datatable(dat9, extensions = c('Scroller', 'FixedColumns'), options = list(
  deferRender = TRUE,
  scrollY = TRUE,
  scrollX = TRUE,
  fixedColumns = list(leftColumns = 2, rightColumns = 1)
))
```

Table 38 shows the partial display by journal name.

Table 38. Partial display by journal name

	Serial	2008	2009	2012	2013	2014	2015	2016	2017	2018	2019
1	Accident Analysis and Prevention	1	0	0	0	0	0	0	2	0	0
2	Air Transport World	0	0	0	0	0	0	2	0	0	0
3	Human Factors	0	0	0	0	1	0	0	0	0	0
4	IEE Transactions on Intelligent Transportation Systems	0	0	0	0	0	0	1	1	0	0

Code Chunk 7 (Display Paper Title and First Author)

```
dat4 <- dat1[,c("title", "author")]
dat4a <- dat4[!duplicated(dat4[,c(1:2)]),]
dat5 = melt(dat4a, id.vars = c("title" ))

dat6 = dat5[complete.cases(dat5), ]
dat7= dat6 %>% group_by(title, variable) %>% mutate(rowind = row_number())
dat7a= subset(dat7, rowind==1)
dat2e <- dat1[,c("title", "serial", "year")][complete.cases(dat1[,c("title", "serial",
"year")]), ][!duplicated(dat1[,c("title", "serial", "year")][complete.cases(dat1[,c("title",
"serial", "year")]), ][,c(1:3)]),]
dat8= left_join(dat7a, dat2e, by="title")
colnames(dat8)[3] <- "first_author"

datatable(
  dat8[,c(6, 1, 3, 5)], extensions = c('Select', 'Buttons'), options = list(
    select = list(style = 'os', items = 'row'),
    dom = 'Blfrtip',
    rowId = 0,
    buttons = c('selectRows', 'csv', 'excel')
  ),
  selection = 'none'
)
```

Table 39 shows the partial display by first author and paper title.

Table 39. Partial display by first author and paper title

	Year	Title	First_ author	Serial
1	2019	Text Mining Tweets on Driving Safety and Cellphone Use	Qian, Chao	Proceedings of the Human Factors and Ergonomics Society Annual Meeting
2	2019	Voice of airline passenger: A text mining approach to understand customer satisfaction	Sezen, Eren	Journal of Air Transport Management
3	2019	Insight from Scientific Study in Logistics using Text Mining	Hong, Jungyeol	Transportation Research Record: Journal of the Transportation Research Board
4	2019	Fuzzy Ontology and LSTM-Based Text Mining: A Transportation Network Monitoring System for Assisting Travel	Ali, Farman	Sensors
5	2018	Transport Analysis Approach Based on Big Data and Text Mining Analysis from Social Media	Serna, Alnhoa	Transportation Research Procedia

Appendix I

Example of Self-Organizing Maps

Problem Statement

The self-organizing map is one of the most commonly used dimension reduction methods. The following example shows how Pedestrian and Bicycle Crash Analysis Tool (PBCAT) data from FARS can be used in determining important clusters. At first, 36 clusters are developed. Based on the parameter tuning, three super clusters are developed. Figures 100-103 show the clusters, associated information in each cluster, and different cluster distance measures.

Code Chunk 1

```
## Please check my RPUBS for additional codes: https://rpubs.com/subasish

library(SOMbrero)
setwd("~folder_location")

new <- read.csv("Ped_RulesNew3.csv")
names(new)

new1 <- subset(new, Tot >40)
dim(new1)


dat1 <- new1[,c(10:61)]

dat2 <- dat1[,-1]
rownames(dat2) <- dat1[,1]
head(dat2)
dim(dat2)
library(SOMbrero)
korresp.som <- trainSOM(x.data=dat2, dimension=c(6,6),
```

```
        type="korresp", scaling="chi2", nb.save=10,
        radius.type="letremy")

plot(korresp.som, what="obs", type="hitmap")
plot(korresp.som, what="obs", type="names")

plot(korresp.som, what="obs", type="names", scale=c(0.6,0.5))

plot(korresp.som, what="prototypes", type="lines", view="r", print.title=TRUE)
plot(korresp.som, what="prototypes", type="lines", view="c", print.title=TRUE)

par(mfrow=c(1,2))
plot(korresp.som, what="prototypes", type="poly.dist", print.title=TRUE)
plot(korresp.som, what="prototypes", type="umatrix", print.title=TRUE)
plot(korresp.som, what="prototypes", type="smooth.dist", print.title=TRUE)
plot(korresp.som, what="prototypes", type="mds")


plot(superClass(korresp.som))

my.sc <- superClass(korresp.som, k=3)
summary(my.sc)
plot(my.sc, plot.var=FALSE)
plot(my.sc, type="grid", plot.legend=TRUE)
plot(my.sc, type="hitmap", plot.legend=TRUE)
plot(my.sc, type="lines", print.title=TRUE)
plot(my.sc, type="lines", print.title=TRUE, view="c")
plot(my.sc, type="mds", plot.legend=TRUE)
plot(my.sc, type="poly.dist")
```

	IN NJ AL		NC LA	VA	MS
OK CO NV	MD	KY NM		AZ MI	
UT IA KS	ME AR DE		TN		FL
HI AK RI ID NH VT		IL OH	GA		TX
CT	WA MN OR	PA			
SC MA	WI	NY			CA

Figure 100. Clusters of states.

Rule0010 Rule0032 Rule0065 Rule0018 Rule0019 Rule0046	IN NJ AL Rule0043 Rule0050 Rule0021	Rule0015 Rule0063 Rule0036 Rule0029 Rule0062 Rule0045	Rule0009 LA NC Rule0023	VA	MS Rule0044
NV CO OK MO	Rule0008 MD	Rule0035 Rule0026 Rule0012 KY NM Rule0059		AZ MI	
IA Rule0048 KS UT Rule0053 Rule0034 Rule0054	ME DE AR	Rule0067 Rule0025 Rule0057 Rule0058 Rule0027	Rule0020 Rule0014 Rule0017 TN		Rule0001 FL
Rule0039 Rule0060 WV Rule0056 ND AK DC HI ID NH Rule0022 SD Rule0051 RI MT NE VT Rule0038 WY Rule0030	Rule0040 Rule0047 Rule0066	Rule0042 IL OH	Rule0024 GA Rule0013	Rule0005 Rule0003	TX
CT Rule0068 Rule0037 Rule0041 Rule0031	Rule0064 Rule0069 MN OR WA	PA	Rule0016 Rule0011	Rule0007 Rule0006	Rule0002
Rule0061 Rule0055 SC MA Rule0049	WI	Rule0033 Rule0052 Rule0028 NY		Rule0004	CA

Figure 101. Cluster items.

Cluster 6	Cluster 12	Cluster 18	Cluster 24	Cluster 30	Cluster 36
Cluster 5	Cluster 11	Cluster 17	Cluster 23	Cluster 29	Cluster 35
Cluster 4	Cluster 10	Cluster 16	Cluster 22	Cluster 28	Cluster 34
Cluster 3	Cluster 9	Cluster 15	Cluster 21	Cluster 27	Cluster 33
Cluster 2	Cluster 8	Cluster 14	Cluster 20	Cluster 26	Cluster 32
Cluster 1	Cluster 7	Cluster 13	Cluster 19	Cluster 25	Cluster 31

Cluster 6	Cluster 12	Cluster 18	Cluster 24	Cluster 30	Cluster 36
Cluster 5	Cluster 11	Cluster 17	Cluster 23	Cluster 29	Cluster 35
Cluster 4	Cluster 10	Cluster 16	Cluster 22	Cluster 28	Cluster 34
Cluster 3	Cluster 9	Cluster 15	Cluster 21	Cluster 27	Cluster 33
Cluster 2	Cluster 8	Cluster 14	Cluster 20	Cluster 26	Cluster 32
Cluster 1	Cluster 7	Cluster 13	Cluster 19	Cluster 25	Cluster 31

Figure 102. Neighboring distance and average distance measures of the clusters.

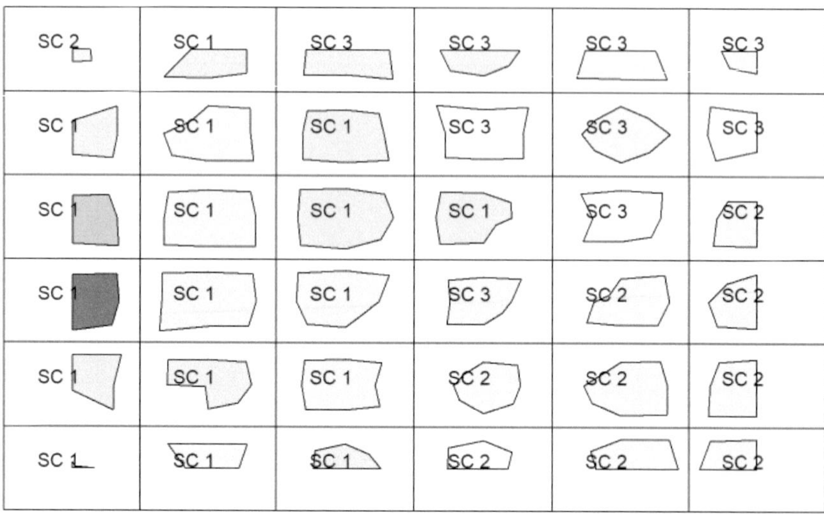

Figure 103. Super clusters.

Appendix J

Example of Correspondence Analysis

Problem Statement

Correspondence analysis is one of the popular dimension reduction methods. This example examines the application of correspondence analysis to see the difference of injury types for wet and dry pavement conditions. The codes present several intermediate plots. Figure 104 and Figure 105 show the trends of injury level by the ordered scores.

Code Chunk 1

```
## Please check my RPUBS for additional codes: https://rpubs.com/subasish
setwd("~folder_location")

library(CAvariants)
library(data.table)
library(dplyr)
library(tidyr)

dry1a <- read.csv("C:/Users/subas/Syncplicity/MyProjects_IMP/MY_Papers_V2/TRB 2020/00000 PAPER DATA/Pap01/dry1.csv")
wet1a <- read.csv("C:/Users/subas/Syncplicity/MyProjects_IMP/MY_Papers_V2/TRB 2020/00000 PAPER DATA/Pap01/wet1.csv")

rownames(dry1a) <- dry1a[,1]
rownames(wet1a) <- wet1a[,1]

dry1b <- dry1a[,-c(1)]
wet1b <- wet1a[,-c(1)]

plot(CAvariants(dry1b, catype = "DONSCA", firstaxis = 1, lastaxis = 2))
plot(CAvariants(dry1b, catype = "NSCA", firstaxis = 1, lastaxis = 2))
plot(CAvariants(dry1b, catype = "DOCA", firstaxis = 1, lastaxis = 2))
plot(CAvariants(dry1b, catype = "SOCA", firstaxis = 1, lastaxis = 2))
plot(CAvariants(dry1b, catype = "SONSCA", firstaxis = 1, lastaxis = 2))
```

(*Contd.*)

```
plot(CAvariants(wet1b, catype = "DONSCA", firstaxis = 1, lastaxis = 2))
plot(CAvariants(wet1b, catype = "NSCA", firstaxis = 1, lastaxis = 2))
plot(CAvariants(wet1b, catype = "DOCA", firstaxis = 1, lastaxis = 2))
plot(CAvariants(wet1b, catype = "SOCA", firstaxis = 1, lastaxis = 2))
plot(CAvariants(wet1b, catype = "SONSCA", firstaxis = 1, lastaxis = 2))
```

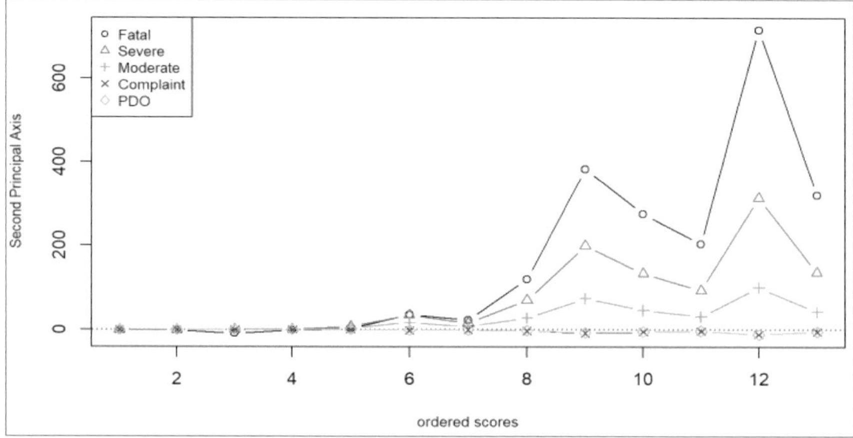

Figure 104. Ordered scores for dry pavement crashes.

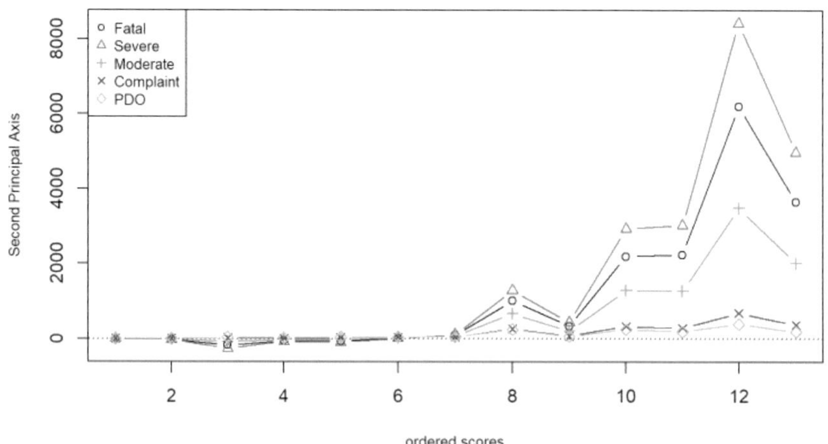

Figure 105. Ordered scores for wet pavement crashes.

Appendix K

Example of Deep Explainer

Problem Statement

Explainable AI has recently gained much attraction from the research community. One of the advanced applications of explainable AI is deep explainer. The following replicable code can be used to perform deep explainable AI on crash count data.

Deep Explainer (Used Google Colab)

```
## Code is uploaded here: https://colab.research.google.com/drive/1veeCupYghsXdHZ-w1UmkAWGRuYTKYy8e#scrollTo=ApF6atTyxNkB

!pip install shap
import pandas as pd
import numpy as np
import matplotlib.pyplot as plt
from collections import Counter
import shap
import seaborn as sns

import warnings
warnings.filterwarnings('ignore')

plt.style.use('fivethirtyeight')
%matplotlib inline

shap.initjs()

import io
df2 = pd.read_csv(io.BytesIO(uploaded['a2.csv']))
```

(Contd.)

```
### LOAD DATA (load segment level crash count data)
from google.colab import files
uploaded = files.upload()

labels= df2['Urban_Rur']
df2 = df2.drop('Urban_Rur', 1)
data=df2
data.loc[:, data.dtypes == 'object'] =\
        data.select_dtypes(['object'])\
        .apply(lambda x: x.astype('category'))

data = pd.get_dummies(data)
data.head()

from sklearn.model_selection import train_test_split

X_train, X_test, y_train, y_test = train_test_split(data, labels, test_size=0.01, random_
state=42)
X_train.shape, X_test.shape

from tensorflow.keras.models import Sequential
from tensorflow.keras.layers import Dropout, Activation, Dense, BatchNormalization
from tensorflow.keras.optimizers import Adam

num_input_features = X_train.shape[1]

dnn_model = Sequential()
dnn_model.add(Dense(256,        input_shape=(num_input_features,),        kernel_
initializer='glorot_uniform'))
dnn_model.add(BatchNormalization())
dnn_model.add(Activation('relu'))

dnn_model.add(Dense(128, kernel_initializer='glorot_uniform'))
dnn_model.add(BatchNormalization())
dnn_model.add(Activation('relu'))

dnn_model.add(Dense(64, kernel_initializer='glorot_uniform'))
dnn_model.add(BatchNormalization())
dnn_model.add(Activation('relu'))

dnn_model.add(Dense(1))
dnn_model.add(Activation('sigmoid'))

dnn_model.compile(loss='binary_crossentropy', optimizer=Adam(lr=2e-5),
            metrics=['accuracy'])
dnn_model.summary()

from sklearn.utils import class_weight
```

```
class_weights = class_weight.compute_class_weight('balanced',
                                np.unique(y_train),
                                y_train)
class_weights = dict(enumerate(class_weights))
class_weights[1] *= 2
class_weights

dnn_model.fit(X_train, y_train, batch_size=128,
        epochs=20, validation_split=0.1, verbose=1, class_weight=class_weights)

shap.explainers._deep.deep_tf.op_handlers["AddV2"] = shap.explainers._deep.deep_
tf.passthrough

explainer = shap.DeepExplainer(dnn_model, data=X_train.values)
shap_values = explainer.shap_values(X_test.values)
shap_values = shap_values[0]

shap.summary_plot(shap_values, X_test, plot_type="bar")
shap.summary_plot(shap_values, X_test)
```

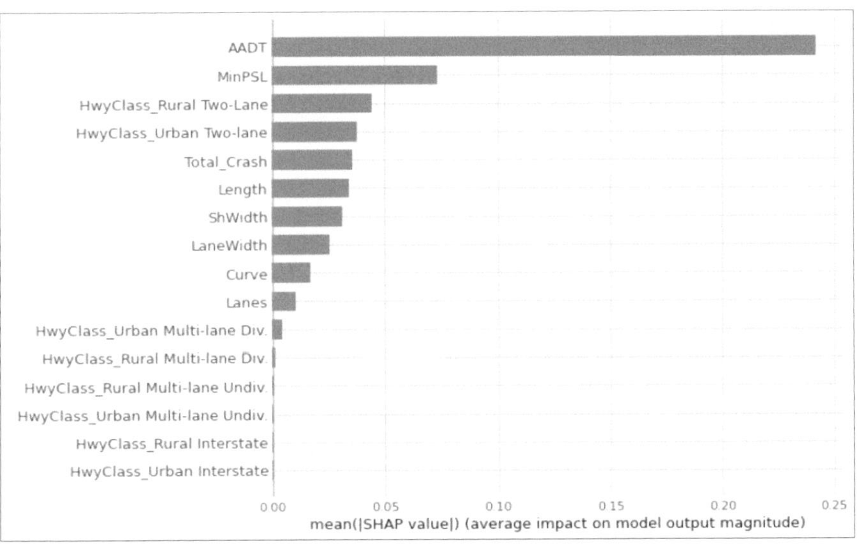

Figure 106. SHAP values on model output magnitude.

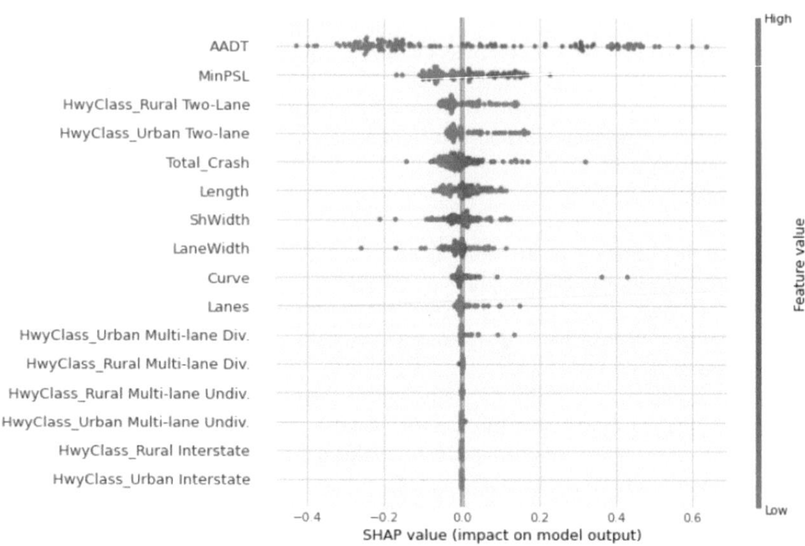

Figure 107. SHAP values on model output.

Appendix L

Road Safety Professional (RSP) Certification Needs

Road Safety Professional (RSP) is a professional certification developed for transportation engineers and practitioners. The certificate holders can claim adequate knowledge in highway safety engineering. As the core competencies of highway safety professionals have been changing, there is a need to add AI-related practice-ready questions for the future curriculum of this certification process. Table 40 shows the current examination format and content of RSP1.

Table 40. Examination format and content of RSP1

Define	Identify	Explain
Domain 1: Foundations of Road Safety		
Define road safety by using an approved reference source	• Identify partners in road safety by listing disciplines and agency types that have a role to play in preventing crashes and reducing their severity. • List road safety-relevant characteristics of different road users	• Describe evidence-based road safety, including the distinction of nominal vs. substantive safety, by using road safety literature. • Describe the complexity of road safety and list the elements that are involved in crash causation and influence the severity of the outcome. • Describe different approaches to road safety management • Describe how to balance safety with other transportation goals by evaluating safety benefits and costs for comprehensive comparison and decision-making. • Describe the elements of a culture that fosters road safety within an organization or discipline and how to achieve it. • Discuss developments in policy and technology that will influence future decisions and actions in road safety.

(*Contd.*)

Table 40. (*Contd.*)

Define	Identify	Explain
Domain 2: Measuring Safety		
	• Identify types, applications, and users of safety data, and discuss the challenges, limitations, and ways to mitigate them by using nontraditional safety data.	• Discuss how the quality of safety data can lead to more effective programs, projects, and initiatives and investments. • Explain how key factors could affect the frequency and severity of crashes. • Explain the primary components of quantitative safety analysis.
Domain 3: Human Behavior and Road Safety		
	• Identify key characteristics and limitations of human behavior that influence how road users interact with the roadway environment.	• Describe multidisciplinary safety strategies to modify human behavior. • Describe the key characteristics of effective educational strategies and discuss their benefits and limitations in modifying human behavior. • Describe the key characteristics of effective enforcement campaigns and discuss their benefits and limitations in modifying human behavior. • Describe and give examples of how roadway infrastructure features and elements affect human behavior. • Describe why human factors should be considered in the process of planning, design, and operations to increase the safety of all road users. • Describe how applying positive guidance principles to road elements can be used to affect road user behavior and improve safety performance.
Domain 4: Solving Safety Problems		
Understand collision patterns and crash contributing factors.	• Identify and describe the steps in a safety management process that uses effective data-driven procedures and methods to reduce fatalities	

	and injuries caused by traffic collisions. • Identify and describe a systemwide approach. • List reliable sources of multidisciplinary countermeasures to reduce fatalities and serious injuries. • List tools used to diagnose safety problems and describe their specific advantages and disadvantages. • Identify how countermeasure costs and benefits can be used to evaluate the effectiveness of program and project investments. • Identify the elements of a countermeasure evaluation by using data to determine its impacts. • Identify techniques for estimating and comparing the safety performance of different project alternatives.	• Describe how multidisciplinary approaches can be used to deploy the most effective solutions. • Describe opportunities for user-focused interventions targeted at different populations.
Domain 5: Implementing Road Safety Programs		
	• Identify elements of successful communication and outreach strategies	• Describe how strategic safety plans are prepared and used. • Explain the role and value of champions in influencing road safety policies and programs.

(*Contd.*)

	that build consensus among decision-makers and lead to increased public acceptance/ awareness about road safety initiatives. • List important elements of successful road safety policies and programs.	• Describe how multidisciplinary teams and partnerships can achieve road safety goals. • Describe the value of safety program evaluation and explain how results influence future program delivery.

Source: https://www.tpcb.org/certification/rsp1/exam-format-and-content/

Index

T

U